Fabergé

IN AMERICA

Fabergé

IN AMERICA

Géza von Habsburg

with contributions by
David Park Curry
Christopher Forbes
Henry Hawley
John Webster Keefe
Anne Odom

———◆———

Thames and Hudson

Fine Arts Museums of San Francisco

Published on the occasion of the exhibition *Fabergé in America*, which has been organized by the Fine Arts Museums of San Francisco and made possible by FABERGÉ CO.

The Metropolitan Museum of Art, New York
February 16–April 28, 1996

Fine Arts Museums of San Francisco
M. H. de Young Memorial Museum
May 25–July 28, 1996

Virginia Museum of Fine Arts, Richmond
August 24–November 3, 1996

New Orleans Museum of Art
December 7, 1996–February 9, 1997

The Cleveland Museum of Art
March 12–May 11, 1997

First published in the United States of America in hardcover in 1996 by Thames and Hudson Inc., 500 Fifth Avenue, New York, New York 10110

First published in Great Britain in 1996 by Thames and Hudson Ltd., London

Library of Congress Catalog Card Number 95-61963

ISBN 0-500-01699-2

British Library Cataloguing-in-Publication data
A catalogue record for this book is available from the British Library.

Fabergé in America
Produced through the Publications Department of the Fine Arts Museums of San Francisco: Ann Heath Karlstrom, Director of Publications and Graphic Design; Karen Kevorkian, Editor.

Editors: Suzanne Kotz and Patricia Draher, Seattle
Designed and produced by Marquand Books, Inc., Seattle
Designer: Brian Ellis Martin with assistance from Noreen Ryan
Typesetter: Susan E. Kelly

Type composed in Didot and Fournier

Printed and bound in Hong Kong

Contents

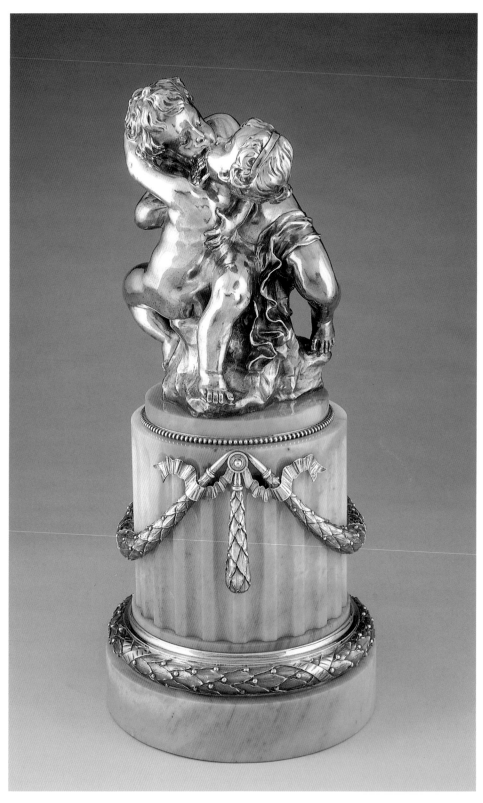

Embracing amorini *in Louis XVI style, Fine Arts Museums of San Francisco*
(cat. no. 39)

Foreword

The remarkable genius of Peter Carl Fabergé and the unsurpassed artistry of the objects made in his workshops have long held a special appeal for American collectors and museum visitors. Some of the world's outstanding collections of Fabergé were assembled by Americans who were attracted by the beauty of the material and, to a lesser extent, to the lingering aura of the Russian imperial family who first patronized this master jeweler. All who see the objects in this exhibition, drawn from a wide range of American public and private collections, will be able to relate to the pleasure and pride that these dynamic individuals experienced in the pursuit of exquisite objects.

This exhibition and catalogue give us the history of American interest in Fabergé through the example of several major collectors: Matilda Geddings Gray (New Orleans Museum of Art), India Early Minshall (the Cleveland Museum of Art), Marjorie Merriweather Post (Hillwood Museum, Washington, D.C.), Malcolm S. Forbes (Forbes Magazine Collection, New York), and Lillian Thomas Pratt (Virginia Museum of Fine Arts, Richmond). The first four institutions are lenders to this exhibition, and we are delighted that the Virginia Museum of Fine Arts is able to circulate an exhibition of its Lillian Thomas Pratt Collection of Fabergé to coincide with *Fabergé in America*, thus providing a more comprehensive picture of this artist. The authors of the catalogue essays have allowed us to share some of the excitement of collecting Fabergé.

Each of the lenders who have agreed to part with their objects for the course of the exhibition has contributed to a rich visual and educational experience for museum visitors. We are fortunate in the generosity of the individual collectors and the dedication of the staffs of the lending institutions, who have been especially resourceful in solving the inevitable obstacles that arise in a project of this scope.

We are grateful indeed to Dr. Géza von Habsburg, who has been associated with several previous Fabergé exhibitions and who has acted as our guest curator and primary author. Through his efforts, the number of privately owned and seldom-seen objects has increased, making this a particularly inclusive exhibition. His expertise and deep involvement in his subject are evident throughout this endeavor.

Assembling more than four hundred objects has been a mammoth undertaking. We have been most fortunate that Patrick J. Choël, President and Chief Executive Officer of FABERGÉ CO., shares our enthusiasm for these unequaled objects; his very meaningful support has made the exhibition and publication possible. We salute Mr. Choël and FABERGÉ CO. for their willingness to undertake a public education project of such magnitude as we commemorate the 150th anniversary of Fabergé's birth.

Finally, appreciation goes to the staff of the Fine Arts Museums of San Francisco for the organization of the exhibition and the supervision of catalogue publication. In particular, I wish to thank Lee Hunt Miller, Curator of European Decorative Arts and Sculpture, who first brought the concept of the exhibition to my attention. Others who have contributed their skills to this highly complex undertaking are Lesley Bone, Objects Conservator; Therese Chen, Chief Registrar; Kathe Hodgson, Coordinator of Exhibitions; and Ann Heath Karlstrom, Director of Publications and Graphic Design. Their energetic commitment to this project has been key to its realization.

—Harry S. Parker III
Director of Museums
Fine Arts Museums of San Francisco

*The 1953 installation of the Lillian Thomas Pratt Collection of Fabergé,
made possible by John Lee Pratt, remained on view at the
Virginia Museum of Fine Arts for nearly thirty years.*

Foreword

The Lillian Thomas Pratt Collection of Fabergé

The Virginia Museum of Fine Arts is pleased to join the Fine Arts Museums of San Francisco in presenting the work of Peter Carl Fabergé in American collections. Within the Commonwealth of Virginia, the extensive collection formed by Lillian Thomas Pratt during the 1930s and 1940s needs no introduction. Since she bequeathed her Russian treasures to the Virginia Museum of Fine Arts in 1947, they have drawn thousands of visitors to Richmond every year.

Now an opportunity to reach a wider audience has presented itself. The museum is proud to introduce Lillian Thomas Pratt as a significant collector of Fabergé's work to museum visitors throughout the United States. In her will, Mrs. Pratt stipulated that the Virginia Museum of Fine Arts was never to lend the wonderful objects she gathered together. The Virginia Museum of Fine Arts itself, therefore, presents the Pratt collection. Doing so within the parameters expressed by Mrs. Pratt's will required the able guidance of the Honorable Randall G. Johnson of the Circuit Court of the City of Richmond and Attorney General James S. Gilmore III. Also important in assuring the successful tour of the collection were John D. Butzner, Mrs. Richard S. Reynolds III, and, at the museum, Associate Director for Exhibitions and Planning Richard B. Woodward, Deputy Director Carol Amato, Director of Protective Services Michael Dougherty, Registrar Elizabeth Hancock, and Associate Director for Communications and Marketing Michael Smith.

The exhibitions *Fabergé in America* and *The Lillian Thomas Pratt Collection of Fabergé* represent a milestone in understanding and cooperation among the participating museums. We are especially grateful to our colleagues at the Fine Arts Museums of San Francisco, who organized *Fabergé in America*, which was made possible by FABERGÉ CO.; and to the Metropolitan Museum of Art, New York; the New Orleans Museum of Art; and the Cleveland Museum of Art. We also wish to acknowledge the help and expertise of Géza von Habsburg, upon whose creative and scholarly talents this joint enterprise rests.

Lillian Thomas Pratt takes her place among the major American collectors of the work of Carl Fabergé on the 150th anniversary of the Russian imperial court jeweler's birth. At the same time, the Virginia Museum of Fine Arts is celebrating its sixtieth anniversary as an institution committed to sharing wonderful works of art with the general public. This opportunity to share Lillian Thomas Pratt's sparkling legacy with visitors in New York, San Francisco, New Orleans, and Cleveland, as well as Richmond, at once provides fitting recognition of the two significant anniversaries and of Mrs. Pratt as a devoted collector of Fabergé.

—Katharine C. Lee
Director
Virginia Museum of Fine Arts

Sponsor's Statement

◆

FABERGÉ CO. is proud to be the national sponsor of *Fabergé in America,* a pioneering exhibition documenting the history of Fabergé collecting by Americans over the past one hundred years. The exhibition showcases some of the finest works of the great Russian artist-jeweler Peter Carl Fabergé, including sixteen extraordinary imperial Easter eggs acquired by American collectors. The catalogue text describes the social context in which a number of great collections were formed and provides a unique insight into America's ongoing fascination with imperial Russia.

The Fine Arts Museums of San Francisco, its director, curators, and staff deserve great credit for the organization of this extraordinary exhibition and for the dedication with which they have gathered nearly four hundred precious examples of the master's oeuvre. Special thanks must go to Géza von Habsburg, guest curator, to whom we owe the concept of the exhibition, the selection of objects, and a large part of the catalogue. I would also like to thank those fine institutions that have agreed to host this exhibition, including the Metropolitan Museum of Art, New York; the Fine Arts Museums of San Francisco; the Virginia Museum of Fine Arts, Richmond; the New Orleans Museum of Art; and the Cleveland Museum of Art. Thanks must also go to the individuals who have loaned objects from their private collections. Without them, there would not be a *Fabergé in America.*

Carl Fabergé is undoubtedly the best known artist-jeweler of all time. He must be admired for the spirit of innovation and the unparalleled perfection found in every one of his objets d'art. We are hopeful that through exhibitions such as *Fabergé in America,* which marks the 150th anniversary of Fabergé's birth, the renowned artist's legacy will extend well into the next century.

—Patrick J. Choël
President, Chief Executive Officer
FABERGÉ CO.

List of Lenders

———◆———

A La Vieille Russie, New York

Elizabeth Blake

Louise and David Braver

The Brooklyn Museum, New York

The Cleveland Museum of Art

De Guigné Collection

Gerald M. de Sylvar

Fine Arts Museums of San Francisco

The Estate of Mr. Malcolm S. Forbes Sr.

The Estate of Mrs. Roberta Forbes

The Forbes Magazine Collection, New York

Raphael and Joyce Gregorian

Hillwood Museum, Washington, D.C.

Collection of Sydney and Frances Lewis

The Metropolitan Museum of Art, New York

New Brunswick Museum, St. John, Canada

New Orleans Museum of Art:
Matilda Geddings Gray Foundation Loan

William Dean Rasco

Joan and Melissa Rivers

Andre Ruzhnikov, Palo Alto, California

John Traina

Virginia Museum of Fine Arts, Richmond

The Walters Art Gallery, Baltimore

Mr. and Mrs. Steven Westerman

The Estate of James A. Williams

Private Collections

Peter Carl Fabergé, ca. 1918. Photo: Courtesy Alexander Morgan Gunst.

Introduction and Acknowledgments

Fabergé in America is the first representative exhibition dedicated to the extraordinary objets d'art, silver, and jewelry crafted by the Russian goldsmith and jeweler Peter Carl Fabergé and amassed by American collectors over nearly a hundred years. Rather than focusing on the craftsmanship of Fabergé's objects, as has been done previously, this exhibition places the social history of American collecting against the backdrop of America's ongoing fascination with imperial Russia. Viewers and readers will witness the interaction between collectors in this country and the art of one of the greatest jewelers of all time.

The art of imperial Russia under its last two czars has captivated the public imagination for many decades. This interest in the opulence, pomp, and splendor of czarist Russia has been amply demonstrated by the success of such pioneering exhibitions as *Treasures from the Kremlin*, held at the Metropolitan Museum of Art, New York, in 1979 (a similar exhibition, which attracted over 500,000 visitors, was held in St. Petersburg, Florida, in 1995) and *Catherine the Great: Treasures of Imperial Russia from the State Hermitage Museum, Leningrad*, shown in Memphis, Dallas, and Los Angeles in 1991.

The only substantial Fabergé display in the United States since the 1960s took place in New York in 1983, with parallel exhibits held at the Cooper-Hewitt Museum and A La Vieille Russie. In the west, San Francisco's single Fabergé showing dates back to 1964. Selections from the Matilda Geddings Gray Foundation collection of New Orleans and the collection of Forbes Magazine have traveled nationwide since 1972. A few exhibitions have highlighted specific aspects of Fabergé's art, such as *Fabergé: The Imperial Easter Eggs* (San Diego, 1989) and *The World of Fabergé: Russian Gems and Jewels* (Houston, 1994).

These exhibitions have kept Fabergé in the public eye, as have appearances in wider-reaching media. The James Bond film *Octopussy* (1983) featured an imperial Easter egg by Fabergé, and a Fabergé Easter egg heist in Oshkosh, Wisconsin, hit the headlines in 1983. Spectacular record prices have been achieved at auction: an American paid $3.19 million in New York in 1992 for an imperial Easter egg, and another American paid $5.5 million in Geneva in 1994 for the long-lost Winter egg of 1913. The sheer number of symposia, books, articles, lectures, auctions, and exhibitions devoted to Fabergé reveals a distinct preference for his art over that of all other jewelers,[1] with the exception, in this country, perhaps, of Tiffany.

The love affair between the American public and Fabergé's art was first documented by Christopher Forbes in 1987,[2] followed by Paul Schaffer in 1994,[3] both in connection with exhibitions held overseas. The present exhibition seeks to examine systematically the history of American collecting and to present the art of Fabergé as seen through the eyes of each generation and each major collector.

The first section of the book is dedicated to the period before World War I and all hitherto traceable objects acquired by Americans in St. Petersburg and London during Fabergé's lifetime. American interest in Carl Fabergé's virtuoso objects dates back to 1900, when millionaire Henry C. Walters of Baltimore visited St. Petersburg. He was followed by Consuelo Vanderbilt, duchess of Marlborough, in 1902 and J. P. Morgan Jr. in 1905. American socialites and their families continued to acquire Fabergé items in large quantities from the firm's London outlet until its closing in 1917. In Appendix II a list of sixty-eight American Fabergé buyers in London is given, together with more than 450 objects they purchased. Only a handful of these items are accounted for today. Some might have been acquired as presents for English friends; others presumably lie unrecognized in family vaults or jewel boxes in the United States, probably separated from their telltale Fabergé boxes. It is expected that this listing and exhibition will bring more of these to light.

The second section of the catalogue is dedicated to the period from 1920 to 1950. In the aftermath of the Russian Revolution, members of the imperial family and a wave of Russian nobility brought to the United States their salvaged treasures, including many objects by Fabergé. These were used as currency and as gifts, and a number have been handed down through inheritance. Interest in things Russian was stimulated in the early 1930s, when Armand and Victor Hammer astutely marketed their Russian treasures, initially through department stores and later at the Hammer Galleries. It was through the Hammers, and Alexander and Ray Schaffer of A La Vieille Russie, that the great American collections of Fabergé were formed, including those of Matilda Geddings Gray, India Early Minshall, Marjorie Merriweather Post, and Lillian Thomas Pratt.

Two of Fabergé's grandchildren, both children of his son Alexander, were among the Russians to settle in the United States. Alexander (1912–88), born in Moscow, was a geneticist and professor emeritus at the University of Texas. Irina (1925–87), born in Paris, married Morgan Arthur Gunst in 1947 and settled in California in the 1950s. Morgan Alexander Gunst and Marina Aline Gunst, great-great-grandchildren of Peter Carl, reside in the United States today.

The final section of the book spans the period from 1950 to the present, covering such celebrated collectors as Jack and Belle Linsky and Helen and Lansdell K. Christie. An attempt has been made to reconstruct part of their collections, the finest of their kind in the United States prior to the appearance of Malcolm S. Forbes. Forbes, with some justice dubbed the "king of Fabergé collectors," from 1963 until his death in 1990 amassed what is without doubt the premier Fabergé collection in the world. Fine Fabergé collections are still being formed today, although their owners generally prefer anonymity.

The success of *Fabergé: Imperial Jeweler* (1993–94), underwritten by Unilever/FABERGÉ CO. and coorganized by the Fabergé Arts Foundation, Washington, D.C.,

and St. Petersburg, and the State Hermitage Museum, St. Petersburg, was one of the factors that led to the development of this exhibition and catalogue in the United States. Original plans developed by this author, the foundation's curator, were amplified as exhibition arrangements moved forward. Thanks to the kind intervention of Peter Schaffer of A La Vieille Russie, a first exchange of letters concerning a choice of venues took place in early 1994 with Harry S. Parker III, director of the Fine Arts Museums of San Francisco, who, from the beginning, gave the project his full support.

The organization of this exhibition and the publication of its catalogue have been a labor of love for all involved. First and foremost, thanks must go to the national tour organizer, the Fine Arts Museums of San Francisco, Director Harry S. Parker III, and Curator of European Decorative Arts and Sculpture Lee Hunt Miller. Ms. Miller has been unflagging in her dedication to this project. The staff at the Fine Arts Museums of San Francisco has been exemplary in its efficiency. These include Kathe Hodgson, Coordinator of Exhibitions; Ann Heath Karlstrom, Director of Publications and Graphic Design; Therese Chen, Chief Registrar; and Lesley Bone, Objects Conservator.

No exhibition is possible without the full cooperation and generosity of lenders, who in this case have been asked to part with their precious objects for almost eighteen months. This is a major concession, especially for those institutions where Fabergé collections are focal points of attraction. Particular thanks therefore are extended to the following institutions, their directors, curators, and staff: Katharine C. Lee, Director, and David Park Curry, Curator of American Arts, Virginia Museum of Fine Arts, Richmond, for circulating their exhibition concurrently; Robert P. Bergman, Director, William Talbot, Deputy Director, and Henry Hawley, Chief Curator, Later Western Art, the Cleveland Museum of Art; E. John Bullard III, Director, and John Webster Keefe, Curator of Decorative Arts, New Orleans Museum of Art; Frederick Fischer, Director, and Anne Odom, Chief Curator, Hillwood Museum, Washington, D.C.; the Metropolitan Museum of Art, New York, Philippe de Montebello, Director, and Clare Le Corbeiller, Curator of European Sculpture and Decorative Arts; the Forbes family, in particular Christopher Forbes, Vice Chairman, Forbes Inc., as well as Margaret Kelly, Director, and Robyn Tromeur, Assistant Curator, Forbes Magazine Collection. Further thanks must go to Gary Vikan, Director, and William R. Johnston, Associate Director, the Walters Art Gallery, Baltimore; and Robert T. Buck, Director, and Kevin Stayton, Curator of Decorative Arts, the Brooklyn Museum. The organizers are grateful particularly to all private lenders, both named and anonymous, especially Joan Rivers, the de Guigné family, and John Traina. Brothers Paul and Peter Schaffer of A La Vieille Russie have been most generous with loans of objects from their holdings formerly in the collection of Lansdell K. Christie. The former, together with dealer Andre Ruzhnikov of Palo Alto, California, also have been helpful in filling other gaps, allowing a full and comprehensive showing of the Russian craftman's art.

Substantial research has gone into this exhibition. Sadly, the archives of the Hammer Galleries apparently no longer exist, precluding any serious study of Fabergé sales by the Bolsheviks in America between 1927 and 1938. Future research in KGB and FBI archives may offer alternative sources. The archives of A La Vieille Russie, another potential mine of information about this period, have yet to be researched. This exhibition must therefore be considered but a first step in an ongoing process of discovery.

Those who have assisted in the research for this project include Leslie P. Symington and Kathleen Luhrs, who investigated the first generation of Fabergé collectors; Christopher Forbes, who contributed an illuminating chapter on his late father; the curators of the lending institutions, Anne Odom of the Hillwood Museum, David Park Curry of the Virginia Museum of Fine Arts in Richmond, Henry Hawley of the Cleveland Museum of Art, and John Webster Keefe of the New Orleans Museum of Art, who contributed catalogue descriptions as well as valuable, often

unpublished information and photographs concerning the respective benefactors of their museums. Fabergé dealers A. Kenneth Snowman and Geoffrey Munn of Wartski, London, and Messrs. Schaffer of A La Vieille Russie also have supplied information about their former clients, as far as their proverbial discretion permitted. Robert Woolley and Gerard Hill of Sotheby's, Anthony Phillips of Christie's, and Alice Ilich, consultant, have all kindly shared their knowledge of the American Fabergé market.

The national sponsor of the exhibition, FABERGÉ CO., owner of the Fabergé trademark, must be especially thanked. As with the last European exhibition of Fabergé, sponsored by Unilever/Fabergé of London and Paris, *Fabergé in America* owes its realization primarily to Patrick J. Choël, President and Chief Executive Officer of FABERGÉ CO. It is due entirely to his enthusiasm that such an ambitious enterprise could be brought to a safe conclusion. Those who have actively participated in this project at FABERGÉ CO. include Bill Ecker, Jean-Denis Voin, and Marie Tully. Day-to-day work on the exhibition in all its stages on behalf of the sponsor was performed by Annemarie Cairns, Ruth Sarfaty, Susan Prout, Steven Burtch, Diana Buchanan, Mindy Krufky, and Céline Gilg of Cairns and Associates.

—Géza von Habsburg
Guest Curator

NOTES

1. A recently published Fabergé bibliography (McCanless 1994), includes 1,772 items and covers "a century of published literature" on the subject, which has since grown by several hundred more entries.

2. Christopher Forbes, in Habsburg 1987, pp. 100–3.

3. Paul Schaffer, in Habsburg/Lopato 1994, pp. 160–64.

Note to the Reader

All catalogue entries are written by Géza von Habsburg, with the exception of entries for the Cleveland Museum of Art, by Henry Hawley; the Virginia Museum of Fine Arts, by David Park Curry; the Hillwood Museum, by Anne Odom; and the Forbes Magazine Collection, by Robyn Tromeur.

Most but not all Fabergé objects bear stamped or engraved marks of the firm. As a rule items made in St. Petersburg are marked Fabergé, in Cyrillic letters, and with the initials of the workmaster or maker. In general objects produced in Moscow are marked in Cyrillic with Fabergé's name and initial or with his initials only, given herein as KF. Objects from Moscow usually carry the firm's Imperial Warrant but do not show workmaster initials. Assay marks indicate the gold or silver alloy used; these marks are sometimes followed by the assay master's initials. Fabergé objects can be associated with their city of manufacture according to variations in the assay marks. The most common gold alloy is 56 *zolotniki* (14 karats), and the most common silver alloy is 84 *zolotniki* (875/1000). Only *zolotniki* of 72 or above for gold (18 karats) and of 88 or above for silver (916/1000) are given here. Unless otherwise indicated, inscriptions on the pieces are in Cyrillic characters.

Russian names, particularly those of the imperial family, that are familiar to general readers are given herein with their Western spellings, such as Nicholas II, Alexandra, and Alexei (in association with the czarevitch). Other names are transliterated according to a modified Library of Congress system.

Fabergé

IN AMERICA

Fig. 1. *Peter Carl Fabergé sorting a parcel of gemstones, ca. 1900.*
Photo: Hugo Oeberg, courtesy Géza von Habsburg.

History of
the House of Fabergé

Peter Carl Fabergé (1846–1920; fig. 1) was born in St. Petersburg, Russia, son of jeweler Gustav Fabergé.[1] Educated first in St. Petersburg and later in Dresden, as a jeweler and businessman, Carl Fabergé in the mid-1860s began working for his father's firm at 16 Bolshaya Morskaya Street, St. Petersburg. By 1866 Fabergé was active for the Imperial Cabinet, the body that oversaw the czar's treasure house and all new jewelry orders. Fabergé repaired and appraised objects in precious stones and metals free of charge to the Imperial Cabinet, thus ingratiating himself with the officials who later would help his ascent to fame.

By 1872 Fabergé was married and had taken over his father's shop. Between 1874 and 1884, four sons, Eugène, Agathon, Alexander, and Nicholas, were born, all later to enter the family business as designers. Fabergé's brother, Agathon (1862–95), a little-known but important influence on the early production of the firm, collaborated with Carl from 1882 until his untimely death.

Contrary to popular belief, the Fabergés themselves did not make jewelry. No object or jewel has survived that is known to have been crafted by either brother, or by the sons. The Fabergés stood at the apex of a pyramid, overseeing a design studio and delegating production to a head workmaster, who in turn supervised the execution of all important commissions and farmed out lesser or specialist pieces to subsidiary workshops. Final approval of the finished item, however, lay with Carl Fabergé himself.

An exceptionally gifted entrepreneur, Carl Fabergé selected and cultivated the best artisans for his specialized workshops by assuring job security, supplying all professional needs, and guaranteeing the sale of their production. In return, Fabergé demanded from his employees a technical perfection hitherto unheard of, a quality that became the hallmark of the firm's entire production. The genius of the Fabergé workshop is based primarily on this craftsmanship and on the family's innovative designs.

During the first fifteen years under Carl Fabergé's stewardship, the firm's jewelry designs followed those of the European mainstream, imitating various revivalist styles from antiquity to the Renaissance, from Louis XV to Marie Antoinette. Fabergé's early works in the archaeological-revivalist style resemble those of the Castellani family in London, and his diamond-set floral brooches and pendants follow traditional French originals in the manner of Oscar Massin. His more expensive creations can be compared to contemporary works by Chaumet and Boucheron. His first objets d'art, crafted by head workmaster Erik Kollin (active 1870–84), are antiquarian in taste.

From the beginning Fabergé, forever the accomplished businessman, was prepared to cater to a diversified clientele. For the Imperial Cabinet, the Fabergé silver factory in St. Petersburg produced monumental silver services, each priced at 50,000 rubles, as well as official presentation gifts. For his newly rich clients he crafted lavish silver services in the neo-Gothic style and expensive diamond necklaces. His Muscovite clients, most of them from the wealthy traditional merchant class, clamored for silver and cloisonné enamel wares in the Russian seventeenth-

Fig. 2. *Fabergé's premises at 24 Bolshaya Morskaya, St. Petersburg, ca. 1905. Photo: Courtesy Géza von Habsburg.*

century revivalist style, in the art nouveau idiom, or in the neo-Russian style.

The year 1882 marked Fabergé's debut as a leading Russian jeweler. His display of objects in the archaeological-revivalist style at the Pan-Russian Exhibition in Moscow attracted the attention of the press, which hailed him as an innovator who had brought the craft "back to its lofty stand," opening "a new era in the art of jewelry."[2] Maria Feodorovna, wife of Czar Alexander III, acquired the first of many objects from Fabergé, a pair of cicada-shaped cuff links inspired by Greek fourth-century B.C. originals in the Hermitage.

In 1884–85 Fabergé gave his firm a significant new direction. He replaced Kollin, his old-fashioned head workmaster, with Mikhail Perkhin (active 1884–1903), a brilliant, self-taught craftsman. Together with his brother Agathon, Fabergé introduced a new line of objects crafted from gold and semiprecious stones, and enameled in the French eighteenth-century manner. The inspiration for many of Fabergé's early creations came from the Hermitage and its

treasury of eighteenth-century art objects collected or received by the czars. A snuffbox dated 1884,[3] a first example of this new style, shows Fabergé's workmaster still testing his somewhat shaky skills on an object of dubious design and displaying a surfeit of large diamonds, probably supplied by the Imperial Cabinet. Many other French-inspired objects were to follow: fans, opera glasses, snuffboxes, bonbonnières, scent bottles, *carnets de bal*, parasol and cane handles, seals, and entire toilet services.

What differentiated Fabergé from all his contemporaries was his constant quest for novelty. He proudly declared in his brochures that "old items, which are out of fashion, are not kept in stock: once a year they are collected and destroyed."[4] This gives credence to the belief that most of Fabergé's objects are one of a kind. There are a few exceptions to this rule, usually popular items that stood in high demand. Shopping at Fabergé's must have been a delight; each object was an amusing, ingenious invention bound to charm its recipient. Indeed the very essence of a Fabergé object was less the object itself than the pleasure of choosing and giving it. Many of the objects issuing from the Fabergé workshops were made to order.

Fabergé rapidly achieved recognition: a first gold medal for his 1882 exhibits; the title of Supplier to the Imperial Court (1885); gold medals for exhibits in Nürnberg (1885)

Fig. 3. *Fabergé's sales room, St. Petersburg, ca. 1905. Photo: Courtesy Géza von Habsburg.*

Fig. 4. Fabergé's shop at Kuznetzki Bridge, Moscow, 1890.
Photo: Courtesy Géza von Habsburg.

and Copenhagen (1888); the Order of St. Stanislas 1st Class (1889); the title of Appraiser of the Imperial Cabinet (1890). Simultaneously imperial orders ensued: the first Easter egg (1884–85); a series of jewels and snuffboxes to accompany the Czarevitch Nicholas on his 1890 world tour; the grand 1891 silver wedding anniversary clock for the czar and czarina;[5] the impressive presents created in 1892 for the golden wedding anniversary of the king and queen of Denmark;[6] the betrothal present of Czarevitch Nicholas to his bride, the future Czarina Alexandra Feodorovna, a magnificent diamond necklace; and a lavish pearl and diamond necklace given by the czar and czarina to their future daughter-in-law (1894).

Within thirty years Fabergé succeeded in supplanting his major competitors. By the time of Czar Nicholas II's coronation in 1896, most official presents to the imperial couple and gifts to visiting heads of state and family members were ordered from Fabergé. But the year 1900 marked the crowning achievement of Fabergé's career. He was singled out to represent the art of Russian jewelry at the

great Paris Exposition Universelle. By imperial command, he exhibited the finest of the Easter eggs crafted for the czars. Fifty million visitors passed through the world's fair. Fabergé reaped a gold medal for his exhibits, the Order of the Legion of Honor for himself, a sellout of his stock, worldwide recognition, and innumerable commissions for his firm.

In Russia, too, Fabergé's success was marked in 1900 with the opening of new premises in a large custom-built house at 24 Bolshaya Morskaya, St. Petersburg (figs. 2, 3). In 1902 a public exhibition in St. Petersburg of objects crafted by Fabergé for the imperial family was acclaimed by the press. With a production center in Moscow (opened 1887; figs. 4, 5); outlets in Odessa (1900), London (1903), and Kiev (1906–10); and with regular sales trips to the Far East, Paris, Cannes, and Rome (from 1908), the three hundred craftsmen in St. Petersburg and two hundred in Moscow barely kept abreast of orders (figs. 6, 7). In 1913, in a last flowering of Russian pomp and splendor, the lavish festivities for the Romanov tercentenary were marked by hundreds of souvenirs designed by Fabergé.

Fabergé's fame was spread by his two chief patronesses, both daughters of King Christian IX of Denmark: Czarina (later Dowager Empress) Maria Feodorovna and her sister, Alexandra, princess of Wales (queen of England [1901–10], wife of Edward VII). The former kept her

Fig. 5. Fabergé's sales room, Moscow, 1890s. Charles Bowe, the manager, is on the left. Photo: Courtesy Géza von Habsburg.

Top: Fig. 6. *The Holmström jewelry workshop, St. Petersburg, ca. 1903. August Holmström is the third figure from the left; behind him stands his son Albert. Photo: Courtesy Fersman Mineralogical Institute, Moscow.* Bottom: Fig. 7. *The silver factory at Ekaterinski Canal, St. Petersburg, ca. 1903. Photo: Courtesy Fersman Mineralogical Institute, Moscow.*

peerless collection of Fabergé eggs, animals, and flowers at the Anichkov Palace, St. Petersburg. The collection of Queen Alexandra, augmented by Queen Mary, once kept at Sandringham and now at Buckingham Palace, is presently the world's biggest, numbering more than 700 pieces, of which approximately 250 are animals.[7]

From the beginning Fabergé saw himself not simply as a jeweler (or silversmith), but as a producer of virtuoso objects. Large ostentatious objects or vulgar diamond-set jewels (as he felt his competitors Tiffany, Cartier, and Boucheron produced) did not interest him. Instead, he offered his highly sophisticated clients and foreign buyers elegant objects of exquisite design but not necessarily of great intrinsic value.

Fabergé's worldwide reputation is due chiefly to his incomparable series of imperial Easter eggs, generally thought to have numbered fifty-six, produced from 1884 to 1916. Eleven of these eggs fall into the reign of Czar Alexander III, from 1884 until 1894, and all were presents from the czar to his wife (fig. 8). From 1895 onward Nicholas II continued the tradition, giving a further forty-four eggs to both his mother and his wife (fig. 9). One unfinished egg made in 1917 has survived. From this imperial series, forty-four eggs still exist, and two additional eggs are known from photographs. Recent research in Russian archives has upset their established chronology.[8] Descriptions of more than eight unknown or lost eggs have surfaced. Many datings have been altered by the appearance of original invoices or lists of purchases from Fabergé by the Imperial Cabinet. Some eggs, hitherto accepted as "imperial," are now in doubt; others, previously questioned, have been reinstated.

Fabergé's first eggs were inspired by prototypes of the eighteenth century, but by the early 1890s Fabergé's creativity asserted itself. Eggs as celebrated as the Coronation egg of 1897 (cat. no. 285) and the Lilies of the Valley egg of 1898 (cat. no. 284) show the master in full possession of his art. Masterpieces were created year after year, some taking more than two years to complete. The series reached its pinnacle in 1913–14 with such inventions as the Winter egg and the Catherine the Great egg (cat. no. 175), but took a more muted note with two 1915 Red Cross eggs (cat. nos. 99, 153), which evoked the suffering of the Russian nation during World War I.

From a technical point of view, Fabergé's virtuosity resided in the quality of his enamels, and it is for these that he was justly acclaimed at the Paris world's fair in 1900. Based on his studies of French art objects in the treasury of the Hermitage, Fabergé mastered the difficult technique of enameling *en ronde bosse* (in the round). By continuous experimentation, he developed an incredibly varied palette of more than 140 enamel colors. Up to seven consecutive coats of a glasslike fluid were applied to objects in precious metals, often painted or decorated under the last layer (see cat. nos. 16, 207). Given the limited technical means at the disposal of Fabergé's craftsmen, their achievements verge on the miraculous. The brilliant colors and the lustrous surfaces of Fabergé enamels have few parallels among the work of his competitors.

After the Easter eggs, Fabergé's flowers were his most popular item. Both Dowager Empress Maria Feodorovna and Grand Duchess Vladimir held extensive collections of Fabergé flowers; Queen Elizabeth II today owns the most celebrated group of twenty-five flowers, many of which were collected by Queen Alexandra. These flowers were inspired by nature studies popular toward the middle of the nineteenth century in China, Western Europe, and Russia. The best-known models are single flower sprays made of gold and precious and/or semiprecious stones set in vases of rock crystal carved to simulate water—such as the dandelion puff ball actually made with carefully tied seeds of the natural flower (cat. no. 186). A sumptuous Fabergé basket of lilies of the valley (cat. no. 59), Czarina Alexandra's favorite flower and arguably the firm's finest work of art now in the United States, stood on the empress's desk until the Russian Revolution.

Fabergé's world of hardstone animals was largely inspired by Japanese netsuke, of which the master had a substantial collection. Carved from specimen semiprecious stones mostly from Russian mines, they are endearing humoristic renderings carefully observed from nature. The collection of the dowager empress at the Anichkov Palace counted more than one hundred examples of these delightful creations. Today they find their fullest expression in the collection of some 250 animal carvings belonging to Queen Elizabeth II. Queen Alexandra once owned the majority of these, too. Many were specially commissioned portraits of her pets at Sandringham.

Fig. 8. *Czar Alexander III and Czarina Maria Feodorovna,*
ca. 1890. Photo: Courtesy Yuri Shelaev, St. Petersburg.

bers of society were presented with more lavish Fabergé objects. A room in the Hermitage, reserved for imperial presents, was well stocked with items from Fabergé's shop, from which the Imperial Cabinet selected appropriate gifts for visiting heads of state. State gifts for the sultan of Turkey, the shah of Persia, the emir of Bukhara, and the emperors of China and Japan were specially ordered from the jeweler.

Among the favorite clients of Fabergé was Swedish-born Emanuel Nobel, who surprised his lady guests at dinner with miniature Fabergé eggs hidden in their napkins. According to Franz Birbaum, Fabergé's chief designer, Grand Duke Aleksei Aleksandrovich "every year went to France, taking with him as presents a good quantity of our works, and he created a very good reputation for us by distributing them in high society."[9] Stanislas Poklewski-Koziell, counselor at the Russian embassy in London, "went off to country house parties . . . loaded with things

The imperial family also assiduously collected Fabergé's hardstone statuettes, some of which represented Russian folkloristic types, while others were caricatures or portrait figures. Their origin lies in Florentine *pietre dure* sculptures of the seventeenth century. The polychrome stone elements were carved in a hardstone cutting factory and then assembled in the head workmaster's atelier. The Russian branch of the Nobel family owned a large group of such figures, some of which, in their exaggerated realism, have truly painterly qualities. One of the most celebrated of these figures is a portrait of Vara Panina, a well-known Moscow gypsy singer (cat. no. 197).

At the peak of Fabergé's success, the firm supplied most of the gifts exchanged by relatives of the imperial family in Russia, Denmark, Germany, and England for christenings, name days, birthdays, Christmas, and Easter. On their travels, members of the imperial family bestowed Fabergé cigarette cases and pins to equerries and ladies-in-waiting, policemen, and detectives. Higher-ranking mem-

Fig. 9. *The future Czar Nicholas II and his fiancée, Princess*
Alix of Hessen-Darmstadt, the future czarina, 1894.
Photo: Courtesy Yuri Shelaev, St. Petersburg.

from Fabergé; two large suitcases filled with them."[10] The firm's fame in Russia was such that it was synonymous with luxury. To "bring out the Fabergé" meant to deck a table with the choicest finery. On the eve of World War I, the firm, one of the largest in Europe, had produced more than 150,000 jewels, silver items, and art objects.

The decline came rapidly: World War I, tragic for Russia, brought about rigorous measures of austerity. Jeweled articles were replaced by much simpler works made of steel, brass, and copper. Most of Fabergé's specialist craftsmen were drafted into the army, and his workshops were converted into factories for making hand grenades and artillery shells. After the 1917 October Revolution, the Bolshevik takeover, and the murder of the imperial family, Fabergé fled to Switzerland in 1918 and died there two years later.

—Géza von Habsburg

NOTES

1. For the history of the house of Fabergé, see Habsburg/Lopato 1994, pp. 20–37. A detailed chronology of the firm can be found on pp. 38–53.

2. *Niva*, no. 40 (1882), pp. 952–54, quoted in Habsburg/Lopato 1994, pp. 57–58.

3. Habsburg 1987, cat. 404.

4. Solodkoff 1984, p. 36.

5. Habsburg/Lopato 1994, cat. 4.

6. Ibid., cats. 79, 80.

7. See Queen's Gallery 1995, cats. 1–38, 66–117, 176–96, 279–341, 425–59, 512–15, 529–43.

8. Lopato 1991, pp. 91–93; Habsburg/Lopato 1994, pp. 71–75; Tatiana Muntian, in Solodkoff 1995, pp. 24–26.

9. Habsburg/Lopato 1994, p. 454.

10. Bainbridge 1966, pp. 82–83.

Fig. 1. Ostrich Feather Fan, *signed Fabergé, initials of workmaster Henrik Wigström,*
l. 20½ inches. Forbes Magazine Collection, New York. The American Walter Winans
acquired the fan from Fabergé's London branch for £90 on September 19, 1908 (see
Appendix II). Photo: H. Peter Curran, courtesy Forbes Magazine Collection.

Carl Fabergé and
His American Clients

◆

1900–1917

The story of Fabergé's sales to American clients is closely linked to the economic histories of Britain, Russia, and America at the turn of the twentieth century. By 1892 there were 4,047 American millionaires, of whom more than one hundred had fortunes exceeding $10 million. These millionaires of the Gilded Age paid an average of $300,000 per year to maintain their city mansions and country homes, and $50,000 per year to keep their yachts afloat. They lived notoriously ostentatious lives; traveled to London, Paris, the Côte d'Azur, and St. Petersburg; and lavishly spent their rapidly gained fortunes. European antique dealers, auction houses, jewelers, and fortune hunters welcomed this influx of American money. Fabergé, too, experienced the power of the dollar.

Acquisitions by Americans from
Fabergé in Russia

Russia's vast reservoir of mineral wealth and its immense economic potential attracted more than one American financier or entrepreneur at the turn of the century. Europeans were already vying with each other for Russian mining and industrial concessions. Some Americans, however, were drawn by the sumptuous lifestyle of the fabulously rich Russian imperial family and their court at St. Petersburg. Inspired by the sophisticated taste of Russian society, visiting Americans discovered Fabergé's shop on fashionable Bolshaya Morskaya and brought back a number of the jeweler's creations to the United States (fig. 1).

Because Fabergé's Russian archives are missing, our chief sources of information are the autobiographies and biographies of the rich and famous of the period. The first documented American visitor at Fabergé's shop in Russia was Princess Cantacuzène (née Julia Grant, granddaughter of President Ulysses S. Grant; fig. 2), who crossed the Atlantic in 1900 to visit her husband's Russian domains. During her stay in St. Petersburg, she visited Dowager Empress Maria Feodorovna at Anichkov Palace: "Her Majesty asked me to sit down. There were several comfortable chairs, with little tables by them. The latter seemed covered with bits of old silver, tiny animals carved in precious stones by Fabergé, or various enamels of his making, a small clock among others—things such as any one might have in a sitting-room."[1]

Princess Cantacuzène had crossed the ocean in the company of millionaire Henry C. Walters (fig. 3) of Baltimore and his favorite niece, Laura Delano, on board Walters's 224-foot yacht *Narada*. This summer cruise would be Walters's only visit to Russia. He derived his fortune from the Atlantic Coast Line, one of America's largest railways. Following in the footsteps of his father, he collected Salon paintings of the nineteenth century, and in three decades he amassed some 22,000 works of art (now housed in the Walters Art Gallery, Baltimore). Walters, who also collected jeweled objects, including exquisite Lalique and Tiffany brooches, was taken to the Fabergé shop by Princess Cantacuzène. Apparently he returned several times "to

Fig. 2. *Princess Cantacuzène, née Julia Grant,*
ca. 1918. Photo: Courtesy Simon and Schuster.

spend many happy hours with Fabergé and bought pieces for his collection, for his family, and friends."² He acquired a number of small animal carvings for himself and some parasol handles for his niece (see cat. nos. 1–6). Later, in 1930, Henry Walters was to buy the exquisite Gatchina Palace egg of 1901 and the Rose Trellis egg (cat. no. 7) from the Paris dealer Polovtsov.

Consuelo Vanderbilt (fig. 4), granddaughter of American railroad magnate Cornelius Vanderbilt, was married against her will to the ninth duke of Marlborough in 1894.³ In 1902 she traveled to Russia prior to the coronation of Edward VII, for which she had been asked by Queen Alexandra to be one of four canopy bearers. She described the lavish balls, including a *bal des palmiers* at the Winter Palace at which dinner was served on "gold and silver plate fashioned by Germain—chased and beautiful in shape and color." After a dinner with Grand Duke and Grand Duchess Vladimir, she was shown the celebrated jewels of the grand duchess "set out in glass cases in her dressing-room." She visited the dowager empress at the Anichkov

Fig. 3. *Henry C. Walters and Mrs. Pembroke Jones (later*
Mrs. Walters), photographed ca. 1905 by Laura Delano, Walters's
niece. Photo: Courtesy The Walters Art Gallery, Baltimore.

Fig. 4. *Consuelo Vanderbilt, duchess of Marlborough,*
at her wedding, 1895. Photo: Courtesy New York
Public Library Picture Collection.

Palace and, as Princess Cantacuzène had two years before, must have admired her Fabergé objects. Certainly she was aware of the popularity of this Russian master craftsman, for although she makes no mention of the acquisition, the duchess of Marlborough commissioned a pink enamel Easter egg–clock from Fabergé (cat. no. 8). Crafted by Mikhail Perkhin, it bears her crowned monogram. She was to sell it in 1926, after her divorce from the duke of Marlborough and her marriage to Jacques Balsan, to help finance a hospital in Paris: "An auction of gifts, including a Fabergé clock I had brought back from Russia and an automobile, brought lively bidding." The successful bidder was Polish soprano Ganna Walska, second wife of the president and chairman of the board of the International Harvester Company of Chicago, Harold Fowler McCormick. The egg was later sold on her behalf by Parke-Bernet in 1965.

A Fabergé frame dating from before 1896 (fig. 5), once in a Liechtenstein princely collection, by tradition also has a McCormick provenance. It contains a miniature by Vasilii Zuiev of a lady whose traits are those of Edith Rocke-

Fig. 6. *Edith Rockefeller McCormick and Harold F. McCormick on their honeymoon, Rome, 1896. Photo: Courtesy Rockefeller Archive Center, North Tarrytown, New York.*

Fig. 5. *Fabergé frame with miniature by Vasilii Zuiev of Edith Rockefeller McCormick (workmaster Mikhail Perkhin, St. Petersburg before 1896, h. 4⅞ inches). Collection Ambassador William Kazan, Paris.*

feller, third child of John D. Rockefeller Sr., who was described as "a thin dark woman with haunted eyes" (fig. 6).[4] In 1895 she became the first wife of Harold McCormick. They traveled to Europe on their honeymoon and might have acquired the Fabergé frame in St. Petersburg. A leader of Chicago society, Edith supported numerous philanthropies. Her notable collection of jewels and silver, with an estimated value of $5 million, included emeralds of Catherine the Great (for which she paid $1.5 million) and the gold dinner service of Napoleon. In 1913 she became a disciple of Carl Jung and lived for a number of years in Zurich. McCormick divorced her in 1921 to marry Walska, and Edith spent her remaining years in Chicago. McCormick also acquired a number of Fabergé objects in London in 1913 (see Appendix II).

Another McCormick-Fabergé connection was made by Robert Sanderson McCormick. He was named American ambassador to the Russian imperial court in St. Petersburg from 1902 to 1905[5] and was later *en poste* in Paris. One of his Paris aides was Robert Woods Bliss, a later client of Fabergé (see Appendix II). During McCormick's tenure in Russia, President Theodore Roosevelt was instrumental in

Fig. 7. Decanter, *Imperial Warrant mark of Ivan Khlebnikov,*
Moscow 1896–1908, silver and champlevé enamel, h. 20½ inches.
Sagamore Hill National Historic Site, National Park Service.
Presented on the behalf of Nicholas II to President
Theodore Roosevelt in 1905, the decanter is inscribed
"Given in peace and friendship."

of his father in 1913, Morgan became head of the family firm. Like his father, he was a well-known collector of rare books and manuscripts. In 1923 he transformed the family collection into a permanent, endowed institution, the Morgan Library. He donated art objects to the Metropolitan Museum of Art, New York, and the Wadsworth Athenaeum, Hartford, Connecticut.

Acquisitions by Americans from Fabergé's London Shop

In Britain the decline of agriculture and a population shift in the late 1800s from farmlands to industrial centers led to a loss in rents for many aristocrats, obliging them to dispossess themselves of both land and chattels. At about this time rich Americans flocked to England in droves. For these families with marriageable daughters, the court of Albert Edward, Prince of Wales, son of Queen Victoria, and his circle, known as the Marlborough House set, was

bringing about the peace treaty between Russia and Japan signed at Portsmouth, New Hampshire, on September 5, 1905. For this achievement Czar Nicholas II presented Roosevelt with a commemorative silver tankard (fig. 7), which hitherto has been attributed to Fabergé but is in fact by the silver manufacturer Ivan Khlebnikov.

John Pierpont Morgan Jr. (fig. 8) was another of Fabergé's early American clients.[6] The only son of financier and industrialist John Pierpont Morgan Sr., he graduated from Harvard in 1889. In 1892 he became a partner in his father's firm, J. P. Morgan and Company. Sent to St. Petersburg in October 1905 to negotiate a crucial loan to the Russian government, Morgan witnessed the city's joyous reception of Nicholas II's October Manifesto and the birth of a constitutional monarchy. During his stay, Morgan visited Fabergé's shop; his purchases included a miniature sedan chair (cat. no. 16) and a miniature chair (cat. no. 15), as well as six Fabergé snowflake brooches, four of which he presented to his children (cat. nos. 10–13). After the death

Fig. 8. *J. P. Morgan Sr. and J. P. Morgan Jr., 1912.*
Photo: Courtesy The Archives, The Pierpont Morgan
Library, New York.

Fig. 9. *Lady Bache Cunard, ca. 1890s. Photo: Bettmann Archive, New York.*

Fig. 10. *Mrs. William Bateman Leeds, ca. 1913. Photo: Bettmann Archive, New York.*

an obvious attraction. As Victorian stuffiness evaporated, social life in London became positively ebullient, and the European aristocracy recognized the appeal of American money. American-born Lady Paget, née Mary Fiske Stevens of New York, is said to have run a marriage bureau in her London drawing room, angling for rich brides for impoverished noblemen. In all, between 1870 and 1914, more than one hundred marriages were recorded between the sons of British peers and American heiresses. It was suggested that a tax be put on Chicago and New York heiresses who were considered to be the most considerable exports from the New World to the Old. Of the millions of dollars that left the United States for Britain during these decades, some were spent on restoring country homes and on lavish entertainment, but much was frittered away frivolously in gambling and at the races.

Among the most celebrated Anglo-American matches were those of Sir Bache Cunard and Maud (Emerald) Burke (fig. 9); the earl of Craven and Cornelia Bradley Martin; Prince Hatzfeldt and Clara Prentice Huntington;

the duke of Manchester and Helena Zimmerman; and the duke of Roxburghe and Mary Wilson Goelet. All were Fabergé clients listed in the sales ledgers of the jeweler's London store. One of Fabergé's most important and richest American-born clients in London was Mrs. William Bateman Leeds (née Nancy Stewart, fig. 10). Between 1913 and 1916 she acquired more than sixty pieces from the London shop (see Appendix II). She was known for her extravagant shopping sprees in Paris and London and for her love of lavish jewelry. Other fashionable Anglo-American couples included Lord Camoys and Mildred Sherman; Lord Curzon and Mary Leiter; the earl of Granard and Beatrice Ogden Mills; the earl of Essex and Adela Beach Grant; Sir Thomas Fermor-Hesketh and Flora Sharon of San Francisco; and Lord Tankerville and Leonora Sophie van Marter. Some of these brides reputedly came with dowries as high as $5 million and annual allowances exceeding $75,000; others inherited vast sums of money.

The so-called first American families of the time were as conscious of their rank as their European counterparts.

Fig. 11. *Mrs. Bradley Martin Sr., at her 1897 ball, wearing Marie Antoinette's stomacher. Photo: Courtesy Mr. and Mrs. Richard J. Hutto.*

C. W. de Lyon Nichols's 1904 society spoof, *The Ultra-Fashionable Peerage of America*, classified them into exclusive groupings of the "ultra-smart 150," the "400 ultra-fashionables" of the provincial cities, and the "outer fringe 400."[7] The four hundred "coroneted" families were usually identified as those who had obtained an invitation to an Astor ball or, better still, an Astor dinner. Among the old guard, the Astors, Goelets, Whitelaw Reids, and Vanderbilts were Fabergé clients. Further Fabergé listings from among the "400" include the names of the Brice, Crocker, Dodge, Drexel, Munn, and Thompson families.

Some American Fabergé clients were obliged to expatriate themselves to Britain for having dared to live too ostentatiously, thus arousing the unwelcome curiosity of tax assessors. Among those who took up residence in Britain and in France were the Bradley Martins and James Hazen Hyde, the former known for a notorious ball in 1897 at the

Waldorf Astoria Hotel, New York (fig. 11), reputed to have cost $350,000, and the latter for a similar affair in 1905 at Sherry's.

Unlike J. P. Morgan Jr., the Vanderbilts, and Henry C. Walters, who sailed to London on board their own yachts, American society generally traveled by luxury ocean liner. The times to be present in London were summer—June and July, which coincided with the thoroughbred horse races, culminating with Ascot Week, followed by shooting in August—and winter—from October through January, months given over to rounds of parties at country homes. For those who "belonged," the pursuit of pleasure was a consuming pastime. Weekend parties and sumptuous receptions demanded lavish presents, and this gay fin de siècle was the heyday for gifts from Fabergé and Cartier, whose sales ledgers in both London and Paris are filled with the names of the same fashionable clientele.

—Géza von Habsburg

NOTES

The author would like to thank Leslie P. Symington and Kathleen Luhrs for their unflagging help in identifying many American buyers and for their painstakingly compiled biographies and family trees, which provided background for this chapter and for Appendix II.

1. Julia Grant Cantacuzène, *My Life Here and There* (New York: Charles Scribner, 1921), pp. 205, 229–30.

2. Ross 1952, pp. 2, 4–10. Marvin C. Ross dedicated this volume to Princess Cantacuzène, "who first aroused the interest of Henry Walters in Fabergé and later my own."

3. Balsan 1952, pp. 89–90, 122–29, 199–200.

4. Edward T. James and Janet Wilson James, eds., *Notable American Women, 1607–1950*, vol. 2 (Cambridge: Belknap Press of Harvard University Press, 1975), p. 452.

5. Frank C. Waldrop, *McCormick of Chicago: An Unconventional Portrait of a Controversial Figure* (Englewood Cliffs, N.J.: Prentice Hall, 1966), pp. 51ff.

6. John D. Forbes, *J. P. Morgan Jr., 1867–1943* (Charlottesville: University Press of Virginia, 1981), pp. 56ff.

7. C. W. de Lyon Nichols, preface to *The Ultra-Fashionable Peerage of America* (New York: George Harjes, 1904).

Catalogue

1900–1917

This section includes items acquired by Americans from a Fabergé outlet, most often in St. Petersburg or in London.

— 1 —

RHINOCEROS
Jasper
L: 4⅝ inches

This standing figure is of variegated reddish-brown hardstone.

Provenance: Henry C. Walters, Fabergé, St. Petersburg, 1900

Bibliography: Ross 1952, p. 10; Snowman 1962, ill. 244; Habsburg/Lopato 1994, cat. 193, p. 314

Exhibitions: ALVR 1949, cat. 37; Hammer 1951; San Francisco 1964, cat. 23, cat. 45; St. Petersburg/Paris/London 1993–94

The Walters Art Gallery, Baltimore, 27.480

— 2 —

ANTEATER
Jasper, diamonds
L: 3½ inches

Provenance: Henry C. Walters, Fabergé, St. Petersburg, 1900

Bibliography: Ross 1952, p. 10 (ill.)

Exhibitions: ALVR 1949, cat. 1; Hammer 1951, cat. 1

The Walters Art Gallery, Baltimore, 42.354

━ 3 ━

CHIMPANZEE
Agate, diamonds
H: 3½ inches

Provenance: Henry C. Walters, Fabergé, St. Petersburg, 1900

Bibliography: Ross 1952, p. 9; Snowman 1962, ill. 243

Exhibitions: ALVR 1949, cat. 7; Hammer 1951, cat. 16(?); WAG 1959

The Walters Art Gallery, Baltimore, 42.353

━ 4 ━

PINK ENAMEL PARASOL HANDLE
Gold, enamel, diamonds, glass
L: 3⅛ inches
Marks: Fabergé, initials of workmaster Mikhail Perkhin,
assay mark of St. Petersburg before 1896, inv. no. 14137

The parasol handle is in the French eighteenth-century taste, painted with dendritic motifs under the pink *guilloché* enamel. The top opens to reveal a mirror.

Provenance: Henry C. Walters, Fabergé, St. Petersburg, 1900, for his sister Mrs. Warren Delano; gift of Laura Delano

Bibliography: Ross 1952, p. 8; Snowman 1953, ill. 174, appendix D, p. 145; Snowman 1962, ill. 195; Habsburg 1987, cat. 483, pp. 241–42

Exhibitions: Hammer 1951; Munich 1986–87

The Walters Art Gallery, Baltimore, 44.620

— 5 —

NEPHRITE PARASOL HANDLE
Nephrite, stones, diamonds, enamel, gold
L: 1¾ inches
Marks: Initials of workmaster Mikhail Perkhin, assay mark of
St. Petersburg 1896–1908, inv. no. 3224

Provenance: Henry C. Walters, Fabergé, St. Petersburg 1900,
for his niece Laura Delano; gift of Laura Delano, 1950

Bibliography: Ross 1952, p. 9

The Walters Art Gallery, Baltimore, 57.1841

— 6 —

ONYX PARASOL HANDLE
Onyx, enamel, diamonds, pearls
H: 2 inches
Marks: Initials of workmaster Mikhail Perkhin
Original fitted case stamped Fabergé, St. Petersburg, Moscow

Provenance: Henry C. Walters, Fabergé, St. Petersburg, 1900;
gift of Mrs. Frederick B. Adams

Exhibitions: ALVR 1961; WAG 1984, cat. 168, p. 80

The Walters Art Gallery, Baltimore, 57.1862

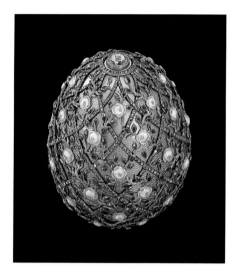

— 7 —

IMPERIAL ROSE TRELLIS EASTER EGG
Gold, enamel, diamonds
H: 3¹⁄₁₆ inches
Marks: Fabergé, initials of workmaster Henrik Wigström

The egg is of pale green translucent enamel over an engine-turned ground and latticed with bands of rose-cut diamonds. Applied on each segment is a painted pink opaque enamel bloom with translucent enamel leaves. A portrait diamond at the apex covers the date 1907; the diamond at the base has lost its device. The egg originally contained a (lost) surprise in the form of a jeweled locket.

Provenance: Presented by Czar Nicholas II to his wife, Czarina Alexandra Feodorovna, Easter 1907; Henry C. Walters, from dealer Polovtsov, Paris, 1930

Bibliography: Bainbridge 1949, pl. 42, note p. 65; Ross 1952, p. 6; Snowman 1962, p. 97, pls. 351–52; Habsburg/Solodkoff 1979, cat. 47; Snowman 1979, p. 101; Forbes 1980, p. 65; Solodkoff 1984, p. 92

Exhibitions: ALVR 1949, cat. 120; Hammer 1951, cat. 171; Cooper Union 1954, cat. 166; V&A 1977, cat. M19; WAG 1982; San Diego/Moscow 1989–90, cat. 29

The Walters Art Gallery, Baltimore, 44.501

— 8 —

DUCHESS OF MARLBOROUGH EASTER EGG
Gold, enamel, diamonds, pearls
H: 9¼ inches
Marks: Stamped Fabergé and engraved K Fabergé 1902, initials of
workmaster Mikhail Perkhin, assay mark of St. Petersburg 1896–1908

The egg is very similar to the Serpent Clock egg, an imperial Easter egg presented to Czarina Maria Feodorovna prior to 1889. In addition to minor decorative variations, the Duchess of Marlborough egg differs from its imperial counterpart by its larger size and color; the Serpent Clock egg is enameled translucent navy blue (see Snowman 1962, pl. LXVIII).

Provenance: Purchased on the occasion of the visit to Russia in 1902 of the duke and duchess of Marlborough (American-born heiress Consuelo Vanderbilt); sold by the duchess to aid a hospital in Vincennes, on Grand Prix Day, 1926, at the Cercle Interallie auction, Paris; Ganna Walska; Parke-Bernet, New York, May 14–15, 1965, lot 326, p. 50

Bibliography: Balsan 1952, p. 252; Waterfield/Forbes 1978, p. 30 (ill.); Habsburg/Solodkoff 1979, cat. 68 (ill.), pp. 118, 120, 126, 158, pl. 142; Forbes 1980, pp. 5, 26, 42, ill. 43; Solodkoff 1984, p. 185 (ill.); Forbes 1986, p. 53; Solodkoff 1986, p. 3, ill. p. 36; Solodkoff 1988, pp. 25, 40, 47, frontispiece; Hill 1989, pp. 14, 21, pl. 4

Exhibitions: ALVR 1983, cat. 552, pp. 16, 140, ill. p. 141; Florida 1995, p. 3, ill. p. 3, cover

The Forbes Magazine Collection, New York

— 9 —

VASE IN RENAISSANCE-STYLE MOUNT
Nephrite, gold, enamel, rubies, diamonds
H: 10 inches
Marks: Fabergé, initials of workmaster Mikhail Perkhin,
assay mark of St. Petersburg 1896–1908, inv. no. 4400,
original price tag for 3,250 rubles
Original fitted case stamped with Imperial Warrant,
St. Petersburg, Moscow

Renaissance-style mounts were used by Fabergé primarily for major presentation pieces (rock crystal vase, collection of Queen Elizabeth II [Habsburg/Lopato 1994, cat. 168]; rock crystal charger, State Hermitage Museum, St. Petersburg [ibid., cat. 111]; Dutch Colony tray, private collection, Buenos Aires [Habsburg/Solodkoff 1979, ill. pl. 45]). The shape of this vase, an opening lotus flower, might suggest that the piece was originally planned as an imperial presentation to King Chulalongkorn (Rama V) of Siam, but it was sold instead to an American client in 1903.

Provenance: Lydia Morris of Philadelphia, 1903

Bibliography: Habsburg/Solodkoff 1979, pl. 46;
Habsburg/Lopato 1994, p. 161

Exhibitions: ALVR 1983, cat. 310

Lent by courtesy of A La Vieille Russie,
New York (lent to New York only)

*The original price tag for the vase.
Photo: Courtesy A La Vieille Russie.*

— 10 —

SNOWFLAKE BROOCH-PENDANT
Platinized silver, diamonds, gold
Diam: ¹⁵⁄₁₆ inch
Marks: Initials of workmaster A. Holmström, assay mark of
St. Petersburg 1896–1908, inv. no. 73647

J. P. Morgan Jr. purchased six snowflake brooches, which
could be worn on a necklace. Four of these brooches, belonging to his grandchildren, are shown here. It is interesting to note that they all have the same stock number.
These brooches were designed for Fabergé by Alma
Theresia Pihl. The technique of platinizing silver utilized here is described by Snowman (1993, pp. 14–15),
who illustrates designs for a number of such brooches
(pp. 158–59).

Provenance: J. P. Morgan Jr., Fabergé, St. Petersburg, 1905

Private Collection

— 11 —

SNOWFLAKE BROOCH-PENDANT
Platinized silver, diamonds, gold
Diam: ¹⁵⁄₁₆ inch
Marks: Initials of workmaster A. Holmström, assay mark of
St. Petersburg 1896–1908, inv. no. 73647

Provenance: J. P. Morgan Jr., Fabergé, St. Petersburg, 1905

Private Collection

— 12 —

SNOWFLAKE BROOCH-PENDANT
Platinized silver, diamonds, gold
Diam: ¹⁵⁄₁₆ inch
Marks: Initials of workmaster A. Holmström, inv. no. 73647

Provenance: J. P. Morgan Jr., Fabergé, St. Petersburg, 1905

Private Collection

— 13 —

SNOWFLAKE BROOCH-PENDANT
Platinized silver, diamonds, gold
Diam: ¹⁵⁄₁₆ inch
Marks: Initials of workmaster A. Holmström, assay mark of
St. Petersburg 1896–1908, inv. no. 73647

Provenance: J. P. Morgan Jr., Fabergé, St. Petersburg, 1905

Private Collection

— 14 —

PIGLET
Agate, diamonds
L: 2¼ inches
Original fitted case stamped with Imperial Warrant,
St. Petersburg, Moscow, Odessa

The striated brown agate pig has rose-cut diamond eyes.

Provenance: J. P. Morgan Jr., Fabergé, St. Petersburg, 1905

Private Collection

— 15 —

MINIATURE CHAIR
Gold, silver gilt, enamel, rubies, diamonds
H: 4⅛ inches
Marks: Fabergé, Imperial Warrant, assay marks of Moscow 1896–1908,
assay master Ivan Lebedkin, inv. no. 25196

The style of this chair is nineteenth-century Louis XVI
revival. An almost identical piece is illustrated in Henri
Havard, *Dictionnaire de l'Ameublement*, vol. 1 (Paris:
Maison Quantin, n.d.), col. 646, fig. 448. A clever device
permits the top of the chair's seat to be raised slightly,
then moved forward on its hinges, in order to entirely
open the compartment within the seat without hitting
the cover against the lower rail of the back.

Provenance: J. P. Morgan Jr., Fabergé, St. Petersburg, 1905;
J. P. Morgan Sr., New York; J. P. Morgan Jr., sale, Parke-Bernet,
New York, March 22–25, 1944, lot 595

Bibliography: Snowman 1962, pl. LI; Hawley 1967, no. 54;
Snowman 1979, p. 26

Exhibitions: San Francisco 1964, cat. 130, pp. 40, 41;
V&A 1977, cat. M7, p. 77

The Cleveland Museum of Art, The India Early Minshall Collection,
66.454

— 16 —

MINIATURE SEDAN CHAIR
Gold, enamel, rock crystal
H: 3½ inches
Marks: Fabergé, initials of workmaster Mikhail Perkhin, assay mark of
St. Petersburg 1896–1908, assay master Iakov Liapunov, 72

This miniature sedan chair was acquired by J. P. Morgan
Jr., from Fabergé's St. Petersburg shop as a gift for his
famous financier father. An almost identical sedan chair
was sold at Christie's, Geneva, on April 28, 1978, lot 382
(private collection, Helsinki). While the present example
is painted in sepia *camaïeu*, the Finnish example is decorated with gilt *paillons*.

Provenance: J. P. Morgan Jr., Fabergé, St. Petersburg, 1905;
J. P. Morgan Sr., New York; J. P. Morgan Jr., New York; Parke-Bernet,
New York, January 6–8, 1944, lot 430; Mr. and Mrs. Jack Linsky,
New York; Lansdell K. Christie, Long Island

Bibliography: Snowman 1953, ill. 519; Snowman 1962, pl. L; McNab
Dennis 1965, pp. 234–36, ill. p. 235; Waterfield/Forbes 1978, pp. 13, 48,
139, ill. pp. 48, 139; Habsburg/Solodkoff 1979, p. 77, ills. 89–90;
Solodkoff 1984, p. 164 (ill.); Habsburg 1987, cat. 485, p. 243

Exhibitions: ALVR 1949, cat. 183, p. 20; Hammer 1951, cat. 293, p. 42,
ill. p. 43; ALVR 1961, cat. 269, p. 76, ill. p. 56; Corcoran 1961, cat. 9,
pp. 14, 31, ill. p. 30; MMA 1962–65, L.62.8.9; ALVR 1968, cat. 357,
p. 134, ill. p. 135; V&A 1977, cat. L14, p. 74; Munich 1986–87; Lugano
1987, cat. 45, p. 66 (ill.); Paris 1987, cat. 45, pp. 6, 8, 62, ill. p. 62

The Forbes Magazine Collection, New York

— 17 —

RECTANGULAR BOX
Nephrite, gold, rubies
L: 3 5/16 inches
Marks: Fabergé, initials of workmaster Henrik Wigström, assay mark
of St. Petersburg 1908–17, inv. no. 21457

The nephrite panels are mounted *en cage,* with bright-cut gold borders. The three clasps are set with two cabochon rubies.

Provenance: Princess Francis Hatzfeldt (Clara Prentice Huntington), Fabergé, London, December 4, 1911, for £40 (see Appendix II)

Exhibitions: ALVR 1983, cat. 168

Lent by courtesy of A La Vieille Russie, New York

— 18 —

CIGARETTE CASE
Silver gilt, enamel, gold, diamonds
L: 3¾ inches
Marks: Initials of workmaster Henrik Wigström, assay mark of
St. Petersburg 1896–1908

This oval case is of waved green *guilloché* enamel. The monogram CV is set in diamonds.

Provenance: Cornelius Vanderbilt III, whose wife was one of Fabergé's London clients (see Appendix II)

John Traina

The Legacy of the Czars

1920s–1930s

In the 1920s and 1930s various members of the Russian imperial family settled in the United States. In 1921 Prince Vasilii Romanov, son of Grand Duchess Xenia, sister of the murdered Czar Nicholas II, moved to California, where he ran a canning enterprise and grew prize tomatoes. In 1931 he married Princess Natalia Galitzine. Vasilii's brother, Prince Rostislav, in 1928 married Princess Alexandra Galitzine and lived in Chicago; another brother, Prince Nikita, for a time taught for the U.S. Army in Monterey, California. These princes, along with their mother, father, and grandmother, Dowager Empress Maria Feodorovna, left Russia in 1919 and were able to save many of their belongings, including the only Fabergé Easter egg kept by the imperial family, the Cross of St. George egg of 1916 (Forbes Magazine collection, New York). Grand Duke Dmitri, one of the murderers of Rasputin, who had been exiled by Nicholas II, in 1926 married an American heiress in Biarritz and was for a while, in the 1930s, a champagne salesman in Palm Beach.

Other Russian families who arrived in the United States included the Cantacuzènes, Galitzines, Obolenskys, and Trubetzkoys. The displaced aristocracy brought with them what valuables they could: jewels, art, and Fabergé objects. The Fabergé items had little intrinsic value but often were given as mementos in gratitude for services rendered. Thus there were, and are, pockets of Fabergé objects in California, including a substantial group of frames formerly belonging to Prince Vasilii.

Russian applied arts were known to collectors in the United States well before the turn of the century through the great 1876 Philadelphia Centennial exhibition, where the firms of Sazikov, Ovchinnikov, Khlebnikov, and Postnikov exhibited their silver and enamel wares. Russian paintings were shown at the World's Columbian exhibition of 1893 in Chicago. At the Louisiana Purchase exhibition, held in St. Louis in 1904, twenty million visitors could take a simulated trip on board a Trans-Siberian railway car and view some six hundred Russian works of art by 148 artists. Later, in the 1920s, Christian Brinton, a Philadelphia art critic and specialist in Russian art, mounted several shows in New York for Russian émigré and Bolshevik artists, including Nicholas Roerig and Archipenko. In 1924 Brinton helped to organize an exhibition of Suprematist art at the Société Anonyme Gallery, New York, and a show of 940 paintings, watercolors, and drawings by eighty-four Soviet artists at the Grand Central Palace, New York, which traveled throughout the country. The organizers of the latter, much like Armand Hammer in the late 1920s, were interested in encouraging Congress to recognize Soviet Russia. These exhibitions, together with the initial success of Russia's first Five-Year Plan at a time when America was suffering a severe economic depression, added to the American public's growing interest in all things Russian.

—Géza von Habsburg

Catalogue

1920s–1930s

A number of the objects in this section were brought to America by Prince Vasilii Romanov. Other Fabergé objects arrived with the first wave of Russian emigrants to reach the United States. Fabergé's art is still treasured by descendants of the imperial family and by those Russians who were able to save some of their precious works of art. Many of these objects are still in the possession of Russian émigré families, who, understandably, find it difficult to part even temporarily with the souvenirs of their past.

— 19 —

CLOISONNÉ ENAMEL BOX
Silver gilt, enamel
L: 1⅞ inches
Marks: Imperial Warrant, assay mark of Moscow 1908–17

The box is painted *en plein* with a view of Étienne-Maurice Falconet's statue of Peter the Great, within a double ogival frame decorated in the neo-Russian style with silver gilt scrolls and geometric patterns.

Provenance: Prince Vasilii Romanov

Private Collection

— 20 —

COCKEREL
Purpurine, agate, obsidian, gold
H: 1⅝ inches
Original fitted case stamped with Imperial Warrant,
St. Petersburg, Moscow, London

The cockerel has a purpurine crest and wattles, agate back, obsidian tail feathers and front, and gold feet (beak replaced).

Provenance: Prince Vasilii Romanov

Private Collection

— 21 —

EGG-SHAPED FRAME
Bowenite, enamel, gold, diamonds, ivory
H: 2¾ inches
Marks: Fabergé, initials of workmaster Mikhail Perkhin,
assay mark of St. Petersburg before 1896

The egg-shaped frame is set on one side with an oval
miniature of Czarina Maria Feodorovna, in a diamond-
set border surmounted by a red enamel bow. The frame
sits on a domed red enamel foot, the upper part of which
is trimmed with green enamel laurel leaves and opaque
white enamel ties; the lower edge is an opaque white
enamel band with gilt laurel leaves.

Provenance: Dowager Empress Maria Feodorovna;
her daughter, Grand Duchess Xenia Aleksandrovna;
her son, Prince Vasilii Romanov

Private Collection

— 22 —

BELL PUSH
Gold, enamel, moonstone
H: 2 inches
Marks: Fabergé, initials of workmaster Mikhail Perkhin,
assay mark of St. Petersburg before 1896

The pink *guilloché* enamel globe on a gold stiff-leaf base
is decorated with a white *guilloché* enamel band and gold
laurel leaves. A cabochon moonstone finial is set in a gold
sun-ray mount.

Provenance: Prince Vasilii Romanov

Private Collection

— 23 —

DIAMOND-SHAPED CLOCK
Gold, silver gilt, enamel, seed pearls, ivory
W: 3½ inches
Marks: Fabergé, initials of workmaster Mikhail Perkhin,
assay mark of St. Petersburg before 1896

The clock is of opalescent pink *guilloché* enamel. The dial is surrounded by a seed pearl border, surmounted by an opaque enamel ribbon. A green gold outer palmetto border is tied with red gold ribbons.

Provenance: Prince Vasilii Romanov

Private Collection

— 24 —

CIRCULAR CLOCK
Silver gilt, enamel, seed pearls, ivory
Diam: 3 inches
Marks: Fabergé, initials of workmaster Mikhail Perkhin,
assay mark of St. Petersburg 1896–1908

The opalescent pale blue enamel dial with black Arabic numerals and gold hands is set in a panel of opalescent pale blue enamel surrounded by a palmetto border. The back is of ivory.

Provenance: Prince Vasilii Romanov

Private Collection

— 25 —

RECTANGULAR FRAME
Gold, enamel, ivory
H: 4 inches
Marks: Fabergé, initials of workmaster Henrik Wigström, assay mark
of St. Petersburg 1896–1908, inv. no. 14369

Provenance: Presented by Count Nikolai Lamsdorff to his wife,
Countess Sophie Lamsdorff, on the occasion of the birth of their
daughter Aleksandra in 1913

Elizabeth S. Blake

— 26 —

ICON OF CHRIST PANTOCRATOR
Silver gilt, rubies, wood
H: 3¼ inches
Marks: Initials of workmaster Hjalmar Armfelt, inv. no. 20112
Original fitted case stamped with Imperial Warrant,
St. Petersburg, Moscow, London

Provenance: Given to Countess Aleksandra Lamsdorff by her
grandmother and godmother, Princess Aleksandra Trubetzkoy, née
Obolensky, on her birthday on February 17, 1913. According to the
present owner, Princess Aleksandra purchased the icon from Fabergé.
On the condition that the design be reserved for her, she ordered six
more for her other grandchildren, but without the cabochon rubies,
which she considered too ostentatious for little children.

Elizabeth S. Blake

— 27 —

FROG ON AGATE STAND
Serpentine, agate, diamonds, silver
H: 4½ inches
Marks: Initials KF engraved under base

The yellow-green serpentine frog with diamond eyes in silver mounts is realistically portrayed climbing a tapering gray agate stand.

This is one of a series of such frogs, each one differing in details. A nephrite example on a pink cane handle is in the collection of Prince Charles of England; a second example on a white handle was with Wartski. A similar frog on an agate stand is illustrated in Solodkoff 1988, p. 78.

Provenance: Christian de Guigné II

Exhibitions: San Francisco 1964, cat. 17

De Guigné Collection

— 28 —

FROG ON MARBLE STAND
Serpentine, marble, diamonds, silver
H: 4½ inches

Provenance: Christian de Guigné II

Exhibitions: San Francisco 1964, cat. 18

De Guigné Collection

— 29 —

DRAFT HORSE

Marble, sapphires

H: 3⅛ inches

The horse is of flecked reddish marble, with darker coloration at mane and hooves. Its eyes are cabochon sapphires. The piece is related to an aventurine quartz figure of a Percheron stallion in the collection of Queen Elizabeth II (Habsburg/Lopato 1994, cat. 87) and to an obsidian Percheron stallion with A La Vieille Russie (ALVR 1983, cat. 446, p. 121).

Provenance: Christian de Guigné II

Exhibitions: San Francisco 1964, cat. 2

De Guigné Collection

— 30 —

TOAD

Serpentine, agate, enamel

H: 2¾ inches

Realistically portrayed in yellowish mottled hardstone, the toad is covered with warts. Its eyes are of brown agate, with pupils of black enamel.

Provenance: Christian de Guigné II

Exhibitions: ALVR 1961, cat. 421, ill. p. 31

De Guigné Collection

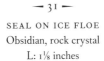

SEAL ON ICE FLOE
Obsidian, rock crystal
L: 1⅛ inches

This miniature carving is of a black seal seated on a rock crystal ice floe.

Provenance: Christian de Guigné II

Exhibitions: ALVR 1983, cat. 428, ill. p. 29

De Guigné Collection

— 32 —
RABBIT
Lapis lazuli, rubies
L: 1½ inches

Provenance: Christian de Guigné II

De Guigné Collection

— 33 —
POTATO-SHAPED BOX
Marble, gold
L: 3½ inches
Marks: Initials of workmaster Mikhail Perkhin, assay mark of
St. Petersburg before 1896, inv. no. 5078

The pinkish flecked breccia marble box has a hinged partial cover and reeded gold mounts.

Provenance: King Farouk of Egypt; Christian de Guigné II

Exhibitions: San Francisco 1964, cat. 44

De Guigné Collection

— 34 —

QUATREFOIL GOLD BADGE
Gold, enamel
L: 1¾ inches
Original fitted case stamped with Imperial Warrant,
St. Petersburg, Moscow

The badge is inscribed "To the esteemed Justice of the
Peace, City of Odessa," around an enameled double-
headed eagle; the reverse is inscribed "In token of gratitude, to Grigori Salomonovich Gurievich, 1871."

Provenance: Christian de Guigné II

De Guigné Collection

— 35 —

RHINOCEROS MATCH HOLDER AND STRIKER
Sandstone, silver, garnets
L: 4 inches
Marks: Initials of workmaster Julius Rappoport, assay mark of
St. Petersburg before 1896

This whimsical animal caricature demonstrates Fabergé's
use of nonprecious materials. The ovoid body is of gray
sandstone; the feet, horn, tail, and ears are of silver; and
the eyes are garnets. The cavity for matches is silver
lined. For an identical figure, see ALVR 1983, cat. 409.

Provenance: Christian de Guigné II

De Guigné Collection

— 36 —

RENAISSANCE-STYLE *KOVSH*
Rock crystal, silver gilt, enamel, garnet, citrine,
quartz, glass, pearl
L: 8¾ inches
Marks: Imperial Warrant, assay mark of Moscow, inv. no. 10031

The rock crystal body of this traditional Russian drinking vessel is carved with a foliate rosette and mounted in
silver gilt. The *kovsh* is decorated with cloisonné enamel
foliage and cabochon stones. A pearl is set on the "prow."

Provenance: Christian de Guigné II

De Guigné Collection

— 37 —

IMPERIAL PRESENTATION CIGARETTE BOX
Nephrite, gold, diamonds, ivory
L: 3¾ inches
Marks: Fabergé, initials of workmaster Henrik Wigström,
assay mark of St. Petersburg 1908–17
Fitted case stamped with Imperial Warrant, St. Petersburg, Moscow

The rectangular box has canted corners, and the rim is
set with rose-cut diamonds. An oval miniature of Czar
Alexander II is placed within a border of rose-cut diamonds, below a diamond-set crown.

Provenance: Christian de Guigné II

De Guigné Collection

— 38 —

EMPIRE-STYLE TEA SERVICE AND TEA TABLE
Silver, ivory, Karelian birchwood
H: (table) 28¼ inches; (kettle) 13½ inches
Marks: K Fabergé, double-headed eagle, initials of workmaster
Julius Rappoport, assay mark of St. Petersburg 1896–1908;
engraved with crowned initials VM

The ten-piece silver tea set comprises a kettle with ivory handle, stand cast and chased with swans and snakes, and burner; a teapot with ivory handle; a creamer, covered sugar bowl, small bowl, strainer, and sugar tongs (a pickle fork has been lost); and a large fruit bowl. Silver decoration is applied to the oval Empire-style galleried birchwood table. The large fruit bowl stands on the galleried stretcher.

The tea service and table were presented by Grand Duchess Kirill to Alma Spreckels of San Francisco. An accompanying letter reads "Cannes, 11th February 1922. Dear Mrs. Spreckels—Having heard of your wonderful new museum, & of all you are doing to help my sister the Queen of Roumania [Alma Spreckels raised money for medical supplies for Romania], I wish to present you with a golden [sic] tea service made by our famous Russian artist 'Fabergé.'—It is one of our few treasures saved & I am glad if it can find a place in the glorious monument you are building to the memory of your California soldiers.

"It has always been a tradition in the Russian Imperial family to help whenever they could, . . . & . . . as at this moment we cannot build anything in remembrance of our own millions of fallen brave, who fought & fell for the same cause, I am happy to offer a token of respect & regard to your 3,600 California sons whom you are immortalizing. Yours very sincerely, Victoria Melita, Grand Duchess Kirill of Russia."

Provenance: Grand Duchess Kirill (Victoria Melita, princess of Saxe-Coburg and Great Britain, 1876–1936, first married to Ernst Ludwig, grand duke of Hessen-Darmstadt, brother of Czarina Alexandra Feodorovna, divorced 1901; in 1905 married Grand Duke Kirill Vladimirovich, who in August 1922 proclaimed himself head of the imperial house of Romanov); presented in 1922 to Alma Spreckels and the California Palace of the Legion of Honor (now one of the Fine Arts Museums of San Francisco)

Exhibitions: San Francisco 1964

Fine Arts Museums of San Francisco, 1945.366.1, 1945.355–65

— 39 —

EMBRACING *AMORINI* IN LOUIS XVI STYLE
Silver, aventurine quartz
H: 23½ inches
Marks: K Fabergé, double-headed eagle, initials of workmaster
Julius Rappoport, assay mark of St. Petersburg 1896–1908

Two embracing putti of cast and chased silver are seated on rockwork. The aventurine quartz base is shaped as a truncated, fluted column, decorated with laurel and berry swags suspended from tied ribbons and a laurel wreath below.

This example of Fabergé's work is related to a clock dated 1891 (Habsburg/Lopato 1994, cat. 4) and to his Colonnade egg in the collection of Queen Elizabeth II (ibid., cat. 20). The *amorini* on the clock, close in style to the present examples, were designed by Alexandre Benois and modeled by Arthur L. Aubert.

Provenance: Alma de Bretteville Spreckels; gift in 1969 of Mrs. Charles A. Munn (Dorothy Constance Spreckels, daughter of Alma Spreckels); California Palace of the Legion of Honor (now one of the Fine Arts Museums of San Francisco)

Fine Arts Museums of San Francisco, 1969.4

Fig. 1. *Twenty-four-year-old Armand Hammer, disembarking in New York on his return from the Soviet Union, 1922. Photo: UPI/Bettmann Archive, New York.*

The Hammer Years

1930s–1950s

Armand Hammer (1898–1990; fig. 1) was born in New York, the son of Russian Jewish immigrant Julius Hammer, who in 1919 had helped to establish the first revolutionary Leninist organization in the United States. Julius collaborated with Ludwig Martens, who headed the Russian Soviet Bureau, an unofficial diplomatic mission for the fledgling Bolshevik government in the United States. Armand, named for the arm-and-hammer symbol of the Socialist Labor Party, graduated as a medical student and made his first trip to the Soviet Union in 1921. Hammer declared the visit to be humanitarian in nature ("planning field hospital relief work among the famine refugees"),[1] but in reality he went to collect a business debt on behalf of his father, then serving a prison sentence for performing an unsuccessful abortion.

While in Moscow, Hammer, with the acquiescence of Lenin, succeeded in obtaining asbestos mining rights in the Urals for twenty years, the first such concession awarded by the Soviets to an American. Further agreements with Hammer's firm, Allied Drug and Chemical, covered a shipment of 18,000 tons of American surplus grain to the Soviet Union in exchange for Siberian furs, precious stones, hides, lace, rubber, and caviar for sale in America. Quite by chance Hammer's first office, rented at $30 per month, was located on Kuznetzki Bridge in a building that once had housed Fabergé's Moscow shop.

By 1923 Hammer had built an import-export empire. He was a purchasing agent for American agricultural ma-

chinery and exclusively represented up to three dozen American companies in the Soviet Union. During Lenin's New Economic Policy of the early 1920s, Hammer was treated like royalty by the Soviets, who hoped to attract other Western investors. In the absence of U.S. diplomatic relations, Brown House, the opulent Moscow domicile occupied by the Hammer family, became an unofficial American embassy, housing visiting politicians, film stars, and celebrities.

Following Lenin's demise in 1924, the revenues from Hammer's import-export business fell from $6 million in 1924 to $1.5 million in 1925 due to restrictions imposed by the Soviets on foreign businesses. This loss was offset by revenues from a newly acquired pencil manufacturing concession, which in 1925 produced 72 million graphite pencils and 95 million steel pens, and grossed 8.5 million rubles (1 ruble = 52 cents) by 1927. This business, in turn, was confiscated in 1930.

In 1928 Armand and his antique-dealer brother, Victor, began to dabble in Russian art.[2] Anastas Mikoyan, then commissar for domestic and foreign trade, first offered them exclusive rights to American sales of paintings from the State Hermitage Museum, for which they would receive a 10 percent commission. The same year the Hammers unsuccessfully bid $5 million on behalf of a consortium of dealers, headed by Joseph Duveen, for forty masterpieces from the Hermitage. To handle their Russian art sales, Hammer founded the Ermitage Galleries at

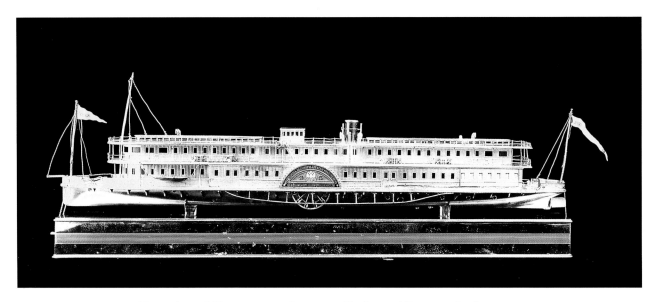

Fig. 2. *Armand Hammer arranged to present this silver paddle steamer (workmaster
Henrik Wigström, assay mark of St. Petersburg 1896–1908, l. 29 inches, Forbes
Magazine Collection, New York) to President Franklin D. Roosevelt in commemora-
tion of the inception of diplomatic relations between the United States and the USSR in
1933. The steamer originally had been given to Czarevitch Alexei in 1913 by a group of
Volga shipbuilders. Photo: H. Peter Curran, courtesy Forbes Magazine Collection.*

3 East 52nd Street in New York. He claims to have collected several warehouses full of Russian art throughout
the 1920s, which he was permitted to export against payment of a 15 percent customs duty. Hammer probably also
reached an agreement with the Soviets concerning an exclusive agency for the sale of Russian works of art in
America. The Bolsheviks welcomed Hammer's help at a
time when the lack of diplomatic recognition by the U.S.
Congress in principle barred Americans from doing business with the fledgling communist republic.

In 1930–31 Hammer transferred what he described as
his private collection of imperial treasure from the Soviet
Union to the United States, including ten Fabergé imperial
Easter eggs from the Kremlin armory. This was possibly
the first shipment of goods he would sell on behalf of the
Soviets as compensation for the loss of his businesses to
nationalization. In January 1931, a three-day auction of
Russian art, reputedly the former property of the imperial
family, was held in New York, but it elicited little interest
except for an unsuccessful temporary injunction slapped
on the sale by the Grand Duchesses Olga and Xenia, sis-
ters of Czar Nicholas II.

For a time business was exceedingly slow in a deeply
depressed economy, and Hammer found himself unable
to sell the Easter eggs. Then, in 1932, Hammer developed
an astute strategy of selling "Russian imperial treasure"
through local department stores on a six-month tour of the
United States. The traveling exhibition began in January at
Scruggs Vandervoort Barney in St. Louis; continued to
Marshall Field's in Chicago, Halle Brothers in Cleveland,
Kaufman's in Pittsburgh, William Hengerer Company in
Buffalo, J. L. Hudson in Detroit, Thalheimer's in Richmond, the Dry Goods Store in Denver, Frederick and
Nelson in Seattle, the Emporium in San Francisco; and, in
June, ended at Young Quinian in Minneapolis. Heralded
with great fanfare by the press, each stop hosted two lectures on the adventures of the Hammers in Russia, given
by either Victor or Armand. In January 1933 a similar
show at Lord and Taylor in New York was a resounding
success, resulting in a three-year contract for Hammer to
sell Russian art objects in the store. These activities culmi-
nated in the founding of the Hammer Galleries of New
York in 1934 and later in Palm Beach. The gallery became
a primary source of Russian applied arts in the United

States. At Lord and Taylor Hammer sold what was probably an unrecognized imperial Easter egg whose description ("No. 4524—Miniature Amour [Cupid] holding wheelbarrow with Easter egg. Made by Fabergé")[3] corresponds to an egg created by Fabergé for Czar Alexander III and recorded in the archives of the Imperial Cabinet ("In 1888—Angel pulling a chariot with an egg—1,500 rubles.") This egg probably exists today, unrecognized, in an American collection.

In Chicago a later showing of Hammer's "imperial treasure" at Marshall Field's ran concurrently with the world's fair of 1933–34. It was here that Matilda Geddings Gray, who would become a serious collector, fell in love with Fabergé's art. In late 1933 Hammer arranged the presentation of a Fabergé silver model of a Volga steamship to President Franklin D. Roosevelt, to mark the opening of Soviet-American diplomatic relations (fig. 2). The Hammers held important Fabergé exhibitions in 1937, 1939, and 1951.

All items sold by Hammer—icons, liturgical implements, and second-rate works of art as well as fine objects by Fabergé—regardless of their provenance, were accompanied by parchment certificates emblazoned with the Russian imperial double-headed eagle, stating that the object originated from the private apartments of the imperial family. With his innovative marketing techniques, Hammer attracted a new class of rich collectors, including celebrities such as Mrs. Harrison Williams, one of America's most glamorous women. Noted for her ice blue eyes and her numerous marriages, Williams was later known as Countess Mona Bismarck. Her Paris collection was sold anonymously at auction in Geneva in the 1970s. Hammer's Fabergé-style fitted cases and his certificates are widely diffused throughout America, testifying to his successful salesmanship. According to Hammer, by 1940 his galleries had turned over $11 million in Russian art.

Beginning in 1933, Russian Imperial Treasures, Inc., a competing firm run by Alexander Schaffer (d. 1972) and his wife, Ray (d. 1993), exhibited the "Schaffer Collection of Authentic Russian Imperial Art Treasures" in New York (fig. 3).[4] The Schaffer collection was first shown in premises at 36 West 50th Street and in 1936 moved to 15 West 50th Street in Rockefeller Center. A former professional

soccer player, Schaffer fled Hungary in the 1920s and settled first in Paris and then in New York. Traveling between New York and Moscow during the 1920s and 1930s, he worked closely with A La Vieille Russie in Paris when France was the hub of Russian art sales by both impoverished émigrés and the cash-starved Bolsheviks. In 1941 the Schaffer gallery became A La Vieille Russie of New York, in partnership with the Paris firm, and moved to 785 Fifth Avenue at 60th Street. Alexander and Ray Schaffer were instrumental in the formation of all the premier Fabergé collections in the United States.

From the late 1920s to early 1930s Schaffer and Hammer worked together, with Schaffer acting as Hammer's adviser. Soon, however, their interests clashed, and their competing advertisements appeared in the same issues of *Connoisseur* magazine in the mid-1930s. At the time impressive quantities of Fabergé were available to buyers. For example, during 1936 and 1937, 100 Fabergé animals were offered for sale by Wartski of London, 500 Fabergé objects were shown by the Schaffer Galleries, and 350 items were displayed in the Hammer Galleries (valued at $2 million, this exhibition included eleven Easter eggs, seven of which were loaned by private owners).

The advertisements and exhibits run by Armand Hammer and Alexander Schaffer were to incite four great American women to begin collecting Russian art in the 1930s. These were Matilda Geddings Gray of New Orleans; India Early Minshall of Cleveland; Lillian Thomas Pratt of Fredericksburg, Virginia; and Marjorie Merriweather Post of Washington, D.C. (Their large-scale Fabergé collections, now held by public institutions, are discussed separately.)

Besides A La Vieille Russie, Paris (active from 1920), the premier European dealer in Fabergé was Wartski of London, run by Emanuel Snowman and, subsequently, by his son, A. Kenneth Snowman. As early as 1927, even before Hammer and Schaffer, Emanuel Snowman made acquisitions from the Soviets. In 1935 Wartski held a substantial loan exhibition of Fabergé objects. A. Kenneth Snowman organized a further exhibition in 1949 to mark the publication of the first monograph on Fabergé, written by Henry C. Bainbridge, Fabergé's London representative. This exhibition attracted American interest: "A fair

Fig. 3. *Alexander and Ray Schaffer, 1960. Photo: Laszlo Schaffer, courtesy A La Vieille Russie.*

sprinkling of Americans waited in the rain for 45 minutes or more to gaze at the Fabergé exhibition at Wartski."[5] The London dealer began to advertise in the American edition of *Connoisseur* in 1952. In the postwar years the firm's clients included an American president (who remains anonymous) and film stars as well as every major

American Fabergé collector. A. Kenneth Snowman curated the landmark 1977 Fabergé exhibition held at the Victoria and Albert Museum, London, and has written a number of seminal monographs on Fabergé.

In 1949 A La Vieille Russie, New York, held a major Fabergé exhibition that featured three hundred pieces, including seven imperial Easter eggs. By the 1950s, when the Hammer Galleries shifted its emphasis from Russian art to modern paintings, the Schaffers remained the sole major source of Fabergé objects in the United States. In a final move in 1961, A La Vieille Russie took up residence at 781 Fifth Avenue, where it still is located. The store organized major Fabergé exhibitions in 1961, 1968, and 1983, and today is run by Paul and Peter Schaffer, sons of Alexander and Ray, and by Paul's son Mark.

—Géza von Habsburg

NOTES

1. Armand Hammer, *The Quest of the Romanoff Treasure* (1932), quoted in Joseph Finder, *Red Carpet* (New York: Holt, Rinehart, Winston, 1983), p. 19.

2. For Armand Hammer and the sales of Russian art, see Robert C. Williams, *Russian Art and American Money* (Cambridge: Harvard University Press, 1980), pp. 191–229; Finder, *Red Carpet*, pp. 11–50, 63–90, 219, 235; Steve Weinberg, *Armand Hammer: The Untold Story* (Boston: Little, Brown, 1989), pp. 46, 83; Carl Blumay with Henry Edwards, *The Dark Side of Power: The Real Armand Hammer* (New York: Simon and Schuster, 1992), pp. 63, 101–7. For further information, see also p. 177, note 3.

3. Lord and Taylor 1933, p. 11, cat. 4524.

4. For A La Vieille Russie, see Helen Harris, "A Shop Fit for a Czar," *Town & Country* (December 1975), pp. 156–57; Paul Schaffer, in Habsburg/Lopato 1994, pp. 160–64. See also Paul Schaffer, in Solodkoff 1984, pp. 131–37.

5. *The Evening Standard* (London), November 19, 1949; for Wartski, see also A. Kenneth Snowman, in Solodkoff 1984, pp. 123–29.

Catalogue

1930s–1950s

This section covers the period of the first sales of Russian art by the Soviet government, from 1927 to 1938. Americans began buying Russian art in about 1930. The catalyzer was Armand Hammer, whose sales exhibition of "Russian imperial treasure" toured to department stores from 1932 to 1934. He was closely followed by Alexander and Ray Schaffer of A La Vieille Russie, who, together with Hammer, were instrumental in developing the earliest Fabergé collections in the United States. The sections that follow cover the four major collections formed in America, beginning in the 1930s, by Matilda Geddings Gray, India Early Minshall, Lillian Thomas Pratt, and Marjorie Merriweather Post.

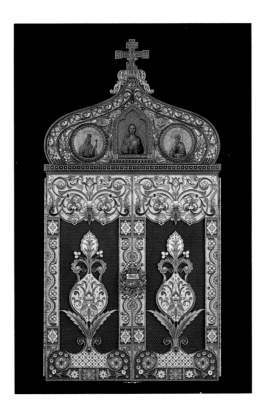

— 40 —

PRESENTATION TRIPTYCH ICON
Silver gilt, enamel
H: 14 inches, W: 14⅝ inches (open)
Marks: Imperial Warrant, assay mark of Moscow 1896–1908
(and see below)
Fitted case stamped "Hammer, New York"

Painted *en plein*, the icon depicts St. Aleksei, the Metropolitan of All Russia (center), the Guardian Archangel (left), and St. Seraphim of Sarov (right). The onion-shaped upper part, surmounted by a Russian Orthodox cross, shows Christ Pantocrator flanked by St. Aleksandra (left) and St. Nikolai (right). The borders are decorated in pastel-colored shaded cloisonné enamels. The outer doors, which have panels of red *guilloché* enamel, are bordered by similar shaded cloisonné enamels. The crowned coat of arms of the city of Uralsk is applied to the clasp.

Three of the saints are the patron saints of Czarevitch Alexei and of his parents Czar Nicholas and Czarina Alexandra Feodorovna; St. Seraphim of Sarov was the favorite saint of the imperial family (the czar and grand dukes carried his coffin at the ceremony of his canonization in 1903).

The reverse is inscribed "A blessing from the city of Uralsk to His Imperial Highness, the Heir Apparent, the Czarevitch and Grand Prince Alexei Nikolaievich, the most august hetman of the cossack forces, the year 1904, October the 5th day, on the occasion of his first name-day; presented in the presence of the hetman of the Uralsk cossack forces lieutenant-general Stavrovsky and the delegation of the citizens of the city of Uralsk consisting of the senior member of the command of the supply unit of the Uralsk cossack forces. Colonel Kolovertov and a senior member of the Uralsk military trade delegation, the cossack Shaposhnikov, and the citizens; the cossack Ovchinnikov and the merchant Makarychev."

Provenance: Czarevitch Alexei, 1904; government of the USSR, 1918; Armand Hammer, 1930s; Paul Fekula, New York

Raphael and Joyce Gregorian

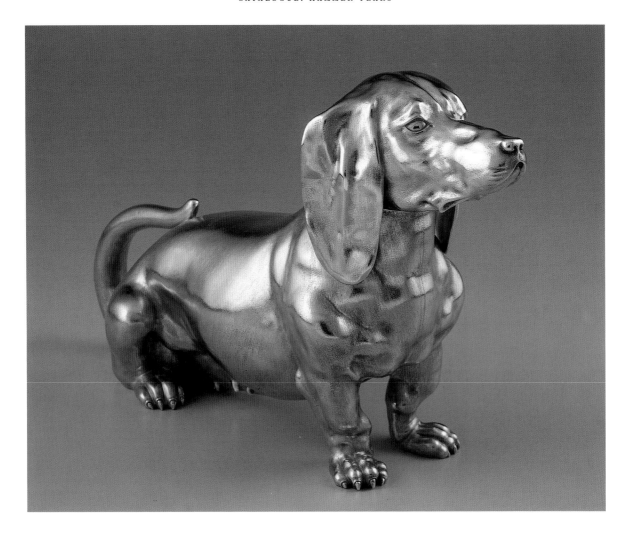

— 41 —

DACHSHUND PITCHER
Silver
L: 14½ inches
Marks: Fabergé, initials of workmaster Julius Rappoport,
assay mark of St. Petersburg before 1896
Fitted case stamped "Russian Imperial Treasures Inc.
The Schaffer Collection"

The seated female dachshund with hinged head is realistically chased and portrayed. The curved tail serves as the handle.

Provenance: Said to come from the imperial collection at the
Alexander Palace, Tsarskoe Selo; Alexander Schaffer, New York;
Viscountess de Bonchamps, mother of the present owner

Exhibitions: ALVR 1949, cat. 43 (ill.); San Francisco 1964, cat. 11

Private Collection

— 42 —

RABBIT
Quartz, rubies, gold
H: 1 1/16 inches

The seated rabbit has large ears and gold-mounted faceted ruby eyes.

Provenance: Hammer Galleries, New York

Mr. and Mrs. Steven Westerman

— 43 —

RHINOCEROS
Bowenite, emeralds, gold
L: 1 1/2 inches

The standing rhinoceros is set with gold-mounted faceted emerald eyes.

Provenance: Hammer Galleries, New York

Private Collection

— 44 —

RUSSIAN PEASANT GIRL
Purpurine, eosite, chalcedony, agate, jade, sapphires
H: 6¼ inches
Marks: "C Fabergé" engraved in English under sole of one slipper
Original fitted case

This is one of a series of Russian folkloristic figures composed of Siberian hardstones. The mark "C Fabergé" in
English indicates that the object was destined for the
London shop. The figure was acquired from Fabergé by
Sir John Baring, second Lord Revelstoke (d. 1929). Bainbridge (1949, p. 85) described him as "among the foremost of Fabergé's discerning customers. Traveling con-
stantly between St. Petersburg and London nothing new
happened in the workshops of the craftsman without
his knowledge. He was the first to bring to London the
figurines."

Provenance: Lord Revelstoke; A La Vieille Russie, New York;
R. Thornton Wilson (nephew of Mrs. Cornelius Vanderbilt III
and of Mrs. Robert Goelet; see Appendix II)

Bibliography: Snowman 1952; Snowman 1962, ill. 269;
Habsburg 1987, cat. 387 (ill.)

Exhibitions: Munich 1986–87

The Metropolitan Museum of Art, New York, Gift of
R. Thornton Wilson, in memory of Florence Ellsworth Wilson,
1954, 54.147.107

Fig. 1. *Matilda Geddings Gray, ca. 1940. Photo: Dorothea Thorp,*
courtesy Matilda Geddings Gray Foundation.

Matilda Geddings Gray

A Louisiana Collector

Carl Fabergé likely would have delighted in the response of Louisianian Matilda Geddings Gray (fig. 1) to his beautifully designed, exquisitely wrought objects. She was possessed of keen intelligence, taste, a developed aesthetic sensibility, style, and the means to acquire almost any object that attracted her attention. An American aristocrat, Gray was not unlike the sophisticated clients Fabergé had sought in czarist Russia.

Matilda Geddings Gray was inordinately fond of travel and availed herself of every opportunity to do so. On a visit to the 1933 Century of Progress exhibition in Chicago, she first encountered the work of Fabergé at Armand and Victor Hammer's display of Russian art. It was a fateful encounter, for Gray was so struck by Fabergé's *objets de fantaisie* that she determined to assemble a collection. The meeting commenced a thirty-year association with Victor Hammer of Hammer Galleries, New York.

That such a chance encounter should inaugurate so refined a collection is perhaps startling until one realizes that Matilda Gray was already a knowledgeable and seasoned collector. A friend recalled that she was "a collector of fine houses and commensurate things with which to furnish them appropriately."[1] Armand Hammer, of course, was one of the few American entrepreneurs with sufficient connections to have access to the newly formed Soviet government and the former imperial and aristocratic collections over which it held jurisdiction. From the 1920s Hammer purchased significant quantities of period jewelry, porcelains, icons, textiles, czarist accoutrements such

as orders and medals, and *objets de vertu*, among which were works by the Fabergé firm. Like other American collectors, Gray was attracted to Hammer's objects because of an interest in both the deposed and storied Romanov dynasty and the objects themselves, apart from any historical context.[2] This is indicated by her acquisition of these pieces long before Fabergé had gained his present international acclaim. In the words of Malcolm S. Forbes, a later collector of Fabergé, the result of her collecting was "one of the most sumptuous and beautifully chosen collections of Fabergé in the United States."[3]

That a well-developed aesthetic sensibility was a motivating force in Gray's buying is reflected in her attendance at H. Sophie Newcomb Memorial College in New Orleans, the women's division of Tulane University and producer of the celebrated Newcomb College art pottery. As a student from 1906 to 1909 Gray decorated this quintessential American art pottery and was well acquainted with the American arts and crafts movement. Since the Newcomb pottery featured native floral motifs, it is not surprising that Gray later selected floral subjects for her skilled watercolors. She was an accomplished bookbinder and for many years participated in the activities of the New Orleans Arts and Crafts Club. Possessed of a restless intelligence, she later studied with the Parisian sculptor and painter Athanase Apartis (fl. ca. 1921–38), himself a follower of the sculptor Émile-Antoine Bourdelle (1861–1929) and an exhibitor with the Société des Artistes Indépendants and at the Salon d'Automne from the early

1920s until 1938. Working in bronze and terra-cotta, Gray produced a number of attractive busts of family, friends, and members of her household staffs. Her artistic endeavors were accompanied by an astute business sense, for Gray further developed her father's timber, cattle, and petroleum interests, thus providing the means to finance her wide-ranging collecting interests.

The Chicago encounter with Armand Hammer's arresting display and a passion for collecting inevitably led Gray to all the leading purveyors of Fabergé works. She became a well-known figure at A La Vieille Russie in New York and at Wartski and Bloom in London. As time passed, she encountered considerable competition from other American collectors such as Marjorie Merriweather Post of Washington, D.C.; Lillian Thomas Pratt of Fredericksburg, Virginia; and India Early Minshall of Cleveland. She also formed a friendship with another pioneering Fabergé collector and rival, Lansdell K. Christie of Long Island, and was his frequent guest.[4]

In common with her American rivals and fellow collectors, Gray did not restrict her acquisitions to works by Fabergé. Not content with French eighteenth-century furniture and gold boxes, English Regency silver, and an extensive collection of works by Mexican painter Diego Rivera, she also collected residences in the grand manner, restoring and sometimes altering them to suit her particular desires. The houses eventually included the Gauche House on New Orleans's Esplanade Avenue, one of the most important Creole structures in the Vieux Carré; Evergreen, the most complete plantation complex on the great River Road; a large Georgian-revival house in her native Lake Charles, Louisiana; a colonial farm-estate in Antigua, Guatemala; a New York townhouse; and a rue Royale apartment in Paris. All were lovingly maintained and furnished with carefully selected objects. The Guatemalan house, for example, contained an important collection of Spanish Colonial decorative arts and paintings.

Collections of any significance inevitably reveal the personalities of their owners, and Gray's collection of Fabergé objects is no exception. The overall quality of the objects is testimony to her possession of that elusive attribute, an "eye," and to her commitment to seek the best. It is equally evident that Gray assembled the collection according to her personal taste and interests and devoted little thought to forming a comprehensive group of Fabergé works. Part of the present-day charm of the Gray collection is its idiosyncrasy and revelation of character. Gray was a committed gardener, and prior to World War II she maintained a 40-acre garden at her Lake Charles house, whose care occupied seventeen full-time gardeners.[5] Her dinner parties always were accompanied by astounding floral arrangements. It is not surprising that her Fabergé collection eventually contained eighteen floral groups. The hardstone animals, which had so enthralled the Edwardians, held little appeal for Gray, and the collection included but two examples. As a woman accustomed to supervising her numerous employees, she was self-assured and occasionally willful. When she acquired an imperial hand seal in the form of a chameleon (originally made as a cane handle) from the Hammer Galleries (cat. no. 55), she had the cipher replaced with her own monogram. Unfortunately, the imperial cipher was not preserved, as Gray's instructions specified that the original metal be melted down and incorporated into her new seal.

Collectors also leave their mark with dealers, fellow collectors, and curators. Matilda Geddings Gray is fondly remembered by everyone in the Fabergé world. In Louisiana, it is still customary to address women of a certain age by the prefix of "tante," or aunt. This pseudofamilial title recalls the days of great extended Creole families and certainly invokes recollections of the now mythical antebellum Deep South. Although Gray was indubitably a grande dame, such was the warmth and force of her personality that she was called "Aunt Matilda" as far from Louisiana as London and New York. After her death on June 8, 1971, her Fabergé collection passed to a foundation bearing her name, with the intention that these rarified objects be placed on public exhibition. Following an extensive tour of American museums, in 1983 the Matilda Geddings Gray Foundation collection of Fabergé works was placed on extended loan at the New Orleans Museum of Art. The gallery in which the collection is installed is the most attended in the building, and a visit to view Gray's collection of the great artist-jeweler's work remains an enduring memory for thousands of visitors annually.

—John Webster Keefe
Curator of Decorative Arts
New Orleans Museum of Art

NOTES

1. Interview with Elinor Bright Richardson, New Orleans, a longtime friend of Gray and her family, September 1992.

2. This dual interest of American collectors is discussed thoroughly by Paul Schaffer, in Habsburg/Lopato 1994, pp. 160–61.

3. Malcolm S. Forbes commenting on the Matilda Geddings Gray Foundation Collection, n.d.

4. Interview with Matilda G. Stream, New Orleans, niece of Matilda Gray, April 20, 1995.

5. Ibid.

Catalogue

◆

Matilda Geddings Gray Collection

The following twenty-six items form part of the Matilda Geddings Gray Foundation collection, New Orleans. They are the finest from her collection of fifty-three objects by, or in the style of, Fabergé and include three imperial Easter eggs and the celebrated basket of lilies of the valley (cat. no. 59).

— 45 —

SILVER CIGARETTE CASE
Silver, silver gilt, gold
L: 3¾ inches
Marks: Imperial Warrant, initials KF, assay mark of Moscow 1908–17,
inv. no. 24464; cover inscribed "War, 1914 * 1915, K. Fabergé"

The cover is embossed with a stylized double-headed eagle in a roundel. The case was made to commemorate the patriotic effort of the Russian armies during World War I, which was to have such tragic effects for the imperial family and their country. The war made it difficult to obtain precious materials; therefore many objects were produced in base metals, including cigarette cases and bowls of similar design in copper and brass. For identical cases see Habsburg 1994, cats. 52 and 54; Habsburg/Lopato 1994, cat. 123.

Bibliography: Fagaly 1972, cat. 42; Keefe 1993, cat. XXIX

New Orleans Museum of Art: Matilda Geddings Gray
Foundation Loan

— 46 —

PEN TRAY
Silver, enamel
L: 10¾ inches
Marks: K Fabergé, double-headed eagle, initials of workmaster
Stephan Wäkeva, assay marks of St. Petersburg 1896 and before 1896

The oblong tray of red enamel is set with a 1732 silver
ruble of Czarina Anna Ivanovna. On the reverse is a
presentation inscription for a twenty-fifth anniversary,
1872–97.

Bibliography: Fagaly 1972, cat. 72; Keefe 1993, cat. XVIII

New Orleans Museum of Art: Matilda Geddings Gray
Foundation Loan

— 47 —

PRESENTATION CIGARETTE CASE
Gold, diamonds
L: 3⅝ inches
Marks: Fabergé; cover inscribed "His majesty Nicholas II,
emperor and autocrat of all the Russias"

On the cover of this cast, ribbed box is a gold medal with
the profile of Czar Nicholas II. The reverse shows the
figure of Empress Catherine the Great in an allegory of
art and industry.

The box was made to commemorate the Pan-Russian
Artistic and Manufacturing Exhibition held in 1896 at
Nizhny Novgorod, at which the czarina was presented
with the lilies of the valley basket (cat. no. 59).

Bibliography: Fagaly 1972, cat. 41; Keefe 1993, cat. XXVIII

New Orleans Museum of Art: Matilda Geddings Gray
Foundation Loan

— 48 —

CIRCULAR BONBONNIÈRE
Gold, silver, agate, diamonds
Diam: 1⅝ inches
Marks: Fabergé, initials CF in English, initials of workmaster
Henrik Wigström, assay mark of St. Petersburg 1896–1908,
London import marks

The cover of this Louis XVI–style gold box is inset with
panels of dendritic agate over pink foil, separated by
borders of rose-cut diamonds. The English initials CF
for Carl Fabergé indicate the piece was made for the
London outlet.

Provenance: Hammer Galleries, New York

Bibliography: Fagaly 1972, cat. 33; Keefe 1993, cat. VIII

New Orleans Museum of Art: Matilda Geddings Gray
Foundation Loan

— 49 —

PERPETUAL CALENDAR
Nephrite, gold, platinized silver, enamel, diamonds
H: 3¹⁵⁄₁₆ inches

Three enameled cylinders are inscribed with the days of
the week, dates of the month, and months of the year.
The central apertures are surrounded by rose-cut diamond borders. The cylinders are rotated by turning gold
knobs on either side.

Provenance: Hammer Galleries, New York

Bibliography: Fagaly 1972, cat. 64; Keefe 1993, cat. XIV

New Orleans Museum of Art: Matilda Geddings Gray
Foundation Loan

— 50 —

OVAL CLOCK-FRAME
Aventurine quartz, silver, gold, diamonds,
sapphires, ivory
H: 7⅝ inches
Marks: Fabergé, initials of workmaster Mikhail Perkhin,
assay mark of St. Petersburg before 1896; miniature signed
and dated "Zehngraf, Berlin '91"

A combination of the functions of frame and clock invented by Fabergé (see also cat. no. 333), this clock-
frame is inset with a miniature of the Princess Albert of
Sachsen-Altenburg (née Duchess Helene of Mecklenburg), dated 1891, the year of her marriage. For a chalcedony clock-frame with an identical miniature, also dated
1891, formerly in the Lansdell K. Christie collection, see
Parke-Bernet, December 7, 1967, lot 47.

Provenance: Said to have been given by the sitter to Czarina Alexandra
Feodorovna, a cousin and frequent correspondent;
Hammer Galleries, New York

Bibliography: Fagaly 1972, cat. 65; Keefe 1993, cat. XI

New Orleans Museum of Art: Matilda Geddings Gray
Foundation Loan

— 51 —

RECTANGULAR BOX
Nephrite, diamonds, platinum, gold
L: 3¹³⁄₁₆ inches
Marks: Fabergé, initials of workmaster Mikhail Perkhin, assay mark of
St. Petersburg 1896–1908, inv. no. 6415

The cover of this plain hinged box is inset with the
crowned diamond-set monogram EK.

Provenance: Count Kinski, Vienna; Hammer Galleries, New York

Bibliography: Fagaly 1972, cat. 32; Keefe 1993, cat. IX

New Orleans Museum of Art: Matilda Geddings Gray
Foundation Loan

— 52 —

GLOBE-SHAPED CLOCK
Aventurine quartz, silver gilt, silver, gold, enamel, glass
H: 3⅞ inches
Marks: Fabergé, initials of workmaster Mikhail Perkhin, assay mark of
St. Petersburg before 1896, inv. no. 50390

Carved from a block of hardstone, the clock stands on
four paw feet. It is decorated with bands of yellow gold
laurel leaves and crowned with a pinecone finial.

Bibliography: Fagaly 1972, cat. 66; Keefe 1993, cat. X

New Orleans Museum of Art: Matilda Geddings Gray
Foundation Loan

— 53 —
LILY OF THE VALLEY LEAF
Nephrite, gold, pearls, diamonds
L: 5⅝ inches

The lily of the valley leaf is carved with veins and set on one side with tiny flowers fashioned of pearls and diamonds. The lily of the valley was Czarina Alexandra Feodorovna's favorite flower.

Provenance: Said to have come from the imperial apartments; Hammer Galleries, New York

Bibliography: Snowman 1952, pl. 86; Fagaly 1972, cat. 20; Keefe 1993, cat. XVI

Exhibitions: Hammer 1951, cat. 299

New Orleans Museum of Art: Matilda Geddings Gray Foundation Loan

— 54 —
CHESTNUT LEAF
Nephrite, gold, almandite
L: 5⁹⁄₁₆ inches

The five-pointed leaf is naturalistically carved. One of the three prickly gold conkers contains a red almandite chestnut.

Provenance: Said to have come from the imperial apartments; Tessier, London; Dr. James Hasson; Hammer Galleries, New York

Bibliography: Bainbridge 1949, pl. 26; Bainbridge 1966, pl. 29; Fagaly 1972, cat. 19; Keefe 1993, cat. XV

Exhibitions: Hammer 1951, cat. 300

New Orleans Museum of Art: Matilda Geddings Gray Foundation Loan

— 55 —
CHAMELEON HAND SEAL
Nephrite, diamonds, gold, silver, enamel
H: 3⅝ inches

The nephrite reptile with diamond eyes is perched on a pink *guilloché* enamel handle that was transformed into a hand seal. Gray had an imperial cipher replaced with her own monogram. A similar but smaller chameleon handle is in the Traina collection. A pink enamel handle with a frog is in the collection of the Prince of Wales.

Provenance: Said to have come from the imperial apartments; Hammer Galleries, New York

Bibliography: Fagaly 1972, cat. 71; Keefe 1993, cat. XIX

New Orleans Museum of Art: Matilda Geddings Gray Foundation Loan

— 56 —
HAWTHORN
Jasper, agate, gold, nephrite, jade
H: 5½ inches
Marks: Fabergé, initials of workmaster Henrik Wigström, 72

The hawthorn is planted in simulated gold earth, in a vase of white agate resting on a white jade plinth. Ripe berries of red jasper, unripe berries of white jade, and nephrite leaves issue from a gold stalk.
　　Other examples of this plant exist in the collection of the late Bing Crosby and with Ermitage Ltd., London.

Bibliography: Fagaly 1972, cat. 16; Keefe 1993, cat. XLVIII

Exhibitions: New Orleans 1971, cat. 371

New Orleans Museum of Art: Matilda Geddings Gray Foundation Loan

— 57 —

DANDELION PUFF BALL
Asbestos fiber(?), gold, diamonds, nephrite, rock crystal
H: 6½ inches
Marks: Fabergé, initials of workmaster Henrik Wigström, 72

According to Fabergé's chief designer Franz Birbaum in his 1919 memoirs, "The dandelions were particularly successful: their fluff was natural and fixed on a golden thread with a small uncut diamond. The shining points of the diamonds among the white fluff were marvelously successful and prevented this artificial flower from being too close a reproduction of nature" (Habsburg/Lopato 1994, p. 458, where another example is illustrated). For another dandelion puff ball, see cat. no. 186.

Bibliography: Fagaly 1972, cat. 9; Keefe 1993, cat. XXXIX

Exhibitions: New Orleans 1971, cat. 368

New Orleans Museum of Art: Matilda Geddings Gray
Foundation Loan

— 58 —

CORNFLOWERS
Gold, silver, enamel, glass
H: 8¼ inches
Marks: Inv. no. 167680 on stem, 08971 on vase

Eight cornflowers of gold, with trumpet-shaped opaque blue enamel blossoms and purple enamel pistils, stand in a blown art nouveau glass by the imperial glass factory. For examples of art nouveau glass by Tiffany used by Fabergé, see the piece formerly in the Robert Strauss collection (Snowman 1962, ill. 58) and a vase in the Forbes Magazine collection (Christie's, London, *Designs from the House of Fabergé*, April 27, 1989, no. 474, illustrates the drawing for the vase).

Provenance: Said to have come from the imperial apartments; Brooks Bromley, Berwyn, Pennsylvania; Hammer Galleries, New York

Bibliography: Fagaly 1972, cat. 6; Keefe 1993, cat. XXXII

Exhibitions: ALVR 1949, cat. 134; New Orleans 1971, cat. 373

New Orleans Museum of Art: Matilda Geddings Gray Foundation Loan

— 59 —

IMPERIAL LILIES OF THE VALLEY BASKET
Gold, silver, nephrite, pearls, diamonds
H: 7½ inches
Marks: Fabergé, initials of workmaster August Hollming(?),
assay mark of St. Petersburg before 1896; inscribed on base "To Her
Imperial Majesty, Czarina Alexandra Feodorovna, from the ironworks
management and dealers in the Siberian iron section of the Pan-Russian
Artistic and Manufacturing Exhibition in the year of 1896"
Original fitted case with the czarina's cipher on blue *guilloché* enamel field

Apart from the imperial Easter eggs, this is arguably Fabergé's finest creation, an absolute masterpiece of gold work, jewelry, and hardstone carving. It was presented to Czarina Alexandra Feodorovna on the occasion of a visit to the Pan-Russian Exhibition at Nizhny Novgorod in 1896. The basket was her favorite object by Fabergé and stood on her desk until the 1917 Revolution. A photograph of a basket of lilies of the valley (see fig.), may have served as inspiration.

Provenance: Czarina Alexandra Feodorovna; Wartski, London; Brooks Bromley, Berwyn, Pennsylvania; Hammer Galleries, New York

Bibliography: Bainbridge 1949, pl. XI; Snowman 1952, pl. XXI; Snowman 1962, pl. XLIII; Snowman 1966, pl. 18; Fagaly 1972, cat. I; Habsburg 1987, cat. 401 (ill.); Solodkoff 1988, p. 60; Keefe 1993, cat. XLII (ill.)

Exhibitions: Hammer 1951, cat. 129; New Orleans 1971, cat. 367; Munich 1986–87

New Orleans Museum of Art: Matilda Geddings Gray
Foundation Loan

Late nineteenth-century photograph of a lilies of the valley basket from a Fabergé album. Photo: Courtesy Fersman Mineralogical Institute, Moscow.

— 60 —

BONBONNIÈRE WITH ARTICULATED FIGURES
Gold, ivory, enamel, glass
Diam: 2⅞ inches
Marks: Fabergé, initials of workmaster Henrik Wigström, assay mark
of St. Petersburg 1908–17

On the cover of this red *guilloché* enamel box are articulated figures of John Bull and an English bobby. A similar box with Swedish peasant figures is with A La Vieille Russie (Habsburg 1987, cat. 504); one is illustrated in Snowman 1962, pl. XV; another is in the collection of the State Hermitage Museum, St. Petersburg.

Bibliography: Fagaly 1972, cat. 34; Keefe 1993, cat. IV;
Habsburg/Lopato 1994, cat. 258

Exhibitions: St. Petersburg/Paris/London 1993–94

New Orleans Museum of Art: Matilda Geddings Gray
Foundation Loan

— 61 —

NÉCESSAIRE
Gold, silver, enamel, mirror glass, ivory, moonstones
L: 3½ inches
Marks: Fabergé, initials of workmaster August Hollming,
assay mark of St. Petersburg 1908–17

Of waved steel gray *guilloché* enamel, the *nécessaire* has four moonstone push pieces and an interior compartment for cigarettes. It holds a mirror, an ivory tablet, and a pencil with a cabochon moonstone finial.

Bibliography: Fagaly 1972, cat. 36; Keefe 1993, cat. II

New Orleans Museum of Art: Matilda Geddings Gray
Foundation Loan

— 62 —

IMPERIAL PRESENTATION BRIDAL FAN
Gold, enamel, diamonds, gouache on parchment, mother-of-pearl
L: 14 inches
Marks: Fabergé, initials of workmaster Mikhail Perkhin, assay mark of
St. Petersburg 1896–1908; signed and dated "Sergei Solomko 1901"

The monogram OA and double-headed eagles alternate on the yellow *guilloché* enamel front guard. On the reverse are graduated heart-shaped diamond centers and the date 1901. The painted scene depicts the wedding in 1901 of Grand Duchess Olga Aleksandrovna, sister of Czar Nicholas II, with Prince Peter of Oldenburg. The fan is further decorated with a view of Pavlovsk Palace, Egyptian-style motifs, and the crowned initials O and P.

The fan was exhibited in St. Petersburg in 1902 and was mentioned in the newspaper *Novoye Vremya* of March 10: "An artistically made fan painted by Solomko is the gem of Grand Duchess Olga Aleksandrovna's collection," and again in *Niva* magazine: "Charming is the fan made by the artist Solomko and belonging to Grand Duchess Olga Aleksandrovna" (Habsburg/Lopato 1994, pp. 66, 69). The marriage was an unhappy one, ending in divorce in 1916. Grand Duchess Olga married Nikolai Kulikovsky in 1916 (see Ian Vorres, *The Last Great Duchess* [London: Finedawn Publishers, 1985]).

Provenance: Presented by Czar Nicholas II as a wedding present to his sister Grand Duchess Olga Aleksandrovna; Hammer Galleries, New York

Bibliography: Bainbridge 1966, pl. 44; Fagaly 1972, cat. 62; Keefe 1993, cat. III

Exhibitions: St. Petersburg 1902; Hammer 1951, cat. 181

New Orleans Museum of Art: Matilda Geddings Gray Foundation Loan

— 63 —

DESK CALENDAR
Silver, gold, enamel, glass, ivory, paper
H: 3⅜ inches
Marks: Fabergé, initials of workmaster Henrik Wigström, assay mark
of St. Petersburg 1908–17, inv. no. 20792

The shaped panel contains a calendar page of November
1910.

Provenance: Said to have come from the imperial apartments;
Wartski, London; Brooks Bromley, Berwyn, Pennsylvania;
Hammer Galleries, New York

Bibliography: Snowman 1952, pl. 133; Fagaly 1972, cat. 63;
Keefe 1993, cat. XIII

New Orleans Museum of Art: Matilda Geddings Gray
Foundation Loan

— 64 —

IMPERIAL PRESENTATION CIGARETTE CASE
Silver gilt, gold, enamel, moonstone
L: 3½ inches
Marks: Fabergé, initials of workmaster A. Holmström, assay mark of
St. Petersburg 1896–1908

Mauve translucent enamel covers a *guilloché* sunburst.
The case is decorated with a chased gold imperial eagle
and has a moonstone push piece. The interior is inscribed "To Arthur E. Bradshaw, a man who radiates
happiness and charm. Emanuel Snowman 1935."

Provenance: Presented by Emanuel Snowman, Wartski, London,
to Arthur E. Bradshaw

Bibliography: Fagaly 1972, cat. 39; Keefe 1993, cat. XXVI

New Orleans Museum of Art: Matilda Geddings Gray
Foundation Loan

— 65 —

TRIANGULAR FRAME
Silver gilt, silver, enamel, holly, glass
H: 9¾ inches
Marks: K Fabergé, initials of workmaster Anders Nevalainen,
assay mark of St. Petersburg 1896–1908, inv. no. 11309

Laurel wreaths tied with ribbons in each corner decorate this frame of pink translucent enamel over *guilloché*
concentric circles. The original photograph is of Grand
Duchess Tatiana, second daughter of Czarina Alexandra
and Czar Nicholas II.

Bibliography: Fagaly 1972, cat. 73; Keefe 1993, cat. XII

New Orleans Museum of Art: Matilda Geddings Gray
Foundation Loan

— 66 —

OPERA GLASSES
Silver gilt, gold, enamel, diamonds
W: 3 3/16 inches
Marks: Fabergé, initials of workmaster Mikhail Perkhin, assay mark of
St. Petersburg 1896–1908

The barrels of white *guilloché* enamel are chased with
swirling palmetto bands and set on each side with borders of rose-cut diamonds. A pair of yellow gold opera
glasses is in the collection of the late Bing Crosby. For a
pink example see cat. no. 263.

Provenance: Said to have belonged to Czarina Alexandra Feodorovna;
Hammer Galleries, New York

Bibliography: Fagaly 1972, cat. 61; Keefe 1993, cat. I

Exhibitions: Hammer 1951, cat. 274

New Orleans Museum of Art: Matilda Geddings Gray
Foundation Loan

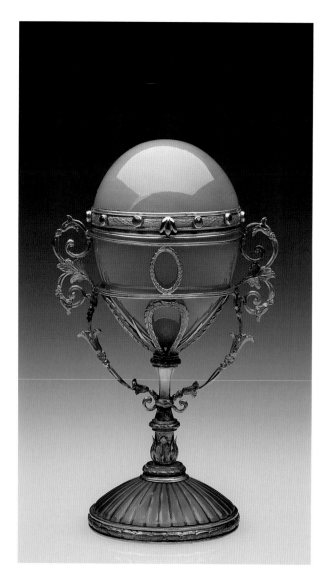
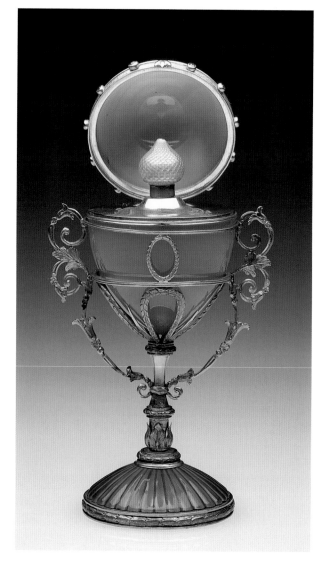

— 67 —

PERFUME BOTTLE
Agate, gold, enamel, rubies
H: 4½ inches
Marks: Fabergé, assay mark of St. Petersburg, 1896–1908

The agate egg opens to reveal a perfume bottle. The egg's rim is banded with green *guilloché* enamel and set with cabochon rubies. The Renaissance-style mount with scrolling handles sits on a domed red *guilloché* enamel foot. An "egg of gilded silver and enamel containing a *flacon*" was listed among the items belonging to Dowager Empress Maria Feodorovna that were removed from the Anichkov Palace in 1917 (see Solodkoff 1995, p. 26).

Bibliography: Fagaly 1972, cat. 27; Keefe 1993, cat. L

Exhibitions: ALVR 1949, cat. 232; Hammer 1951, cat. 164

New Orleans Museum of Art: Matilda Geddings Gray
Foundation Loan

— 68 —

IMPERIAL CAUCASUS EASTER EGG
Gold, silver, platinum, enamel, diamonds, seed pearls,
rock crystal, ivory
H: 3⅝ inches
Marks: Fabergé, initials of workmaster Mikhail Perkhin,
assay mark of St. Petersburg before 1896; miniatures signed
and dated "Krijitski: 1891"
Later gold stand

Hidden behind four hinged doors are the surprises of this egg: four views of the imperial hunting lodge at Abastuman, signed by Konstantin I. Krijitski and dated 1891. Abastuman became the residence of Grand Duke Georgi Aleksandrovich, younger brother of Nicholas II, after he was diagnosed with tuberculosis in 1891. His portrait is visible under the table-cut diamonds at the apex and base. In spite of the healthy air of the Caucasus, the grand duke died there six years later.

The crimson *guilloché* enamel shell is decorated with four-color gold swags suspended from diamond-set tied bows. The oval windows are decorated with diamond-set numerals forming the date 1893 and are surrounded by seed pearls and flanked by fluted columns.

Provenance: Presented by Czar Alexander III to his wife, Czarina Maria Feodorovna, Easter 1893; government of the USSR, 1918; sold to Armand Hammer, 1930, for 5,000 rubles; Hammer Galleries, New York

Bibliography: Snowman 1962, pl. LXXI, p. 83; Bainbridge 1966, pl. 57; Fagaly 1972, cat. 24; Waterfield/Forbes 1978, p. 116; Habsburg/Solodkoff 1979, cat. 10; Snowman 1979, p. 91; Forbes 1980, pp. 34, 35; Solodkoff 1984, p. 67; Hill 1989, ill. 23; Pfeffer 1990, pp. 28, 29; Keefe 1993, cat. LII

Exhibitions: Hammer 1937, cat. I; Hammer 1939, cat. 155; V&A 1977, cat. M12; San Diego/Moscow 1989–90, cat. 3

New Orleans Museum of Art: Matilda Geddings Gray
Foundation Loan

— 69 —

IMPERIAL DANISH PALACES EASTER EGG
Gold, enamel, star sapphire, emeralds, diamonds, mother-of-pearl,
rock crystal, velvet
H: 4 inches
Marks: Fabergé, initials of workmaster Mikhail Perkhin, assay mark of
St. Petersburg before 1896; miniatures signed "Krijitski"

In Louis XVI style, of pink translucent enamel over *guilloché* pellet crosses, the egg has twelve panels divided by borders of laurel leaves and rose-cut diamonds, with an emerald at each intersection. The finial is a star sapphire surrounded by rose-cut diamonds. The surprise in the egg is a ten-leaf screen painted on mother-of-pearl, depicting the imperial Russian yachts *Polar Star* and *Tsarevna;* the royal Danish palaces Amalienborg, Kronborg, Bernsdorff, Hvidore, and Fredensborg; and the Russian residences Alexandria at Peterhof, and two dachas at Gatchina.

Provenance: Presented by Czar Alexander III to his wife, Czarina Maria Feodorovna, Easter 1895; government of the USSR, 1918;

sold to Armand Hammer, 1930, for 1,500 rubles; Hammer Galleries, New York; Mr. and Mrs. Nicholas H. Ludwig

Bibliography: Bainbridge 1966, pl. 65; Fagaly 1972, cat. 25; Habsburg/Solodkoff 1979, cat. 12; Snowman 1979, p. 95; Solodkoff 1984, pp. 70ff; Habsburg 1987, cat. 537; Solodkoff 1988, p. 26; Hill 1989, ill. 28; Pfeffer 1990, p. 38

Exhibitions: Hammer 1937, cat. 3; Hammer 1939; ALVR 1949, cat. 129; Hammer 1951, cat. 157; V&A 1977, cat. M8; Munich 1986–87; San Diego/Moscow 1989–90, cat. 6

New Orleans Museum of Art: Matilda Geddings Gray Foundation Loan

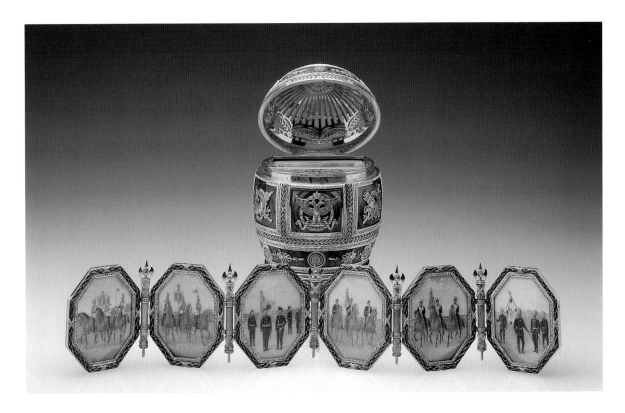

— 70 —

IMPERIAL NAPOLEONIC EASTER EGG
Gold, enamel, diamonds, platinum, ivory, velvet, silk
H: 4⅝ inches
Marks: Fabergé, initials of workmaster Henrik Wigström,
assay mark of St. Petersburg 1908–17; miniatures signed and
dated "V. Zuiev 1912"

The egg commemorates the centenary of the Russian victory over the armies of Napoleon, which were defeated in 1812 at the hands of Prince Kutuzov following the battle of Borodino. The festivities for this centenary were used to enhance Russian patriotism. Fabergé's green *guilloché* enamel Easter egg is decorated in the Empire style with double-headed eagles and trophies of war. Diamonds at the apex and base cover the cipher of the dowager empress and the date 1912.

As in the Danish Palaces Easter egg (cat. no. 69), the surprise is a folding screen. On six panels Vasilii Zuiev has painted the regiments of which the dowager empress was honorary colonel. From left to right these are Her Majesty's Regiments of the Eleventh Eastern Siberian Sharpshooters, the Eleventh Ulan Chuguevskis, the Second Pskov Dragoons, the Naval Guards, the Kirasirki Life Guards, and the Cavalry Guards. The panels are framed within green enameled laurel-leaf and diamond borders; the hinges are shaped as ax-topped fasces. The reverses each show the crowned cipher of Maria Feodorovna on a green *guilloché* enamel disk in the center of an opalescent white enamel panel.

Provenance: Presented by Czar Nicholas II to his mother, Dowager Empress Maria Feodorovna, Easter 1912; government of the USSR, 1918; sold to Armand Hammer, 1930, for 5,000 rubles; Hammer Galleries, New York

Bibliography: Snowman 1953, pls. 370–72; Snowman 1962, p. 103; Fagaly 1972, cat. 26; Waterfield/Forbes 1978, p. 125; Habsburg/Solodkoff 1979, pl. 132; Snowman 1979, p. 110; Solodkoff 1984, pp. 98–99; Habsburg 1987, cat. 542; Hill 1989, ill. 54; Pfeffer 1990, pp. 100–1; Keefe 1993, cat. LIV

Exhibitions: Hammer 1937, cat. 8; Hammer 1939; Hammer 1951, cat. 160; V&A 1977, cat. O26; Munich 1986–87; San Diego/Moscow 1989–90, cat. 21

New Orleans Museum of Art: Matilda Geddings Gray
Foundation Loan

Fig. 1. *India Early Minshall as a young matron, mid-1920s(?).*

India Early Minshall

Portrait Sketch of a Russophile

India Early Minshall (fig. 1) was born in 1885 in Columbus, Ohio, into a family headed by her father, Lewis Mortimer Early, a successful physician with business interests in photographic supplies and automobiles. Her mother, older sister, and paternal grandparents were part of her extended, upper-middle-class family. All her life India seems to have been a warmhearted person, open and accepting of those around her. Her niece has described her as "kind, compassionate, and generous to a fault."[1] Like many women of her generation, India had a limited formal education. In 1906 she married Thaddeus Ellis Minshall, who became a successful businessman after some false starts and an interruption occasioned by military service during World War I. In 1920 India and her husband moved to Cleveland, Ohio, and the following year he established a petroleum marketing firm, the Pocahontas Oil Company.[2] In 1928 the company was sold to the Hickok Oil Company, although it operated as an independent subsidiary for more than twenty years.[3]

T. Ellis Minshall died in 1930. An obituary stated that he had made $1 million from Pocahontas Oil,[4] and though the amount is perhaps not precisely accurate, he evidently left enough for his widow to live comfortably. When she died some thirty-five years later, in 1965, her estate was valued at just less than $1.5 million, roughly two-thirds of that amount in intangible property—stocks, bonds, and bank deposits—and the remainder mostly accounted for by her collection of works of art and historical artifacts

made in Russia before the 1917 Revolution.[5] That India Early Minshall chose to form this collection, and then pursued her objective with vigor and tenacity over roughly a quarter of a century, is an amazing aspect of her life. The hows and whys can never be entirely explained, but documents and the recollections of those close to her provide enough evidence to suggest an outline of her methods.

As a girl, India Early is said to have been a voracious reader. She began with fairy stories and went on to tales of the lives of kings and queens, later narrowing her interest to the history of the Russian czars and the art and culture of that country. After her marriage, she shared this interest with her husband, and together they built a library devoted to prerevolutionary Russia. India became an expert on the anecdotal minutiae of Russian imperial history and said of herself, "I have a queer loyalty to the country of Russia itself, inexplicable, for I have never been there."[6] It was, however, only after her husband's death that she began to form her collection of Russian art and artifacts. In 1934 Minshall saw in an advertisement of the Hammer Galleries a pair of bottles that reportedly once belonged to Czar Alexander III. She went to New York to visit the gallery, and there she met a young Russian, Prince Mikhail Aleksandrovich Gundorov, whom she described a few years later as "having been born plain Bill Jones, would still be a Prince in any language."[7] Minshall seems to have been equally enraptured by the contents of the Hammer Galleries, but she decided she could not afford the bottles that had brought her there. With Gundorov's help, she aquired instead a carved wooden presentation bread-and-salt platter given to Czar Nicholas II and Czarina Alexandra in 1896, an icon reputed to have come from Alexandra, and a small medal of 1825. For less than $300, thus began the India Early Minshall collection (fig. 2).[8]

The Romanov czars of Russia present a varied if always colorful cast of historical figures. Minshall had her favorites. For Nicholas II and Alexandra, "about whom I have read everything I can find," she felt enormous sympathy. She admired Catherine the Great for her political acumen. But perhaps Minshall was most intrigued by Alexander II, whom she described as "so human and kind," and his longtime mistress and briefly, at the end of his life, morganatic wife, Princess Katherine Yurievsky. Of them she said,

"Their life together was simple and ideally happy," a view perhaps both naive and romantic, but revealing for what it tells of Minshall's own attitudes.[9] Through Prince Gundorov, Minshall was introduced in New York in 1938 to Countess Sophie de Berg, the daughter-in-law of Princess Yurievsky's sister. From her, Minshall obtained a number of items associated with Alexander II and Katherine. Minshall remained on intimate terms with the countess, and later with her daughter, Princess Obolensky.[10] She greatly valued the personal contacts with the ancien régime of Russia provided through these New York acquaintances.

In the meantime, Minshall's collection was growing apace. Minshall made further purchases from the Hammer Galleries in 1935, and from the same source she bought her first Fabergé piece in 1937, for $250, a charming little

Fig. 2. *India Early Minshall in her living room, 1951. Behind her, in a shadow-box frame, is a carved wooden platter, which was among the first Russian objects she acquired. Photo: Rudolph G. Muller.*

Fig. 3. *Fabergé firm*, Clock, *workmaster Henrik Wigström, rhodonite, silver, enamel, diamonds, h. 2¹⁄₁₆ inches. The Cleveland Museum of Art, The India Early Minshall Collection, 66.476. Acquired in 1937, this clock was India Minshall's first piece of Fabergé.*

clock made of rhodonite with an enamel face inscribed "Fabergé" and surrounded by tiny diamonds (fig. 3).[11]

In 1939 India Early Minshall wrote a short essay entitled "The Story of My Russian Cabinet," and in the same year a photograph was made of her standing beside that cabinet and displaying some of its contents—Russian porcelain and glass and a silver samovar (fig. 4). Minshall carefully preserved records of her early dealings with the Hammer Galleries, and we therefore know that most of the items in the cabinet did not come from that firm, nor do other documents reveal their origins.[12] Clearly, she early on began to tap more than one or two sources to augment her collection. As both the photograph and the essay of 1939 make clear, by that year Minshall had begun to identify herself with her collection of Russian material.

Though by 1939 Minshall had bought only one Fabergé piece, her essay indicates her great admiration for the products of the jeweler's firm, especially the imperial eggs. She says, "Fabergé was called the Cellini of the North, but I do not think any jeweler can ever be compared to him."[13] Four years later, in an addendum to the 1939 essay, she described the latest additions to her collection.[14] In a section

headed "And Now to Fabergé," she first briefly recounted the history of the Fabergé firm and then listed twelve recent purchases. First came three flower subjects and four animals carved from hardstones. These pieces are specifically noted as "all signed," though in fact the only two apparently still in the collection today, a jade rabbit and a topaz bulldog, are not signed. These two animals came from the Hammer Galleries, but the vendor of the others is not known. Since Fabergé's flowers and animals usually are not signed and the source of the now missing pieces is undetermined, one wonders if perhaps Minshall bought them from an unreliable dealer, discovered they were not genuine, and eliminated them from her collection (learning in the process that not all Fabergé objects are signed and that all objects signed Fabergé are not necessarily authentic). The last item on this list, which is dated January 16, 1943, was the great Fabergé tea set with enamel decoration (fig. 5) which Minshall purchased from Alexander Schaffer for $1,925, far and away the largest sum she had spent to date for a Fabergé item.[15] A few months later, she

Fig. 4. *India Early Minshall standing beside a cabinet filled with Russian objects, 1939. Photo: Courtesy* Cleveland Press.

Fig. 5. *Fabergé firm, Moscow branch,* Tea Set, *silver gilt with cloisonné enamel decoration, greatest h. 7⅛ inches. The Cleveland Museum of Art, The India Early Minshall Collection, 66.500–.510.*

purchased the Red Cross egg from Schaffer for $4,400 (cat. no. 99).[16] The India Early Minshall collection of Fabergé was off and running. She was no longer willing only to admire the imperial eggs at the Hammer Galleries.

For several years after 1943, Minshall's purchases of Fabergé seem to have been few. Invoices do not survive for about a dozen Fabergé pieces in the collection, and some or all might have been acquired at this time. From 1948 to 1951 the pace probably quickened, with at least eighteen objects acquired, chiefly from the Hammer Galleries. From them Minshall purchased in 1951 a beautiful green jade presentation box with portrait miniatures of Nicholas II and Alexandra. It cost more than the Red Cross egg but was discovered to be the work not of Fabergé but of his rivals, Cartier in Paris (for the box) and probably the Hahn firm in St. Petersburg (for the enframement of the miniatures).

Another comparatively quiet period of collecting seems to have occurred in the mid-1950s, but it was at this time, in 1954, that Minshall purchased from A La Vieille Russie the piece that is aesthetically perhaps the finest in the col-

lection, a miniature bidet from the Wigström workshop of the Fabergé firm, with its almost miraculous enamels in the Louis XVI style (cat. no. 97).[17] A drawing for this object dated May 26, 1915, has recently been discovered in a stock book from the Wigström atelier.[18]

Minshall's collecting of Fabergé again increased in 1957, and this tempo lasted until 1961, but after that year no further additions were made to the collection as it now exists. There is extant a 1959 receipt for several pieces, no longer in the collection, that she might have given to friends and family.[19] During this period, Minshall's Fabergé purchases seem to have been made entirely from A La Vieille Russie. Perhaps attempting to round out her collection, Minshall purchased several hand seals, of which she had previously had only one example. In 1959 she acquired a set of enameled buttons with tiny diamonds, the only jewelry by Fabergé that she seems ever to have owned. She bought some quite unusual pieces, such as a Lukutin lacquer box with Fabergé mounts (cat. no. 73). In general, the quality and interest of these last acquisitions were very high, but there was at least one serious mistake, the purchase of a green jade egg and stand. The stand is marked Fabergé and is probably genuine, but the unmarked egg is less well made than the stand and was likely produced only a few years before its purchase by Minshall.[20]

As she herself told me, India Early Minshall was a woman of comparatively modest means. She lived comfortably in a suite in a residential hotel. She chose to spend most of her surplus income on her collection. She said, for example, that when presented with the choice of European travel or a Fabergé object, she customarily opted for the latter, despite the fact that exploring new places was a great pleasure for her. In the beginning, Minshall had focused on artifacts that might be associated in some way or another with one of the Romanov czars. Though she retained many of her earlier purchases and remained interested in Russian imperial history, Fabergé came to dominate her

Fig. 7. *India Early Minshall standing beside a cabinet containing Russian material, ca. 1960.*

collecting activities in later life. If the Fabergé objects also had associations with the Romanovs, so much the better, but that was no longer a necessity. In 1949 India lent some Fabergé pieces to an exhibition at A La Vieille Russie, and her name is recorded among those of other distinguished Russian and American collectors.[21] Henceforth she seems to have classified herself primarily as a collector of Fabergé, and her other Russian material became of secondary interest. In 1965 an elaborate folio catalogue of her Fabergé collection was produced for Minshall, with entries for each piece printed on heavy stock and original color photographs used as illustrations.[22] For at least one copy, a large box covered in red leather was provided.[23]

It was perhaps in the 1950s that Minshall began to consider the eventual disposition of her collection. Her residence overlooked the Cleveland Museum of Art and the park that it faces, and in 1950 she became a life member of the museum. The building in which she lived was also home to William M. Milliken, then director of the museum.

Fig. 6. *A corner of the Minshall living room, 1951. The cabinet contains much of Minshall's Fabergé collection as it existed at that date, including the Red Cross egg on the center shelf. Photo: Rudolph G. Muller.*

Fig. 8. *India Early Minshall shortly before her death in 1965.*
Photo: Courtesy Cleveland Press.

It is reported that at some time before his retirement in 1958, Minshall approached Milliken and asked him to come to see her collection of Fabergé and other Russian artifacts. This he point-blank refused to do.[24] Milliken was a man of broad tastes in the visual arts, but he had a blind spot when it came to the decorative arts of around 1900. It is also possible that for political reasons he was disinclined to look with favor upon the relics of the Russian czars. Milliken was succeeded as director by Sherman E. Lee in 1958, and two years later I arrived at the museum to take charge of European and American decorative arts made after 1600. Shortly after coming to Cleveland, I was approached by Minshall's nephew by marriage, Harry Jackson, who asked me to see her collections. This I did, and I was impressed with their quality, particularly that of the Fabergé material. Dr. Lee also visited Minshall, and he too looked favorably on the pieces made by the Fabergé firm.

There remained, however, one problem. In addition to the Fabergé objects, the Minshall collection included a large number of other Russian artifacts in a variety of materials, some with imperial and other historical associations, but many of limited aesthetic interest and hence of, at best, marginal relevance to an art museum. The suggestion was made that perhaps the Fabergé material might be bequeathed to the Cleveland Museum of Art and the remainder of the collection left to a nearby sister institution, the Western Reserve Historical Society. In 1963 Minshall gave to the art museum the Red Cross egg, with life interest retained, and following her death in 1965, her collections were distributed between these two Cleveland institutions. In 1967 a catalogue entitled *Fabergé and His Contemporaries: The India Early Minshall Collection of the Cleveland Museum of Art* was published, and both parts of the collection were exhibited in their entirety by their respective owners.[25] Since that time, at least a part of the Fabergé collection always has been on view at the art museum, and pieces from it frequently have been lent to important exhibitions of Fabergé's work. After 1967 the group of objects bequeathed to the Western Reserve Historical Society were placed in storage at that institution, and on April 12, 1988, this part of the Minshall collection was sold in its entirety at auction in New York in a hundred lots for a total of $364,606. The catalogue prepared by Christie's for this sale offers a detailed description of these Russian objects from the Minshall collection, many of them illustrated, some in color.

Without doubt, India Early Minshall was a remarkable human being. Her personal virtues are proven by the affection and respect with which she was regarded by those who knew her. She was an exemplar of an increasingly rare species, the intellectual hobbyist. An intense interest in Russian imperial history resulted first in her building a distinguished library of books on that subject, much of which was unfortunately destroyed in a fire in the 1940s. Next, she began to collect memorabilia of the czars and a bit later objects produced by the Fabergé firm. And toward the end of the 1930s, she undertook to learn the Russian language, a task that few have attempted without the encouragement of impelling professional necessity.[26]

Though not of enormous size, Minshall's Fabergé collection includes representative examples of every significant variety of object that Fabergé made. It is the remark-able degree of concurrence of historic importance, technical quality, and beauty of the particular pieces that makes this Fabergé collection a distinguished one. But the factor of overriding importance is that India Early Minshall, through the formation of her Fabergé collection, engaged in an activity that gave pleasure and meaning to her own life and that will substantially enrich those of us who are able to experience it now and in the future.

— Henry Hawley
Chief Curator, Later Western Art
The Cleveland Museum of Art

NOTES

1. Betty Bonnet Shepherd (Mrs. Frank), "India Early Minshall," manuscript, October 1994, curatorial files, Cleveland Museum of Art. Unless otherwise specified, the biographical information on India Early Minshall is derived from this source.

2. The Minshall residences in Cleveland can be traced from 1920 to 1932 in Cleveland city directories. After that date, Mrs. Minshall's address is only sporadically listed. The Pocahontas Oil Company is also listed in Cleveland city directories.

3. *Cleveland News,* June 27, 1951, clipping in the files of the Business Economics and Labor Department, Cleveland Public Library.

4. *Cleveland Plain Dealer,* June 11, 1930, p. 2.

5. Estate of India E. Minshall, State of Ohio, Cuyahoga County, no. 682589.

6. India Early Minshall, "The Story of My Russian Cabinet," typescript dated February 5, 1939, Archive of the Western Reserve Historical Society, p. 15.

7. Ibid., p. 1.

8. Ibid., p. 2; Hammer Galleries invoice, Christmas 1937, curatorial files, Cleveland Museum of Art.

9. Minshall, "Russian Cabinet," pp. 5–6.

10. Ibid., pp. 7–8.

11. Hammer Galleries invoice, dated March 7, 1939, but including all purchases made between 1934 and 1939, curatorial files, Cleveland Museum of Art.

12. Ibid.

13. Minshall, "Russian Cabinet," p. 10.

14. Minshall, addendum to "Russian Cabinet," dated January 16, 1943, pp. 16–18.

15. Alexander Schaffer invoice, 1942, curatorial files, Cleveland Museum of Art.

16. A La Vieille Russie invoice, March 16, 1943, curatorial files, Cleveland Museum of Art.

17. A La Vieille Russie invoice, December 15, 1954, curatorial files, Cleveland Museum of Art.

18. Habsburg/Lopato 1994, pp. 92–93.

19. A La Vieille Russie invoice, February 11, 1959, curatorial files, Cleveland Museum of Art.

20. Hawley 1967, no. 52.

21. Millicent Stow, "Fabergé's Wondrous Works of Gold and Jewels Exhibited," *New York Sun,* November 18, 1949, clipping file, Ingalls Library, Cleveland Museum of Art.

22. *Fabergé: From the Collection of India Minshall* (Cleveland, 1965).

23. Now Ingalls Library, Cleveland Museum of Art.

24. Winsor French, column in *Cleveland Press,* April 4, 1967.

25. See n. 20. The exhibitions were widely reported in Cleveland newspapers for March 1967. See, for example, *Cleveland Press,* March 14, and *Cleveland Plain Dealer,* March 15 and 19.

26. Letter from Armand Hammer to India Early Minshall, March 7, 1939, curatorial files, Cleveland Museum of Art.

Catalogue

India Early Minshall Collection

The Cleveland Museum of Art has loaned a selection of thirty Fabergé objects (cat. nos. 15, 71–99) from those donated to the museum by India Early Minshall.

— 71 —

ROUND BOX
Silver gilt, enamel
Diam: 2¼ inches
Marks: Fabergé, Imperial Warrant, assay mark of
Moscow 1908–17, inv. no. 25477

The style of this box is very close to the work of Fedor Rückert, who sometimes sold his enamels through the Fabergé firm.

Bibliography: Hawley 1967, no. 61

The Cleveland Museum of Art, The India Early Minshall Collection,
66.497

— 72 —

PAIR OF CANDELABRA
Silver
H: 11 3/16 inches
Marks: K Fabergé, double-headed eagle, initials of workmaster
Julius Rappoport, assay mark of St. Petersburg before 1896.
Original fitted case stamped with Imperial Warrant,
St. Petersburg, Moscow

A drawing of a related piece is illustrated in Snowman
1962, fig. 35.

Bibliography: Hawley 1967, no. 26

The Cleveland Museum of Art, The India Early Minshall Collection,
66.494–.495

— 73 —

LACQUER BOX
Lacquer, papier-mâché, gold, diamonds
L: 5¹¹⁄₁₆ inches
Marks: Initials KF; interior inscribed "Factory N. Lukutin"

The Lukutin factory near Moscow was famous for the production of lacquer boxes. N. Lukutin succeeded his father as head of the factory in the late 1880s and continued in that capacity until the factory closed in 1904. The gold crown in the center of the cover reproduces the design of the Russian imperial crown.

Provenance: Said to have been made for Grand Duke Aleksandr

Bibliography: Hawley 1967, no. 55

The Cleveland Museum of Art, The India Early Minshall Collection, 66.464

— 74 —

BAROMETER
Palisander, silver gilt, garnet
H: 5½ inches
Marks: Fabergé, initials of workmaster Victor Aarne, assay mark of St. Petersburg 1896–1908, assay master Iakov Liapunov; barometer mechanism appropriately inscribed and with monogram GL, presumably the mark of its maker

Bibliography: Hawley 1967, no. 20

The Cleveland Museum of Art, The India Early Minshall Collection, 66.484

— 75 —

MINIATURE CUP
Gold, diamonds, sapphires
H: 1 11/16 inches
Marks: Fabergé, initials of workmaster Mikhail Perkhin, assay mark of
St. Petersburg before 1896, inv. no. 40139

Opposite the handle is a double-headed eagle in rose-cut
diamonds with the arms of Russia in gold superimposed
on it.

Provenance: Said to come from the Alexander Palace, Tsarskoe Selo

Bibliography: Hawley 1967, no. 5

Exhibitions: Hammer 1951, cat. 69, p. 14

The Cleveland Museum of Art, The India Early Minshall Collection,
66.483

— 76 —

KREMLIN TOWER CLOCK
Rhodonite, silver, enamel, emeralds, sapphires
H: 11⅜ inches
Marks: Fabergé, Imperial Warrant, assay mark of
Moscow 1908–17, inv. no. 16419

The form of this clock recalls in a general way several
towers within the Kremlin, particularly the Toinitskaia.

Provenance: Said to have been made in 1913 for Czar Nicholas II to
commemorate the tercentenary of the Romanov dynasty

Bibliography: Bainbridge 1935, 87–90; Garvey 1945, 2–4; Bainbridge
1949, pl. 17; Hawley 1967, no. 57; Habsburg/Lopato 1994, cat. 118

Exhibitions: St. Petersburg/Paris/London 1993–94

The Cleveland Museum of Art, The India Early Minshall Collection,
66.477

— 77 —

FRAME FOR NINE MINIATURES
Gold, silver gilt
H: 8½ inches
Marks: Fabergé, initials of workmaster Victor Aarne, assay mark of
St. Petersburg 1896–1908, assay master Iakov Liapunov; three
miniatures signed "I. Goffert," one signed "Vegner"

Almost certainly this frame was designed to display an already existing group of miniatures. The subjects are (top row, left to right) Alexander II; Maria Feodorovna, wife of Alexander II; Nicholas I; Alexander III; (bottom row, left to right) Alexander III; Nicholas I; Alexander II; Alexander III; Alexander III.

Provenance: Said to have come from the apartments of the Czarina Alexandra Feodorovna, Alexander Palace, Tsarskoe Selo

Bibliography: Hawley 1967, no. 21; Habsburg/Lopato 1994, cat. 2, p. 170

Exhibitions: Hammer 1951, cat. 214, p. 36; San Francisco 1964, cat. 122, p. 23; St. Petersburg/Paris/London 1993–94

The Cleveland Museum of Art, The India Early Minshall Collection, 66.460

— 78 —

TRIANGULAR FRAME
Gold, rubies, diamonds, gouache, ivory, glass
H: 5 3/16 inches
Marks: Fabergé, Imperial Warrant, assay mark of Moscow 1896–1908, assay master Ivan Lebedkin, inv. no. 27280

The portrait is of Czarina Alexandra Feodorovna.

Bibliography: Snowman 1962, pl. XIX; Hawley 1967, no. 56; Habsburg/Lopato 1994, cat. 14, p. 181

Exhibitions: ALVR 1961, cat. 189, p. 63; San Francisco 1964, cat. 115, p. 23; V&A 1977, cat. M1, pp. 76, 77, pl. XIX; St. Petersburg/Paris/London 1993–94

The Cleveland Museum of Art, The India Early Minshall Collection, 66.456

— 79 —

MINIATURE TEAPOT
Jade, gold
L: 4¼ inches
Marks: Fabergé, initials of workmaster Mikhail Perkhin, assay mark of
St. Petersburg before 1896, inv. no. 47274

Like most Fabergé works in the rococo style, this piece
was made before 1903, when Perkhin headed the chief
workshop.

Bibliography: Hawley 1967, no. 1; Snowman 1979, p. 26;
Habsburg/Lopato 1994, cat. 246, p. 354

Exhibitions: ALVR 1961, cat. 275; San Francisco 1964, cat. 131;
V&A 1977, cat. M5, p. 77; St. Petersburg/Paris/London 1993–94

The Cleveland Museum of Art, The India Early Minshall Collection,
66.479

— 80 —

MINIATURE SHOE
Bloodstone, gold, diamonds, silver
L: 3½ inches
Marks: Inv. no. 49194

The rococo style and high-quality workmanship of this
piece suggest that it was made in the workshop of Mikhail Perkhin before 1903. For a similar sabot, see cat.
no. 223.

Bibliography: Hawley 1967, no. 2; Habsburg/Lopato 1994,
cat. 245, p. 354

Exhibitions: ALVR 1961, cat. 276; San Francisco 1964, cat. 132;
St. Petersburg/Paris/London 1993–94

The Cleveland Museum of Art, The India Early Minshall Collection,
66.482

— 81 —

CLOCK

Jade, gold, enamel, diamonds

H: 3 1/16 inches

Marks: Fabergé, initials of workmaster Henrik Wigström, assay mark
of St. Petersburg 1908–17, inv. no. 22681

The parallel bars of diamonds decorating this clock appear to form the Roman numeral three and suggest that
this clock was designed as a third-anniversary gift.

Bibliography: Snowman 1962, p. 147, pl. XXVIII; Hawley 1967, no. 14;
Habsburg/Lopato 1994, cat. 259, p. 362

Exhibitions: Hammer 1951, addenda, cat. 332; ALVR 1961, cat. 178,
pp. 59, 63; San Francisco 1964, cat. 90, p. 34; V&A 1977, cat. M4,
p. 77, pl. XXVIII; St. Petersburg/Paris/London 1993–94

The Cleveland Museum of Art, The India Early Minshall Collection,
66.475

— 82 —

FRAMED MINIATURE OF HAMPTON COURT

Jade, gold, enamel, ivory

L: 4 7/16 inches

Marks: Initials of workmaster Henrik Wigström, assay mark of
St. Petersburg 1908–17, inv. no. 19677; illegible monogram at
lower right corner of miniature

Bainbridge 1949, p. 98, describes monochromatic miniatures of English royal residences framed in nephrite,
ordered from Fabergé's St. Petersburg workshop.

Provenance: Richard Bradshaw, England

Bibliography: Hawley 1967, no. 18

Exhibition: Hammer 1951, p. 36

The Cleveland Museum of Art, The India Early Minshall Collection,
66.461

— 83 —

PAIR OF FRAMED MINIATURES
Gold, jade, rubies, gouache, ivory, glass
H: 6 inches
Marks: Fabergé, initials of workmaster Mikhail Perkhin,
assay mark of St. Petersburg before 1896, inv. no. 54471;
miniatures inscribed "Zehngraf"

The subjects of the miniatures are Czar Nicholas II and
one of his children, probably Grand Duchess Olga. Both
frames are visible on a photograph of the Fabergé exhibition held in 1902 at the von Dervise House in St. Petersburg (see Habsburg/Lopato 1994, cat. 366).

Provenance: Said to come from the Alexander Palace, Tsarskoe Selo

Bibliography: Snowman 1962, pl. XVIII; Hawley 1967, no. 8

Exhibitions: St. Petersburg 1902; Hammer 1951, cat. 215, p. 36;
ALVR 1961, cat. 188, pp. 61, 63; San Francisco 1964, cat. 114, p. 56;
V&A 1977, cat. M3, p. 77, pl. XVIII

The Cleveland Museum of Art, The India Early Minshall Collection,
66.458–.459

— 84 —

HAND SEAL
Gold, enamel, purpurine, diamonds
H: 1⅝ inches
Marks: Initials of workmaster Karl Armfelt, assay mark of
St. Petersburg 1896–1908, assay master A. Richter, inv. no. 14771

This seal is accompanied by its original wooden box, the
lining of which does not bear the location London, indicating that it was made in 1903 or earlier. However, since
Armfelt did not become a workmaster until 1904, the
piece must have been made between 1904 and 1908.

Provenance: The letter A engraved on the seal is said to be in the
handwriting of Czarina Alexandra Feodorovna, suggesting that
the seal was made for her.

Bibliography: Hawley 1967, no. 22

The Cleveland Museum of Art, The India Early Minshall Collection,
66.487

— 85 —

PUPPIES ON A MAT
Agate, chalcedony, marble(?)
L: 4⁹⁄₁₆ inches

The stones were carefully chosen to depict the natural coloration of the animals.

Bibliography: Hawley 1967, no. 28

Exhibitions: ALVR 1961, cat. 24

The Cleveland Museum of Art, The India Early Minshall Collection, 66.451

— 86 —

BEGGING POODLE
Agate, rubies
H: 2½ inches

The poodle is precisely and realistically rendered.

Bibliography: Hawley 1967, no. 29

The Cleveland Museum of Art, The India Early Minshall Collection, 66.448

— 87 —

ELEPHANT BELL PUSH
Jade, gold, rubies, emeralds, diamonds, enamel
L: 3 inches
Marks: Fabergé, initials of workmaster Henrik Wigström,
assay mark of St. Petersburg 1896–1908

The elephant is the heraldic beast of Denmark; Dowager
Empress Maria Feodorovna was born Dagmar, princess
of Denmark.

Provenance: Said to have been made for Dowager Empress
Maria Feodorovna

Bibliography: Hawley 1967, no. 13

Exhibitions: Hammer 1951, cat. 57, p. 13; ALVR 1961, cat. 225,
pp. 60, 80; San Francisco 1964, cat. 91, p. 35

The Cleveland Museum of Art, The India Early Minshall Collection,
66.474

— 88 —

PARROT ON A PERCH
Silver, enamel, jasper, agate, emeralds
H: 6 inches
Marks: Fabergé, initials of workmaster Mikhail Perkhin, assay mark of
St. Petersburg 1896–1908, assay master Iakov Liapunov, inv. no. 6817

The parrot's tail was broken at the time it was sold at
auction in 1958 and was subsequently replaced in agate.

Provenance: Christie's, London, November 25, 1958, lot 152

Bibliography: Hawley 1967, no. 3

The Cleveland Museum of Art, The India Early Minshall Collection,
66.447

89   90   91   92   93

— 89 —

CRANBERRY
Chalcedony, jade, rock crystal, gold
H: 4½ inches

In addition to cranberry, other popular names have been suggested for the species represented, among them partridgeberry and bearberry.

Bibliography: Hawley 1967, no. 34; Booth 1990, p. 122

Exhibitions: San Francisco 1964, cat. 32, pp. 24, 25

The Cleveland Museum of Art, The India Early Minshall Collection, 66.446

— 90 —

FORGET-ME-NOTS
Turquoise, diamonds, rock crystal, silver gilt
H: 3½ inches
Marks: 8100(?)

Bibliography: Hawley 1967, no. 35; Booth 1990, p. 122

Exhibitions: San Francisco 1964, cat. 35, pp. 24, 25

The Cleveland Museum of Art, The India Early Minshall Collection, 66.444

— 91 —

LILY OF THE VALLEY
Pearls, diamonds, jade, rock crystal, silver, gold
H: 4¾ inches

Bibliography: Hawley 1967, no. 36; Booth 1990, p. 123

Exhibitions: Hammer 1951, addenda, cat. 344; San Francisco 1964,
cat. 34, pp. 24, 25

The Cleveland Museum of Art, The India Early Minshall Collection,
66.443

— 92 —

MINIATURE LILY OF THE VALLEY
Pearls, jade, rock crystal, gold
H: 2 inches

Bibliography: Hawley 1967, no. 37; Booth 1990, p. 123

Exhibitions: San Francisco 1964, cat. 33, pp. 24, 25

The Cleveland Museum of Art, The India Early Minshall Collection,
66.445

— 93 —

WILD ROSE
Gold, silver, enamel, diamond, jade, rock crystal
H: 4 inches
Marks: Inv. no. 1132(?)

This flower and botanically similar examples also have
been described as primrose and eglantine.

Bibliography: Hawley 1967, no. 38; Booth 1990, p. 123

The Cleveland Museum of Art, The India Early Minshall Collection,
66.440

— 94 —

LADYBUG BOX
Gold, enamel, diamonds
L: 1 15/16 inches
Marks: Fabergé, initials of workmaster Mikhail Perkhin, assay mark
of St. Petersburg 1896–1908

Another box of this design appeared at auction in the late
1980s (Habsburg, Feldman, Geneva, November 16, 1988,
lot 81).

Bibliography: Hawley 1967, no. 7

Exhibitions: ALVR 1961, cat. 128, pp. 42, 50; San Francisco 1964,
cat. 57, pp. 30, 31

The Cleveland Museum of Art, The India Early Minshall Collection,
66.465

— 95 —

COMPASS
Gold, enamel, glass, steel
H: 2 3/16 inches
Marks: Fabergé, initials of workmaster Mikhail Perkhin, assay mark
of St. Petersburg before 1896

The style of the table mount is early neoclassic, from the
end of the eighteenth century.

Bibliography: Hawley 1967, no. 4

Exhibitions: Hammer 1951, cat. 52, p. 13; ALVR 1961, cat. 277, p. 83;
San Francisco 1964, cat. 98, pp. 40, 41

The Cleveland Museum of Art, The India Early Minshall Collection,
66.480

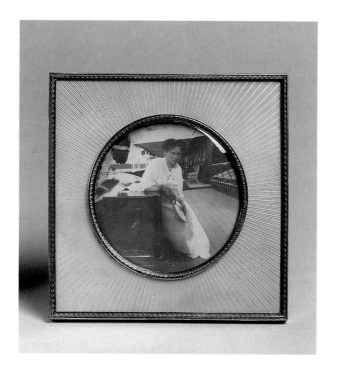

— 96 —

FRAME
Silver, enamel, wood, glass
H: 4½ inches
Marks: Fabergé, initials of workmaster Anders Nevalainen,
assay mark of St. Petersburg 1896–1908, assay master
Iakov Liapunov, inv. no. 9061 or 1906

The subject of the photograph has been identified as
Czarina Alexandra Feodorovna, seated on the deck of
the yacht *Standart*.

Provenance: Said to come from the study of Czar Nicholas II in the
Alexander Palace, Tsarskoe Selo

Bibliography: Hawley 1967, no. 25

The Cleveland Museum of Art, The India Early Minshall Collection,
66.462

— 97 —

MINIATURE BIDET
Gold, jade, enamel, pearls
H: 3¼ inches
Marks: Fabergé in English, initials of workmaster Henrik Wigström,
assay mark of St. Petersburg 1908–17, inv. no. 25256

On this piece the mark Fabergé is in Roman rather than
Cyrillic letters, indicating that it was intended to be sold
outside of Russia, perhaps through Fabergé's London
shop. A drawing for this object dated May 26, 1915, has
recently been discovered in Wigström's book of designs
in Finland.

Provenance: King Farouk of Egypt; Sotheby's, Cairo, March 10, 1954,
no. 126, for £66

Bibliography: Bainbridge 1949, pl. 38; Snowman 1962, pl. LII;
Hawley 1967, no. 12; Snowman 1979, p. 26; Habsburg/Lopato 1994,
cat. 260, pp. 92, 93, 363

Exhibitions: ALVR 1961, cat. 272, pp. 79, 81; San Francisco 1964,
cat. 129, p. 58; V&A 1977, cat. M6, p. 77, pl. LII;
St. Petersburg/Paris/London 1993–94

The Cleveland Museum of Art, The India Early Minshall Collection,
66.455

— 98 —

LAPIS LAZULI EASTER EGG
Gold, enamel, lapis lazuli, pearls, diamonds, rubies
L: 2⁵⁄₁₆ inches

In form this egg most closely resembles the Kelch Hen egg made by Fabergé in 1898 for Barbara Kelch (cat. no. 208); however, the surprise of this lapis lazuli egg, a miniature crown containing a ruby egg, is quite different. The miniature crown recalls the surprise in what is considered to be the first imperial egg, probably made about 1884. A crown containing a ruby egg was also the (lost) surprise of the Rosebud egg (Forbes Magazine collection) presented by Nicholas II to his wife in 1895. Because the miniature crown and ruby egg fit perfectly into this lapis egg, which shows no evidence of alteration, it seems almost certain that the egg was made for a member of the Romanov family. It was probably not intended for Czarina Alexandra or Dowager Empress Maria, however, since they presumably had received eggs containing similar surprises.

Bibliography: Hawley 1967, no. 32; Waterfield 1973, p. 38

Exhibitions: San Francisco 1964, cat. 147, p. 37

The Cleveland Museum of Art, The India Early Minshall Collection, 66.436

— 99 —

IMPERIAL RED CROSS EASTER EGG
Gold, silver, enamel, gold, glass
H: 3⅜ inches
Marks: Fabergé, initials of workmaster Henrik Wigström, 1915,
assay mark of St. Petersburg 1908–17

The Red Cross egg was given by Czar Nicholas II to his wife Alexandra at Easter 1915. Wartime economy prevailed in the making of this egg and its austere decoration. A miniature of the *Harrowing of Hell* appears inside, flanked by St. Olga and St. Tatiana, patron saints of the two eldest grand duchesses. Snowman says that these were painted by Adrian Prachov. On the exterior are portraits of the Grand Duchesses Olga and Tatiana wearing Red Cross uniforms.

Provenance: Presented by Czar Nicholas II to his wife, Czarina Alexandra Feodorovna, Easter 1915

Bibliography: Snowman 1962, p. 107; Hawley 1967, no. 11; Snowman 1979, p. 26; Habsburg/Solodkoff 1979, no. 24; Forbes 1980, p. 68; Solodkoff 1984, p. 105; Hill 1989, no. 59; Booth 1990, pp. 100, 110; Habsburg/Lopato 1994, cat. 129, p. 271

Exhibitions: Hammer 1951, cat. 162, pp. 27, 31; ALVR 1961, cat. 291, p. 91; San Francisco 1964, cat. 144, p. 38; V&A 1977, cat. M2, pp. 76, 77, pls. 378–81; San Diego/Moscow 1989–90, cat. 43, p. 113; St. Petersburg/Paris/London 1993–94

The Cleveland Museum of Art, The India Early Minshall Collection, 63.673

Fig. 1. *Julien Binford*, Portrait of Mrs. John Lee Pratt, *ca. 1971, oil on canvas, 48 x 34½ inches, Virginia Museum of Fine Arts, Richmond, gift of Mr. John Lee Pratt, 1971, 71.19. This portrait was based on a turn-of-the-century family photograph.*

Lillian Thomas Pratt

◆

An Aesthetic Antiquarian

In a gently wistful memorial portrait, Lillian Thomas Pratt (1876–1947) sits before the banks of the Rappahannock River, across from Fredericksburg, Virginia (fig. 1). One might not guess from this ethereal image, commissioned by her husband almost twenty-five years after her death, that Pratt's determined pursuit of Russian decorative arts established her among the leading American collectors of Fabergé.

Lillian Thomas Pratt bequeathed nearly five hundred items to the Virginia Museum of Fine Arts in Richmond. Eighty percent of the collection is Russian decorative arts, much of it by the Fabergé workshops. Like two other important collectors of the 1930s and 1940s—Marjorie Merriweather Post and India Early Minshall—Pratt's interests went beyond Fabergé jeweled enamels and hardstones to include embroidered textiles as well as antique and modern icons. American paintings and furniture, a few Chinese jades, and even some Egyptian antiquities figure in Pratt's legacy.[1]

Pratt's bequest was later augmented by the fiscal support of her husband, John Lee Pratt, a self-made multimillionaire who outlived her by three decades. Thanks to their generosity, the museum, 50 miles south of the estate where Pratt assembled her collection, became one of the largest and best-known public repositories for such material outside Russia.

The donors, however, are as enigmatic as their collection is celebrated.[2] The Pratts were extremely private individuals—old friends recall them as publicity shy. John

Pratt retired in 1937 to devote himself to various philanthropic causes, although he assiduously avoided the limelight. A rare snapshot records the couple in the garden of Chatham Manor, their historic Fredericksburg house (see fig. 2). The photograph captures the no-nonsense posture of a former farm lad—later praised by a General Motors president as "the best businessman I have ever known"—as well as the reassuring solidity of the private secretary who became his wife.[3]

In the absence of confirmed data, the tendency to romanticize Fabergé tinges stories of Pratt's collecting patterns. Over the years, like a game of "telephone," variations on the theme of an eccentric woman squirreling away a hoard of sparkling Russian trinkets purchased with pin money have been constructed from available tidbits and legitimized in print:

> These exquisitely crafted jewels had been assembled by Mrs. John Lee Pratt, who had kept them during her lifetime in her bedroom closet. Upon Lillian Pratt's death, her husband, who had known little of the Fabergé collection, found it stuffed in hat boxes.[4]

The mythology of a clandestine collection is not supported by surviving documents in the Virginia Museum archives, despite some gaps in the available records. John Pratt himself refuted the story that his wife's collection was formed in secret.[5] We might wonder how an accomplished businessman could overlook his wife's steady—and regularly recorded—outlay for Fabergé acquisitions made almost monthly for more than a decade.⁶ Moreover, several display cabinets existed at Chatham Manor. One mirrored cabinet, designed with the help of New York dealer Alexander Schaffer, measured a hard-to-miss 4 by 6 feet. Schaffer wrote to Mrs. Pratt, "You see, I did want you to be able to show off your beautiful treasures to best advantage."⁷

It is hard to believe that John Pratt, a trained engineer, would be completely indifferent to the exquisite crafts-manship and finely tuned mechanisms of Fabergé objects. Indeed he later underwrote an elaborate gallery installa-tion at the Virginia Museum and supported publication of the collection.⁸

Journalistic license embellished the circumstances of the Pratt bequest with a little more cloak-and-dagger mystery than was probably the case. A correspondent for *Time* magazine suggested that Thomas Colt Jr., then di-rector of the museum, had "no idea" of the collection's scope or importance:

> All he knew was that a wealthy Mrs. John Lee Pratt had willed to the museum her collection of the last Russian Czar's family trinkets. Colt drove over to the Pratt home in Fredericksburg, [and] piled the packages in the back of his station wagon. . . . When he recalls how casually he treated these treasures, he shudders.⁹

It is highly unlikely that Colt missed the significance and scope of "a wealthy Mrs. Pratt's" collection any more than her husband did. The Pratts moved in the same Fredericksburg social circle as museum founder Corrine Melchers, wife of the painter Gari Melchers, and major Virginia Museum supporters such as Jessie Ball DuPont. John Pratt was a member of the museum's board of trust-ees, and in 1945 he sat on the executive committee. He also headed the artist fellowship committee, which he had ini-tiated. Five years before Lillian's death, the Pratts had do-nated to the museum a mirrored table with silver gilt mounts attributed to Fabergé.¹⁰ Having himself helped to pack and transport the collection to the Virginia Museum, Colt cannot have been too surprised by the contents, nor did he treat them "casually." Most pieces were stored in a bank vault until special security measures could be insti-tuted at the museum.

Fig. 2. *John and Lillian Pratt in the garden at Chatham Manor, ca. 1933. Photo: Courtesy General Motors Institute, Collection of Industrial History, Flint, Michigan.*

Meanwhile, a few anecdotes help to shed a bit of light on the couple. Mrs. Pratt's household datebooks give the impression that she was a sociable person, actively en-gaged in community affairs; she was a familiar figure in the Rappahannock Valley Garden Club; a woman fond of cards, cocktail parties, and the movies.¹¹ Born as the United States celebrated its centennial with an interna-tional exhibition marking the nation's coming of age as a great industrial power, Lillian Thomas Pratt, like her hus-band, embodied a central component of the American dream: hard work rewarded. Her collecting interests echo patterns of privileged consumption established in America during the last quarter of the nineteenth century.

Lillian Pratt was not always chauffeured in the Cadillac limousine shown in a snapshot of her and her husband (fig. 2). Originally from Philadelphia, she moved with her mother to Tacoma, Washington, sometime before the turn of the century. In various city records she is listed as a ste-nographer, rooming with a family that took boarders.¹²

Sometime in or after 1907, when John Lee Pratt went west to help build a DuPont Company plant south of Tacoma, the couple met.[13] Married in 1917, they moved back east, living in Delaware and New York during John Pratt's Horatio Alger–like rise through E. I. du Pont de Nemours and its affiliate, the General Motors Corporation.

When John Pratt was conducting business in New York, his wife frequently shopped for bric-a-brac, an appropriate activity for the spouse of a corporate executive. By this time, collecting had become a popular pastime for middle- and upper-class women.[14] The status of previously owned goods was rising, as a turn-of-the-century journal illustration of window-shoppers points out: "They don't call them

Fig. 3. "They don't call them second-hand, they call them antiques," *turn-of-the-century American illustration.*
Photo: Denise Lewis, courtesy Virginia Museum of Fine Arts Archive, Richmond.

second-hand, they call them antiques," one woman assures her companion (fig. 3). Americana then existed in a far greater supply than it does now and was much more affordable. The same was true for Fabergé pieces.[15]

Lillian Pratt bought Americana and Fabergé materials consistently, and sometimes simultaneously. What sparked her initial interest in things Russian is not recorded, but by the early 1930s, a fashion for such exotic materials was already under way.[16] It was not unusual for major department stores to stage art and antique exhibitions, and John Pratt later recalled that his wife first encountered the glittering splendors of Russian decorative art at Lord and Taylor, an upscale New York emporium where she maintained a charge account. Her first documented purchase, made on January 25, 1933, was unassuming: a silver gilt fork with a mother-of-pearl handle. Pratt found the fork in an exhibition of Russian imperial objects conducted at Lord and Taylor by Armand Hammer and his brother. Although not attributed to Fabergé, the fork bore an enticing Russian provenance: "from the Winter Palace Collection in St. Petersburg."[17] Shopping, collecting, and remembering were inextricably intertwined as both art and decoration became commodified in late-nineteenth-century America.

The entrepreneurial Armand Hammer, who had been selling art for the Soviet government as early as 1928, made a clever marketing move that put him in close contact with women like Lillian Pratt who "were making period collections for their homes," as the *New York Times* described American attendees at an auction of Russian arts.[18] Taking advantage of the vogue for the department store as an exhibition venue, Hammer closed his offices in Paris and established himself in New York in 1932. He arranged to show his Russian treasures at department stores in several big cities, beginning with the St. Louis firm Scruggs, Vandervoort, and Barney. In early 1933, his exhibition opened at Lord and Taylor. On January 2, the *New York Times* bubbled, "Jewelry of Czar on View This Week . . . Gold Champagne Pails."[19]

Dated invoices suggest that Pratt returned to the exhibition several times after her first visit and made additional purchases in rapid succession. These included more flatware, her first icon, and—significantly for understanding her initial collecting impetus—a silver Fabergé frame containing a photograph of Grand Duke Sergei Aleksandrovich and Grand Duchess Elizaveta Feodorovna, brother-in-law and sister of Czarina Alexandra (cat. no. 101). Pratt's first piece of Fabergé, and many that followed, were intimately linked to the tragic fortunes of the last Russian czar and his family. The frame, made in 1904, commemorated the grand duke's thirteen years as governor-general of Moscow. He was assassinated the following year.

Pratt continued to drop in at Lord and Taylor, making modest acquisitions such as her 1933 Valentine's Day purchase of a silver gilt and enamel caviar spoon from the Alexander Palace.[20] As a group, these early purchases indicate that Pratt's first interest in Russian decorative arts was romantic and associative, not sumptuary. Over time, the quality of her buying suggests that she augmented her historical bent with a concern for aesthetics, but the antiquarianism she first manifested in 1933 was never supplanted.

Originally scheduled to last three weeks, Hammer's exhibition at Lord and Taylor went on and on, replenished from time to time from the entrepreneur's ample stock. On October 31, 1933, only days before the United States government officially recognized the USSR, Pratt made her first purchase of an imperial Easter egg, the Red Cross egg with miniatures (cat. no. 153).[21]

A catalogue inscribed in Pratt's bold hand, "Lord & Taylor, 7th floor to right of elevator," gives us some idea of what she might have encountered during an afternoon's shopping spree: "[The exhibition] comprises crown jeweled objects of art in diamonds, rubies and emeralds; old world antique brocades and fabrics, vestments, copes, chasubles, imperial silverware, porcelain and glassware, Russian icons."[22] The range of Pratt's eventual collection—from textile fragments to icons to imperial Easter eggs—is set out in the catalogue's pages.[23] According to the text, the jeweled Fabergé objects "in themselves constitute an endless source of wonderment" while most of the china, glassware, and porcelain on view was made "in the Royal Imperial Porcelain Factory at St. Petersburg" by order of the czar and was "never offered for sale." Two important works listed in the Lord and Taylor catalogue found their way into Pratt's collection: a gold column frame with Czar Nicholas II's portrait (cat. no. 106), acquired on January 4,

1934, and an imperial lapis Easter egg (cat. no. 151), purchased sometime between the fall of 1933 and the spring of 1934.[24]

Hammer particularly treasured the lapis egg. It was the only imperial Easter egg pictured in his sparsely illustrated best-seller *The Quest of the Romanoff Treasure* (1932), where it is featured as "the famous diamond and lapis Easter egg," competing with such full-page illustrations as "The Imperial Crown of the Romanoffs," "The Author's Passport in Russia," and "Governor Receiving Tractors." Hammer also illustrated the gold column frame acquired by Pratt. And while she did not purchase the imperial crown, with its 763 carats of pearls and three thousand diamonds topped by "the largest ruby in the world," her purchase of a Fabergé brooch similar in shape and materials argues for the impact of published objects on Pratt's thinking (figs. 4, 5).

Pratt bypassed the 1895 imperial Danish Palaces Easter egg with ten miniatures (cat. no. 69), which was exhibited at Lord and Taylor but not illustrated in the catalogue.[25]

Fig. 4. *"Imperial Crown of the Romanoffs," illustration from Armand Hammer,* The Quest of the Romanoff Treasure *(1932).*

She might have felt she had missed an opportunity, for she later acquired the imperial Rock Crystal Easter egg with revolving miniatures (1896), which is somewhat similar in conception and only a year later in execution (fig. 6). As with the lapis egg, she most likely knew the crystal egg from an illustration in an early text regarding Fabergé.[26]

Pratt could not buy every available imperial egg on the market, but she was not immune to lesser objects that combined the skill and artistry of the West with the originality and color of the Far East.[27] Among her purchases from Hammer's showing at Lord and Taylor was a silk runner, which was described in the exhibition catalogue:

> From a collection of brocades which were formerly used in the Imperial Chapels of the Romanoffs as altar covers and priests' robes. They were brought from the various Palaces about St. Petersburg to the Winter Palace. Here soldiers of the present government sorted them for burning so that the precious gold and silver used in weaving many of them could be reclaimed. Fortunately, Dr. Armand Hammer heard of the plan and succeeded in saving a large number of the vestments by purchasing them.[28]

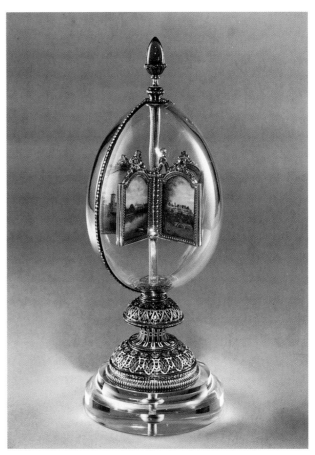

Fig. 6. *Fabergé firm*, Imperial Rock Crystal Easter Egg with Revolving Miniatures, *1896, rock crystal, gold, diamonds, champlevé enamel, cabochon emerald, h. 9¾ inches. Miniatures in watercolor on ivory by Johannes Zehngraf. Virginia Museum of Fine Arts, Richmond, bequest of Lillian Thomas Pratt, 47.20.32. Photo: Katherine Wetzel.*

Fig. 5. *Fabergé firm*, Brooch, *silver gilt with cabochon rubies, sapphires, diamonds, h. 3 inches. Virginia Museum of Fine Arts, Richmond, bequest of Lillian Thomas Pratt, 47.20.138. Photo: Katherine Wetzel.*

Another revealing catalogue entry describes a white batiste handkerchief "embroidered in brown and lace border, with monogram of Czarina Marie Feodorovna. Mendings made by herself; she was known for her thriftiness. From Anitchkov Palace."[29]

As has long been understood by both journalists and scholars—and probably by collectors themselves—a significant part of the charm of collecting Fabergé in America was the exclusivity of these exquisitely crafted objects, and their links to a resplendent monarchy eradicated suddenly amid cataclysmic tragedy. Personal items such as handkerchiefs and cigarette cases and umbrella handles help to humanize royalty in a republic that has none but occasionally seems to wish it had.

Fig. 7. *Entrance Salon, Chatham Manor, after 1930. From Thomas Tileston*
Waterman, The Mansions of Virginia 1706–1776 *(Chapel Hill, N.C.:*
University of North Carolina Press, 1946).

At the same time, the sale of Russian imperial treasures to American buyers followed the collapse of Russia's feudal system and the subsequent struggles of a fledgling communist government. That the Soviets felt obliged to sell royal artifacts for hard cash reinforced the sense that the American economic system was valid despite the Great Depression, during which many imperial items changed hands.

Free-market competition meant that Armand Hammer had rivals for the available supply of Fabergé material. The chief contender for Pratt's acquisition dollars was Alexander Schaffer, whose gallery Pratt had discovered within a year of her first documented purchase from Hammer.[30] As with Hammer, her initial acquisitions from Schaffer were modest in both price and significance, and included a textile cope and an icon as well as Fabergé pieces. Among the latter were an enameled double frame with photographs of Czar Nicholas's brother, Grand Duke

Mikhail Aleksandrovich, and his wife (cat. no. 144), and a diamond-studded frame with a regal photograph of Czarina Alexandra, doubtless intended to complement the jeweled miniature of the czar purchased two months before at Lord and Taylor (cat. no. 140).[31]

While Pratt's spending patterns at the Hammer Galleries are difficult to reconstruct, surviving papers do reveal that she kept a substantial running account with Schaffer.[32] She seems to have been relatively evenhanded in her trade with the two New York dealers, however. If she acquired a larger number of items from Schaffer, she bought four of her five imperial eggs from Hammer, including the Rock Crystal egg. This was probably her last major acquisition.[33]

Pratt would make successive visits to a gallery during the course of a week. Often she bought groups of things— several icons, a number of frames, three elaborate parasol handles (including cat. nos. 129, 133), a large clutch of miniature Easter eggs.[34] An avid gardener, she frequently purchased her hardstone and enamel flowers during the cold winter months. In a childless marriage, she favored photographs, often of the royal children. There is only occasional evidence of "trading up" or deaccessioning and, as yet, no documentary proof of her collecting after 1945.[35]

The formation of Pratt's Fabergé collection coincided with the purchase and furnishing of Chatham Manor, across the Rappahannock River from Fredericksburg. The couple acquired the house in 1931 and lived there permanently after John Pratt's retirement as vice president of General Motors in 1937. The elegant Georgian manor house was built around 1760 and has rich historic associations with colonial America.[36] Resonant with tales of early presidents—the closest Americans come to royalty Chatham Manor provided a context of romantic antiquarianism in which Pratt gathered up the imperial Easter eggs and other Russian decorative objects that now enrich the Virginia Museum of Fine Arts.

An auction catalogue recording the contents of Chatham Manor at the time of John Lee Pratt's demise gives us an idea of the contents of the house, and of the aesthetic environment in which Lillian Thomas Pratt's Fabergé treasures were housed.[37] The Pratts' taste ran to English and American antiques of the late eighteenth and early nineteenth centuries—assorted Chippendale, Federal, and Regency chairs, sofas, and case pieces, augmented by later revival and reproduction objects. This comfortable mix became the hallmark of a proper domestic interior following about 1876 and the Colonial Revival in America (fig. 7).[38]

The kinds of objects the Pratts and many others collected were celebrated in certain conservative American painting circles at this time, notably by the Boston School. In some, such as Edmund Tarbell's *New England Interior* (Museum of Fine Arts, Boston), Americana is prominently featured. Others, including William Paxton's *The New Necklace*, set Americana into a larger pattern of sophisticated international materialism (fig. 8). The model wearing a Chinese silk jacket slumps back, almost obscuring the turned Windsor armchair in which she sits. Her companion's hat and cloak cover most of the Queen Anne or Chippendale side chair at the lower right. Paxton's ladies examine a piece of jewelry with the rapt attention Lillian Pratt might have brought to her consideration of the Rus-

Fig. 8. *William McGregor Paxton,* The New Necklace, *1910, oil on canvas, 35½ x 28½ inches. Museum of Fine Arts, Boston, Zoë Oliver Sherman Collection, 22.644.*

sian pendants, necklaces, and rings in her collection. With its gilt mounts, Paxton's fall-front desk would be as much at home in St. Petersburg or Paris as in the artist's Boston studio. Behind the Japanese screen, a large black-and-gilt-framed painting leaning against a tapestry-covered wall typifies the steady stream of Old Master pictures and hangings flowing from the mansions and palaces of Europe to the houses of wealthy American collectors during the late nineteenth and early twentieth centuries.

In general the arts of the past were seen as a soothing antidote to the often shocking social and economic turmoil of the late nineteenth and early twentieth centuries. Surviving correspondence indicates that strikes at General Motors had a more immediate impact than the Russian Revolution upon Lillian Pratt, but her house on the Rappahannock provided both comfort and shelter in an era of unprecedented change.[39]

Like her Fabergé collection, Pratt's Americana must have satisfied her antiquarian appetite for objects with links to the past. A mahogany lowboy, billed by the dealer who sold it to Pratt as "the finest example of William Savery's work," was said to have belonged to George Washington. A thoroughly modern silver bowl was thought to have belonged to William Fitzhugh, for whom the house originally was built. Pratt also owned a number of portraits, including a depiction of Fitzhugh's mother attributed to Charles Bridges. That some of these pieces have not survived changes in taste or have failed to withstand scholarly scrutiny does not detract from the collector's desire to be surrounded by pieces of Americana that in some way were linked to Chatham Manor. In such an antiquarian atmosphere, her attraction to prerevolutionary Russian arts makes considerable sense.

Not all of Pratt's Fabergé objects currently are accepted as genuine, either. But half a century ago, Western connoisseurship of these pieces was in its infancy, while antiquarianism was in the ascendancy. Documentation of imperial provenance was as likely to accompany an authentic piece, such as Pratt's dandelion seed ball, as a spurious one, such as her hardstone poppy (fig. 9).[40]

One important imperial jewel from the Pratt collection, the imperial Red Cross Easter egg, seems particularly to clarify the collector's antiquarian interests. The egg's resonance with Chatham Manor lies in both its topical subject and its emotional appeal. Chatham Manor survived the Civil War, supposedly because General Robert E. Lee, who met and wooed his bride there, refused to have the house shelled, although it was being utilized as the Union headquarters from whence Generals Sumner, Burnside, and McDowell launched their devastating Fredericksburg and Peninsula campaigns. An eloquently stark photograph by Mathew Brady records the manor at this time (fig. 10).

Certainly not the most beautiful of Fabergé's creations, the Red Cross egg was made and presented during another devastating war, the one that eroded the last vestiges of Russian tolerance for czarist rule. The egg contains miniature portraits of five uniformed women, including Czarina Alexandra, titular head of the Russian Red Cross. Following the 1862 battle of Fredericksburg, Chatham Manor served as a Union hospital. Clara Barton, founder of the American Red Cross, wrote of the beautiful grounds of the stately mansion but soon was ministering to twelve hundred wounded soldiers crammed into its rooms. Shortly thereafter, the poet Walt Whitman visited both battlefield and hospital: "In the door-yard, towards the river, are fresh graves, mostly of officers, their names on pieces of barrel staves or broken boards stuck in the dirt."[41]

When Pratt lent the Red Cross egg to an exhibition in New York in 1939, its topical link with the American Red Cross was picked up by the *New York Sun* (fig. 11). Pratt later seems to have made great efforts to acquire another imperial Red Cross egg (cat. no. 99) through the Schaffers, but it wound up in the hands of rival collector India Early Minshall.[42]

In the end, history lets us understand the motives of Lillian Thomas Pratt as a collector as well as the lasting public appeal of the objects she bequeathed to the Virginia Museum of Fine Arts. Made for royalty, surviving through the patronage of capitalists, and eventually donated to a

Fig. 9. Left: *Fabergé firm*, Dandelion Seed Ball, *rock crystal, gold, nephrite, asbestos, sapphire, h. 6½ inches. Virginia Museum of Fine Arts, Richmond, bequest of Lillian Thomas Pratt, 47.20.235.* Right: *Unknown craftsman*, Poppy, *agate, chalcedony, nephrite, gold, sapphire, topaz, diamond, h. 10¼ inches. Virginia Museum of Fine Arts, Richmond, bequest of Lillian Thomas Pratt, 47.20.217. Photo: Katherine Wetzel.*

Fig. 10. *Chatham Manor, ca. 1864–65. Photo: Mathew Brady, courtesy National Park Service, Fredericksburg and Spotsylvania National Battlefield.*

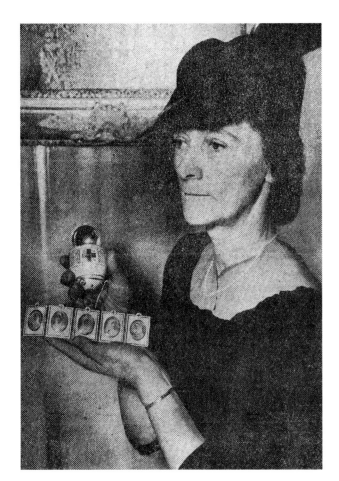

Fig. 11. *The chairwoman of New York's Red Cross chapter holds Pratt's imperial Red Cross Easter egg and its surprise, which were displayed in New York in 1939. "Royal Red Cross Treasure," New York Sun, November 24, 1939. Photo: Denise Lewis, courtesy Virginia Museum of Fine Arts Archive, Richmond.*

state art museum, the Pratt collection's five imperial Easter eggs survey the story of the Romanovs from the early, happiest days of Nicholas and Alexandra to the sad privations of World War I. If some of the miniatures in these pieces touch us with their pathos, they remain, nonetheless, splendid testaments to imaginative craftsmanship. Along with the imperial eggs, Lillian Thomas Pratt's bejeweled frames, boxes, and handles; hardstone flowers and figures; and even the old photographs, let us contemplate splendors that few can experience firsthand. In a sense, American public museums, enriched by collectors such as Pratt, become like giant Fabergé eggs, each filled with surprising treasures.

—David Park Curry
Curator of American Arts
Virginia Museum of Fine Arts

NOTES

1. The will was probated on August 7, 1947. The Virginia Museum's computerized database holds 477 records for the collection, with some multiple entries.

2. The John Lee Pratt Papers, no. 10,125-b, have been held by the University of Virginia, Special Collections, Alderman Library, since John Pratt's death on December 20, 1975. The papers, which include personal correspondence from the 1920s, 1930s, and 1940s, are closed until April 21, 2011. Obituaries for Mrs. Pratt prove somewhat inconsistent. The *Richmond Times-Dispatch* stated that she was "a native of Washington State" (July 22, 1947, p. 21), while the *Tacoma News Tribune* reported that she "came to Tacoma with her mother in the early 1900s" (July 26, 1947, p. 1). Neither is correct. The Twelfth Census of the United States (June 11, 1900) records Lillian Thomas, born December 1876, in Pennsylvania, and further indicates that Pratt was already a resident of Tacoma in 1900. Courtesy Tacoma Public Library.

3. Alfred P. Sloan, former president of General Motors, quoted in "John Lee Pratt Dies, Was Philanthropist," *Richmond Times-Dispatch*, December 21, 1975. For more on John Lee Pratt's humble beginnings, see Guy Friddell, "Learning Was Lifelong Interest," *Richmond News-Leader*, obituary, undated clipping, Virginia Museum archive.

4. Parke Rouse Jr., *Living by Design: Leslie Cheek and the Arts* (Williamsburg, Va.: Society of the Alumni of the College of William and Mary, 1985), p. 106. Another version mentions "the unassuming Lillian Thomas Pratt. Her Fabergé hoard was kept in shoe boxes, and upon her death in 1947 was delivered to the Virginia Museum in the back of a station wagon"; see Christopher Forbes, "On Hunting for Easter Eggs," in Solodkoff 1984, p. 10.

5. He wrote, "It is not correct to say that they were kept in boxes and not displayed until given to the Museum" (John Lee Pratt to Leslie Cheek, February 4, 1965, Virginia Museum archive). Tales of

Mr. Pratt's ignorance of his wife's collecting activities may have been fostered by his dislike of dealers. On June 2, 1936, dealer Alexander Schaffer wrote to Mrs. Pratt, "I would like you to let me know when you are entirely alone on a Saturday or a Sunday, as I would not want to examine your things when anyone, especially Mr. P., is at home. That is, I don't think you would want it" (Virginia Museum archive).

6. Between March 1934 and November 1945, Pratt spent just under $100,000 with Alexander Schaffer alone. Simultaneously she was purchasing a large number of Russian pieces, including four imperial eggs, from the Hammer Galleries. The Virginia Museum archive does not hold receipts for every piece acquired, so the total outlay for the collection can only be estimated. Clearly, however, it was substantial enough to exceed pin money from even the most unsuspecting husband.

7. Schaffer apparently based the design on cases in his gallery. The cabinet was paid for by December 29, 1939. Letters, Virginia Museum archive.

8. This dramatic and much-beloved installation opened in 1953 and did not close until the early 1980s. It cost $25,000, a healthy sum for a museum installation at the time. Pratt also funded Parker Lesley's *Handbook of the Lillian Thomas Pratt Collection: Russian Imperial Jewels* (Richmond: Virginia Museum of Fine Arts, 1960). His estate funded a more elaborate catalogue in 1976.

9. "Royal Haul," *Time* (November 24, 1947), p. 61.

10. Curatorial file 42.19.1.

11. Pratt's datebooks are currently missing according to personnel at Chatham Manor, Fredericksburg, which now belongs to the National Park Service. The Rappahannock Valley Garden Club yearbooks show that Pratt joined in 1932, serving as a narcissus tester, property custodian, and eventually a vice president. She hosted meetings at Chatham Manor on October 23, 1941, and in November 1943. Courtesy Rappahannock Valley Garden Club.

12. The circumstances of Lillian Thomas Pratt's birth are ambiguous. Her mother, Susan E. Thomas, was born in Pennsylvania on June 7, 1818. She married Robert S. Thomas, a tailor (*Gospeill's Philadelphia City Directory*, 1876). A Philadelphia birth certificate records the birth on January 2, 1875, of a Lillie M. Thomas to William Thomas and Annie (no last name given) of 302 Wyoming Avenue. The birth of another female child with the last name Thomas also is recorded on January 2 at 1310 Green Street; no other birth certificates have been located. According to the Twelfth Census of the United States, 1900, Lillian M. Thomas was born in Pennsylvania in December 1876. Susan E. Thomas first appears in Tacoma's 1893 directory as the widow of Robert S. Thomas, residing at Washington College Building; Lillie M. Thomas is listed as a stenographer for Rev. William M. Jefferis, the president of Washington College (R. L. Polk and Company, *Tacoma City Directory*, 1893, p. 761). Susan E. Thomas died on May 31, 1894, and is buried in Tacoma. Her obituary listed her maiden name as "Elton." The Twelfth Census shows Lillian Thomas living at the home of David Huggins. Already an experienced stenographer,

the future Mrs. Pratt worked for Ralph B. Smith, agent for the Puget Sound Flouring Mill (*Tacoma City Directory*, 1900, p. 613).

13. John Lee Pratt "came to Tacoma in 1907 as a $100-a-month engineer" according to the *Seattle Daily Times*, December 20, 1947. The Washington DuPont plant was built on a 2,700-acre site next to Fort Lewis. Construction began in 1906–7.

14. See Susan Porter Benson, *Counter Cultures: Saleswomen, Managers, and Customers in American Department Stores, 1890–1940* (Urbana, Ill.: University of Illinois Press, 1986).

15. Géza von Habsburg, "When Russia Sold Its Past," *Art & Auction* 17, no. 8 (March 1995); pp. 94–97, 128. See also Robert C. Williams, *Russian Art and American Money, 1900–1940* (Cambridge, Mass.: Harvard University Press, 1980).

16. "Romanoff Sale Nets $69,136," *The Art News* 29, no. 23 (March 7, 1931), p. 19.

17. Curatorial file 47.20.381. The pseudo-parchment gallery description, imprinted with exhibition title, is dated January 25, 1933. Pratt also acquired a knife of similar design and an antique brocade runner. Neither has been securely identified in the collection.

18. "Vase of a Czarina Auctioned for $780," *New York Times*, March 1, 1931, p. 2.

19. "Jewelry of Czar on View This Week," *New York Times*, January 2, 1933, p. 25.

20. Curatorial file 47.20.382.

21. By late 1933, Hammer's object descriptions, many of which survive in the Virginia Museum archive, were typed on special stationery that lists Lord and Taylor on the letterhead rather than Hammer's offices at 3 East 52nd Street. Changes in the letterhead style have been useful in establishing the chronology of Pratt's purchases.

22. Lord and Taylor 1933, p. 2.

23. Neither Parker Lesley's 1960 handbook nor his *Fabergé: A Catalog of the Lillian Thomas Pratt Collection of Russian Imperial Jewels* (1976) gives the full range of Pratt's holdings. The textiles are not mentioned at all, and there is no discussion of her collecting activities apart from Fabergé.

24. Curatorial files 47.20.303 and 47.20.367. The column frame is discussed in Lord and Taylor 1933, no. 4765, p. 4; for the lapis egg, see no. 4756, p. 3. No gallery description has been found for the lapis egg, but we know Pratt purchased other objects from the Hammer exhibition at Lord and Taylor on the following dates: October 2, October 31, December 4, 1933; January 4, February 1, March 26, May 3, 1934. Virginia Museum archive.

25. Lord and Taylor 1933, no. 4396, p. 2.

26. Henry C. Bainbridge's *Twice Seven* (New York: E. P. Dutton, 1934) was revised in 1937. Pratt's copy, autographed by the author, is the 1937 edition.

27. Lord and Taylor 1933, p. 2.

28. Curatorial file 47.20.393, purchased December 4, 1933.

29. Lord and Taylor 1933, no. H-3785, p. 6. We have evidence that Pratt bought a kerchief, although not this one.

30. Pratt left no record of dealing with Wartski in London, or with A La Vieille Russie in Paris, although code marks suggest that a few items came to her from the Paris shop via Schaffer.

31. Curatorial file 47.20.333.

32. Her first documented purchase from Schaffer was made in March 1934, her last known payment on November 8, 1945. Virginia Museum archive.

33. An exhibition catalogue confirms that by 1939 she owned three imperial eggs, all acquired through the Hammer Galleries; see Hammer 1939. A dedication page thanks Pratt for lending the Pelican, Czarevitch, and Red Cross Easter eggs. The Rock Crystal egg was included in the exhibition but she did not yet own it. Changes in Hammer's gallery letterhead let us date this purchase to sometime after 1940.

34. Pratt bought twenty-three miniature eggs from Schaffer on December 4, 1934, and twenty-nine more on June 1, 1935.

35. "I am sorry that I haven't sold any of your pieces yet, but I am sure I will" (Alexander Schaffer to Pratt, June 23, 1941, Virginia Museum archive). Her trade-ins were pieces of jewelry.

36. Erected for William Fitzhugh (1741–1809), Chatham Manor was noted for hospitality and sheltered such prominent visitors as Presidents Washington, Madison, and Monroe. "I have put my legs oftener under your mahogany at Chatham than anywhere else in the world and have enjoyed your good dinners, good wine, and good company more than any other," George Washington wrote to Fitzhugh, who is remembered as a member of the House of Burgesses and the Continental Congress, and as an avid horse racer as well as a genial host. See Robert A. Lancaster Jr., *Historic Virginia Homes and Churches* (Philadelphia and London: J. P. Lippincott, 1915), pp. 349–51.

37. *Historic Chatham Manor*, sale catalogue, Sotheby Parke Bernet, May 1976, sale number 3869. The Pratt sale included forty-three case pieces and sixty-eight chairs and sofas.

38. For a general discussion, see Alan Axelrod, ed., *The Colonial Revival in America* (New York: W. W. Norton, 1985).

39. Dealer Alexander Schaffer sympathized with Pratt: "Thank you for your letter of the first, and for your check on account. We weren't very happy to read about the strike GM had, but it is just one of those things that one has to put up with today" (Schaffer to Mrs. Pratt, June 3, 1941, Virginia Museum archive).

40. Curatorial files 47.20.235 (dandelion), 47.20.217 (poppy).

41. *Historic Chatham Manor*, n.p.

42. Alexander Schaffer wrote, "Now that I realize that you wanted the red cross egg so much, I am sorry that it is sold. I would much rather if you had it" (Schaffer to Mrs. Pratt, December 8, 1941, Virginia Museum archive).

Catalogue

The Lillian Thomas Pratt Collection of Fabergé

Thanks to the bequest of Lillian Thomas Pratt, the Virginia Museum of Fine Arts in Richmond possesses the largest collection in an American museum of art objects by, or in the style of, Carl Fabergé, numbering 328 pieces. Among the objects included here are four of the five imperial Easter eggs Pratt owned. Three objects at the end of this section (cat. nos. 154, 155, 156) are not part of the Pratt collection but appear by special arrangement with the Virginia Museum of Fine Arts.

— 100 —

RABBIT PITCHER
Silver, rubies, silver gilt
H: 10 inches
Marks: K Fabergé, Imperial Warrant, assay mark of Moscow 1894,
assay master LO, 88, inv. no. 4639

Animal-shaped containers were made of everything from ceramic to papier-mâché during the nineteenth century, but here semiprecious materials are used to make a somewhat unwieldy pitcher. The hinged head of this lifelike silver rabbit tilts back to reveal a silver gilt interior with a soft lip suitable for pouring.

Provenance: Said to be from the Alexander Palace, Tsarskoe Selo; The Schaffer Collection of Russian Imperial Art Treasures, New York, December 4, 1934

Bibliography: Lesley 1976, p. 23, pl. 22; Curry 1995, no. 39

Exhibitions: ALVR 1983, pp. 111–13, pl. 401

Virginia Museum of Fine Arts, Richmond, bequest of Lillian Thomas Pratt, 47.20.214

— 101 —

OCTAGONAL FRAME
Silver, enamel, ivory
H: 7½ inches
Marks: KF, assay mark of St. Petersburg 1896–1908,
assay master Iakov Liapunov

Ornamented with an enamel plaque showing St. George killing a dragon, this frame was Pratt's first piece of Fabergé. Like many of the Fabergé objects she subsequently acquired, the frame was intimately linked to the tragic fortunes of the last Russian czar and his family. Grand Duke Sergei Aleksandrovich, czar Nicholas's uncle, is shown here with his wife, Elizaveta Feodorovna, sister of Czarina Alexandra. In 1905, the year after the frame was made to commemorate Sergei's thirteen years as governor-general of Moscow, the grand duke was assassinated. A virtually identical frame, lacking only the crown atop the enamel image of St. George, is owned by the Cleveland Museum of Art (Hawley 1967, cat. 51).

Provenance: Said to be from the Winter Palace, St. Petersburg; Hammer Galleries, New York, January 26, 1933

Bibliography: Lesley 1976, p. 95, pl. 198; Curry 1995, no. 12

Exhibitions: Lord and Taylor 1933, cat. H-4108, p. 8; NCMA 1979

Virginia Museum of Fine Arts, Richmond, bequest of Lillian Thomas Pratt, 47.20.355

— 102 —

GOLD *KOVSH*
Gold, ruble
H: 3½ inches
Marks: Initials of workmaster Erik Kollin, assay mark of
St. Petersburg before 1896, inv. no. 40297

Catherine the Great's portrait on a five-ruble gold coin embellishes this ceremonial cup, engraved with stylized Old Russian motifs. An avid collector of Americana as well as Russian decorative art, Pratt would not have failed to note that the coin is dated 1776.

Provenance: Hammer Galleries, New York, December 4, 1940

Bibliography: Lesley 1976, p. 153, pl. 321

Virginia Museum of Fine Arts, Richmond, bequest of
Lillian Thomas Pratt, 47.20.298

— 103 —

ROCK CRYSTAL *KOVSH*
Rock crystal, gold, pearl, rubies, diamonds
H: 2³⁄₁₆ inches
Marks: Initials KF, assay mark of Moscow 1896–1908,
assay master Ivan Lebedkin

The art nouveau style of this elaborate ceremonial cup demonstrates the ability of the Fabergé designers to work in modern as well as historical styles.

Provenance: The Schaffer Collection of Russian Imperial
Art Treasures, New York, 1940–41

Bibliography: Lesley 1976, p. 153, pl. 320

Virginia Museum of Fine Arts, Richmond, bequest of
Lillian Thomas Pratt, 47.20.297

— 104 —

KOVSH WITH SAPPHIRES
Gold, sapphires
H: 1 5⁄16 inches
Marks: Initials of Vasilii Finikov, assay mark of
St. Petersburg before 1896, inv. no. 36643

Four sapphires, shaped and polished to a dull sheen, are
set into the sides of this cup to imitate fish jumping in the
chased golden waves. Although the cup was believed to
be by the Fabergé workshops, recent scholars have identified Vasilii Finikov as an independent artisan who specialized in work featuring cabochon sapphires (Solodkoff
1995, p. 95).

Provenance: The Schaffer Collection of Russian Imperial
Art Treasures, New York, 1940

Bibliography: Lesley 1976, p. 151, pl. 313

Virginia Museum of Fine Arts, Richmond, bequest of
Lillian Thomas Pratt, 47.20.292

— 105 —

TREFOIL CUP
Gold, gold coins
H: 1 1⁄8 inches
Marks: Fabergé, initials of workmaster Erik Kollin, assay mark of
St. Petersburg before 1896, no. 1.24, French import mark ET

Three eighteenth-century gold coins stamped with the
likeness of Catherine the Great are worked into this resplendent trefoil cup, bearing witness to the Romanov
family's lengthy reign.

Provenance: The Schaffer Collection of Russian Imperial
Art Treasures, New York, 1941

Bibliography: Lesley 1976, p. 153, pl. 318

Exhibitions: NCMA 1979

Virginia Museum of Fine Arts, Richmond, bequest of
Lillian Thomas Pratt, 47.20.374

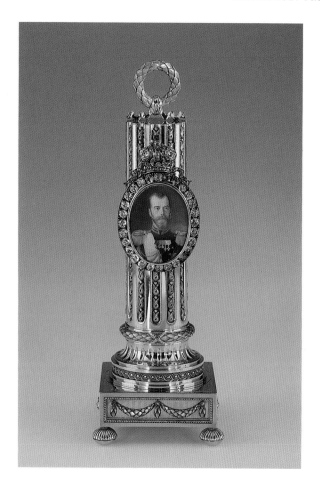

— 106 —

IMPERIAL COLUMN FRAME
Gold, diamonds, watercolor, ivory
H: (column) 6 inches; (miniature) 2 3/16 inches
Marks: Fabergé, initials of workmaster Henrik Wigström,
assay mark of St. Petersburg 1896–1908; miniature marked
on reverse "no. 289/200p"
Original fitted case

Among Pratt's earliest acquisitions, this imperial commission column was one of the few pieces illustrated by Armand Hammer in his romantic *The Quest of the Romanoff Treasure* (1932). The diamond-mounted frame contains a miniature of Nicholas II. According to Hammer, Czarina Alexandra commissioned the piece as a birthday gift for the czar in 1907.

Provenance: Presented by Czarina Alexandra Feodorovna to Czar Nicholas II, 1907, Alexander Palace, Tsarskoe Selo; Hammer Galleries, New York, January 4, 1934

Bibliography: Hammer 1932, pp. 216–17; Lesley 1976, p. 95, pl. 196; Curry 1995, no. 13

Exhibitions: Lord and Taylor 1933, cat. 4765, p. 4

Virginia Museum of Fine Arts, Richmond, bequest of Lillian Thomas Pratt, 47.20.303, 47.20.367

— 107 —

MINIATURE EGG PENDANT
Purpurine, gold
H: ¾ inch
Marks: Initials of workmaster Erik Kollin, assay mark of St. Petersburg before 1896

Unlike much gaudier bejeweled miniature eggs by the Fabergé workshop and other makers, this acornlike piece offers simple contrasts of color and texture. Light glances off the smooth surface of the dark purpurine but is broken up by the bright gold wire cap.

Provenance: Said to be from the apartments of Grand Duchess Tatiana, Alexander Palace, Tsarskoe Selo; The Schaffer Collection of Russian Imperial Art Treasures, New York, November 1, 1935

Bibliography: Lesley 1976, p. 53, pl. 70; Curry 1995, no. 42a

Virginia Museum of Fine Arts, Richmond, bequest of Lillian Thomas Pratt, 47.20.55

— 108 —

SCARAB BROOCH
Rhodolite garnet, enamel, gold, diamonds, rubies, sterling silver
L: 1⅜ inches
Marks: Initials KF, illegible punch marks

Long associated with enduring power, Egyptian artifacts inspired this regal brooch in the form of a large scarab set between two lotus flowers of diamond, enamel, and ruby. The brooch has an imperial Russian provenance, but it was equally appropriate for an American collector living in a country that assiduously built Egyptian-revival structures.

Provenance: Said to have belonged to Czarina Alexandra Feodorovna; The Schaffer Collection of Russian Imperial Art Treasures, New York, August 18, 1937

Bibliography: Lesley 1976, p. 135, pl. 270; Curry 1995, no. 6

Virginia Museum of Fine Arts, Richmond, bequest of Lillian Thomas Pratt, 47.20.143

— 109 —

OCTAGONAL BOX
Nephrite, gold, rubies, diamonds
H: 1¼ inches
Marks: Fabergé, initials of workmaster Mikhail Perkhin, assay mark of St. Petersburg before 1896

Room was found on the gold lid of this tiny box to accommodate minute cherubs and flower garlands chased in low relief, classical egg-and-dart and beaded borders, and even a series of minuscule diamonds and rubies. The workmaster executed the complex design without making the box look busy.

Provenance: Said to be from the apartments of Czarina Alexandra Feodorovna, Alexander Palace, Tsarskoe Selo; The Schaffer Collection of Russian Imperial Art Treasures, New York, October 29, 1936

Bibliography: Lesley 1976, p. 143, pl. 291

Virginia Museum of Fine Arts, Richmond, bequest of Lillian Thomas Pratt, 47.20.275

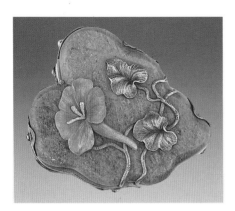

⊸ 110 ⊷
LEAF BOX

Feldspar, gold, diamond, ruby, emerald, sapphire, pearl, enamel
H: 1¹⁄₁₆ inches
Marks: Initials KF, assay mark of Moscow 1896–1908,
partial initials of assay master Ivan Lebedkin, inv. no. 16795

On rare occasions, Fabergé workers shaped a box to echo its floral ornament. Thought to be a snuffbox, this small container takes on the heart-shaped leaf form of the chased gold foliage entwined on its sides and top. Small precious stones stud a bright golden band of leaves that edge the opening, giving one's fingers a better grip on the tightly fitted lid. The dominant blossom, from the trumpet vine, is symbolic of fame. For another art nouveau leaf-shaped box, see cat. no. 163.

Bibliography: Lesley 1976, p. 143, pl. 290; Curry 1995, no. 31

Exhibitions: NCMA 1979; ALVR 1983, p. 66, pl. 154

Virginia Museum of Fine Arts, Richmond, bequest of
Lillian Thomas Pratt, 47.20.274

⊸ 111 ⊷
DESK CALENDAR

Nephrite, gold, enamel, pearls, agate, sterling silver
H: 3⅜ inches
Marks: Fabergé, initials of workmaster Henrik Wigström,
assay mark of St. Petersburg 1896–1908,
assay master Iakov Liapunov

The numbers in this perpetual calendar can be manipulated by using the knobs on either side. The names of the months are engraved in French on gilt plaques held in place by red enamel and milky white agate mounts. The piece is thought to have belonged to Nathalie Cheremetevskaya, an alluring divorcée who married the czar's younger brother Mikhail Aleksandrovich against the ruler's wishes. The czar granted his new sister-in-law the title of Countess Brassova, but he and Czarina Alexandra were not on speaking terms with her.

Provenance: Said to have belonged to Countess Brassova;
The Schaffer Collection of Russian Imperial Art Treasures,
New York, August 18, 1937

Bibliography: Gems and Minerals 1961, pp. 16–18, p. 18 (ill.);
Lesley 1976, p. 147, pl. 300

Virginia Museum of Fine Arts, Richmond, bequest of
Lillian Thomas Pratt, 47.20.286

— 112 —

EGG FRAME
Bowenite, gold, rock crystal
H: 2¼ inches
Marks: Initials of workmaster Mikhail Perkhin, assay mark of
St. Petersburg before 1896; French import mark ET

Known as "the little pair," the two youngest daughters
of Czar Nicholas shared a room in the Alexander Palace
at Tsarskoe Selo. Viewed through rock crystal, photographs of Maria and Anastasia share an egg-shaped frame
worked in cool green stone with warm gold mounts. The
stone egg is nearly solid, but room was hollowed out for
two gold easels that fold out to support it.

Provenance: The Schaffer Collection of Russian Imperial
Art Treasures, New York, 1940

Bibliography: Lesley 1976, p. 103, pl. 210

Virginia Museum of Fine Arts, Richmond, bequest of
Lillian Thomas Pratt, 47.20.306

— 113 —

BOWENITE COLUMN FRAME
Bowenite, gold, rubies, pearl, rock crystal
H: 4½ inches
Marks: Initials of workmaster Henrik Wigström, assay mark of
St. Petersburg 1908–17, inv. no. 17259

Easily overlooked details reinforce the power of Fabergé
designs. Here, a tiny oval pearl used as a finial in a bowknot set with rubies echoes the oval shape of this gold
double-sided frame on a neoclassical stone column. The
frame contains photographic reproductions of Frederick
August von Kaulbach's 1903 pastels of Grand Duchesses
Olga and Tatiana. Rock crystal instead of glass covers
the images.

Provenance: Said to be from the Alexander Palace at Tsarskoe Selo;
The Schaffer Collection of Russian Imperial Art Treasures,
New York, November 1, 1935

Bibliography: Ross 1965, p. 48; Lesley 1976, p. 101, pl. 209

Virginia Museum of Fine Arts, Richmond, bequest of
Lillian Thomas Pratt, 47.20.304

— 114 —

COUPE

Nephrite, silver gilt, rubies, sapphires

H: 11 inches

Marks: Fabergé, initials of workmaster Mikhail Perkhin,
assay mark of St. Petersburg before 1896, 88

Held aloft by a trio of powerfully modeled sea horses,
this spinach-colored nephrite cylinder rises dramatically
to a domed lid topped with a head and trident suggesting
Neptune. During the eighteenth century the Romanov
dynasty furthered its power by establishing several outlets to the sea, including St. Petersburg, founded in 1703
by Peter the Great.

Provenance: Hammer Galleries, New York, September 25, 1939

Bibliography: Lesley 1976, p. 151, pl. 312

Virginia Museum of Fine Arts, Richmond, bequest of
Lillian Thomas Pratt, 47.20.300

— 115 —

TERRESTRIAL GLOBE
Rock crystal, gold
H: 5⅛ inches
Marks: Initials of workmaster Erik Kollin, assay mark of
St. Petersburg before 1896

The terrestrial globe rests on a rather plain, solid gold tripod with a compass in the base. The engraved rock crystal sphere can be tilted and is encircled by wide gold bands engraved to show latitude and longitude, months of the year, and signs of the zodiac. The gold caps marking the poles are engraved with the hours of the day. Also initialed by Kollin, a related globe on a much more elaborate base is in the royal collection at Sandringham. A nephrite desk clock marked by Henrik Wigström, in the Forbes Magazine collection, is topped by a similar rock crystal terrestrial globe (see p. 230, fig. 2).

Provenance: Said to be from the imperial Russian collection;
Hammer Galleries, New York, January 5, 1940

Bibliography: Lesley 1976, p. 147, pl. 302; Curry 1995, no. 10

Exhibitions: ALVR 1983, pp. 92–93, pl. 293

Virginia Museum of Fine Arts, Richmond, bequest of
Lillian Thomas Pratt, 47.20.285

— 116 —

PRESENTATION BOX
Nephrite, gold, diamonds, sterling silver
H: 1⅝ inches
Marks: Fabergé, initials of workmaster Mikhail Perkhin, assay mark of
St. Petersburg 1896–1908, assay master Iakov Liapunov

Worked in diamonds, the initials of the last Russian czar sparkle against the spinach green stone of this gold-mounted box, possibly intended to hold snuff. Similarly designed boxes were sometimes used as presentation gifts by the czar (see Habsburg/Lopato 1994, cats. 101, 108, 147).

Provenance: Said to be from the apartments of Czar Nicholas II, Alexander Palace, Tsarskoe Selo; The Schaffer Collection of Russian Imperial Art Treasures, New York, February 8, 1937

Bibliography: Lesley 1976, p. 143, pl. 287

Exhibitions: ALVR 1983, p. 80, pl. 220

Virginia Museum of Fine Arts, Richmond, bequest of
Lillian Thomas Pratt, 47.20.271

— 117 —

POLAR BEAR
Marble, foil-backed glass
L: 5⅝ inches

The lolling tongue and lumbering gait of this polar bear typify the individuality that Fabergé's carvers captured in their hardstone animals. On the gallery sheet that accompanied the piece, Armand Hammer attributed the work to "Kremlev the Younger" (Petr Mikhailovich Kremlyev), one of the firm's most talented stone carvers.

Provenance: Said to be from the apartments of Czar Nicholas II, Alexander Palace, Tsarskoe Selo; Hammer Galleries, New York, April 19, 1939

Bibliography: Lesley 1976, p. 19, pl. 5

Virginia Museum of Fine Arts, Richmond, bequest of
Lillian Thomas Pratt, 47.20.239

— 118 —

EAGLE
Agate, gold, diamonds
H: 1 11/16 inches
Marks: Initials of workmaster Henrik Wigström, assay mark of
St. Petersburg 1896–1908, illegible assay marks, 72

Crisp carving gives a lively presence to this alert little
predator with its cocked head and diamond eyes.

Provenance: The Schaffer Collection of Russian Imperial
Art Treasures, New York, 1940

Bibliography: Lesley 1976, p. 25, pl. 27

Virginia Museum of Fine Arts, Richmond, bequest of
Lillian Thomas Pratt, 47.20.257

— 119 —

OSTRICH
Agate, gold, diamonds, quartzite
H: 4 9/16 inches

No two of the Fabergé hardstone animals are precisely
alike. This ostrich, accurately carved from striated agate,
strikes a slightly more dignified pose than a related ostrich in the royal collection at Sandringham.

Provenance: Hammer Galleries, New York, June 1, 1939

Bibliography: Lesley 1976, p. 31, pl. 35

Exhibitions: ALVR 1983, pp. 118–19, pl. 435

Virginia Museum of Fine Arts, Richmond, bequest of
Lillian Thomas Pratt, 47.20.262

— 120 —

SAILOR
Aventurine quartz, lapis lazuli, sapphires, onyx, jadeite
H: 4¾ inches
Original fitted case

"His piercing blue eyes each set with a . . . sapphire sparkle with loyalty and sincerity," says the Hammer Galleries catalogue of this hardstone sailor. The name Zarnitsa carved on the figure's hatband links him to one of the imperial yachts. Sailors on the *Zarnitsa* are said to have remained loyal to the crown during one of the mutinies that marked the crumbling power of czarist Russia.

Provenance: Hammer Galleries, New York, December 9, 1937

Bibliography: Lesley 1976, p. 147, pl. 301; Curry 1995, no. 19

Exhibitions: Hammer 1937; ALVR 1983, p. 132, pl. 481

Virginia Museum of Fine Arts, Richmond, bequest of
Lillian Thomas Pratt, 47.20.268

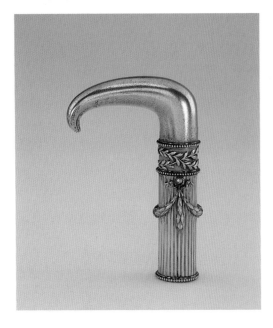

— 121 —

GOLD PARASOL HANDLE
Gold, diamonds
H: 2¼ inches
Marks: Initials KF, assay mark of Moscow 1896–1908, partial initials
of assay master Ivan Lebedkin, inv. no. 20636

Only two tiny diamonds enhance the skillful metalwork of this miniature handle worked in three shades of gold. The delicately fluted shaft, overlaid with a green gold swag, ends with a bead-edged collar of chased leaves. The smooth curved handle provides a textural counterpoint.

Provenance: Said to have belonged to Czarina Alexandra Feodorovna; The Schaffer Collection of Russian Imperial Art Treasures, New York, August 18, 1936

Bibliography: Lesley 1976, p. 109, pl. 217

Virginia Museum of Fine Arts, Richmond, bequest of
Lillian Thomas Pratt, 47.20.185

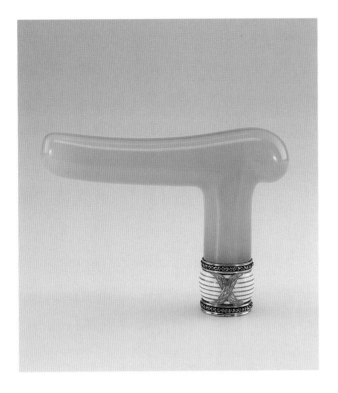

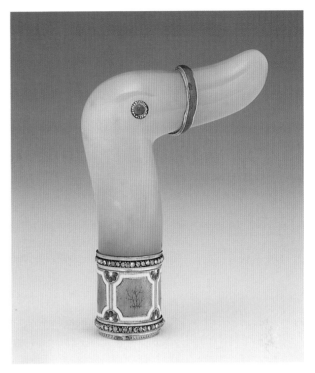

— 122 —

BOWENITE CANE HANDLE
Bowenite, enamel, gold, diamonds
H: 2½ inches
Marks: Initials of workmaster Mikhail Perkhin

Bands of minuscule rose-cut diamond chips edge the
white enameled mount of this smooth stone handle. The
sparkling bands are paralleled by slender stripes of gold.
Crossed ribbons chased in greenish gold and enameled
with translucent orange provide a complementary color
contrast to the milky green stone.

Provenance: Said to have belonged to Czarina Alexandra Feodorovna;
The Schaffer Collection of Russian Imperial Art Treasures,
New York, October 29, 1936

Bibliography: Lesley 1976, p. 117, pl. 242

Virginia Museum of Fine Arts, Richmond, bequest of
Lillian Thomas Pratt, 47.20.168

— 123 —

DUCK PARASOL HANDLE
Bowenite, enamel, rubies, diamonds, gold, sterling silver
H: 3¼ inches
Marks: Initials of workmaster Mikhail Perkhin, assay mark of
St. Petersburg before 1896

A saucy duck's head with bright ruby eyes and a beak
ringed with green enamel forms a whimsical handle for
a parasol. The fresh pink, white, and green enamel of the
diamond-banded collar demonstrates the skill of enamel-
ists in the Fabergé workshops. Underneath the translucent pink is a mosslike pattern found on other Fabergé
handles and picture frames.

Provenance: Said to have belonged to Czarina Alexandra Feodorovna;
The Schaffer Collection of Russian Imperial Art Treasures,
New York, April 9, 1936

Bibliography: Lesley 1976, p. 117, pl. 243; Curry 1995, no. 16

Virginia Museum of Fine Arts, Richmond, bequest of
Lillian Thomas Pratt, 47.20.169

— 124 —

LILY OF THE VALLEY HAND SEAL
Bowenite, gold, pearls, chalcedony
H: 3 inches
Marks: Initials of workmaster Mikhail Perkhin, assay mark of
St. Petersburg before 1896

The curved surfaces of individual pearls set into this jade
seal convincingly replicate the bell-shaped blossoms of
the lily of the valley, a spring flower that grows profusely
in northern European forests.

Provenance: The Schaffer Collection of Russian Imperial
Art Treasures, New York, March 18, 1937

Bibliography: Lesley 1976, p. 149, pl. 308; Curry 1995, no. 29

Virginia Museum of Fine Arts, Richmond, bequest of
Lillian Thomas Pratt, 47.20.204

— 125 —

ROCK CRYSTAL HAND SEAL
Rock crystal, enamel, gold, silver, diamonds
H: 3 inches
Marks: Fabergé, initials of workmaster Mikhail Perkhin, assay mark
of St. Petersburg before 1896

Daisylike sterling silver flowers set with diamonds and
gold embellish the enameled base of a rock crystal seal.
The translucent stone is carved with birds and flowering
branches that recall eighteenth-century chinoiserie patterns. A plated cap has been added where the original
seal would have been.

Bibliography: Lesley 1976, p. 149, pl. 305; Curry 1995, no. 28

Virginia Museum of Fine Arts, Richmond, bequest of
Lillian Thomas Pratt, 47.20.201

— 126 —

PINK ROCK CRYSTAL CANE HANDLE
Rock crystal, enamel, gold, emeralds, diamonds
H: 2¹⁵⁄₁₆ inches
Marks: Initials of workmaster Mikhail Perkhin, assay mark of
St. Petersburg before 1896, illegible inv. no.

Set on a diamond-banded pink enamel collar enriched
with gold swags suspended from small emeralds, the
clear rock crystal of this handle takes on a roseate glow.
A somewhat clumsy crowned initial of Czar Nicholas II
and the date 1912 were added later.

Bibliography: Lesley 1976, p. 115, pl. 237

Virginia Museum of Fine Arts, Richmond, bequest of
Lillian Thomas Pratt, 47.20.188

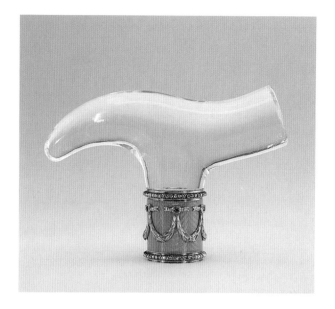

— 127 —

SNAKE HANDLE
Chalcedony, gold, ruby
H: 4³⁄₁₆ inches
Marks: Initials of workmaster Henrik Wigström, assay mark of
St. Petersburg 1896–1908, assay master A. Richter, inv. no. 14939

The gold snake slithering up this pale green stone handle
was made in two sections that are joined under the lip of
the disk-shaped knob. Wigström used color to knit the
design together. Made of red gold washed with yellow
gold, the snake is set with a pink cabochon ruby that echoes the red gold collar at the base of the handle.

Provenance: Said to have belonged to Czarina Alexandra Feodorovna;
The Schaffer Collection of Russian Imperial Art Treasures,
New York, April 9, 1936

Bibliography: Bainbridge 1935, pp. 87–90, pl. VII;
Lesley 1976, p. 119, pl. 250

Exhibitions: NCMA 1979

Virginia Museum of Fine Arts, Richmond, bequest of
Lillian Thomas Pratt, 47.20.187

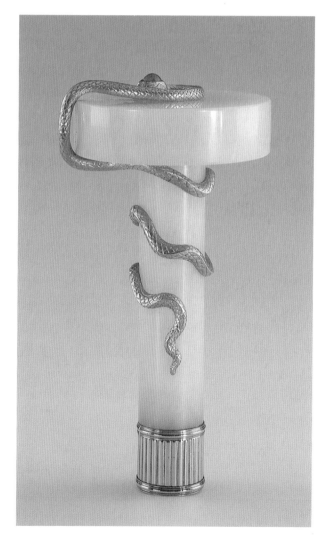

— 128 —

ROCOCO CANE HANDLE
Chalcedony, gold, diamonds, sterling silver
H: 3⅛ inches
Marks: Initials of workmaster Mikhail Perkhin, assay mark of
St. Petersburg before 1896, inv. no. 46856

The Russian court's lasting appetite for French design is
distilled in this handle of yellow-green stone held in a
golden rocaille cage. Pratt bought the handle the year
after Henry C. Bainbridge published the piece, describ-
ing its gold work as "admirably adapted to the round
contours of the stone," and attributing the design to
Agathon Fabergé, Carl Fabergé's younger brother.

Provenance: Said to have belonged to Czarina Alexandra Feodorovna;
The Schaffer Collection of Russian Imperial Art Treasures,
New York, April 9, 1936

Bibliography: Bainbridge 1935, pp. 87–90, pl. VII; Ross 1965, p. 33;
Lesley 1976, p. 119, pl. 245

Exhibitions: NCMA 1979

Virginia Museum of Fine Arts, Richmond, bequest of
Lillian Thomas Pratt, 47.20.183

— 129 —

NEPHRITE PARASOL HANDLE
Nephrite, diamonds, gold
H: 3⅜ inches
Marks: Fabergé, initials of workmaster Mikhail Perkhin, inv. no. 1225

With the pent-up energy of a fiddlehead fern about to
open, this nephrite handle furls tightly upon itself. Sinuous curves are heightened with lines of rose-cut diamonds. The dark green color of the stone is set off by the
warm red gold collar.

Provenance: Said to be from the apartments of Czarina Alexandra
Feodorovna, Alexander Palace, Tsarskoe Selo; Hammer Galleries,
New York, January 5, 1940

Bibliography: Lesley 1976, p. 111, pl. 226

Exhibitions: NCMA 1979

Virginia Museum of Fine Arts, Richmond, bequest of
Lillian Thomas Pratt, 47.20.178

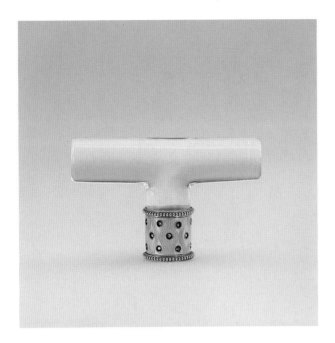

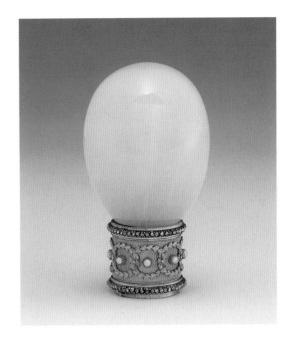

— 130 —

BLUE ROCK CRYSTAL CANE HANDLE
Rock crystal, enamel, gold, diamonds
H: 1⅜ inches
Marks: Initials KF, assay mark of Moscow 1896–1908, partial initials
of assay master Ivan Lebedkin, illegible inv. no.

Unusually diminutive, this handle features a piece of rock crystal quartz set on an enameled collar studded with diamonds and edged with yellow gold. The sky blue enamel tinges the clear stone with a bluish glow. The dealer's description that accompanied Pratt's purchase assured her that the handle was "worthy of the most discriminating taste."

Provenance: Said to be from the apartments of Czarina Alexandra Feodorovna, Alexander Palace, Tsarskoe Selo; The Schaffer Collection of Russian Imperial Art Treasures, October 29, 1936

Bibliography: Lesley 1976, p. 115, pl. 236

Virginia Museum of Fine Arts, Richmond, bequest of
Lillian Thomas Pratt, 47.20.177

— 131 —

EGG PARASOL HANDLE
Chalcedony, enamel, gold, diamonds, pearls
H: 2⅞ inches
Marks: Initials of workmaster Mikhail Perkhin, assay mark of
St. Petersburg before 1896

The simplicity of this handle's unadorned pale stone egg is reinforced by an elaborate collar worked in rich pink enamel, bordered with tiny diamond fillets, and embellished with overlapping wreaths of gold leaves centered with pearls.

Bibliography: Lesley 1976, p. 119, pl. 245; Curry 1995, no. 17

Virginia Museum of Fine Arts, Richmond, bequest of
Lillian Thomas Pratt, 47.20.175

— 132 —

MAUVE EGG PARASOL HANDLE
Enamel, gold, diamonds
H: 2¾ inches
Marks: Initials of workmaster Mikhail Perkhin, assay mark of
St. Petersburg before 1896

Radiating from a large diamond, spirals of smaller rose-
cut stones descend around a voluptuous egg-shaped
handle. Worked in mauve enamel, the egg is set on a yellow enamel collar with two horizontal fillets of diamonds.
The sinuous bejeweled curves are echoed by swags of
red and green gold accented with additional diamonds.

Provenance: Said to have belonged to Prince Aleksandr Romanovski,
duke of Leuchtenberg; Hammer Galleries, New York,
December 6, 1939

Bibliography: Lesley 1976, p. 109, pl. 213; Curry 1995, no. 18

Exhibitions: ALVR 1983, p. 81, pl. 226

Virginia Museum of Fine Arts, Richmond, bequest of
Lillian Thomas Pratt, 47.20.172

— 133 —

ENAMELED PARASOL HANDLE
Enamel, gold, diamond
H: 3 inches
Marks: Fabergé, initials of workmaster Henrik Wigström,
assay mark of St. Petersburg 1896–1908, 72

A faceted diamond punctuates the tip of this handle, and
handsome enamel work articulates the tapering cylindrical form. Transparent blue enamel fields, animated by
underlying *guilloché* surfaces, shimmer in contrast to
white-bordered areas of gold enriched with opaque red
flowers and green leaves.

Provenance: Said to be from the imperial Russian collection;
Hammer Galleries, New York, January 5, 1940

Bibliography: Lesley 1976, p. 109, pl. 216; Curry 1995, no. 27

Virginia Museum of Fine Arts, Richmond, bequest of
Lillian Thomas Pratt, 47.20.199

— 134 —

ENAMELED SNUFFBOX
Gold, enamel, carnelian, diamonds
H: 1¾16 inch
Marks: Fabergé, initials of workmaster Mikhail Perkhin, assay mark
of St. Petersburg 1896–1908, inv. no. 5805

Edged with diamonds, an oval carnelian engraved with
Arabic script tops this brightly enameled gold box. Taken
from the Koran, sura 2, verse 256, the inscription can be
translated "God, there is no God but He; the Living, the
Self-subsisting. Neither slumber seizeth Him, nor sleep;
His, whatsoever is in the Heavens and whatsoever is in
the Earth! Who is he that can intercede with Him, but by
His own permission? He knoweth what is present with
his creatures and what is yet to befall them; yet naught
of His knowledge do they comprehend, save what He
willeth. His Throne reacheth over the Heavens and the
Earth, and the upholding of both burdeneth Him not;
and He is the High, the Great!"

Provenance: The Schaffer Collection of Russian Imperial
Art Treasures, New York, October 29, 1936

Bibliography: Lesley 1976, p. 143, pl. 292

Exhibitions: ALVR 1983, p. 66, pl. 153

Virginia Museum of Fine Arts, Richmond, bequest of
Lillian Thomas Pratt, 47.20.276

— 135 —

CYLINDRICAL CONTAINER
Silver gilt, gilt copper, enamel
H: 3½ inches
Marks: K Fabergé, double-headed eagle, initials of workmaster
Anders Nevalainen, assay mark of St. Petersburg
1908–1917, 88, inv. no. 18258

Probably intended to hold cigarettes, this simply shaped
container depends on brilliant red enamel enriched with
gilt ornament for its visual impact.

Provenance: The Schaffer Collection of Russian Imperial
Art Treasures, New York, August 26, 1936

Bibliography: Lesley 1976, p. 157, pl. 326

Virginia Museum of Fine Arts, Richmond, bequest of
Lillian Thomas Pratt, 47.20.291

— 136 —

CROSS OF ST. ANDREW FRAME
Silver gilt, enamel, silk ribbon, wood
H: 5¾ inches
Marks: K Fabergé, initials of workmaster Anders Nevalainen,
assay mark of St. Petersburg 1896–1908, assay master
A. Richter, 91, inv. no. 15647
Original fitted case

On November 28, 1698, Peter the Great founded Russia's
highest order, the imperial Order of St. Andrew, as part
of an effort to westernize Russia. The blue ribbon saltire,
a heraldic device, derives from the Scottish version of St.
Andrew's X-shaped cross. The photograph captures the
grand duchesses Tatiana, Anastasia, and Olga and their
governess in 1916.

Provenance: Said to be from the Winter Palace, St. Petersburg;
Hammer Galleries, New York, October 2, 1933

Bibliography: Lesley 1976, p. 91, pl. 189

Exhibitions: Lord and Taylor 1933, no. 4404, p. 9

Virginia Museum of Fine Arts, Richmond, bequest of
Lillian Thomas Pratt, 47.20.357

— 137 —

STAR-SHAPED FRAME
Gold, enamel, pearls, ivory
H: 3 3/16 inches
Marks: Fabergé, initials of workmaster Mikhail Perkhin, assay mark
of St. Petersburg before 1896

A pearly white enamel triangle, superimposed on a bright yellow one, gives this gold-edged frame its striking geometric form. The opening is edged by a circle of tiny seed pearls that echoes the string of pearls Grand Duchess Tatiana wears in the photograph, taken about 1912, when she was fifteen.

Bibliography: Lesley 1976, p. 95, pl. 195

Virginia Museum of Fine Arts, Richmond, bequest of
Lillian Thomas Pratt, 47.20.352

— 138 —

DIAMOND-SHAPED FRAME
Rock crystal, gold, rubies, emeralds, ivory
H: 3 7/8 inches
Marks: Initials KF, assay mark of Moscow before 1896, inv. no. 15234

A bust-length photograph of Grand Duchess Tatiana floats serenely in this rock crystal frame, which is given substance by a circle of channel-cut emeralds. Sinuous gold work set with rubies forms graceful flowers.

Provenance: The Schaffer Collection of Russian Imperial
Art Treasures, New York, 1940–41

Bibliography: Lesley 1976, p. 101, pl. 208; Curry 1995, no. 30

Virginia Museum of Fine Arts, Richmond, bequest of
Lillian Thomas Pratt, 47.20.351

— 139 —

RED, WHITE, AND BLUE FRAME
Enamel, gold, silver, silver gilt, ivory
H: 2⅜ inches
Marks: Fabergé, initials of workmaster Henrik Wigström, assay mark
of St. Petersburg 1908–17, 91, inv. no. 19762

One of the flags designed for the imperial Order of St.
Andrew, instituted by Czar Peter I in 1698, was the imperial standard. The red, white, and blue standard, possibly
intended to resemble the British Union Jack, provides
the color scheme for this frame, which encloses a uniformed image of Czar Nicholas II.

Provenance: The Schaffer Collection of Russian Imperial
Art Treasures, New York

Bibliography: Lesley 1976, p. 95, pl. 194

Virginia Museum of Fine Arts, Richmond, bequest of
Lillian Thomas Pratt, 47.20.334

— 140 —

TENTH ANNIVERSARY FRAME
Enamel, silver, diamonds, ivory
H: 3⁷⁄₁₆ inches
Marks: Fabergé, initials of workmaster Henrik Wigström, assay mark
of St. Petersburg 1896–1908, 91 (frame), 88 (stand), inv. no. 16167

Pratt may have acquired this pale blue enamel frame containing a regal photograph of Czarina Alexandra Feodorovna in court dress as a companion piece to the imperial
column frame with miniature portrait of Czar Nicholas,
purchased only two months earlier (cat. no. 106).

Provenance: Said to have been presented by Czarina Alexandra to
Czar Nicholas II, Alexander Palace, Tsarskoe Selo, on the tenth
anniversary of their marriage; The Schaffer Collection of Russian
Imperial Art Treasures, New York, March 1, 1934

Bibliography: Lesley 1976, p. 77, pl. 163
Exhibitions: PFAC 1981

Virginia Museum of Fine Arts, Richmond, bequest of
Lillian Thomas Pratt, 47.20.333

— 141 —

GRAY ENAMELED FRAME
Gold, enamel, ivory
H: 3⁵⁄₁₆ inches
Marks: Fabergé, initials of workmaster Mikhail Perkhin, assay mark
of St. Petersburg before 1896, inv. no. 45843

Rococo-style gold work glitters against subdued gray enamel. The frame contains a photographic reproduction of Grand Duchess Olga's childhood pastel portrait by Frederick August von Kaulbach.

Provenance: The Schaffer Collection of Russian Imperial
Art Treasures, New York, 1945

Bibliography: Lesley 1976, p. 77, pl. 160

Virginia Museum of Fine Arts, Richmond, bequest of
Lillian Thomas Pratt, 47.20.318

— 142 —

IVORY FRAME
Gold, ivory
H: 3¼ inches
Marks: Initials of workmaster Mikhail Perkhin, assay mark of
St. Petersburg before 1896
Original fitted case

Instead of translucent enamel, smooth ivory adds color and texture to this frame, which opens from the front by lifting the oval bezel. The frame contains a photograph of the czar's youngest daughter, Grand Duchess Anastasia, at about the age of eight.

Bibliography: Lesley 1976, p. 97, pl. 199

Virginia Museum of Fine Arts, Richmond, bequest of
Lillian Thomas Pratt, 47.20.316

— 143 —

MAUVE ENAMELED FRAME
Enamel, silver gilt, rock crystal, wood
H: 4⅝ inches
Marks: (stand) Fabergé, 84

A pronounced *guilloché* pattern is overlaid with translucent enamel in mauve, one of Czarina Alexandra Feodorovna's favorite colors. Protected by a large sheet of rock crystal, her photograph in court dress fills the frame. The name Victoria is worked into the curvaceous wirework that supports the frame, suggesting that the original owner might have been Victoria Melita, who was the wife of Grand Duke Kirill Vladimirovich.

Provenance: Said to be from the Alexander Palace, Tsarskoe Selo; The Schaffer Collection of Russian Imperial Art Treasures, New York, April 2, 1936

Bibliography: Lesley 1976, p. 83, pl. 174

Virginia Museum of Fine Arts, Richmond, bequest of Lillian Thomas Pratt, 47.20.314

── 144 ──

DOUBLE-SIDED FRAME
Silver gilt, enamel
H: 4³⁄₁₆ inches
Marks: Fabergé, initials of workmaster Hjalmar Armfelt, assay mark of
St. Petersburg 1908–17, 88, inv. no. 18194

Signed and dated photographs here capture Czar Nicholas's younger brother Mikhail Aleksandrovich and his inamorata, Nathalie Cheremetevskaya, in 1909. The double-sided frame, elegantly enameled in mauve on one side and pale gray on the other, swings in its silver gilt stand, allowing the user to choose which photograph to display. For a similar double frame, see Habsburg/Lopato 1994, cat. 47.

Provenance: Said to be from the apartments of Czar Nicholas II, Alexander Palace, Tsarskoe Selo; The Schaffer Collection of Russian Imperial Art Treasures, New York, March 1, 1939

Bibliography: Lesley 1976, p. 95, pl. 192

Virginia Museum of Fine Arts, Richmond, bequest of Lillian Thomas Pratt, 47.20.312

— 145 —

FRAME WITH DIAMOND BOWKNOT
Enamel, gold, silver, diamonds, ivory
H: 2⅝ inches
Marks: Fabergé, initials of workmaster Mikhail Perkhin, assay mark
of St. Petersburg before 1896, inv. no. 54500

Shallow curves edged in gold soften the geometry of this
triangular frame centered with a bowknot of diamonds
set in silver. Grand Duchess Tatiana looks out from the
jewel-encrusted opening.

Provenance: Said to be from the Alexander Palace, Tsarskoe Selo;
The Schaffer Collection of Russian Imperial Art Treasures,
New York, March 2, 1936

Bibliography: Lesley 1976, p. 81, pl. 167

Virginia Museum of Fine Arts, Richmond, bequest of
Lillian Thomas Pratt, 47.20.349

— 146 —

SEAWEED FRAME
Gold, enamel, pearls, ivory
H: 3 3/16 inches
Marks: Fabergé, initials of workmaster Henrik Wigström, assay mark
of St. Petersburg 1896–1908, inv. no. 11884

Seaweedlike tendrils float under bluish white enamel on
this delicate frame enhanced with a circle of pearls. The
ivory-backed frame contains an image of Czarevitch
Alexei.

Provenance: Said to be from the Alexander Palace, Tsarskoe Selo;
The Schaffer Collection of Russian Imperial Art Treasures,
New York, September 30, 1935

Bibliography: Lesley 1976, p. 91, pl. 186

Virginia Museum of Fine Arts, Richmond, bequest of
Lillian Thomas Pratt, 47.20.336

— 147 —

FRAME WITH MINIATURE
Gold, platinum, enamel, watercolor, ivory
H: 2¼ inches

A small circular frame of shimmering white enamel ornamented with a delicate golden bowknot and floral
swags contains a profile miniature of Queen Alexandra,
sister of Dowager Empress Maria Feodorovna and herself an avid patron of the Fabergé workshops. The cellu-
loid back is fitted with both a loop for hanging and an
easel for standing.

Provenance: Said to have belonged to Prince Felix Yusupov;
Hammer Galleries, New York, February 26, 1941

Bibliography: Lesley 1976, p. 91, pl. 191

Virginia Museum of Fine Arts, Richmond, bequest of
Lillian Thomas Pratt, 47.20.359, 41.20.365

— 148 —
TRIANGULAR FRAME
Gold, enamel, diamonds, ivory
H: 2¼ inches
Marks: Initials KF, assay mark of Moscow 1896–1908,
assay master Ivan Lebedkin

One of the most beautiful of all Pratt's frames, this gold
and white triangular easel holds three deliciously enameled pink ovals, each studded with a tiny diamond. The
element of surprise comes into play when the hinged
ovals are lifted to reveal tiny photographs of the daughters of Nicholas and Alexandra. For a circular frame with
similarly engineered covered openings, see Habsburg/
Lopato 1994, cat. 235.

Bibliography: Lesley 1976, p. 91, pl. 188; Curry 1995, no. 38

Exhibitions: ALVR 1983, p. 48, pl. 85

Virginia Museum of Fine Arts, Richmond, bequest of
Lillian Thomas Pratt, 47.20.347

⟵ 149 ⟶

OPENWORK FRAME
Silver gilt, enamel, holly
H: 5⁹⁄₁₆ inches
Marks: Fabergé, initials of workmaster Victor Aarne,
assay mark of St. Petersburg 1896–1908,
assay master Iakov Liapunov, 88

Vivid red and green enamels punctuated by white strip-
ing and silver gilt leafage distinguish this frame. It holds
a photograph of Czar Alexander II, grandfather of Czar
Nicholas II, in his study. The image is older than its
frame and shows that the fashion for desks and tables
crammed with framed pictures of friends and family was
well established by the third quarter of the nineteenth
century.

Provenance: The Schaffer Collection of Russian Imperial
Art Treasures, New York, 1939–40

Bibliography: Lesley 1976, p. 83, pl. 178; Curry 1995, no. 23

Virginia Museum of Fine Arts, Richmond, bequest of
Lillian Thomas Pratt, 47.20.308

— 150 —

IMPERIAL PELICAN EASTER EGG
Gold, diamonds, enamel, pearls, ivory, watercolor
H: (egg) 4 inches; (with stand) 5¼ inches
Marks: Fabergé, initials of workmaster Mikhail Perkhin, assay mark
of St. Petersburg before 1896; miniatures signed Zehngraf,
stand marked Fabergé

The Pelican Easter egg is a visual allegory celebrating charity and good works. The pelican nesting on the top is an ancient symbol of self-sacrifice: raising her diamond-studded wings, the sculpted and enameled mother bird protects her little nestlings. As they clamor for food, she plucks at her own breast to feed them. Near the top of the shell an engraving of the pelican family repeats the sculptural motif, while an inscription on the rose gold exterior reads, "Visit our vineyards, O Lord, and we shall live in Thee."

The little nestlings in this case were actually the daughters of the aristocracy. Engraved on the shell are the celebratory dates 1797–1897. Following the coronation of Czar Paul I in 1796, a Society for Bringing Up the Young Ladies of Noble Families was headed by his wife, Maria Feodorovna. In 1797 it became the Department of Institutions of the Empress Maria, which oversaw various educational entities. The mother of Czar Nicholas II, for whom the Pelican egg was made, was also named Maria Feodorovna, and she, too, was interested in charitable works.

Most of Fabergé's Easter eggs contain separate surprises that move within the shell or can be taken out completely, but the entire Pelican egg itself is the surprise.

The egg unfolds in vertical slices to become a screen of golden oval frames, each rimmed with seed pearls. The frames hold eight miniatures by Johannes Zehngraf showing buildings in St. Petersburg that housed educational institutions for women of privilege. The second miniature from the left is the Razumovsky Palace, which sheltered the Nikolai Orphanage. Over the palace gates, a figure of a pelican tears its breast to feed its young, symbolizing the ideals of charity celebrated by the egg.

Provenance: Presented by Czar Nicholas II to Dowager Empress Maria Feodorovna, 1897, Anichkov Palace, St. Petersburg; Hammer Galleries, New York

Bibliography: Bainbridge 1939; Bainbridge 1949, pl. 66; Snowman 1953, pp. 80–81, pls. 298, 299; Snowman 1962, pp. 87–88, pls. 330, 331; Lesley 1976, p. 40, pl. 49; Forbes 1979, p. 1231; Solodkoff 1984, p. 75; Hill 1989, p. 57, pls. 33, 34; Pfeffer 1990, pp. 48–51 (ill.); Curry 1995, no. 2

Exhibitions: San Diego/Moscow 1989–90, p. 98, fig. 13

Virginia Museum of Fine Arts, Richmond, bequest of Lillian Thomas Pratt, 47.20.35

— 151 —

IMPERIAL CZAREVITCH EASTER EGG
Egg: Lapis lazuli, gold, diamonds
Frame: Diamonds, gold, platinum or silver, lapis lazuli,
watercolor, ivory
H: (egg) 4¹⁵⁄₁₆ inches; (frame) 3¾ inches
Marks: Engraved Fabergé, initials of workmaster
Henrik Wigström, inv. no. 17547

Six sections of lapis lazuli are encased in gold latticework that covers the joints of this imposing piece, making it look as if it was carved from a single block of stone. An imperial eagle motif, also used for the diamond-studded surprise picture frame, adds continuity to the eclectic assemblage of rococo decorative motifs. The golden double-headed eagles vie for space with double-winged caryatids. Hanging chinoiserie canopies, florid scrolls, graceful garlands, and flower baskets festoon the remaining space. Trios of robust anthemion surround an opulent diamond solitaire at the bottom of the shell and a large table diamond at the top. The inscriptions AF and 1912, visible under the table diamond, record the recipient—Czarina Alexandra Feodorovna—and the date of her husband's lavish Easter gift. The regal gold and blue egg makes a suitable container for a miniature portrait on ivory of the eight-year-old Czarevitch Alexei. The egg's original stand, which is known from a vintage photograph, is currently unlocated and apparently was not brought out of Russia by Armand Hammer when he acquired the egg.

Provenance: Presented by Czar Nicholas II to Czarina Alexandra Feodorovna, Easter 1912, Alexander Palace, Tsarskoe Selo; Hammer Galleries, New York, by 1939

Bibliography: Hammer 1932, p. 184 (ill.); Bainbridge 1934, p. 299, fig. 1; Bainbridge 1935, pp. 87–90, fig. 408; Bainbridge 1939; Bainbridge 1949, pl. 49; Snowman 1953, pp. 96–97, pls. 336–38; Snowman 1962, pp. 102–3, pls. 367–69; Haydon 1967, p. 101 (ill.); Lesley 1976, pp. 42–43, pl. 48; Forbes 1979, p. 1232 (ill.), p. 1234; Williams 1980, fig. 20; Solodkoff 1984, p. 98 (ill.); Hill 1989, p. 60, pl. 53; Pfeffer 1990, p. 98, p. 99 (ill.); Curry 1995, no. 4

Exhibitions: Lord and Taylor 1933, no. 4756, p. 3 (ill.); NCMA 1979; San Diego/Moscow 1989–90, p. 110, fig. 37

Virginia Museum of Fine Arts, Richmond, bequest of Lillian Thomas Pratt, 47.20.34, 47.20.368 (miniature)

— 152 —

IMPERIAL PETER THE GREAT EASTER EGG
Egg: Gold, platinum, diamonds, rubies, enamel, bronze,
sapphire, watercolor, ivory, rock crystal
Statue: Gold, sapphire
H: (egg) 4⅜ inches; (statue) 1⁹⁄₁₆ inches
Marks: Engraved K Fabergé 1903, initials of workmaster
Mikhail Perkhin, assay mark of St. Petersburg 1896–1908, 72

Fabergé workmaster Mikhail Perkhin's last egg for Czarina Alexandra Feodorovna links the past glories of the Romanov dynasty to the regime of her husband, Czar Nicholas II. The form of this historicizing artwork was inspired by an eighteenth-century *nécessaire* in the Hermitage. The egg is lavishly worked in the rococo-revival style, using four-color gold set with rubies and diamonds to create an extravagant celebration of St. Petersburg's two-hundredth anniversary.

The diamond-studded dates 1703–1903 establish the egg's central theme. Four miniatures, one signed B. Byalz, and each covered with rock crystal and mounted on the shell in a gold cartouche, offer telling contrasts— Czar Nicholas's portrait corresponds to that of his illustrious ancestor, Peter the Great, while Peter's humble log hut, one of the first buildings in the Russian capital, is offset by the majestic Winter Palace. The localized focus is further reinforced by naturalistic bullrushes that spread gracefully over the egg, their channel-cut rubies winking against the richly worked surface. These recall the marshy grounds on which Peter built his new capital city to gain strategic access to the sea.

As the egg opens, a miniature gilt bronze statue rises from the interior and is silhouetted against a sunburstlike dome of rich yellow enamel. The tiny bronze, perched on a substantial sapphire, copies Étienne-Maurice Falconet's statue of Peter the Great commissioned by Catherine the Great. This equestrian monument, which still stands on the banks of the Neva River, has been a landmark in St. Petersburg since it was unveiled in 1782. Both the original monument and the miniature copy are inscribed "Peter I, Catherine II, 1782."

Provenance: Presented by Czar Nicholas II to Czarina Alexandra Feodorovna, 1903; The Schaffer Collection of Russian Imperial Art Treasures, New York, February 2, 1942

Bibliography: Stolitsa y Usadba 1916; *Art News* 1936, p. 16; *Comstock* 1936; *New York Sun* 1936, p. 17; Bainbridge 1949, pl. 50; Snowman 1953, pp. 88–89, pl. 311; Snowman 1962, pp. 93–94, pl. 341; Lesley 1976, p. 40, pl. 47; Forbes 1979, p. 1230, p. 1231 (ill.); Swezey 1980, pp. 23–31; Demerest 1983; Solodkoff 1984, p. 87; Habsburg 1986, p. 96 (ill.), p. 310; Hill 1989, p. 59, pls. 43, 44; Pfeffer 1990, pp. 78–81 (ill.); Habsburg/Lopato 1994, pp. 77–78, p. 78 (ill.); Curry 1995, no. 3

Exhibitions: V&A 1977; ALVR 1983, pp. 147–48, pl. 564; SAM 1984; San Diego/Moscow 1989–90, p. 103, pl. 23

Virginia Museum of Fine Arts, Richmond, bequest of
Lillian Thomas Pratt, 47.20.33

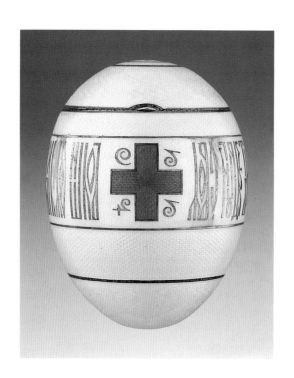

— 153 —

IMPERIAL RED CROSS EASTER EGG
Enamel, silver, gold, mother-of-pearl, watercolor, ivory
H: 3 inches
Marks: Engraved Fabergé 1915, initials of workmaster
Henrik Wigström, assay mark of St. Petersburg 1908–17, 88

Deceptively simple at first glance, the Red Cross egg rewards intense scrutiny. Just underneath its pearly surface, a host of engraved *guilloché* patterning causes the egg to shimmer with nuanced, broken light. On opposite sides of the egg, equilateral crosses in brilliant red enamel dominate the central band; one carries the date 1914, the other 1915. The central portion of the shell is further embellished by the inscription "Greater love hath no man than this, that a man lay down his life for his friends."

On Easter 1915, Czar Nicholas II presented this egg to his mother, Dowager Empress Maria Feodorovna, who officially headed the Russian branch of the international Red Cross. By 1915 hundreds of thousands of Russian soldiers had been captured, killed, or wounded in World War I. While Nicholas was at the front, his wife and two eldest daughters nursed wounded soldiers at a hospital in Tsarskoe Selo. Miniature portraits of the three women, flanked by the czar's sister, Olga Aleksandrovna, and his cousin, Maria Pavlovna, are set in a gold and mother-of-pearl screen that folds to nestle inside the egg. All the women wear Red Cross nursing uniforms.

One of the few immediate members of the czar's family to escape the Bolsheviks, the dowager empress fled Russia for her native Denmark in April 1919, leaving behind her, in the Anichkov Palace at St. Petersburg, this austere Easter egg, whose message of selflessness transcends the turbulent political background against which it was created.

Provenance: Presented by Czar Nicholas II to Dowager Empress Maria Feodorovna, Easter 1915, Anichkov Palace, St. Petersburg; Edgar Philip Everhard; Hammer Galleries, New York

Bibliography: Bainbridge 1939; *New York Sun* 1939; Bainbridge 1949, pl. 56; Snowman 1953, no. 352, p. 104; Snowman 1962, p. 108, pl. 382; Lesley 1976, p. 47, pl. 50; Forbes 1979, p. 1233 (ill.), p. 1234; Hill 1989, p. 61, pl. 59; Curry 1995, no. 5

Virginia Museum of Fine Arts, Richmond, bequest of
Lillian Thomas Pratt, 47.20.36

→ 154 ←

CHAMPAGNE FLUTE
Glass, gold
H: 7⅜ inches
Marks: Fabergé, initials of workmaster Mikhail Perkhin, assay mark
of St. Petersburg 1896–1908, assay master Iakov Liapunov
Original fitted case

A recently auctioned sheet of designs for gold-stemmed
glassware bearing the initial L includes a drawing for this
elegant champagne flute (Christie's, London, April 27,
1989, lot 416). A related crochet hook is also recorded
(Habsburg/Lopato 1994, cat. 75). The L may be the
monogram of Czar Nicholas's grandmother, Louisa,
queen of Denmark, whose daughters were Maria Feodorovna and Queen Alexandra of England.

Provenance: D. M. Blair, Richmond, Hammer Galleries, New York;
Lelia Blair Northrop

Bibliography: Curry 1995, no. 7

Virginia Museum of Fine Arts, Richmond, bequest of
Lelia Blair Northrop, 78.78.2

— 155 —

TUREEN ENSEMBLE
Silver, silver gilt, garnet, amethyst, chalcedony
H: 22 inches
Marks: K Fabergé, Imperial Warrant, assay mark of
Moscow 1908–17, inv. no. 16798

Stylized swans dominate this unusual covered tureen of
chased silver set with semiprecious stones. The birds'
heads serve as handles, while their wings fan out over the
vessel. The domed cover is chased with oak leaves, dol-
phins, and geometric patterns, and the flared base is covered with stylized seaweed. Despite the aquatic nature of
the ornamental program, from a distance, the tureen recalls the helmet of a medieval Russian *bogatyr* warrior.

Provenance: Sotheby's, London, May 8, 1972, lot 221z
(urn and cover only)

Collection of Sydney and Frances Lewis

— 156 —

MONUMENTAL *KOVSH*
Silver, chrysoprase, amethysts
H: 15 inches
Marks: K Fabergé, Imperial Warrant, assay mark of
Moscow 1896–1908, French import mark

Armored *bogatyr* warriors astride galloping horses charge off this enormous silver cup made in the shape of a traditional wooden drinking vessel. Worked in the Old-Russian style, the piece was possibly inspired by the epic paintings of Viktor Vasnetsov. A similar *kovsh*, also dominated by the legendary warriors of medieval Russia, has been linked to Vasnetsov's paintings and is now in the Forbes Magazine collection (Habsburg/Lopato 1994, cat. 232). Fabergé's Moscow workshops regularly responded to the demand for Old-Russian-style pieces,

made as part of a Slavic revival that affected literature, architecture, and fine arts during the second half of the nineteenth century. Chunky semiprecious stones and stylized Old-Russian motifs invest the cup with additional barbaric richness.

Provenance: Christie's, New York, October 18, 1994, lot 642

Private Collection

Fig. 1. *Marjorie Merriweather Post and Ambassador Joseph E. Davies in front of*
Spasso House, Moscow, 1937. Photo: Courtesy Associated Press.

Marjorie Merriweather Post

A Collector Discovers Imperial Russia

In 1935 Marjorie Merriweather Post (1887–1973),[1] sole heiress to the Post cereal empire, philanthropist, and art collector, married her third husband, Joseph E. Davies, a political friend and supporter of Franklin D. Roosevelt. In November 1936 Roosevelt appointed Davies the second U.S. ambassador to the Soviet Union. Davies, a lawyer, had no background in matters dealing with the Soviet Union or even with foreign policy in general. While his eighteen-month tenure in Moscow has been viewed with disdain by foreign service officers and historians ever since, the adventure was a major turning point in Post's life, and it would change dramatically the direction of her art collecting (fig. 1).

Post was a collector by nature, having been encouraged by her father, a collector of Victoriana from many countries. In the 1920s, at the time of her marriage to Edward F. Hutton, she began to assemble French eighteenth-century furniture, tapestries, and Sèvres porcelain. She had outgrown the heavy neo-Renaissance furnishings with which she had begun her married life with Edward Close in 1905, and started to develop a preference for the style of interior decoration she would retain for the rest of her life (fig. 2). In these years she received advice and encouragement from the art dealer Joseph Duveen, from whom she bought furniture, and attended classes on tapestries and textiles at the Metropolitan Museum of Art. Even when she later began to focus on Russian art, Post preferred the Louis XVI style for most of her rooms.

In addition to collecting antiques for furnishings and porcelains to use on her dinner tables, Post favored small, finely crafted objects, such as gold boxes and etuis of various shapes. It was probably because of this interest that she purchased in 1926 her first piece of Fabergé, a box with a spinel carving of a lion mounted in diamonds on an amethyst quartz box (cat. no. 162). The box came from the Yusupov collection, which was being dispersed, as were those of many émigré aristocrats. After the 1917 Russian Revolution émigrés often said that they "ate their jewels" to survive after escaping to the West.

For Post new collecting possibilities opened up when she went to the Soviet Union in 1937. In the early 1920s the Soviet government had sold off some of the gems and jewelry confiscated from the imperial family and nobility following the revolution. By 1928, as he consolidated his power, Joseph Stalin authorized much broader sales of imperial treasure. Attempts had been made to interest Western antique dealers in everything from chandeliers to Fabergé to linens from the imperial household to liturgical objects and icons removed from churches.[2] Armand Hammer, who had business interests in the USSR, played the largest role in helping the Soviets dispose of what they considered the detritus of the imperial court. Hammer claimed that by 1929 the future of his pencil factory in Moscow was uncertain and that he exchanged the factory for permission to export his art collection. It is more likely that he sold art for the Soviet government.[3] Once back in

Fig. 2. *Drawing Room, Hillwood, 1960s. Photo: Courtesy Hillwood Museum.*

New York, Hammer began selling Russian objects, which would soon appear in the collections of Lillian Thomas Pratt, India Early Minshall, Matilda Geddings Gray, and later, Marjorie Merriweather Post.

By the time the ambassador and his wife arrived in Moscow in January 1937, the sale of Russian objects in commission shops in both Moscow and Leningrad was on the decline; Davies complained to his daughter Eleanor that "in general the supply has been well picked over."[4] Collecting Russian art appears to have been initially Joe Davies's passion. He noted in his diary on January 27, 1937, "Went to a Commission Art Store and had a field day seeing canvases by modern Soviet artists. They are fascinatingly interesting."[5] The very next day he indicated that he and Marjorie had been to see an art exhibition again and that he "secured several fascinating oils (snow, revolu-

tionary, etc.) for my University of Wisconsin Collection."[6] On March 9 he wrote Governor La Follette of Wisconsin of his desire to give a collection of icons and paintings to the university, his alma mater. The Associated Press reported that although the Davieses had made numerous shopping trips to the commission shops, "their purchases, except for contemporary paintings, have not been great."[7]

It was in these commission shops, which operated like thrift shops for antiques, where individuals could bring their treasures to sell, that Post found the objects which became the nucleus of her Russian collection. (Later the Davieses would be taken to government storerooms as well.) She often talked about purchasing silver gilt chalices for the equivalent of five cents per gram weight, the going price of silver, and finding vestments in heaps on the floor in some corner. These now form an important part of her collection. She purchased porcelain, some glass, many silver vodka cups and tumblers, and most of the Russian furniture now at Hillwood, her Washington residence, at this time. There is no evidence that Post purchased any of the approximately ninety pieces of Fabergé (and certainly none of the major ones) now in the collection during her stay in the Soviet Union. The possible exception is a Fabergé display case, which was purchased in the Moscow years, although precisely where is unknown (see fig. 5).[8] She even shopped in Fabergé's St. Petersburg store, then converted to a commission shop, but few if any Fabergé treasures were left. Most Fabergé items had already been bought up by Hammer (whose brother Victor continued to make buying trips throughout the 1930s), Alexander Schaffer of A La Vieille Russie, Emanuel Snowman of Wartski in London, and others.

The Davieses spent the summer of 1937 traveling around the Baltic on the *Sea Cloud*, Post's yacht, visiting the leaders of the Baltic capitals to fulfill FDR's request for reports on the prospects of war with Germany. Post and Davies punctuated diplomatic meetings with shopping trips to antique stores. It is more likely that Post found a few pieces of Fabergé in Helsinki, Stockholm, Oslo, Riga, or Tallinn than in Russia. In London in 1938 Davies purchased a fifty-first birthday present for his wife, a Fabergé clock mounted as a miniature table (cat. no. 174), and later that year he gave her a grand birthday in Moscow.

Only after she left the Soviet Union and returned to Washington, and especially after the war, did Post begin to collect Russian art in earnest. As she began a new social life in the capital, she realized her Russian objects not only attracted great interest but were unlike anything other Washington collectors owned. In 1943 she exhibited paintings (mostly twentieth century), icons, vestments, and porcelain at the War Relief Center in Washington for a fund-raiser.[9] This public attention surely quickened her desire to pursue collecting things Russian.

Post divorced Davies in 1955, bought and renovated Hillwood, and in 1957 moved in. By this time she had decided to give her collection to the nation; thus she designed her new home to suit her lifestyle and to show off her collection of French and Russian objects (fig. 3). Post presented Hillwood to the Smithsonian Institution in 1968, retaining a lifetime residency. She died in 1973. After man-

Fig. 3. *Icon Room, Hillwood, 1960s. Photo: Courtesy Hillwood Museum.*

aging Hillwood for three years, the Smithsonian decided to return the property to the Marjorie Merriweather Post Foundation of the District of Columbia, which administers the Hillwood Museum today.

Post's Fabergé treasures should be considered in the context of her entire collection, particularly the Russian objects, which constitute about one-third of the total collection. She was recognized initially as a collector of icons, liturgical objects, porcelain, glass, and silver. Of the articles written about her in the 1940s and 1950s which take notice of her collection, only one, a *Vogue* article of 1945, mentions her Fabergé vitrine and the one imperial egg then in her collection (cat. no. 175). Journalists might have focused on icons and liturgical objects, which were Davies's particular interests, because these items, not Fabergé, best represented Post's Moscow collecting.

Further, the name of Fabergé had not yet acquired the cachet it possesses today. Dealer A. Kenneth Snowman's first book on Fabergé only appeared in 1952. Hammer Galleries had mounted an exhibition the year before, to which Post loaned 335 Russian objects, approximately 40 of which were (or she thought were) by Fabergé. Of these, 25 are definitely by Fabergé and remain at Hillwood. Aside from two imperial Easter eggs, most of the pieces are small boxes and picture frames. Post was generous with loans of her Russian objects to both Hammer Galleries and A La Vieille Russie during the 1950s and early 1960s. In 1955

Fig. 4. *Marjorie Merriweather Post at Tregaron, her Washington estate, 1945. Photo: Courtesy* Vogue.

both galleries compiled lists of sales to Post at the time Davies and Post divorced. These lists indicate that between 1940 and 1955, Post had purchased porcelain in large quantities and only a very few pieces of Fabergé.[10]

Post was fascinated by the members of European royalty and the Russian imperial family who frequented New York and Palm Beach, Florida.[11] In 1923 she was among those who welcomed Grand Duchess Xenia Aleksandrovna, sister of Czar Nicholas II, to Palm Beach, which probably explains her interest in a cane handle (cat. no. 165) that once had belonged to the grand duchess.[12] In 1929 Post gave a lunch at Palm Beach for Grand Duke Aleksandr Mikhailovich,[13] and Grand Duchess Maria Pavlovna gave a talk in New York in 1931 at Post's home to aid a hospital charity.[14] Both Aleksandr and Maria had written books that were then circulating in the United States.[15]

Post's interest in the Russian imperial family was not immediately reflected in purchases of Fabergé objects.

Unlike Pratt, Minshall, and Gray, Post did not buy at Armand Hammer's department store sales or from the Hammer Galleries in the 1930s. Once she began collecting Russian art, however, she acquired portraits of the czars and many objects that the czars, from Peter the Great to Nicholas II, had owned, commissioned, or presented as gifts to others.

Post appears to have acquired only three pieces of Fabergé before she went to the Soviet Union. Her appreciation of these objects, for both their neoclassical style and fine workmanship, was an extension of her response to eighteenth-century French gold boxes, which she had collected in the 1920s. Of the two imperial eggs at Hillwood, the 1914 egg (cat. no. 175) with pink enamel panels in the style of François Boucher (a gift from her second daughter, Eleanor, in 1931) happily combines her love of the French Louis XVI style and Fabergé's brilliant handling of four-color gold and enameling techniques.[16] She kept the imperial eggs, with other special treasures such as the nuptial crown worn by Alexandra at her marriage to Nicholas II in 1894, in her Fabergé vitrine (fig. 5).

Fig. 5. *Fabergé vitrine, Icon Room, Hillwood, 1960s. Photo: Courtesy Hillwood Museum.*

Post purchased frames by both Fabergé and Cartier for her own use (cat. nos. 167, 171–73). Although she acquired frames with photographs of members of the imperial family, she used many for miniatures of herself and her daughters. In an age when photographs were rendering miniatures on ivory obsolete, Post commissioned hand-painted miniatures of her family members. Some of these are copies of oil paintings or even photographs (see cat. nos. 171, 172).

On the basis of the many fine objects she collected, especially by Fabergé, it seems fair to say that Post had a real love for carved hardstones. The rococo clock of bowenite mounted in silver (cat. no. 170), the quartz basket (cat. no. 160), and a seal with an emerald quartz handle (cat. no. 164) are just a few examples. Post assembled a special collection of objects made from bloodstone, her birthstone, which she kept, along with eighteenth-century English etuis and boxes, on a table in her bedroom (fig. 6).

Post preferred to display a mass of similar objects together—a wall vitrine with cups and saucers, or pink Sèvres porcelain, or Russian figurines; a table full of bloodstone objects or military orders. She wrote a young collector, "When I began I did it for the joy of it, and it was only as the collections grew and such great interest was evidenced by others, that I came to the realization that the collection should belong to the country."[17]

In 1958 Post hired a curator, Marvin C. Ross, to catalogue her Russian collection. Ross, who had been a curator of Byzantine and decorative arts at the Walters Art Gallery, Baltimore, attempted to direct Post's acquisitions of Russian art toward styles and periods not represented in her collection. Post often took his advice, but not always. There are frequent notes on Ross's memos (Post was quite deaf toward the end of her life, and Ross's communication with her was by memo): "not interested," "too expensive," "I don't need that." In 1963 Ross suggested that she

Fig. 6. *Post's bedroom, Hillwood, 1960s. Photo: Courtesy Hillwood Museum.*

Fig. 7. Marjorie Merriweather Post in the Icon Room at Hillwood, late 1960s.
Photo: Courtesy Hillwood Museum.

might add extra vitrines in the pavilion of her home; she had recently placed one there. Her response was, "This I do not like at all. I think you have heard me hold forth quite a number of times about not getting Hillwood too crowded and too full. It is bad enough the way it is and I am definitely in the mood to stop any further acquisition, unless there is some very outstanding article."[18] (There are now six vitrines in the pavilion.) Post, like so many collectors before her who have vowed to stop, could not. Ross persisted with suggestions, and she continued to buy, making many significant purchases in the late 1960s.

In 1964 Ross was writing his book *The Art of Peter Karl Fabergé and His Contemporaries* (1965). It is clear that his research led him to suggest more Fabergé objects to Post, and she bought at least six Fabergé pieces in 1964 and at least twenty between 1964 and 1969. One of the most important of these later items is the Yusupov music box (cat. no. 207) purchased from the estate of Lansdell K. Christie

in 1966. Ross rightly called it a "true museum piece—and historic" when he successfully convinced Post to pay the asking price. As had been the case when she found Washington society interested in her Russian collection in the 1940s, the public fascination for Fabergé in the 1960s led Post to collect his work with more vigor.

Marvin Ross and Post together gave several public lectures on her collection, including one in 1963 at Williamsburg and one in 1968 at Palm Beach. In both Ross discussed everything from her French furniture to her silver chalices, while Post told stories about their acquisition. As if saving the best for last, they finished both talks with illustrations of her two imperial eggs, the first Fabergé box she had acquired, and a bloodstone bell push with an elephant (cat. no. 166). In sheer quantity, however, the number of Fabergé objects illustrated was small in comparison to the liturgical objects and porcelain. Fabergé remained for Post a treasured part of a much larger whole. Fabergé's creations represented the culmination of two centuries of imperial art, and they attained the technical virtuosity of eighteenth-century French boxes, which had been Post's first love. To the end Post admired the perfectly crafted object.

—Anne Odom
Chief Curator
Hillwood Museum, Washington, D.C.

NOTES

1. Post married four times. Davies was her third husband. After her divorce from her last husband, Herbert May, she took back her maiden name, which is how we refer to her today. In books written between 1958 and 1964, objects from her collection are identified as from the collection of Mrs. Herbert May.

2. See Sir Martin Conway, *Art Treasures in Soviet Russia* (London: Edward Arnold, 1925), and Germain Seligman, *Merchants of Art, 1880–1960: Eighty Years of Professional Collecting* (New York: Appleton-Century-Crofts, 1961), for two accounts of the Soviets' attempts to entice Western dealers into buying Russian objects in the 1920s.

3. Armand Hammer with Neil Lyndon, *Hammer* (New York: G. P. Putnam's Sons, 1987), p. 189. No one who knew Hammer in the 1920s, when he held court in Brown House, recalls a Russian collection, although there is mention of the general opulence of the house and the many paintings on its walls. Robert C. Williams, *Russian Art and American Money* (Cambridge: Harvard University Press, 1980), chap. 6, and Joseph Finder, *Red Carpet* (New York: Holt Rinehart and Winston, 1983), pp. 67–69, explore whether Hammer was buying and warehousing art objects for future use, taking them in trade for his factory, or selling on commission. It seems increasingly obvious in light of new information on Hammer's role in laundering money for the Soviet government that he sold art for them as well; see Harvey Klehr, John Earl Haynes, and Fridrikh Igorovich Firsov, *The Secret World of American Communism* (New Haven: Yale University Press, 1995),
pp. 26–30.

4. Joseph E. Davies, *Mission to Moscow* (New York: Simon and Schuster, 1941), p. 131.

5. Ibid., p. 29.

6. Ibid., p. 30.

7. Associated Press, April 17, 1937. Post subscribed to a clipping service, and all newspaper and magazine articles about the family were pasted into albums. These are now in the Bentley Historical Library at the University of Michigan with the Post family papers.

8. Knowledge of what Post acquired in the Moscow period comes from several sources, but there are no invoices for these purchases. Post told many stories of her discovery of chalices and vestments, and she annotated her Moscow scrapbooks, which are also part photo albums. Thus we know Davies gave her a Fabergé clock (cat. no. 174) for her birthday. An additional source is an inventory of the contents of the ambassador's residence in Belgium, dated May 9, 1939 (Davies became ambassador to Belgium after leaving Moscow in June 1938), although only large items are listed. The Fabergé vitrine appears on this inventory.

A missing invoice, however, does not necessarily indicate that an object was purchased during the Moscow years (this applies to Post's entire collection). Post received many items, including Fabergé, as gifts. After her death, Marvin Ross, her curator, tried to collect all invoices relating to the collection from her downtown Washington business office but was only partially successful. Furthermore, some surviving bills are not specific enough to be enlightening ("one Fabergé box," "one Fabergé frame").

9. *Washington Star*, April 4, 1943.

10. When the Davies divorced, their Russian collection was split between them. In some cases Post later bought back objects from the Davies estate.

11. Nancy Rubin titles her biography of Post *American Empress* (New York: Villard, 1995) with good reason.

12. *New York Herald*, February 17, 1923. A note signed by Grand Duchess Xenia in 1927 states that the cane handle came from her collection. It is unclear if Post acquired it in that year.

13. *New York Herald-Tribune*, March 1, 1929.

14. *New York Sun*, June 18, 1931.

15. Grand Duchess Maria's memoir, *Education of a Princess* (New York: Viking Press) was published in 1930, Grand Duke Aleksandr's *Once a Grand Duke* (New York: Farrar and Rinehart) in 1932.

16. Post purchased the other imperial egg, with diamond monograms on blue enamel of Alexander III and his wife, Maria Feodorovna, in 1949 from an Italian collector, a Mrs. G. V. Berchielli, who might have been a friend of Frances Rosso, wife of the Italian ambassador in Moscow from 1936 to 1941. Rosso, an American, and Post remained friends until the former's death in 1969.

17. Post family papers, Michigan Historical Collections, Bentley Historical Library, University of Michigan, reel 13.

18. Memorandum from Ross to Post, dated August 1, 1963. Hillwood's archives are still in the process of being organized, and further citation of some materials is not possible. Ross's papers about the Post collection are at Hillwood.

Catalogue

Marjorie Merriweather Post Collection

Marjorie Merriweather Post's Fabergé collection today numbers about ninety pieces. From these, twenty-one have been selected that best reflect her life as a collector (cat. nos. 157–75, 193, 207), including the celebrated Catherine the Great egg (cat. no. 175).

— 157 —

KOVSH
Silver gilt, enamel
L: 4 inches
Marks: Fabergé, Imperial Warrant, assay mark of
Moscow 1908–17, 88, inv. no. 32770

This *kovsh* (drinking vessel) is in the neo-Russian style of dark, muted enamels and stylized ornament typical of the work of Fedor Rückert, Fabergé's chief enameler in the Russian style. The miniature is a detail of the bridal couple from Konstantin Makovski's most famous painting, *The Boyar Wedding Feast*, now at the Hillwood Museum. Post had the *kovsh* long before the painting, which came to Hillwood in 1968. Although she preferred the rococo and neoclassical styles of Fabergé's St. Peters-

burg workshops, Post had a large collection of Moscow enamels as well.

Bibliography: Ross 1965, p. 84, pl. 31

Exhibitions: Hammer 1951; Hammer 1952

Hillwood Museum, Washington, D.C., 15.36

— 158 —

VASE

Silver

H: 12 ⁷⁄₁₆ inches

Marks: Fabergé, initials of workmaster Julius Rappoport, assay mark of
St. Petersburg before 1896, 88, inv. no. 3471

The vase, mounted with coins and medals of the Russian
emperors and empresses from Peter I to Alexander III,
must have been a presentation gift at some ceremony related to St. Petersburg, perhaps to a delegation coming
to the city in the 1890s.

Provenance: Parke-Bernet, New York, 1952

Bibliography: Taylor 1983, p. 19

Hillwood Museum, Washington, D.C., 12.184

— 159 —

WATCH FOB
Gold
L: 5⅞ inches
Marks: Initials of workmaster Erik Kollin, assay mark of
St. Petersburg before 1896; on clasp, initials MD in Roman letters
and assay mark of St. Petersburg before 1896

Kollin made a specialty of using gold coins in his creations, very often as the handle of a small *charka*. Here he devised a watch fob with three coins from the reign of Catherine II in ascending order of size, with a smaller one from the reign of Empress Elizaveta Petrovna dangling off to the side. Post received this as a Christmas gift from her husband, Joseph E. Davies, in 1951.

Provenance: Wartski, London, 1951

Bibliography: Ross 1965, pp. 35–36; Taylor 1983, p. 37

Hillwood Museum, Washington, D.C., 11.79

— 160 —

BASKET
Gold, rose quartz, diamonds, emerald, pearl
H: 1⅝ inches
Marks: Fabergé, initials of workmaster Mikhail Perkhin, assay mark of
St. Petersburg before 1896

Perkhin perfectly harmonized a green emerald thumb piece with the rose quartz in this small basket, which was a gift from Davies to Post, probably in the 1940s.

Bibliography: Taylor 1983, p. 41

Exhibitions: Hammer 1952

Hillwood Museum, Washington, D.C., 11.240

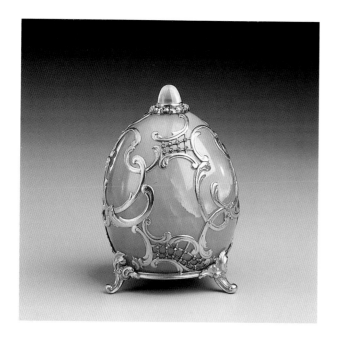

— 161 —

EGG-SHAPED BELL PUSH
Gold, bowenite, diamonds, moonstone
H: 2¹⁵⁄₁₆ inches
Marks: Fabergé, initials of workmaster Mikhail Perkhin,
assay mark of St. Petersburg before 1896, inv. no. 50466

This egg-shaped bell push is typical of rococo-revival
pieces by Mikhail Perkhin in the 1890s. An agate egg at
Hillwood is similarly mounted (Ross 1965, p. 26). Davies
bought this bell push in London and gave it to Post in
1951.

Provenance: Wartski, London, 1951

Bibliography: Taylor 1983, p. 20

Exhibitions: Hammer 1951; ALVR 1961, cat. 228; Zurich 1989, cat. 89

Hillwood Museum, Washington, D.C., 11.74

— 162 —

BOX WITH LION
Gold, diamonds, emeralds, amethyst quartz, spinel
H: 2⁹⁄₁₆ inches
Marks: Fabergé, initials of workmaster Mikhail Perkhin, assay mark
of St. Petersburg before 1896

This box is the first Fabergé object acquired by Post. Purchased from the Yusupov collection at Cartier in 1926,
the box is a composite. The lid is composed of a lion
carved from a spinel, surrounded by an irregular circle of
emeralds and large, crudely cut diamonds. The lion is
most likely a Mogul piece of jewelry, possibly a family
heirloom, which Perkhin mounted onto an amethyst
quartz base.

This box was probably made for Felix Sumarokov-
Elston, who took the name Yusupov when he married
Zenaïde Yusupov, the last in the family line. He was the
father of the better-known Felix Yusupov, one of the
murderers of Rasputin.

Provenance: Felix Yusupov; Cartier, New York, 1926

Bibliography: Ross 1965, p. 17; Taylor 1983, p. 48

Exhibitions: Hammer 1952; ALVR 1961, cat. 98; Zurich 1989, cat. 1

Hillwood Museum, Washington, D.C., 11.62

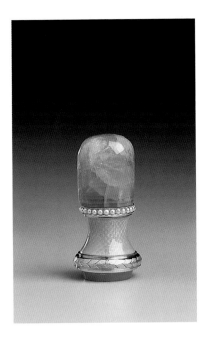

— 163 —

LEAF-SHAPED BOX
Gold, bloodstone, diamonds
D: 2⁹⁄₁₆ inches
Marks: Initials KF, assay mark of Moscow 1896–1908, assay master
Ivan Lebedkin, inv. no. 17117

Fabergé converted ordinary bloodstone, Post's birth-stone, to an art nouveau leaf-shaped box. This is a very unusual and sophisticated box for the Moscow work-shops, which were better known for silverware and enameling in the Russian style. For another leaf-shaped box see cat. no. 110.

Provenance: The Antique Porcelain Company, New York, 1968

Bibliography: Taylor 1983, p. 41

Exhibitions: Zurich 1989, cat. 3

Hillwood Museum, Washington, D.C., 11.219

— 164 —

HAND SEAL
Gold, emerald quartz, enamel, pearls
H: 1½ inches
Marks: Initials of workmaster Henrik Wigström; assay mark of
St. Petersburg 1908–17, 72

This small hand seal is a fine example of Fabergé's har-monious combination of hardstone and enamel, en-hanced with just a row of small pearls and a gold band of chased laurel leaves. Post and her husband, Joseph Davies, assembled a very large collection of seals, mostly of hardstone, while they were in the Soviet Union.

Bibliography: Ross 1965, p. 43, pl. 15

Exhibitions: Hammer 1951; Hammer, 1952

Hillwood Museum, Washington, D.C., 11.221

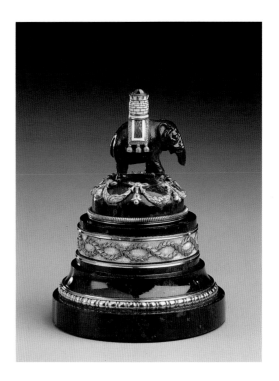

— 165 —

CANE HANDLE

Nephrite, gold, diamonds, rubies, enamel

H: 3⅝ inches

Marks: Initials of workmaster Mikhail Perkhin, assay mark of
St. Petersburg 1896–1908, assay master Iakov Liapunov

This cane handle came with a note dated November 5,
1927, signed by Grand Duchess Xenia Aleksandrovna,
saying that it had been part of her Fabergé collection.
Xenia was the daughter of Alexander III and the sister of
Nicholas II; Post met her in the 1920s.

Provenance: Grand Duchess Xenia Aleksandrovna

Bibliography: Ross 1965, p. 19, pl. 6; Taylor 1983, p. 28

Exhibitions: Hammer 1952; Zurich 1989, cat. 42

Hillwood Museum, Washington, D.C., 11.66

— 166 —

ELEPHANT BELL PUSH

Bloodstone, gold, diamonds, ruby, enamel

H: 2¹¹⁄₁₆ inches

Marks: Initials of workmaster Mikhail Perkhin, assay mark of
St. Petersburg 1896–1908, assay master Iakov Liapunov

Elephants were popular in Fabergé's work, particularly
during the reign of Alexander III, whose wife, Maria
Feodorovna, was a Danish princess. (The Order of the
Elephant was the highest award of Denmark.) This bell
push reportedly once was among Maria Feodorovna's
belongings at the Anichkov Palace. This is only one of
many objects at Hillwood in bloodstone, Post's birth-
stone.

Provenance: Czarina Maria Feodorovna (unverified)

Bibliography: Ross 1965, p. 19, pl. 5

Exhibitions: Hammer 1952; ALVR 1961, cat. 226

Hillwood Museum, Washington, D.C., 11.65

— 167 —

BOWENITE FRAME
Bowenite, gold, ivory
H: 3⁷⁄₁₆ inches
Marks: Fabergé, initials of workmaster Mikhail Perkhin, assay mark
of St. Petersburg before 1896

The bowenite panel of the frame is mounted in gold.
Framing the miniature is an oval ring of red gold intertwined with a garland of leaves in green gold. The miniature of Post, signed by a Russian-born American, Sonia
Engalicheff, is after a 1952 painting by Douglas Chandor
(1897–1953), which now hangs at Hillwood.

Bibliography: Ross 1965, p. 22, frontispiece; Taylor 1983, p. 6

Hillwood Museum, Washington, D.C., 11.70

— 168 —

FRAME ON STAND
Agate, gold, diamonds, rubies, enamel, ivory, mother-of-pearl
H: 3⁷⁄₁₆ inches
Marks: Fabergé, initials of workmaster Victor Aarne, assay mark of
St. Petersburg 1896–1908, assay master Iakov Liapunov, inv. no. 3358

This tiny salmon-colored frame is decorated with Victor
Aarne's ornate bowknots and green gold leaves, top and
bottom. Post purchased this frame without a miniature.
In 1970 her curator, Marvin C. Ross, located this miniature on ivory of Nikolai Yusupov. The portrait is identical to one of three formerly in the Yusupov egg (see
Snowman 1953, ills. 392, 393). When Maurice Sandoz
purchased the egg, the miniatures were removed and replaced by the letters MYS, his initials. It is thus likely that
this miniature was originally in the Yusupov egg.

Bibliography: Ross 1965, p. 48

Exhibitions: Hammer 1943; Hammer 1951; Hammer 1952; ALVR 1961,
cat. 194; ALVR 1983, cat. 86; Zurich 1989, cat. 108

Hillwood Museum, Washington, D.C., 11.86

— 169 —

BOX

Nephrite, gold, ivory

D: 3⅛ inches

Marks: Fabergé, initials of workmaster Henrik Wigström, assay mark
of St. Petersburg 1896–1908, assay master A. Richter, inv. no. 311099

A Hillwood curatorial file photograph shows this box
holding a miniature of a woman in early nineteenth-
century dress. The present miniature of the Czarevitch
Alexei, dated about 1916, was apparently substituted
sometime before 1955, when Post purchased it.

Provenance: Mrs. Humphrey Butler, London, 1935

Bibliography: Ross 1965, p. 24, pl. 13

Exhibitions: London 1935, cat. 596; ALVR 1961, cat. 97;
Zurich 1989, cat. 2

Hillwood Museum, Washington, D.C., 11.82

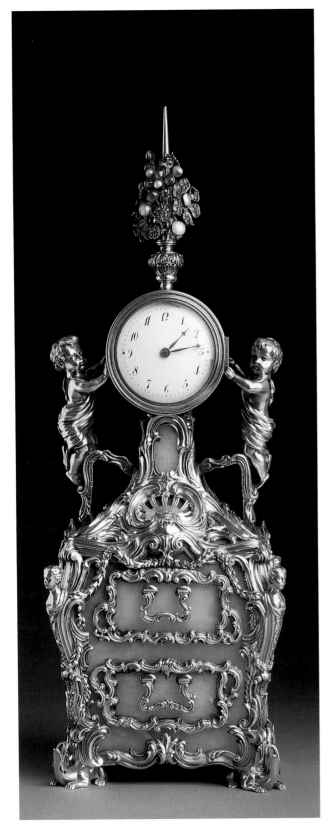

— 170 —

IMPERIAL TABLE CLOCK
Silver gilt, bowenite, ivory
H: 11¼ inches
Marks: Initials of workmaster Julius Rappoport, assay mark of
St. Petersburg 1896–1908; works marked "H. Moser & Cie"

Inspired by a clock attributed to James Cox (now in the Walters Art Gallery, Baltimore), which had belonged to Czarina Alexandra, this clock is a splendid example of how Fabergé both copied and altered models. Both clocks are in the shape of commodes and have figures at the top supporting the works. The Fabergé clock has drawers and side panels that open to reveal portraits on ivory of Nicholas and Alexandra.

This clock is visible in a photograph of the dowager empress's case in the 1902 exhibition of Fabergé in the von Dervise House on the English Embankment in St. Petersburg. The photograph shows a small bird perched on the top of the finial, holding a baroque pearl in its beak (see Habsburg/Lopato 1994).

Provenance: Dowager Empress Maria Feodorovna;
Hammer Galleries, 1956

Bibliography: Ross 1965, pp. 65–66; Taylor 1983, p. 51; Habsburg 1987, cat. 280; Habsburg/Lopato 1994, cat. 3

Exhibitions: St. Petersburg 1902; Munich 1986–87, cat. 280; St. Petersburg/Paris/London 1993–94, cat. 3; WAG 1995

Hillwood Museum, Washington, D.C., 12.155

— 171 —

FRAME WITH FLOWER BASKET
Gold, diamonds, rubies, pearls, ivory
H: 4⁵⁄₁₆ inches
Marks: Fabergé, initials of workmaster Mikhail Perkhin, assay mark
of St. Petersburg 1896–1908, assay master Iakov Liapunov,
inv. no. 8003; side engraved "Nedenia 1936"

The surface of the frame is in white *guilloché* enamel. A basket of flowers, in diamonds and rubies, hangs from a bowknot of gold. The miniature of Nedenia Hutton (actress Dina Merrill), Post's third daughter, was painted by M. Rae of New York from a photograph of her as a young girl.

Bibliography: Ross 1965, p. 29

Exhibitions: Hammer 1937

Hillwood Museum, Washington, D.C., 11.68

— 172 —

FRAME WITH OAK AND LAUREL LEAVES
Gold, enamel, ivory
H: 3⁷⁄₁₆ inches
Marks: Initials of workmaster Mikhail Perkhin, assay mark of
St. Petersburg before 1896

Two sprays, one of oak leaves, the other of laurel leaves, mounted on a blue-gray translucent enamel background decorate the frame. These sprays, symbols of strength and victory respectively, imply that the frame was originally intended for a portrait of a military figure. Italian artist Altea Luzi painted the miniature of Nedenia Hutton (actress Dina Merrill), Post's daughter, after a Hollywood studio photograph.

Bibliography: Ross 1965, p. 24

Exhibitions: ALVR 1961, cat. 192

Hillwood Museum, Washington, D.C., 11.69

— 173 —

GREEN ENAMELED FRAME
Gold, enamel, pearls
H: 3⅛ inches
Marks: Fabergé, initials of workmaster Victor Aarne, assay mark of
St. Petersburg 1896–1908, assay master Iakov Liapunov,
French import mark ET (1893–1938)

The delicate but lush swags of flowers and leaves and the
ornate bowknot at the top are typical of Victor Aarne's
workmanship. The photograph depicts an unknown
woman.

Bibliography: Ross 1965, p. 49; Taylor 1983, p. 46

Hillwood Museum, Washington, D.C., 11.87

— 174 —

ENAMELED CLOCK
Silver gilt, gold, pearls, enamel
H: 3½ inches
Marks: Fabergé, initials of workmaster Henrik Wigström,
assay mark of St. Petersburg 1908–17, 88

This pink enameled clock is mounted to create a miniature table. The neoclassical ornamentation of two-color
gold swags, Corinthian columns, and crossed scepters
is typical of Henrik Wigström's style. The clock was
among the first pieces of Fabergé Post owned. It was a
fifty-first birthday gift from Davies when they were in
Moscow in 1938.

Provenance: Wartski(?), London, 1938

Bibliography: Ross 1965, pp. 40–41

Exhibitions: Hammer 1951; Hammer 1952; Zurich 1989, cat. 113

Hillwood Museum, Washington, D.C., 11.89

— 175 —

IMPERIAL CATHERINE THE GREAT EASTER EGG
Gold, diamonds, pearls, enamel
H: 4¾ inches
Marks: Engraved Fabergé, initials of workmaster Henrik Wigström,
assay mark of St. Petersburg 1908–17

A gift from Czar Nicholas II to his mother, Maria Feodorovna, this Easter egg in the French Louis XVI style
was designed by Henrik Wigström. Vasilii Zuiev painted
the two pink and white enamel panels *en camaïeu* with
miniature allegorical scenes of the arts and sciences after
François Boucher. Alternating with smaller enameled
ovals, featuring putti with attributes of the seasons, are
musical instruments, tools of the arts and sciences, and
trophies in four-color gold mounted on cream *guilloché*
enamel. Under a table diamond at the top are the initials
of Maria Feodorovna, and the date 1914 is under a diamond at the bottom.

According to a letter from Maria Feodorovna to her
sister, Queen Alexandra of England (Solodkoff 1984,
p. 78), the surprise in this egg was a mechanical sedan
chair, carried by two African servants, with Catherine
the Great seated inside. At the time the egg was invento-
ried into the Kremlin Armory Museum collection in
1922, its surprise had already been separated from it. Although the sedan chair that was formerly in the Clore
collection (illustrated in Solodkoff, p. 102) fits the de-

scription in Maria Feodorovna's letter, it is too large, and
the colors do not harmonize with the egg.

Provenance: Presented by Czar Nicholas II to his mother, Dowager
Empress Maria Feodorovna, Anichkov Palace, 1914; Kremlin Armory
Museum, 1922; GOKHRAN (State Depository of Valuables), 1927;
Kremlin Armory Museum, 1930; Antikvariat, 1930; acquired by
Armand Hammer for 8,000 rubles; given to Post by her daughter
Eleanor, 1931 (Tatiana Muntian of the Kremlin Armory Museum
has been most helpful in providing information about the
provenance of this egg)

Bibliography: Bainbridge 1949, pl. 57; Snowman 1953, ill. 347;
Ross 1965, pp. 38–39; Habsburg/Solodkoff 1979, cat. 134; Taylor 1983,
p. 48; Solodkoff 1984, p. 101; Habsburg/Lopato 1994, cat. 9

Exhibitions: Hammer 1937, pl. 10; Hammer 1943; Hammer 1951,
cat. 161 (ill.); Hammer 1952; St. Petersburg/Paris/London
1993–94, cat. 9

Hillwood Museum, Washington, D.C., 11.80

Fig. 1. *Ray Schaffer with her sons, Paul and Peter, present-day proprietors of*
A La Vieille Russie, 1984. Photo: Tom Carraway, courtesy
A La Vieille Russie, New York.

The Postwar Years

1950s–1970s

With the beginning of World War II, the chief source of Russian art, the Soviet Union, was cut off. Pieces from secondary sources—Russian émigrés and collections formed throughout the 1930s and 1940s—did appear on the market. During the 1950s Armand Hammer and Alexander Schaffer (fig. 1) helped Jack and Belle Linsky form what Mrs. Linsky liked to call "the second greatest [collection of Fabergé]—next to the English Queen's."[1] The Linskys, Russian Jews who emigrated to New York in the 1920s, sold their Swingline Staple Company for $210 million in 1970 (fig. 2). Today they are known primarily for the extraordinary gift Belle Linsky made in 1982 to the Metropolitan Museum of Art, a wonderful collection of European paintings and decorative arts acquired with great love and discernment. The Linsky collection of Fabergé eggs, snuffboxes, flowers, and animals, begun with a gold cigarette case purchased for $1,100 from Hammer in the early 1950s, was at one time the most important in the United States. But the disdainful attitude of James Rorimer, director of the Metropolitan Museum of Art, toward what he decried as their Fabergé "turn of the century trinkets" influenced the Linskys to dispose of the collection through A La Vieille Russie.[2] Their substantial holdings formed the nucleus of an exhibition held in 1961 by the Russian specialists of 290 Fabergé objects including animals, flowers, boxes, jewels, functional objects, cabinet pieces, figurines, and eggs.

In 1961 Fabergé and American furniture collectors Helen and Lansdell K. Christie (figs. 3, 4) acquired part of the Linsky collection from A La Vieille Russie.[3] Lansdell Christie (1903–65), a self-made man of quiet determination and exacting personality, was the owner of Scow Corporation, which operated the largest fleet of barges on the Hudson River, and of important iron ore mining rights in Liberia. The Christie Fabergé collection was on view and in use at their Long Island home, Les Palmiers. The more precious objects were hidden in Christie's bedroom, under his bed. The Christies first loaned 110 of their Fabergé pieces to an exhibition at the Corcoran Gallery of Art, Washington, D.C., in 1961. By 1962 the collection had grown to 175 pieces, which were put on indefinite loan at the Metropolitan Museum of Art. This exhibition was a late vindication for an infuriated Belle Linsky, who saw many of the objects once spurned by the Metropolitan as part of the display.

When Lansdell K. Christie died in 1965, his executors entrusted A La Vieille Russie with the sale of most of the Fabergé collection, with pieces left after an agreed period to be auctioned. Private sales from the collection included such choice items as the Chanticleer egg (cat. no. 210), the Kelch Hen egg (cat. no. 208), a pink sedan chair (cat. no. 16), a nephrite Nicholas II presentation box (cat. no. 194), a Nicholas II coronation box (cat. no. 203), and the firescreen frame (cat. no. 204), all acquired by Malcolm S. Forbes; the figure of Vara Panina, sold to Robert H. Smith of Bethesda, Maryland (cat. no. 197); and the Yusupov music box, sold to Marjorie Merriweather Post (cat. no. 207). Another Christie object, the Balletta box (fig. 5), a

Fig. 2. *Belle and Jack Linsky, 1964. Photo: Ed Sullivan, New York, courtesy Ms. L. Hecht and Tony Victoria, New York.*

diamond-set vanity case presented by Grand Duke Aleksei Aleksandrovich to Elizabeth Balletta, has a further American connection: Christie presented it to his esteemed friend Eleanor Roosevelt, who had admired it at a private exhibition. Mrs. Roosevelt, irked by the special security measures imposed by the high value of the gift, later asked to return it.

Other American collectors of renown from the entertainment industry in the postwar years included Kathryn and Bing Crosby,[4] who, much like European royalty, gave each other Fabergé objects to mark special occasions, and Frank Sinatra, whose collection of Fabergé comprised two important diamond-set imperial presentation boxes.[5] Robert H. Smith, a builder and developer, began collecting Fabergé in the early 1960s after seeing a Wartski ad in the American edition of *Connoisseur* magazine. He traveled to London, met A. Kenneth Snowman, and acquired a silver Fabergé statuette of a standard-bearer of the dragoon guards on horseback. Smith became a friend of Snowman's father, Emanuel, and later of Alexander and Ray Schaffer's, and was fascinated by their stories of imperial treasure. Over the years he acquired some thirty-

Fig. 3. *Lansdell K. Christie, ca. 1960. Photo: Bacharach, courtesy the Christie family.*

Fig. 4. *Helen Christie. Photo: Beidler-Viken, New York, courtesy the Christie family.*

Fig. 5. Balletta Box, *signed Fabergé, workmaster Henrik Wigström, assay mark of St. Petersburg 1908–17, gold, enamel, diamonds, l. 4 inches. Private collection.*

five major Fabergé objects, including the Cuckoo egg[6] and Dutch Colony tray[7] from Wartski, the figure of Vara Panina, and a yellow sedan chair and the Balletta box at Parke-Bernet. Smith sold his Fabergé in Geneva in 1973–74 for record prices. He is, at present, president of the National Gallery of Art, Washington, D.C., and a celebrated collector of Renaissance bronzes.

The Auction Market

Following World War I and the death of Carl Fabergé in 1920, sales of the jeweler's art temporarily came to a standstill. Seven years later, in 1927, interest revived with the publicity surrounding the acquisition of eighty Fabergé pieces from the Russian imperial collections by Emanuel Snowman of Wartski, London. A first auction dedicated to eighty-seven Fabergé objects was held by Christie's, London, on March 15, 1934, for which an illustrated catalogue was issued. Other sales of jewels and objects of vertu including Fabergé followed in London throughout the 1930s and the 1950s.[8] In Cairo, Sotheby's auctioned 151 Fabergé objects from the collection of King Farouk of Egypt in 1954. The most important recent auction in London was that of the Robert Strauss collection held by Christie's in March 1976.

Throughout the 1940s and early 1950s, American auctions rarely contained more than a few items of Fabergé. Parke-Bernet dispersed the first substantial offering of note on December 11, 1952, as "Gold, Silver, and Enamel, Objects of Vertu, with an extensive group of the work of

Carl Fabergé, Property of Baron Basile de Lemmerman," an aesthete and collector. Sixty-seven items (of which twenty-one were illustrated in the auction catalogue) were labeled Fabergé, many from the collections of Queen Olga and of Prince Christopher of Greece, some still retaining penciled notes from Dowager Empress Maria Feodorovna or other members of the imperial family (cat. no. 215). The top price of $1,600 was paid for a lapis lazuli figure of a dancing bear made for General Petr Aleksandrovich Polovtsov (cat. no. 213).

In New York Fabergé was generally included as part of larger sales of French eighteenth-century furnishings and objects of vertu. In such surroundings we find "Property from the Estate of Prince Vladimir Galitzine, sold by Order of a New York Private Collector" at Parke-Bernet on December 5, 1953, which included twenty-three items by Fabergé, the most expensive of which was a fine obsidian figure of a sea lion that sold for $1,000. Seven items offered at the same sale from another private collection included a nephrite box with diamond swallow ($425) and a circular blue enamel clock ($575) that had been offered originally in the 1952 Lemmerman sale. On January 15, 1955, Mrs. Harrison Williams sold at Parke-Bernet a Fabergé *carnet* with portrait miniature for $2,050 and a Kalgan jasper mouse for $400. Parke-Bernet sold items from the estate of Grand Duchess Olga Aleksandrovna (who died in Toronto in 1960) on March 18, 1967, including five items by Fabergé, among them a rock crystal cup mounted in gold by head workmaster Erik Kollin.

In a landmark auction held on December 7, 1967, Parke-Bernet sold those items in the Lansdell K. Christie collection still held by A La Vieille Russie. The sale totaled $304,375 and achieved exceptionally high prices, which exceeded those of any retail outlet. Sir Charles Clore of London acquired some of the most expensive items, including a miniature cabinet for $39,000 (resold at Christie's, Geneva, in 1985 for $280,000) and a pink enamel presentation box for $40,000 (Geneva price: $120,000).

In 1968 Sotheby's hired Robert Woolley from A La Vieille Russie, who inaugurated new specialized sales of objects of vertu, including Fabergé. They were held twice a year, generally in April and November. Woolley, promoted to head of the decorative arts department in 1974, was succeeded by Gerard Hill, who still presides over

Sotheby's Russian sales in New York. Under Hill substantial Fabergé collections were sold, including those of Fabergé Inc. (1979) and M. T. Heller II of Scottsdale, Arizona (1980).

Christie's held its first Russian sale in New York in April 1978, and from 1979 made regular spring and fall offerings, mostly as part of sales of objets d'art and silver. One exceptional event was the 1988 sale of one hundred Russian works of art from the estate of India Early Minshall of Cleveland, sold on behalf of the Western Reserve Historical Society. These items had been considered not of sufficient merit to join the works of art by Fabergé bequeathed by Minshall to the Cleveland Museum of Art.

In 1969 Christie's, Geneva, began holding auctions containing Fabergé and Russian art which became regular events from 1973. These were organized by this author, later with the help of Alexander von Solodkoff. Following the sale of some exceptional Fabergé items from the Robert H. Smith collection, the Swiss auctions attracted increasing American interest. Smith's 1900 Cuckoo egg was acquired in November 1973 by Bernard C. Solomon of Los Angeles for a then record price of 620,000 Swiss francs (approximately U.S.$250,000). Sold again in 1985 for $1.76 million, it became the eleventh egg in the Forbes collection, which took the lead over the Kremlin Armory Museum's ten eggs. From the late 1970s until the mid-1980s Geneva was a mecca for American Fabergé buyers, with virtually every major collector and dealer making obligatory appearances at the May and November auctions. These sales, which in November 1981 included as many as two hundred pieces by Fabergé, brought many new buyers to the market.

One of these was James Williams, a Fabergé collector and dealer from Savannah, Georgia, who is best known as an unlikely hero of a best-selling history of notorious Savannah celebrities, *Midnight in the Garden of Good and Evil* by John Berendt.[9] Williams was a keen buyer of any object with royal connotations and, most particularly, of any Fabergé with an imperial provenance. His regular visits to the Geneva biannual sales began in 1977, and his most important purchase was an imperial presentation box, acquired in 1980 for $70,000.[10] In May 1981 Williams was arrested for the shooting of a friend, Danny Hansford, at his palatial Savannah mansion. While awaiting trial, he obtained permission to travel to a Geneva auction where he acquired a Fabergé flower. Convicted of murder, he was sentenced to serve a life term. Following an overturned verdict and a retrial, he was jailed from September 1983 until July 1985. His incarceration did not hinder him from bidding by telephone at Christie's Geneva sales, although he masked the origin of his calls. Williams was finally acquitted in May 1989. By this time he had been obliged to sell much of his collection of imperial Fabergé to pay his legal costs. He died in January 1990. Two pairs of imperial cuff links (cat. nos. 351, 352) are relics of this unusual personality.

Daniel Witek of Buffalo, New York, was another of the more colorful figures gravitating to the Geneva Fabergé sales. This self-styled English earl, who claimed to be a godson of the king of Norway, artfully penned his correspondence with old-fashioned quills on cream paper embossed with a crest and coronet, and peppered his conversation with references to his relationship to royalty, including "his cousin" the Queen of England. Witek collected and dealt in Fabergé, and credited himself with building up the collections of several major American clients. He invited friends and clients to excellent dinners, preferably at the Connaught Hotel in London. Here waiters called him "my lord" and catered to his whims. In 1991 he disappeared from the United States, was arrested in Switzerland, extradited, and incarcerated at Riker's Island. According to the tabloid press, he passed bad checks to three New York jewelers for £250,000 worth of diamonds and emeralds, which he claimed to be purchasing as a present for Britain's Princess Margaret.[11] FBI agents investigated the whereabouts of a number of Fabergé objects allegedly consigned to him by clients but never paid for.

In the late 1970s, Sotheby's Russian sales held in Zurich were transferred to Geneva, joining those of Christie's. At present both firms hold biannual sales, but the American buying contingent has virtually evaporated. The last major Fabergé sale in Geneva was that of the collection of Sir Charles Clore, held by Christie's in 1985.

—Géza von Habsburg

NOTES

1. See Gary Graffman, "The Natural," *Connoisseur* (June 1983), p. 90.

2. Ibid., pp. 87–95.

3. The Linsky collection formed the nucleus of the A La Vieille Russie 1961 exhibition. For an intimate portrait of Christie, see A. Kenneth Snowman, in Cooper 1963, pp. 240–49.

4. Susan Colgan, "Kathryn Crosby and the Romance of Fabergé," *Art and Antiques* 6, no. 3 (May/June 1983), pp. 80–83.

5. Auctioned at Christie's, New York, December 1, 1995.

6. Illustrated in Solodkoff 1984, p. 80.

7. Illustrated in Habsburg/Solodkoff 1979, p. 43.

8. Sales held in London by Christie's between 1930 and 1955 include: "A Collection of Objects of Art and Vertu designed by Carl Fabergé formed by Alistair McKelvie, Esq.," July 5, 1937, lots 88–171; "Jewelry, Objects of Art and Vertu designed by Carl Fabergé, the Property of Madame Nicholas Fabergé and a Lady," May 16, 1938, lots 64–104; "The Vagliano Collection of Important Objects of Vertu by Carl Fabergé," July 13, 1955, lots 34–50. Sotheby's finest sale of Fabergé was that of the Eckstein collection, on February 8, 1949.

9. John Berendt, *Midnight in the Garden of Good and Evil* (New York: Random House, 1994). For Williams's Fabergé acquisitions, see pp. 16–17, 294.

10. Christie's, Geneva, May 12, 1980, lot 269.

11. "We Help Trap Royal Diamond Diddler," *News of the World*, January 12, 1992.

Catalogue

---◆---

1950s–1970s

After the Hammer Galleries discontinued sales of Russian art objects in the 1950s, A La Vieille Russie became the chief source of Fabergé pieces for American collectors.

The first fifteen objects in this section (cat. nos. 176–90) form part of the bequest of Helen Babbott Sanders to the Brooklyn Museum, New York. She was a daughter of Frank L. Babbott, member of the Brooklyn Museum board, its president from 1920 until 1928, and one of the chief benefactors of the museum. As a member of the museum's acquisition committee, always interested in excellence in art, Helen Babbott Sanders shared her family's interest in Italian paintings and left to the museum a number of Renaissance works, including Palma Vecchio's *Venus and Mars*. Most of her Fabergé objects were acquired from A La Vieille Russie in the 1950s.

Cat. nos. 191–210 were formerly in the collection of Helen and Lansdell K. Christie. Many of them previously belonged to collectors Jack and Belle Linsky. The Christie collection at one time numbered 175 Fabergé pieces. All of them were on view at the Metropolitan Museum of Art between 1962 and 1965 as the first examples of the art of a twentieth-century jeweler ever shown at that institution.

Cat. nos. 211–16 were acquired by a lady of distinction from Parke-Bernet, New York, in the 1950s.

In addition to several objects once owned by Lansdell K. Christie, Paul and Peter Schaffer have loaned cat. nos. 217–27 from the collection of A La Vieille Russie, New York.

— 176 —

DOG

Agate, diamonds

L: 1½ inches

The barking, playful dog is of honey-colored agate, with rose-cut diamonds for eyes.

Bibliography: Habsburg 1987, cat. 351, p. 203

Exhibitions: ALVR 1983, cat. 432; Munich 1986–87; Houston 1994

The Brooklyn Museum, New York, 78.129.5

— 177 —

MOUSE

Citrine, diamonds

L: 1⅛ inches

Original fitted case stamped with Imperial Warrant, St. Petersburg, Moscow

A mouse with rose-cut diamond eyes is seated on an up-turned saucer. The piece was copied from a Japanese netsuke.

Bibliography: Habsburg 1987, cat. 352, p. 203

Exhibitions: Munich 1986–87; Houston 1994

The Brooklyn Museum, New York, 78.129.7a–b

— 178 —

CAT

Agate, diamonds

L: 1½ inches

A striated agate cat with rose-cut diamond eyes stands with its back arched and tail raised.

Bibliography: Habsburg 1987, cat. 353, p. 203

Exhibitions: ALVR 1983, cat. 432; Munich 1986–87; Houston 1994

The Brooklyn Museum, New York, 78.129.4

— 179 —

BLACK BEAR
Obsidian, rubies
L: 1¼ inches

Seated on its hindquarters, the bear has cabochon ruby eyes.

The Brooklyn Museum, New York, 78.129.12

— 180 —

RABBIT
Obsidian, diamonds
L: 1¾ inches
Original fitted case stamped with Imperial Warrant,
St. Petersburg, Moscow

The seated rabbit has rose-cut diamond eyes.

Bibliography: Habsburg 1987, cat. 357, p. 203
Exhibitions: Munich 1986–87; Houston 1994

The Brooklyn Museum, New York, 78.129.8a–b

— 181 —

BEAR CUB
Bowenite, rubies
L: 2 inches

The cub has cabochon ruby eyes.

Bibliography: Habsburg 1987, cat. 359, p. 203
Exhibitions: Munich 1986–87; Houston 1994

The Brooklyn Museum, New York, 78.129.10

— 182 —

LAMB

Agate, rubies

L: 2 inches

Original fitted case stamped with Imperial Warrant,
St. Petersburg, Moscow

The reclining lamb is of pinkish agate and has cabochon ruby eyes.

Bibliography: Habsburg 1987, cat. 358, p. 203

Exhibitions: ALVR 1983, cat. 369; Munich 1986–87; Houston 1994

The Brooklyn Museum, New York, 78.129.a–b

— 183 —

BULL

Nephrite, diamonds

L: 2⁵⁄₁₆ inches

Original fitted case stamped with Imperial Warrant,
St. Petersburg, Moscow

The bull charges with lowered head. Its eyes are rose-cut diamonds.

Bibliography: Habsburg 1987, cat. 355, p. 203

Exhibitions: Munich 1986–87; Houston 1994

The Brooklyn Museum, New York, 78.129.3a–b

— 184 —

FROG

Jade, rubies, gold

L: 2 inches

The seated green hardstone frog has gold-mounted ruby eyes.

Bibliography: Habsburg 1987, cat. 354, p. 203

Exhibitions: Munich 1986–87; Houston 1994

The Brooklyn Museum, New York, 78.129.11

— 185 —

MISTLETOE SPRIG
Rock crystal, nephrite, moonstones, gold
H: 5½ inches
Original fitted case stamped with Imperial Warrant

A spray of mistletoe, with nephrite leaves, moonstone
berries, and gold stalk, stands in a rock crystal vase
carved to simulate water.

Bibliography: Habsburg 1987, cat. 391, p. 214; Solodkoff 1988, p. 65

Exhibitions: ALVR 1968, cat. 337; ALVR 1983, cat. 460;
Munich 1986–87; Houston 1994

The Brooklyn Museum, New York, 78.129.13a–b

— 186 —

DANDELION PUFF BALL
Asbestos fiber, diamonds, gold, nephrite, rock crystal
H: 7½ inches

This is the finest extant example of a popular floral composition by Fabergé. For a discussion of the use of natural dandelion fluff by Fabergé, see cat. no. 57.

Provenance: A La Vieille Russie, New York

The Brooklyn Museum, New York, 78.129.17a–c

— 187 —

CLOCK

Lapis lazuli, jade, diamonds, enamel, gold

H: 2¾ inches

Marks: Fabergé, initials of workmaster Henrik Wigström, 72

The clock has an opalescent white enamel dial with gold hands and a green jade bezel with diamond-set tied ribbons. The case is carved from a block of lapis lazuli.

Bibliography: Habsburg 1987, cat. 252, p. 174

Exhibitions: ALVR 1983, cat. 104, p. 56; Munich 1986–87; Houston 1994

The Brooklyn Museum, New York, 78.129.1

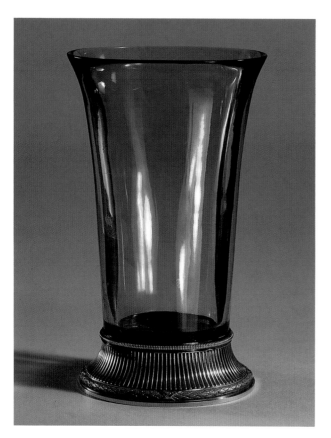

— 188 —

VASE

Topaz, gold

H: 8⅞ inches

Marks: Fabergé, initials of workmaster Mikhail Perkhin, assay mark of St. Petersburg 1896–1908, 72

Original fitted case stamped with Imperial Warrant

This vase was considered by Henry C. Bainbridge (1966) as "perhaps the most beautiful thing Fabergé ever made."

Provenance: Given by Grand Duke Aleksei Aleksandrovich to Elizabeth Balletta, prima ballerina at the Imperial Michael Theater in St. Petersburg

Bibliography: Bainbridge 1966, p. 8, pl. 7; Habsburg 1987, cat. 277, p. 182

Exhibitions: London 1935, cat. 504; ALVR 1961, cat. 261; San Francisco 1964, cat. 135; ALVR 1968, cat. 366; ALVR 1983, cat. 309; Munich 1986–87; Houston 1994

The Brooklyn Museum, New York, 78.129.18a–b

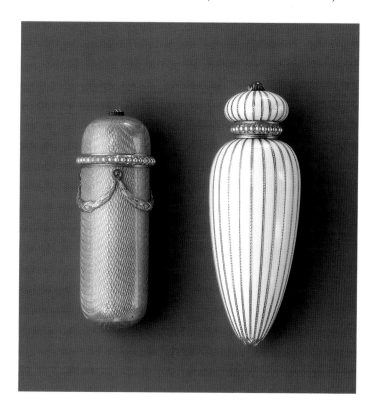

— 189 —

GREEN ENAMEL SCENT BOTTLE
Gold, enamel, diamond, seed pearls
H: 2⅛ inches
Marks: Initials of workmaster Mikhail Perkhin(?), assay mark of
St. Petersburg 1896–1908

This cylindrical scent bottle is of lime green *guilloché*
enamel; it has a seed pearl border and a diamond finial.

The Brooklyn Museum, New York, 78.129.19

— 190 —

WHITE ENAMEL SCENT BOTTLE
Gold, enamel, cork
H: 2¾ inches
Marks: Initials of workmaster Henrik Wigström, assay mark of
St. Petersburg 1896–1908, assay master A. Richter, inv. no. 11232
Original fitted case stamped with Imperial Warrant,
St. Petersburg, London

This ovoid scent bottle is decorated with opaque white
enamel stripes.

The Brooklyn Museum, New York, 78.129.6a–b

— 191 —

DOUBLE MARRIAGE CUP
Gold
H: 3⅝ inches
Marks: Fabergé, initials of workmaster Mikhail Perkhin,
assay mark of St. Petersburg before 1896, inv. no. 41819
Original fitted case stamped K Fabergé

This modern interpretation of a Gothic double marriage
cup is unusual for its geometric elements and its imaginative and technically challenging use of four colors of
gold.

Provenance: Lansdell K. Christie, Long Island;
Sir Charles Clore, London

Bibliography: Snowman 1962, pl. XXIX; Habsburg 1987, cat. 161

Exhibitions: Corcoran 1961, cat. 46; MMA 1962–65;
V&A 1977, cat. O22; Munich 1986–87

Lent by courtesy of A La Vieille Russie, New York

— 192 —

NEPHRITE *KOVSH*
Nephrite, gold, enamel, diamonds, pearl
L: 2½ inches

Provenance: Lansdell K. Christie, Long Island; A La Vieille Russie,
New York

Bibliography: McNab Dennis 1965, p. 234 (ill.); Solodkoff 1984,
p. 165 (ill.); Kelly 1985, p. 23 (ill.)

Exhibitions: MMA 1962–65, L.62.8.160

The Forbes Magazine Collection, New York

— 193 —

STATUETTE OF PETER THE GREAT
Gold, emerald
H: 1⅜ inches
Marks: Fabergé, initials of workmaster Mikhail Perkhin, assay mark of
St. Petersburg 1896–1908, inv. no. 8875

This statuette is a miniature replica of the famous statue
of Peter the Great by Étienne-Maurice Falconet in Senate
Square in St. Petersburg, commissioned by Catherine the
Great to commemorate the centennial of Peter's ascent to
the throne. Engraved in both English and Latin on the
side of the emerald is the inscription found on the Falconet statue, "Peter I, Catherine II, 1782."

Provenance: Elizabeth Balletta, 1935; Lansdell K. Christie, Long Island;
A La Vieille Russie, New York, 1966

Bibliography: Taylor 1983, p. 41

Exhibitions: London 1935, cat. 506; ALVR 1961, cat. 264;
Corcoran 1961, cat. 10, p. 31, ill. p. 45; MMA 1962–65

Hillwood Museum, Washington, D.C., 11.61

— 194 —

IMPERIAL PRESENTATION BOX
Nephrite, gold, diamonds
L: 3¾ inches
Marks: Fabergé, initials of workmaster Henrik Wigström, assay mark
of St. Petersburg 1908–17, inv. no. 4909

The lid of the box is applied with a miniature by Vasilii
Zuiev of Czar Nicholas II wearing the uniform of the
Fourth Rifle Battalion of Guards and the Cross of the
Order of St. George, which he was awarded in 1915.

Provenance: Presented by Czar Nicholas II to an unidentified person,
1915–16; Mrs. J. M. Jacques, England; Lansdell K. Christie,
Long Island; A La Vieille Russie, New York

Bibliography: Bainbridge 1949, pl. 125(b); Snowman 1953, pl. 122;
Snowman 1962, pl. 130; Bainbridge 1966, pl. 127; Waterfield/Forbes
1978, pp. 52, 54, 130, 132, 135, ill. p. 55; Snowman 1979, p. 122 ill.;
Solodkoff 1984, pp. 25, 173, ill. pp. 26, 173; Kelly 1985, p. 23, ill. p. 22;
Hill 1989, pp. 22, 140, pl. 118; Habsburg/Lopato 1994,
cat. 146, p. 280 ill.

Exhibitions: Wartski 1949, cat. 259, pp. 3, 21; Wartski 1953,
cat. 158, p. 16; MMA 1962–65, L.62.8.156; V&A 1977, cat. L9, p. 73;
ALVR 1983, cat. 216, p. 77, ill. p. 79; St. Petersburg/Paris/
London 1993–94

The Forbes Magazine Collection, New York

— 195 —

DANCING PEASANT

Chalcedony, purpurine, marble, agate, jasper, gold, sapphire,
H: 5¼ inches

This figure of a dancing and possibly inebriated peasant is
one of a series of hardstone figures created by Fabergé
portraying the common Russian laborer.

Provenance: Lansdell K. Christie, Long Island;
A La Vieille Russie, New York

Bibliography: Cooper 1963, ill. p. 249; McNab Dennis 1965, p. 236,
cat. 13; Waterfield/Forbes 1978, p. 42, ill. p. 41

Exhibitions: MMA 1962–65, L.62.8.151; V&A 1977, cat. L13, p. 74;
ALVR 1983, cat. 480, p. 132, ill. p. 134

The Forbes Magazine Collection, New York

— 196 —

PEASANT WOMAN

Amazonite, chalcedony, aventurine quartz, nephrite, jasper, purpurine,
and other Russian hardstones, cabochon sapphires, silver gilt
H: 4⅞ inches
Marks: Inv. no. 56003

This peasant woman is one of Fabergé's folkloristic figures, some of which were made for the Russian imperial
family.

Provenance: Lansdell K. Christie, Long Island

Bibliography: Cooper 1963, p. 249; McNab Dennis 1965, p. 236, ill. 13

Exhibitions: ALVR 1961, cat. 478; MMA 1962–65, L.62.8.154

Lent by courtesy of A La Vieille Russie, New York

— 197 —

GYPSY SINGER VARA PANINA
Aventurine quartz, jasper, quartz, purpurine, calcite, and other Russian
hardstones, diamonds, gold, silver
H: 7 inches

This statuette is the largest and best known of approximately sixty to eighty hardstone figures in Fabergé's oeuvre. The figure is a portrait of the celebrated gypsy Vara Panina, who sang at Yar, Moscow's tzigane restaurant. Suffering from unrequited love for a member of zthe Imperial Guard, she committed suicide by taking poison. It is said she died at his feet, singing "My heart is breaking."

Provenance: Lansdell K. Christie, Long Island; Robert H. Smith

Bibliography: Snowman 1962, pl. XLVI; McNab Dennis 1965, fig. 14; Habsburg/Solodkoff 1979, ill. p. 156; Habsburg/Lopato 1994, cat. 194, p. 415

Exhibitions: Corcoran 1961, cat. 91, p. 54 (ill.); MMA 1962–65, L.62.8.91; V&A 1977, cat. N11; ALVR 1983, cat. 482; St. Petersburg/Paris/London 1993–94

Lent by courtesy of A La Vieille Russie, New York

— 198 —

WILD FLOWERS IN ROCK CRYSTAL POT
Chalcedony, nephrite, rock crystal, gold, rubies
H: 4¾ inches

Provenance: Richard Bradshaw; Lansdell K. Christie, Long Island

Bibliography: McNab Dennis 1965, ill. 3

Exhibitions: Corcoran 1961, cat. 85; MMA 1962–65, L.62.8.85

Lent by courtesy of A La Vieille Russie, New York

— 199 —

DAISIES IN ROCK CRYSTAL POT
Gold, rock crystal, diamonds, enamel
H: 4¼ inches

Provenance: Lansdell K. Christie, Long Island

Exhibitions: Corcoran 1961, cat. 86; MMA 1962–65

Lent by courtesy of A La Vieille Russie, New York

— 200 —

LILIES OF THE VALLEY BASKET
Gold, pearls, nephrite
H: 3⅛ inches
Marks: Fabergé, initials of workmaster Mikhail Perkhin,
St. Petersburg before 1896

This piece is similar to the larger basket of lilies of the valley in the collection of the Matilda Geddings Gray Foundation, New Orleans (cat. no. 59).

Provenance: Princess Marina, dowager duchess of Kent (daughter of Grand Duke Vladimir Aleksandrovich, brother of Czar Alexander III); Sotheby's, London, 1960; Lansdell K. Christie, Long Island; A La Vieille Russie, New York

Bibliography: Snowman 1962, pl. LXV; Cooper 1963, p. 244, ill. p. 242; Waterfield/Forbes 1978, p. 49 (ill.); Solodkoff 1984, p. 165 (ill.); Kelly 1985, p. 23 (ill.); Hill 1989, p. 22

Exhibitions: Corcoran 1961, cat. 90, pp. 15, 54, ill. p. 53; MMA 1962–65, L.62.8.90; V&A 1977, cat. L10, pp. 73–74, ill. p. 82

The Forbes Magazine Collection, New York

— 201 —

IMPERIAL SNUFFBOX IN LOUIS XVI STYLE
Gold, enamel, diamonds
L: 3¼ inches
Marks: Fabergé, initials of workmaster Mikhail Perkhin, assay mark of
St. Petersburg before 1896

This box was created in response to Czar Alexander III's
challenge to Fabergé's craftsmen that they could not produce works equal to those of the French master goldsmiths of the eighteenth century. After studying a Louis
XVI snuffbox by Joseph-Étienne Blerzy from the czar's
collection (see fig.), Fabergé workmaster Mikhail Perkhin
supervised the making of a pastiche so visibly finer (the
engine turning is more regular, the enamel less porous)
that the czar ordered both boxes to be displayed in the
Hermitage as a tribute to the extraordinary achievement
of Russian craftsmanship.

Provenance: Czar Alexander III; Czar Nicholas II; Wartski, London;
Lansdell K. Christie, Long Island; A La Vieille Russie, New York

Bibliography: Snowman 1953, pl. VI; Snowman 1962, pl. IX;
Cooper 1963, p. 244, ill. p. 245; Waterfield/Forbes 1978, pp. 13, 54, 57,
ill. p. 56; Snowman 1979, pp. 147–48; Solodkoff 1984, pp. 52, 174 (ill.);
Habsburg 1987, cat. 403, p. 222, ill. p. 223

Exhibitions: Corcoran 1961, cat. 16, p. 33, ill. p. 39; MMA 1962–65,
L.62.8.16; ALVR 1968, cat. 321, p. 122 (ill.); V&A 1977, cat. L17, p. 75;
ALVR 1983, p. 31; Munich 1986–87

The Forbes Magazine Collection, New York

*Joseph-Étienne Blerzy, Snuffbox, 1777, gold, enamel,
l. 3¼ inches. The Forbes Magazine Collection,
New York.*

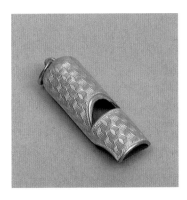

— 202 —

PINK WHISTLE
Silver, silver gilt, enamel
L: 1⅜ inches

Whistles such as this were worn as pendants around the neck.

Provenance: Christie's, London, March 1, 1960, lot 54; Wartski, London; Lansdell K. Christie, Long Island, Parke-Bernet, New York, December 7, 1967, lot 21; A La Vieille Russie, New York

Bibliography: Snowman 1962, ill. 186; Cooper 1963, p. 224 (ill.); McNab Dennis 1965, p. 229, frontispiece; Waterfield/Forbes 1978, p. 77, ill. p. 76; Solodkoff 1984, pp. 31, 169 (ill.)

Exhibitions: Corcoran 1961, cat. 72, p. 46; MMA 1962–65, L.62.8.72; Lugano 1987, cat. 74, p. 82 (ill.); Paris 1987, cat. 74, p. 78 (ill.)

The Forbes Magazine Collection, New York

— 203 —

CORONATION BOX
Gold, enamel, diamonds
L: 3¾ inches
Marks: Fabergé, initials of workmaster August Holmström, assay mark of St. Petersburg before 1896, inv. no. 1067

Similar in design to the Coronation egg (cat. no. 285), this box is thought to have been Czarina Alexandra Feodorovna's reciprocal gift to Czar Nicholas II on Easter 1897, when her husband presented her with the egg. The double-headed eagles of the Romanov family crest decorate the lid of the box, which bears Nicholas's crowned monogram set in diamonds.

Provenance: By tradition presented by Czarina Alexandra Feodorovna to her husband, Czar Nicholas II, Easter 1897; Herr Bomm, Vienna; Sidney Hill, Berry-Hill Galleries, London and New York; Wartski, London; Arthur E. Bradshaw; Lansdell K. Christie, Long Island; A La Vieille Russie, New York

Bibliography: Snowman 1962, frontispiece; Cooper 1963, p. 244, ill. p. 245; Waterfield/Forbes 1978, pp. 52, 130, 132, 135, ill. p. 51; Habsburg/Solodkoff 1979, p. 126, pl. 149; Snowman 1979, pp. 122, 125, ill. p. 122; Forbes 1980, p. 14; Solodkoff 1984, pp. 25, 173, ill. pp. 27, 173; Forbes 1986, ill. p. 57; Habsburg 1987, cat. 513, pp. 254–55, ill. p. 255; Hill 1989, pp. 22, 140, pl. 120, title page; Habsburg/Lopato 1994, cat. 105, p. 252 (ill.)

Exhibitions: Wartski 1949, cat. 5, pp. 3, 9; ALVR 1961, cat. 93, p. 43, ill. p. 49; Corcoran 1961, cat. 14, p. 33, frontispiece; MMA 1962–65, L.62.8.14; V&A 1977, cat. O14, pp. 12, 98, ill. p. 81; Munich 1986–87; Lugano 1987, cat. 95, p. 94, ill. pp. 94–95; Paris 1987, cat. 95, p. 90, ill. pp. 90–91, cover; San Diego/Moscow 1989–90, cat. 27, p. 86 (ill.); St. Petersburg/Paris/London 1993–94

The Forbes Magazine Collection, New York

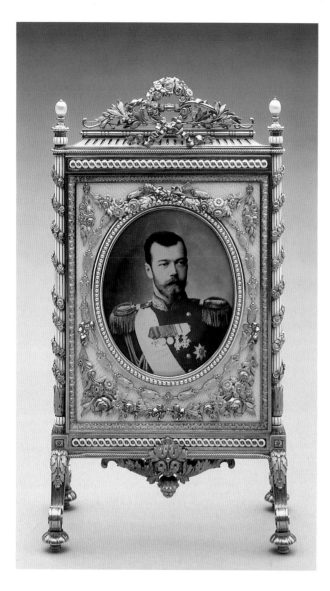

— 204 —

IMPERIAL FIRE-SCREEN FRAME
Gold, enamel, pearls
H: 7⅛ inches
Marks: Fabergé, initials of workmaster Henrik Wigström, assay mark
of St. Petersburg 1908–17, 72

This double-sided frame can be seen in a photograph of
1902 showing items from the collection of the imperial
family exhibited at the von Dervise House in St. Petersburg. It contains late photographs of Czar Nicholas II
and his wife, Czarina Alexandra Feodorovna.

Provenance: Maurice Sandoz, Switzerland; Lansdell K. Christie,
Long Island; A La Vieille Russie, New York

Bibliography: Snowman 1962, p. 147, pl. XXVII; Waterfield/Forbes
1978, pp. 62, 63, 112 (ill.); Solodkoff 1984, p. 170 (ill.); Forbes 1986,
ill. p. 55; Habsburg 1987, cat. 493, p. 245, ill. p. 246; Hill 1989, p. 22;
Habsburg/Lopato 1994, cat. 262, p. 364 (ill.)

Exhibitions: St. Petersburg 1902; ALVR 1961, cat. 183, p. 61, ill. p. 68;
Corcoran 1961, cat. 6, pp. 18, 26, ill. p. 27; MMA 1962–65, L.62.8.6;
ALVR 1968, cat. 365, p. 137 (ill.); V&A 1977, cat. L1, p. 71;
Munich 1986–87; Lugano 1987, cat. 29, p. 56 (ill.); Paris 1987,
cat. 29, p. 52 (ill.); St. Petersburg/Paris/London 1993–94

The Forbes Magazine Collection, New York

— 205 —

CIRCULAR BONBONNIÈRE
Gold, enamel
Diam: 2⅛ inches
Marks: Fabergé, initials of workmaster Henrik Wigström, assay mark
of St. Petersburg 1896–1908, 72, inv. no. 16254

This bonbonnière is a fine example of Fabergé's masterful
enameling technique. Sepia *camaïeu* paintings on an opalescent pink ground depict Falconet's statue of Peter the
Great and a statue of Catherine the Great, both in
St. Petersburg.

Provenance: Lansdell K. Christie, Long Island

Exhibitions: ALVR 1961, cat. 127; MMA 1962–65

Lent by courtesy of A La Vieille Russie, New York

— 206 —

IMPERIAL PRESENTATION *CARNET DE BAL*
Gold, enamel, seed pearls, diamonds, moonstone
H: 2⅞ inches
Marks: Assay mark of St. Petersburg 1896–1908
Original fitted case stamped with Imperial Warrant,
St. Petersburg, Moscow, Odessa

A gold plaque in the interior of this Louis XVI–style
agenda is engraved in French, "Présent de Sa Majesté
l'Empereur Nicholas II, 2 Févr. 1902."

Provenance: Presented by Czar Nicholas II to Elizabeth Balletta
of the Imperial Michael Theater, on the eve of a benefit performance
marking her tenth anniversary on the St. Petersburg stage;
Lansdell K. Christie, Long Island

Bibliography: McNab Dennis 1965, ill. 19;
Habsburg/Lopato 1994, cat. 175

Exhibitions: Corcoran 1961, cat. 73; MMA 1962–65,
L.62.8.73; ALVR 1968, cat. 340; ALVR 1983, cat. 217;
St. Petersburg/Paris/London 1993–94

Lent by courtesy of A La Vieille Russie, New York

— 207 —

YUSUPOV MUSIC BOX
Gold, pearls, enamel
L: 3½ inches
Marks: Fabergé, initials of workmaster Henrik Wigström, 72

This music box in the Louis XVI style was a gift from
Felix and Nikolai Yusupov to their parents, Felix and
Zenaïde, on their twenty-fifth wedding anniversary in
1907. The Roman numerals XXV, set in diamonds, form
the thumb piece. The initials of all four members of the
family appear at the corners. Sepia enameled panels over
a *guilloché* sunburst pattern depict six of the Yusupov
residences. They are (top) Arkhangelskoe palace outside
Moscow; (front) Moika palace, where Felix and Grand
Duke Dmitri murdered Rasputin in 1916; (bottom)
Koreiz palace in the Crimea; (back) dacha at Tsarskoe
Selo; (left) Rakitnoe palace in Kursk; (right) Moscow
palace.

When opened, the music box plays "The White
Lady" by François Boïeldieu, the regimental march of
the horse guard, Prince Felix Yusupov's regiment.

Provenance: Given by Princes Felix and Nikolai Yusupov to their
parents, Prince Felix and Princess Zenaïde Yusupov, 1907; Lansdell K.
Christie, Long Island; A La Vieille Russie, New York, 1966

Bibliography: Bainbridge 1949, pl. 4; Snowman 1962, pl. VIII;
Habsburg/Solodkoff 1979, pp. 153–54; Taylor 1983, p. 8;
Habsburg 1987, p. 256 (ill.); Habsburg/Lopato 1994, cat. 190

Exhibitions: Corcoran 1961, cat. 18, p. 18, ill. p. 32;
MMA 1962–65; ALVR 1983, cat. 222; Munich 1986–87;
St. Petersburg/Paris/London 1993–94

Hillwood Museum, Washington, D.C., 11.80

— 208 —

KELCH HEN EASTER EGG
Gold, enamel, diamonds, rubies, suede
L: (egg) 3¼ inches; (hen) 1⅜ inches
H: (easel) 1⅞ inches
Marks: Fabergé, initials of workmaster Mikhail Perkhin, assay mark of
St. Petersburg 1896–1908; dated 1898

The Kelch Hen egg, a more elaborate conceptualization of Fabergé's design for the first imperial egg, was presented by Aleksandr Ferdinandovich Kelch to his wife, Barbara. The portraits of Nicholas II beneath the table diamond and that of the czarevitch on the easel were added to the egg at a later date.

Provenance: Given by Aleksandr Ferdinandovich Kelch to his wife, Barbara, Easter 1898; Hammer Galleries, New York; King Farouk of Egypt; Sotheby's, Cairo, March 10–13, 17–20, 1954, lot 165; Lansdell K. Christie, Long Island; A La Vieille Russie, New York

Bibliography: Snowman 1953, p. 105, ill. 357; Snowman 1962, ill. pp. 111, 114, pl. LXXXII; Cooper 1963, p. 249, ill. p. 242; McNab Dennis 1965, p. 242, ill. 26; Habsburg/Solodkoff 1979, pp. 108, 120, 139, 158, cat. 58, pl. 141; Forbes 1980, pp. 5, 7, 24, 26, ill. pp. 25, 27; Solodkoff 1984, p. 185 (ill.); Solodkoff 1988, pp. 39, 47, 97; Hill 1989, p. 62, pl. 65

Exhibitions: Hammer 1939 (ill.); Corcoran 1961, cat. 3, p. 26, ill. p. 21; MMA 1962–65, L.62.8.3

The Forbes Magazine Collection, New York

— 209 —

IMPERIAL SPRING FLOWERS EASTER EGG
Egg: Gold, platinum, enamel, diamonds, bowenite
Basket and flowers: Platinum, gold, enamel, chalcedony,
demantoids, wood
H: (egg) 3¼ inches; (basket) 1½ inches
Marks: Fabergé, initials of workmaster Mikhail Perkhin, assay mark of
St. Petersburg before 1896, inv. no. 44374

The shell of the Spring Flowers egg parts to reveal a miniature bouquet of wood anemones in a platinum basket. A similar basket of flowers was used for the surprise of the Winter egg, given by Czar Nicholas II to his mother, Dowager Empress Maria Feodorovna, Easter 1913.

Provenance: Presented by Czar Alexander III to his wife, Czarina Maria Feodorovna, Easter ?; Lansdell K. Christie, Long Island; A La Vieille Russie, New York

Bibliography: Snowman 1962, pp. 81–82, pl. LXIX; Cooper 1963, ill. p. 241; McNab Dennis 1965, pp. 240, 242, ill. 22; Waterfield/Forbes 1978, pp. 8, 19–20, 110, 130, 132, 135, ill. pp. 19, 109, 115, dust jacket; Forbes 1979, p. 1237, pl. XIV; Habsburg/Solodkoff 1979, p. 157, ill. p. 159; Forbes 1980, pp. 5, 8, 10, 12, 61, ill. pp. 9, 11, 13, 61; Solodkoff 1984, pp. 12, 48, 187, ill. pp. 58–59, 187; Kelly 1985, p. 14; Forbes 1986, ill. p. 54; Habsburg 1987, p. 94; Solodkoff 1988, p. 41 (ill.)

Exhibitions: ALVR 1961, cat. 290, p. 91, ill. p. 89; Corcoran 1961, cat. 1, p. 25, ill. p. 24, dust jacket; MMA 1962–65, L.62.8.1; V&A 1977, cat. L8, p. 73; San Diego/Moscow 1989–90, cat. 9, p. 20, ill. pp. 50, 51, 89, 99

The Forbes Magazine Collection, New York

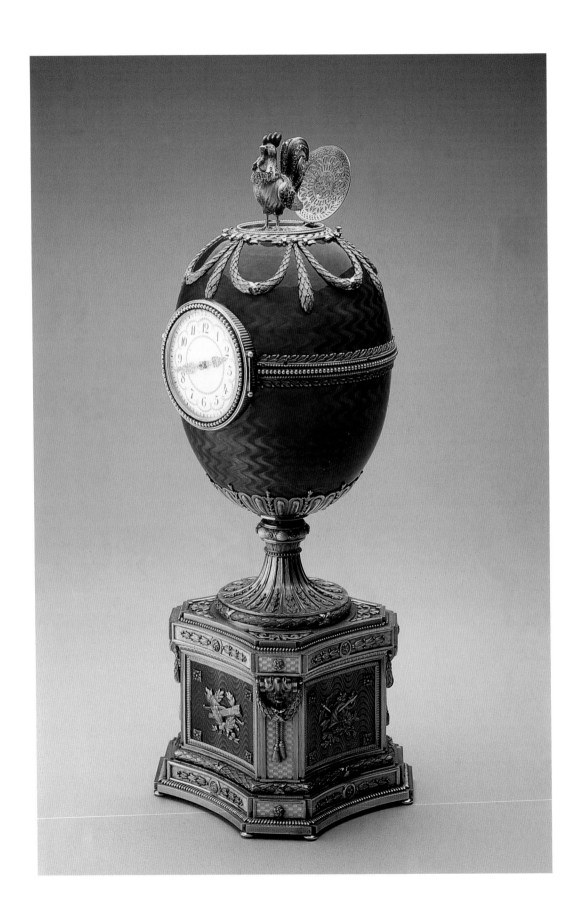

— 210 —

IMPERIAL CHANTICLEER EASTER EGG
Gold, enamel, diamonds, pearls
Original silver key
H: 12⅝ inches (open)
Marks: Fabergé, initials of workmaster Mikhail Perkhin, assay mark of
St. Petersburg 1896–1908, assay master Iakov Liapunov; dated 1903

This monumental egg in the French neoclassical style is, after the Uspensky Cathedral egg of 1904, the largest Fabergé Easter egg known today. The surprise, concealed beneath a gold grille atop the egg, is a naturalistically enameled chanticleer that emerges automatically, bobbing its head and flapping its wings to crow the hour.

Marina Lopato discussed a similar egg with pink enamel at a symposium held in the Hermitage Theater, St. Petersburg, on September 13, 1991. Her comments, combined with photographs taken in Paris in the 1920s, have led to some confusion as to whether one of the two eggs was in fact created for Barbara Kelch, the wife of Aleksandr Ferdinandovich Kelch. Two of Fabergé's sons accepted the blue egg as an imperial one, but until more period documentation becomes available, it is not possible to reach a definite conclusion.

Provenance: Presented by Czar Nicholas II to his mother, Dowager Empress Maria Feodorovna, Easter 1903; Hammer Galleries, New York; Maurice Sandoz, Switzerland; A La Vieille Russie, New York; Lansdell K. Christie, Long Island

Bibliography: Snowman 1962, pp. 94–95, ills. 343–45, pl. LXXVI; Cooper 1963, p. 249, ill. p. 241; Forbes 1979, pp. 1238, 1241, ill. p. 1238, pl. XVII; Habsburg/Solodkoff 1979, cat. 64, pp. 108, 120, 158, pls. 141, 143; Forbes 1980, pp. 5, 16, ill. p. 17, unnumbered page; Solodkoff 1984, p. 187 (ill.); Kelly 1985, p. 14, cover; Forbes 1986, p. 86, ill. p. 57; Solodkoff 1986, p. 3; Solodkoff 1988, pp. 28, 39, 40, 47; Hill 1989, p. 22

Exhibitions: Hammer 1939; ALVR 1961, cat. 295, pp. 16, 94, ill. p. 95; Corcoran 1961, cat. 2, pp. 14, 25, ill. p. 8; V&A 1977, cat. L2, p. 71, ill. pp. 71, 81

The Forbes Magazine Collection, New York

— 211 —

CHARKA
Gold, rubies
W: 3⅛ inches
Marks: Fabergé, initials of workmaster Mikhail Perkhin, assay mark of St. Petersburg before 1896

The circular, hammered bowl is set with cabochon rubies; the scrolling handle is similarly decorated.

Provenance: Czarina Alexandra Feodorovna; Baron Basile de Lemmerman, Parke-Bernet, New York, December 11, 1952, lot 44

Private Collection

— 212 —

SPHERICAL PERFUME BOTTLE
Gold, enamel, seed pearls
H: 2¾ inches
Marks: Fabergé, inv. no. 3282
Original fitted case stamped with Imperial Warrant,
St. Petersburg, Moscow

Of rich aubergine-colored enamel, the bottle is decorated with a yellow gold trelliswork sleeve at the neck and scrolls at the base. The neck and finial are set with seed pearls.

Private Collection

— 213 —

DANCING BEAR
Lapis lazuli, diamonds, silver
H: 4 inches

The wife of General Petr Aleksandrovich Polovtsov commissioned this piece as a present to him. The gift marked his cotton mill's successful production of an extremely fine black thread, known as "blue bear," for Coats, Clark, and Philippi of Edinburgh. A contemporary photograph of this bear is in a Fabergé album of photographs in the archive of the Fersman Mineralogical Institute, Moscow.

Provenance: General Petr Aleksandrovich Polovtsov, St. Petersburg; Baron Basile de Lemmerman; Parke-Bernet, New York, December 11, 1952, lot 63, for $1,600

Exhibitions: ALVR 1961, cat. 53, ill. p. 19

Private Collection

— 214 —

ENAMELED FRAME
Gold, enamel, emerald, ivory
H: 4 inches
Marks: Fabergé, initials of workmaster Mikhail Perkhin, assay mark of
St. Petersburg before 1896, inv. no. 59499

The frame of emerald green *guilloché* enamel is surmounted by a vase-shaped finial and laurel swags. Four-
color gold swags are applied above the oval aperture.

Private Collection

— 215 —

IMPERIAL HEART-SHAPED TRAY
Aventurine quartz, gold, enamel, diamonds, pearls
L: 5 inches
Marks: Inv. no. 3318
Original fitted case stamped with Imperial Warrant, St. Petersburg;
lining inscribed "Noel 1900," penciled note "Mindode, Olga"

The borders of this aventurine quartz tray are chased laurel wreaths tied with four-color gold floral swags. The
wreaths terminate in pearls and are tied with a diamond-
set knot.

Provenance: Czarina Maria Feodorovna; Queen Olga of Greece;
Prince Christopher of Greece; Baron Basile de Lemmerman,
Parke-Bernet, New York, December 11, 1952, cat. 67

Bibliography: D'Otrange 1953, pp. 139–40

Private Collection

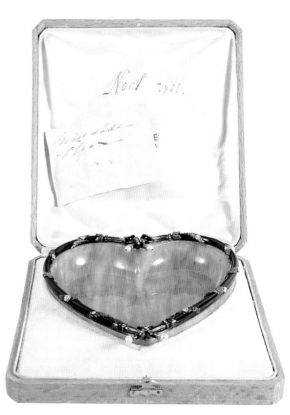

— 216 —

IMPERIAL PRESENTATION BOX
Nephrite, gold, enamel, diamonds
W: 3⅜ inches
Marks: Fabergé, initials of workmaster Mikhail Perkhin, assay mark
of St. Petersburg 1896–1908
Original fitted case

The cover of this square box is adorned with a crowned,
diamond-set cipher of Czar Nicholas II on an oval white
guilloché enamel disk. Diamond-set yellow gold rococo
scrolls are also applied.

Provenance: A La Vieille Russie, New York

Exhibitions: ALVR 1961, cat. 89, ill. p. 50

Private Collection

— 217 —

COOKING POT AND COVER
Copper, brass
H: 5 inches
Marks: Base stamped "K Fabergé, War 1914"

This cooking pot illustrates the effect of austerity measures on the Fabergé workshops during World War I.
Such pots were known to have been used by wealthy patrons to send soup to their children at the front. For an
identical pot from the India Early Minshall collection,
see Habsburg/Lopato 1994, cat. 122.

Bibliography: Habsburg 1987, cat. 19

Exhibitions: ALVR 1983, cat. 10; Munich 1986–87

Lent by courtesy of A La Vieille Russie, New York

— 218 —

MONKEY-SHAPED TABLE LIGHTER
Silver
H: 5 inches
Marks: K Fabergé, double-headed eagle, initials of workmaster
Julius Rappoport, assay mark of St. Petersburg 1896–1908,
inv. no. 7883

The seated monkey, its fur naturalistically chased, holds
its tail, which contains the wick. This is one of a series of
such lighters, most of which are shaped as various types
of monkeys.

Exhibitions: ALVR 1983, cat. 404A

Lent by courtesy of A La Vieille Russie, New York

— 219 —

CLOISONNÉ ENAMEL *KOVSH*
Silver gilt, enamel
L: 4¾ inches
Marks: Initials of workmaster Fedor Rückert, assay mark of
Moscow 1896–1908, inv. no. 20712
Original fitted case stamped with Imperial Warrant,
St. Petersburg, Moscow, Odessa

Although struck only with Rückert's initials, this *kovsh*, a
traditional Russian drinking vessel, was retailed by
Fabergé, as shown by the original fitted case. The style
of the shaded cloisonné enamels denotes an early date in
Rückert's oeuvre, which was later strongly influenced by
neo-Russian motifs.

Lent by courtesy of A La Vieille Russie, New York

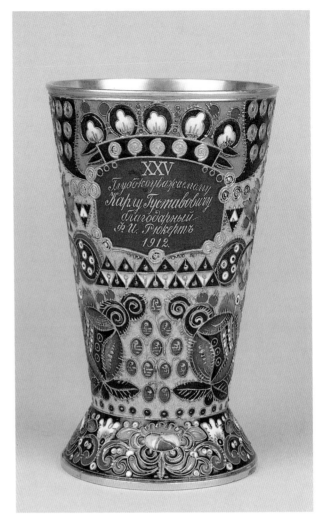

— 220 —

COMMEMORATIVE BEAKER
Silver gilt, enamel
H: 4½ inches
Marks: Initials of workmaster Fedor Rückert

One side of the beaker is painted with a view of Fabergé's
Moscow shop on the Kuznetzki Bridge, the other with the
inscription: "XXV to the highly esteemed Karl Gustav-
ovich in gratitude. F. I. Rückert 1912." This is the only
extant proof of the collaboration of Rückert, Fabergé's
main supplier of cloisonné enamels, as of the opening of
the Moscow branch in 1887.

Bibliography: Habsburg/Lopato 1994, cat. 219

Exhibitions: V&A 1977, cat. S5; ALVR 1983, cat. 55;
St. Petersburg/Paris/London 1993–94

Lent by courtesy of A La Vieille Russie, New York

— 221 —

PANAGIA
Gold, enamel, diamonds, rubies, sapphires, pearls
H: 5⅜ inches (overall)
Marks: Fabergé, initials of workmaster Henrik Wigström, assay mark
of St. Petersburg 1908–17, inv. no. 19428
Original fitted case stamped with Imperial Warrant,
St. Petersburg, Moscow, London

A Christ Pantocrator of polished cloisonné enamel is at
the center of the crowned oval *panagia* (pendant icon
worn by Russian Orthodox clerics). The image derives
from an eleventh-century border medallion on an icon
of Archangel Gabriel from Djumati Monastery in Georgia (see fig.). The icon was in the Zwenigorodski collection in St. Petersburg, where it was accessible to Fabergé.

Bibliography: Bainbridge 1966, pl. 116;
Habsburg/Lopato 1994, cat. 203

Exhibitions: ALVR 1961, cat. 88; ALVR 1983, cat. 312;
St. Petersburg/Paris/London 1993–94

Lent by courtesy of A La Vieille Russie, New York

*Byzantine medallion, 11th century, cloisonné enamel,
diam. 3¼ inches. The Metropolitan Museum of Art, New York,
gift of J. Pierpont Morgan, 1917 (17.190.678).*

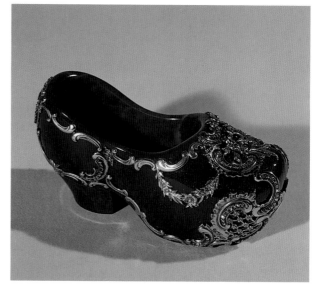

— 222 —

TRIPLE HAND SEAL
Nephrite, gold, enamel, agate, carnelian, bloodstone
H: 4 inches
Marks: Fabergé, initials of workmaster Henrik Wigström, assay mark
of St. Petersburg 1908–17, inv. no. 23818
Original fitted case stamped with Imperial Warrant,
St. Petersburg, Moscow

The triple seal has an outer agate matrix, a central carnelian matrix, and an inner engraved bloodstone seal face.
Closed, it appears to be a single standing seal.

Provenance: Given by Lillian Thomas Pratt to Ray Schaffer on
the birth of her son Paul

Exhibitions: ALVR 1983, p. 13, cat. 224

Lent by courtesy of A La Vieille Russie, New York

— 223 —

SABOT IN LOUIS XV STYLE
Bloodstone, gold, diamonds
L: 3½ inches
Marks: Inv. no. 47132

The sabot is very similar in style, and identical in size, to
a Louis XV–style bloodstone boot in the India Early
Minshall collection (cat. no. 80).

Exhibitions: ALVR 1983, cat. 270

Lent by courtesy of A La Vieille Russie, New York

— 224 —

CHIMPANZEE ON PERCH
Jasper, silver gilt, nephrite, diamonds
H: 3⅞ inches
Marks: Initials of workmaster Mikhail Perkhin, assay mark of
St. Petersburg 1896–1908, inv. no. 4184
Original fitted case stamped with Imperial Warrant,
St. Petersburg, Moscow

The mottled, reddish-brown jasper chimpanzee seated on
a perch scratches its head with its left paw. The square
base is of nephrite.

Bibliography: Snowman 1979, p. 143

Exhibitions: ALVR 1983, cat. 434

Lent by courtesy of A La Vieille Russie, New York

— 225 —

EAGLE
Smoky quartz, gold, diamonds
H: 1⅞ inches
Original fitted case stamped with Imperial Warrant,
St. Petersburg, Moscow

The eagle has rose-cut diamond eyes and chased-gold
legs and claws.

Exhibitions: ALVR 1983, cat. 436

Lent by courtesy of A La Vieille Russie, New York

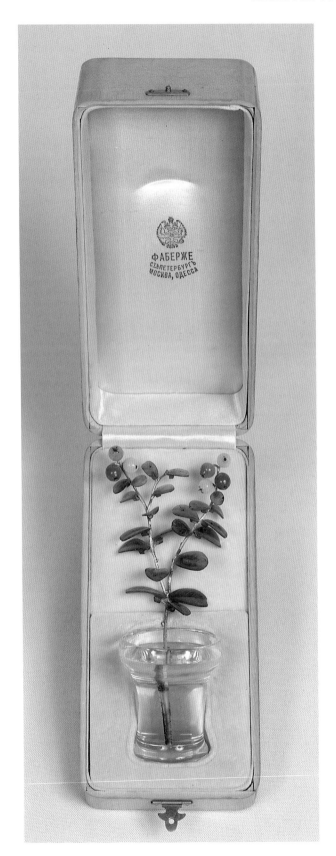

ФАБЕРЖЕ
С.ПЕТЕРБУРГЬ
МОСКВА, ОДЕССА

MOUNTAIN CRANBERRIES
Nephrite, rock crystal, carnelian, gold
H: 4¾ inches
Original fitted case stamped with Imperial Warrant,
St. Petersburg, Moscow, Odessa

A double branch of cranberries show berries in varying stages of maturity. Gold stems with nephrite leaves are in a vase of rock crystal, carved to simulate water. For a similar plant, see cat. no. 89.

Provenance: Lady Sackville West

Bibliography: Bainbridge 1966, pl. 79

Exhibitions: ALVR 1961, cat. 462

Lent by courtesy of A La Vieille Russie, New York

— 227 —

JAPANESE FLORAL COMPOSITION
Nephrite, eosite, gold, enamel, diamonds, copper
H: 6¼ inches
Marks: Inv. no. 5621
Original fitted case stamped with Imperial Warrant,
St. Petersburg, Moscow

Two dwarf pines of red and green gold and a single six-petal white enamel flower are in a nephrite, copper-lined vase. The eosite table with simulated wood grain stands on gold feet. One of Fabergé's best examples of *japonisme*, this piece illustrates the influence of Japanese art on the Russian master (see Habsburg/Lopato 1994, p. 72; see also Habsburg 1987, p. 78 for another "Japanese" flower from the Robert Strauss collection). An original Fabergé photograph of this object exists in an album at the Fersman Mineralogical Institute, Moscow.

Exhibitions: ALVR 1983, cat. 472

Lent by courtesy of A La Vieille Russie, New York
(lent to New York only)

Fig. 1. *Julian Barrow,* The Forbes Family Easter, *1983, oil on canvas,*
30 x 40 inches. Forbes Magazine Collection, New York. The Spring Flowers egg
(cat. no. 209) is displayed on the table.

The Fabergé Collection of Malcolm S. Forbes

More Than He Dreamed

Malcolm Stevenson Forbes was born on August 19, 1919, a little more than a year after Czar Nicholas II and his family were murdered by the Bolsheviks. He was the third of five sons of Bertie Charles Forbes and his wife, the former Adelaide Stevenson.

B. C. Forbes, a Scottish immigrant, achieved acclaim as an author and syndicated business columnist writing for William Randolph Hearst. In September 1917 he launched his own magazine. A month later the October Revolution brought Lenin to power in Russia. From these seemingly unrelated events was laid the foundation for a capitalist/communist competition only slightly less earth shattering than the arms race—the "eggs race."

Malcolm Forbes was an enthusiast of history and politics and, even as a young man, an avid collector. It took the then Princeton undergraduate three years to pay for his first major purchase—a note penned by Abraham Lincoln just days prior to his assassination.

Malcolm, while sharing his father's business acumen, was very different when it came to money. After seeing a swimming pool under construction down the street, he observed that these neighbors must be rich. His father tartly replied, "If they've spent it, they haven't got it anymore." When it came to collecting, Malcolm was much more his mother's son. He would recall that, during a particularly protracted argument about bills, Grandma left her canny husband stunned and speechless when she announced, "But Bert, I *like* to spend money." So did Pop.

This is obvious in his reminiscences about his lifelong fascination with Fabergé:

But, when all is said and done, our best-known collection is the Forbes Fabergé treasury. As in the other cases, we never set out to be collectors of Fabergé. What happened can be traced back to early memories of my being awed as a youngster by the photographs and history of the Russian Revolution, and remembering that some of the work of Fabergé was offered as an example of the waste and extravagance of the imperial Russian court. This made an impression on me because of the obvious irony involved. When you think about it, most reigning families are remembered not for conquests but for their support of the arts. It was the art they supported that often gave their reigns much historical significance.

For Fabergé, great hunks and gobs of precious stones were totally irrelevant. The artistry and fantasy that created these pieces gave them their extraordinary beauty. A Fabergé place setting projects a quality that an ordinary knife and fork just doesn't cut.

I caught the Fabergé bug when I was in London twenty-five or thirty years ago. In one of those totally intriguing, old-fashioned-looking jewelry stores on New Bond Street, I saw a cigarette case by

Fig. 2. *Fabergé firm,* Globe Clock Egg, *workmaster Henrik Wigström, assay mark of St. Petersburg, 1908–17, gold, rock crystal, nephrite, enamel, h. 9 inches. Forbes Magazine Collection, New York. Photo: Larry Stein.*

Fabergé. It was plain gold, decorated with the crest of the imperial Russian double eagle. I went in and bought it—I think it was less than $1,000—a presentation piece to be given by the czar as a "thank-you" for some small service. I gave it to my wife for Christmas, and she was totally thrilled with it [cat. no. 233]. So thrilled that the next Easter I went to A La Vieille Russie, then, as now, the leading Fabergé house in New York, and bought what we call a "jelly bean" egg by Fabergé. It was small, made of white enamel with a red cross [cat. no. 269]. . . .

Our first *major* egg turned out to be a gift to the Duchess of Marlborough, the American heiress Consuelo Vanderbilt, commemorating her visit to

Russia in 1902. . . . It was estimated to go for $15,000. Thirty years ago $15,000 was a lot of money—it still is to me—but I thought it would be wonderful to have such a beautiful thing. At the auction the bidding went a good deal higher than $15,000, until finally I ended up paying $50,000. I didn't sleep at all that night worrying about what auction fever had done to our exchequer. . . . The under-bidder turned out to be Mr. Alexander Schaffer, owner of A La Vieille Russie. After that sale, he introduced himself and said he assumed, because I had bid so high, that I was a "serious" collector. He took me to his shop on Fifth Avenue, opened his vault, and showed me four stunning imperial Easter eggs. I was absolutely bowled over, totally hooked from that moment forward.

So, something that I really couldn't afford led me to build a Fabergé collection that is said to be the greatest in private hands. The Queen of England has a most major collection of Fabergé; it probably numbers overall more pieces than ours. But not as many imperial eggs. She has three and the Kremlin has ten. We have twelve of these ultimate creations.[1]

Pop's pleasure in having won the eggs race was palpable. In front of special guests, he loved to tease the Honorable Caspar Weinberger that one of the reasons Weinberger had joined Forbes was that while secretary of defense he was never sure about missile superiority, whereas at Forbes he *knew* he commanded more imperial eggs.

Malcolm Forbes purchased some incredible Fabergé eggs through Alexander Schaffer, shortly after outbidding him for the Duchess of Marlborough egg (cat. no. 8), including the Renaissance egg (the last egg presented by Czar Alexander III to his wife; cat. no. 283), the Orange Tree egg (cat. no. 286), the Chanticleer egg (cat. no. 210), the Spring Flowers egg (cat. no. 209), and the Kelch Hen egg (cat. no. 208). The latter three were among the more than twenty pieces Pop ultimately acquired from the legendary collection of the late Lansdell K. Christie.

In a 1984 essay I chronicled the addition of six more imperial eggs to the collection:

Next came perhaps one of the most poignant of all the pieces created by Fabergé for his imperial patrons: the egg presented by Nicholas to Alexandra in 1911 on the Easter following the fifteenth anniversary of their coronation. Flanking miniatures of the czar, the czarina, and their five children are nine additional tiny paintings of the major events of Nicholas II's reign. . . .

Since this acquisition, five more eggs from the matchless series created by Fabergé for the imperial family have joined the Forbes Magazine Collection. These include the so-called First Imperial egg, the Resurrection egg, and the Cross of St. George egg. More modest than most of its predecessors, this last egg with its silver shell (a gesture to wartime austerity!) was the final Easter present to be delivered by Fabergé to the imperial family. In the spring of 1916, in a letter to Nicholas II, Dowager Empress Marie Feodorovna wrote:

> Christ has indeed arisen! I kiss you three times and thank you with all my heart for your dear cards and lovely egg with miniatures, which dear old Fabergé brought himself. It is beautiful. It is so sad not to be together. I wish you, my dear darling Nicky, with all my heart all the best things and success in everything.
>
> —Your fondly loving old Mama

The tragic irony of the czarina's wishes for her son's "success in everything" would be only too sadly apparent a few short years later, with the czar and his family bloodily murdered and she herself en route to exile, first in England and later in her native Denmark.

The egg was inherited by her daughter, Grand Duchess Xenia, who in turn bequeathed it to her son, Prince Vassily Romanov. *Forbes* missed its chance to buy this Fabergé egg in the early 1970s and had to wait until it had passed through several collections, including that of the internationally known perfume company of the same name, before it finally came to roost at 60 Fifth Avenue.

After several years of on-again-off-again discussions as delicate as any SALT treaty negotiations, my father was able to persuade Kenneth Snowman of Wartski in London to part with the two eggs purchased by his father in the USSR in 1927. The Coronation egg is perhaps the single best known of Fabergé's fantasies, with its miniature golden carriage which took more than fifteen months to create. The Lilies of the Valley egg is one of the firm's rare essays into the then contemporary art nouveau style.[2]

At the time I noted that "the egg hunt continues." And so it has. At Sotheby's on June 11, 1985, we bid successfully for the Cuckoo egg from the collection of record magnate Bernard C. Solomon. As the gavel came down, auctioneer Gerard Hill intoned, "The score now stands, Forbes 11, Kremlin 10."[3] Shortly afterward, through the good offices of estate jewelry expert Paul Vartanian and London's Fine Art Society, we rounded out our even dozen. The Rosebud egg, Nicholas II's first Easter egg for Czarina Alexandra Feodorovna, was thought to have been destroyed when Henry Talbot de Vere Clifton reputedly threw it at his wife during a heated quarrel (there is no record of what she might have thrown at him!).[4] Slight damage to the top of the egg helped convince me that Vartanian's client had the genuine article.

Since Pop's untimely death in 1990, my brothers and I have added a number of pieces to the collection, but only one egg. The Globe Clock egg is a tour de force of modern design but, to our knowledge, not part of the imperial egg series (figs. 2, 3).

Fig. 3. *The Globe Clock egg (fig. 2) is similar in design to this original Fabergé watercolor, dated 1917, for an Easter egg which was never made. Illustrated in Snowman 1953.*

Fig. 4. *Treasures by Fabergé, including the imperial presentation writing portfolio (cat. no. 291) and desk calendar (cat. no. 292), decorated Malcolm S. Forbes's desk. Photo: Larry Stein.*

But there is much more to Fabergé than eggs, and one of the things Pop enjoyed most about the firm's "practical" objects was their genuine functionality. For him, Fabergé bell pushes were not only a pleasure to look at but a pleasure to use. He never ceased to get a kick out of pushing the cabochon moonstone or garnet buttons of the two bowenite bell pushes that summoned either secretaries or security to his office (cat. nos. 296, 297). The date and time of day both seemed somehow better on a Fabergé nephrite calendar (cat. no. 292) and clock (cat. no. 287). Pens and pencils from a nephrite beaker (cat. no. 288), not to mention paper clips conveniently stashed in a pink agate dish (cat. no. 295), all made working that much more fun. *Forbes*

readers probably never appreciated, as much as did my father, that the drafts of his biweekly "Fact & Comment" column "marinated" in a writing portfolio that had once figured among Nicholas and Alexandra's coronation presents (cat. no. 291).

Pop had the ability to keep his desk from being overwhelmed with the daily flow of paper, so these and other Fabergé pieces reigned unobstructed on the surface (fig. 4). Alas, none of his sons has yet mastered this feat, so the functional Fabergé is no longer being pressed into service, but has joined the display in the galleries on the ground floor of our headquarters. Hopefully they are giving some of the pleasure in the viewing that Pop and other previous owners had in the using.

The Fabergé collection first went on display in the lobby of the Forbes Building after it was remodeled for the magazine's fiftieth anniversary in 1967. A special gallery to accommodate the increasing number of objects was opened in 1978. Then in 1985 my father had the entire ground floor of the building transformed by architect John Blatteau and designers Peter Purpura and Gary Kisner into a series of galleries showcasing Fabergé as well as toy boats, toy soldiers, inscribed trophies, and rotating selections from the autograph, painting, and photograph collections. These galleries are open at no charge Tuesday through Saturday from 10:00 A.M. to 4:00 P.M., and were enjoyed by almost seventy thousand visitors in 1994.

— Christopher Forbes
Vice Chairman
Forbes Inc.

NOTES

1. Malcolm S. Forbes, *More Than I Dreamed* (New York: Simon and Schuster, 1989), pp. 220–22.

2. Christopher Forbes, in Solodkoff 1984, pp. 12–13.

3. D. McGill, "Forbes 11, Kremlin 10, in Faberge Egg Race," *New York Times* (June 12, 1985), p. C21.

4. Forbes 1986, p. 86.

Catalogue

---◆---

The Forbes Magazine Collection

The Fabergé collection formed by the late Malcolm S. Forbes over twenty-five years is considered today to be the finest of its kind. Of the approximately 365 pieces that it comprises, 12 are imperial Easter eggs. Eighty-four objects (cat. nos. 8, 16, 192, 194, 195, 200–4, 208–10, 228–97) have been selected from the collection, including 6 imperial Easter eggs, among them the celebrated Coronation egg (cat. no. 285) and the exquisite Lilies of the Valley egg (cat. no. 284).

— 228 —

DECANTER WITH FABERGÉ STOPPER
Silver, cork, glass
H: (stopper) 4½ inches; (stopper and decanter) 9¾ inches
Marks: Fabergé, initials of workmaster Victor Aarne, assay mark of St. Petersburg 1896–1908

Made in the imperial glass factory in the first quarter of the nineteenth century, the decanter for which this Fabergé stopper is a replacement is etched with a portrait and monogram of Czar Alexander I.

Provenance: A La Vieille Russie, New York

Bibliography: Waterfield/Forbes 1978, p. 97 (ill.); Solodkoff 1984, p. 180 (ill.)

Exhibitions: Forbes 1987–94

The Forbes Magazine Collection, New York

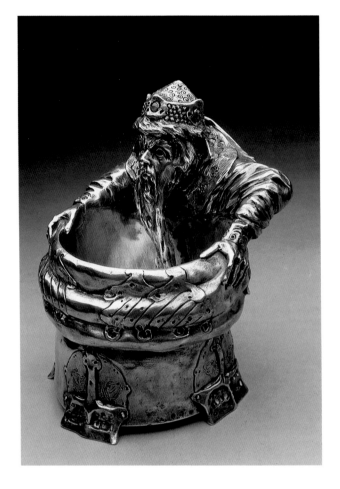

— 229 —

IVAN KALITA BOWL
Silver, silver gilt, emeralds, ruby
H: 6¼ inches
Marks: Imperial Warrant, assay mark of Moscow 1896–1908,
assay master Ivan Lebedkin, inv. no. 21310

Ivan I, caricatured here, became grand prince of Moscow
in 1325 and was grand duke of Russia from 1339–41. His
miserliness earned him the nickname Kalita (money-
bags). An almost identical piece with stone eyes was sold
at Sotheby's, Geneva, May 17, 1990, lot 162.

Provenance: Irving M. Feldstein, Chicago; Christie's, New York,
October 5, 1983, lot 415

Bibliography: Snowman 1979, p. 79, ill. p. 78; Solodkoff 1984,
p. 178 (ill.); Kelly 1985, ill. p. 12; Hill 1989, p. 223, pl. 194

Exhibitions: V&A 1977, cat. S7, pp. 127, 129 (ill.); Lugano 1987,
cat. 2, pp. 23, 24, 26, 28, 40, ill. pp. 28, 29, 40; Paris 1987, cat. 2,
pp. 19, 20, 22, 24, 36, ill. pp. 24, 25, 36; Forbes 1987–94

The Forbes Magazine Collection, New York

— 230 —

BORIS GODUNOV DESK SET
Silver, sapphire, rock crystal, *pâte de verre*
L: (inkwell) 16½ inches
Marks: Imperial Warrant, Moscow 1896–1908 and
1908–16, inv. no. 25323

The desk garniture, which includes an inkwell, a pair of
lamps, a pen rest, a letter opener, and a seal, was created
for set designer Nikolai Roerich (1874–1947) on the occasion of the production of Rimsky-Korsakov's version
of Mussorgsky's opera *Boris Godunov*. Nikolai Roerich
championed the Slavic-revival movement popular at the
turn of the century.

Provenance: Nikolai Roerich

Bibliography: Solodkoff 1984, p. 175 (ill.); Hill 1989, p. 294, pl. 273

Exhibitions: Lugano 1987, cat. 3, pp. 23–24, 26, 30, 32, 34–35, 41,
ill. pp. 32–33, 41; Paris 1987, cat. 3, pp. 19–20, 22, 26–28, 30–31, 37,
ill. pp. 28–29, 37; Forbes 1987–94

The Forbes Magazine Collection, New York

- 231 -

GRAND DUKE KIRILL VLADIMIROVICH *KOVSH*
Silver, silver gilt, amethysts
L: 8½ inches
Marks: Imperial Warrant, assay mark of Moscow 1896–1908,
assay master Ivan Lebedkin; inscribed "1914/Prize/August Patronage/
Teriokski Naval Yacht Club of His Imperial Majesty
Grand Duke Kirill Vladimirovich"

Provenance: Grand Duke Kirill Vladimirovich, son of Alexander III's
brother Vladimir and a member of the Guard Equipage

Bibliography: Solodkoff 1984, p. 173 (ill.)

Exhibitions: Forbes 1987–94

The Forbes Magazine Collection, New York

— 232 —

TWENTY-FIFTH ANNIVERSARY ICON
Silver, holly, pearls
H: 6½ inches
Marks: Fabergé, initials of workmaster Hjalmar Armfelt,
assay mark of St. Petersburg 1908–17, dated 1913, and
inscribed "Blessings from an old friend ZY"

Princess Zenaïde Yusupov was the mother of Prince
Felix Yusupov, who helped murder Rasputin. This icon
depicts the Virgin Mary in the center, flanked by St.
Sophie and St. Matthew.

Provenance: Presented by Princess Zenaïde Yusupov in 1913 to Prince
Mathias and Princess Sophie Cantacuzène on the occasion of their
twenty-fifth wedding anniversary; Dino Yannopoulos, Philadelphia

Bibliography: Solodkoff 1984, p. 172 (ill.); Kelly 1985, ill. p. 12;
Habsburg/Lopato 1994, cat. 192, p. 312 (ill.)

Exhibitions: Forbes 1987–94; St. Petersburg/Paris/London 1993–94

The Forbes Magazine Collection, New York

— 233 —

GOLD IMPERIAL PRESENTATION CIGARETTE CASE
Gold, diamonds, sapphire
L: 3¾ inches
Marks: Initials of workmaster Gabriel Niukkanen, assay mark
of St. Petersburg 1896–1908

The plain polished gold case is decorated at one corner
with the imperial eagle set with rose-cut diamonds and a
single brilliant. The thumb piece is set with a cabochon
sapphire. Similar cases were presented on many occasions to those who had faithfully served members of the
imperial family. This was the first piece of Fabergé purchased by Malcolm S. Forbes in 1960.

Provenance: Bentley & Co., London

Bibliography: Waterfield/Forbes 1978, pp. 7, 54, ill. p. 55; Solodkoff
1984, p. 7, ill. pp. 8, 174; Kelly 1985, p. 13, ill. p. 24; Forbes 1986, p. 53

Exhibitions: Helsinki 1980, cat. B8, p. 24 (ill.)

The Estate of Mrs. Roberta Forbes

— 234 —

FISH *CHARKA*
Gold, sapphire, rubies, ruble
H: 3½ inches
Marks: Fabergé, initials of workmaster Mikhail Perkhin, assay mark
of St. Petersburg before 1896, inv. no. 43596

Six goldfish of red and white gold with ruby eyes swim
around the gold *charka*, which is chased with waves. The
design was inspired by the aesthetic movement and Japanese art. The foot has six chased gold scallop shells, and
the handle is set with a gold ruble of Empress Elizaveta
Petrovna I's reign topped with a cabochon sapphire. The
charka is similar to a bowl produced by Martin Hall and
Company in 1880 which is decorated with a fish and seaweed motif in the Japanese style after Tiffany (see *Japonisme* [London: The Fine Art Society, 1991], unnumbered
catalogue).

Provenance: Sotheby's, London, June 20, 1977, lot 205

Bibliography: Waterfield/Forbes 1978, p. 97, ill. p. 96; Forbes 1980,
p. 40, ill. p. 41; Solodkoff 1984, p. 179 (ill.); Habsburg 1987,
cat. 153, p. 151 (ill.)

Exhibitions: ALVR 1983, cat. 281, p. 89 (ill.); Munich 1986–87;
Lugano 1987, cat. 9, p. 45 (ill.); Paris 1987, cat. 9, p. 41 (ill.)

The Forbes Magazine Collection, New York

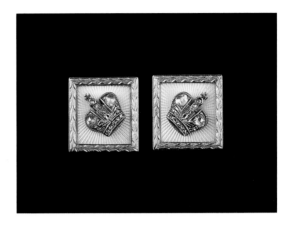

— 235 —

VODKA CUP WITH RUBIES
Gold, rubies
H: 1⅞ inches
Marks: Fabergé, initials of workmaster Mikhail Perkhin, assay mark
of St. Petersburg 1896–1908

Provenance: Wartski, London

Bibliography: Waterfield/Forbes 1978, p. 96 (ill.);
Solodkoff 1984, p. 179 (ill.)

The Forbes Magazine Collection, New York

— 236 —

IMPERIAL CROWN CUFF LINKS
Gold, enamel, diamonds
H: ½ inch (each)

The square cuff links are set with imperial crowns and
embellished with rose-cut diamonds.

Provenance: A La Vieille Russie, New York

Bibliography: Waterfield/Forbes 1978, p. 81 (ill.);
Solodkoff 1984, p. 168 (ill.)

The Estate of Mr. Malcolm S. Forbes Sr.

— 237 —

SCYTHIAN-STYLE BRACELET
Gold
Diam: 2⁵⁄₁₆ inches
Marks: Initials of workmaster Erik Kollin, assay mark
of St. Petersburg before 1896

This piece is modeled after a bracelet that was part of the
Scythian treasure, discovered in the second half of the
nineteenth century at Kerch in the Crimea. Replicas of
the Scythian treasure first won Fabergé recognition and
brought the firm to the attention of Czar Alexander III.
For an illustration of this or an almost identical bracelet
in the catalogue of the Pan-Russian Artistic and Manufacturing Exhibition in Moscow, see Habsburg/Lopato
1994, p. 57, fig. 1. A similar bracelet by Fabergé was sold
at Christie's, Geneva, May 14, 1991, lot 275.

Provenance: A La Vieille Russie, New York

Bibliography: Solodkoff 1984, p. 167 (ill.); Habsburg 1987,
cat. 88, p. 138 (ill.)

Exhibitions: ALVR 1983, cat. 348, p. 105, ill. p. 104; Munich 1986–87;
Lugano 1987, cat. 94, p. 93 (ill.); Paris 1987, cat. 94, p. 89 (ill.);
Houston 1994, p. 34 (ill.)

The Forbes Magazine Collection, New York

— 238 —

ROCK CRYSTAL BOOKMARK
Rock crystal, gold, enamel, pearl
L: 2⁷⁄₈ inches
Marks: Fabergé, initials of workmaster Mikhail Perkhin, assay mark
of St. Petersburg before 1896

Provenance: Mrs. L. D. Hirst-Broadhead

Bibliography: Waterfield/Forbes 1978, p. 90 (ill.);
Solodkoff 1984, p. 177 (ill.)

The Forbes Magazine Collection, New York

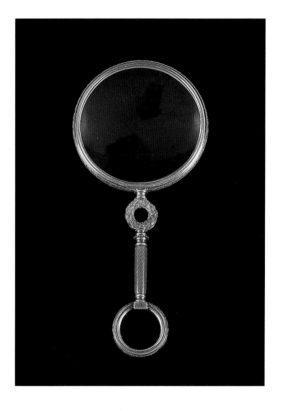

— 239 —

BOOK BLADE AND LOUPE
Rock crystal, gold, enamel
L: 3⅜ inches
Marks: Initials of workmaster Mikhail Perkhin, assay mark
of St. Petersburg before 1896, inv. no. 52664

Provenance: King Farouk of Egypt; Sotheby's, Cairo, March 10–13,
17–20, 1954, lot 117; Robert Strauss; Christie's, London,
March 9, 1976, lot 12; Wartski, London

Bibliography: Waterfield/Forbes 1978, p. 91 (ill.);
Solodkoff 1984, p. 176, ill. pp. 44, 176

The Forbes Magazine Collection, New York

— 240 —

ROUND MAGNIFYING GLASS
Glass, gold, enamel
H: 3 1/16 inches
Marks: Initials of workmaster Henrik Wigström, assay mark
of St. Petersburg 1896–1908, inv. no. 15893

The circular glass within gold mounts is chased with
green gold foliage. The red enamel handle is joined between green gold foliage circlets.

Provenance: Mrs. L. D. Hirst-Broadhead

Bibliography: Waterfield/Forbes 1978, p. 90 (ill.);
Solodkoff 1984, p. 177, ill. pp. 45, 177

The Forbes Magazine Collection, New York

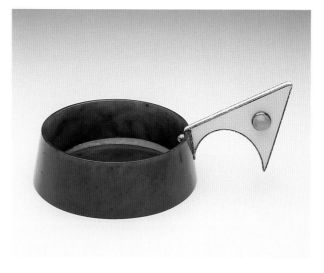

— 241 —

FIGUREHEAD *KOVSH*
Bowenite, gold, diamonds, pearl, moonstone
L: 4½ inches
Marks: Initials of workmaster Erik Kollin, assay mark
of St. Petersburg before 1896

Provenance: Mr. Theodore Case, Connecticut; Sotheby Parke Bernet,
New York, December 11, 1979, lot 340

Bibliography: Solodkoff 1984, p. 179 (ill.)

The Forbes Magazine Collection, New York

— 242 —

STYLE-MODERNE KOVSH
Nephrite, gold, enamel, moonstones
L: 5 inches

The circular nephrite *kovsh* in the modern style with gold
handles is enameled a translucent white and set on both
sides with a foiled moonstone.

Provenance: Wartski, London

Bibliography: Waterfield/Forbes 1978, p. 99 (ill.);
Solodkoff 1984, p. 179 (ill.)

The Forbes Magazine Collection, New York

— 243 —
FROG ASHTRAY
Bowenite, gold, garnets
L: 3½ inches

Provenance: Grand Duke Ernst Ludwig of Hessen-Darmstadt,
brother of Czarina Alexandra Feodorovna; David Geddes;
Christie's, London, July 24, 1979, lot 162
Bibliography: Solodkoff 1984, p. 166 (ill.)

The Forbes Magazine Collection, New York

— 244 —
FLEUR-DE-LYS BOOKMARK
Bowenite, gold, enamel, diamonds
L: 3¼ inches
Marks: Fabergé, initials of workmaster Mikhail Perkhin, assay mark
of St. Petersburg before 1896, inv. no. 56843

The bookmark is in the form of a small knife. A fleur-de-
lys of small diamonds is on the enameled handle.

Provenance: Presented by Queen Mary to her surgeon, Sir Russell
Wilkinson, K.C.V.O.; Jeremy Grantham, Boston
Bibliography: Solodkoff 1984, p. 177, ill. pp. 45, 177

The Forbes Magazine Collection, New York

 245 —

SQUARE ASHTRAY
Bowenite, gold, enamel
W: 2⅞ inches
Marks: Engraved Fabergé, initials of workmaster Henrik Wigström,
assay mark of St. Petersburg 1908–17

The square bowenite ashtray with gold rim is enameled
deep blue and white.

Provenance: Wartski, London

Bibliography: Waterfield/Forbes 1978, p. 100 (ill.);
Solodkoff 1984, p. 179 (ill.)

The Forbes Magazine Collection, New York

— 246 —

HAND SEAL
Lapis lazuli, gold, enamel, diamonds
H: 3½ inches

Provenance: Christie's, London, November 13, 1973, lot 134;
The Fine Art Society, London; A La Vieille Russie, New York

Bibliography: Waterfield/Forbes 1978, p. 91 (ill.);
Solodkoff 1984, p. 176 (ill.)

The Forbes Magazine Collection, New York

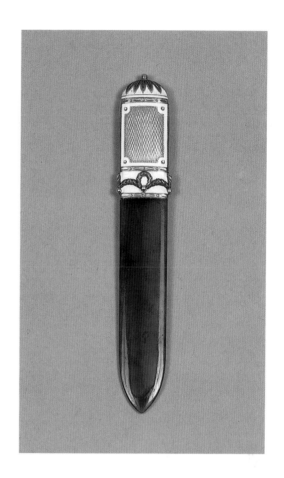

— 247 —

PAPER KNIFE
Nephrite, gold, enamel
L: 3⅜ inches

Provenance: Mrs. L. D. Hirst-Broadhead; Sotheby's, London,
December 8, 1969, lot 108

Bibliography: Waterfield/Forbes 1978, p. 90 (ill.);
Solodkoff 1984, p. 176 (ill.)

The Forbes Magazine Collection, New York

— 248 —

SQUARE MAGNIFYING GLASS
Gold, enamel, diamonds, moonstone, glass
L: 3¹⁵⁄₁₆ inches
Marks: Initials of workmaster Mikhail Perkhin, assay mark of
St. Petersburg 1896–1908, assay master Iakov Liapunov

Provenance: Presented by Queen Mary to her surgeon, Sir Russell
Wilkinson, K.C.V.O.; Jeremy Grantham, Boston

Bibliography: Solodkoff 1984, p. 177, ill. pp. 45, 177

The Forbes Magazine Collection, New York

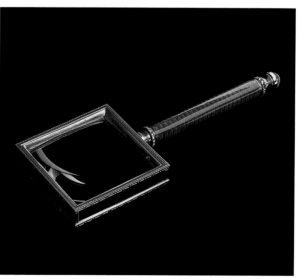

— 249 —

TWENTY-FIFTH ANNIVERSARY CLOCK
Nephrite, gold, silver gilt, enamel, diamonds, pearls
H: 6 inches
Marks: Initials of workmaster Henrik Wigström, assay mark of
St. Petersburg 1908–17, 91, inv. no. 18008

An identically shaped and decorated clock in pale blue and green enamel was formerly in the collection of Sir Charles Clore (see Solodkoff 1986, p. 34).

Provenance: Two anonymous Belgian nuns; Wartski, London; Mr. and Mrs. C. J. Byrne; Sotheby's, London, December 8, 1969, lot 86

Bibliography: Snowman 1953, ill. 130; Snowman 1962, ill. 142; Waterfield/Forbes 1978, pp. 84, 142, ill. p. 85; Solodkoff 1984, ill. p. 177; Kelly 1985, p. 23, ill. p. 22; Solodkoff 1986, p. 35 (ill.); Habsburg 1987, cat. 276, p. 181 (ill.)

Exhibitions: Wartski 1953, cat. 355, p. 29; V&A 1977, cat. L5, p. 72; Munich 1986–87; Lugano 1987, cat. 26, p. 54 (ill.); Paris 1987, cat. 26, p. 50 (ill.); Houston 1994, p. 45 (ill.)

The Forbes Magazine Collection, New York

— 250 —

IMPERIAL PRESENTATION TRAY
Nephrite, gold, enamel, diamonds
W: 23⅜ inches (at handles)
Marks: Initials of workmaster Henrik Wigström on handles,
initials of workmaster Mikhail Perkhin on plate,
assay mark of St. Petersburg 1896–1908

The large nephrite presentation tray with varicolored
gold handles is mounted with the crowned monogram of
Czar Nicholas II and Czarina Alexandra Feodorovna.
Dignitaries of the city of St. Petersburg presented the
tray to the imperial couple at their coronation in 1896. A
design for a very similar tray is in the State Hermitage
Museum, St. Petersburg (see Habsburg/Lopato 1994,
cat. 303, p. 395).

Provenance: Presented by the dignitaries of the city of St. Petersburg to
Czar Nicholas II and Czarina Alexandra Feodorovna on the occasion
of their coronation in 1896; A La Vieille Russie, New York

Bibliography: Koronatsionnyi sbornik 1899; Solodkoff 1984, p. 172 (ill.);
Kelly 1985, p. 23, ill. p. 21; Habsburg/Lopato 1994, cat. 169,
cat. 303 (drawing), pp. 297, 395

Exhibitions: ALVR 1983, cat. 292, p. 90, ill. p. 92

The Forbes Magazine Collection, New York

— 251 —

IMPERIAL REVOLVING FRAME
Silver gilt, bowenite, crystal
H: 9 inches
Marks: Fabergé, initials of workmaster Victor Aarne, assay mark
of St. Petersburg before 1896

The sixteen photographs of members of the Russian,
Danish, British, and Greek royal families are original to
the frame.

Provenance: Czarina Maria Feodorovna; a member of the Danish royal
family; Christie's, Geneva, November 19, 1979, lot 349

Bibliography: Solodkoff 1984, p. 170 (ill.); Forbes 1986, ill. p. 57;
Habsburg 1987, cat. 278, p. 183 (ill.); Hill 1989, p. 170, pl. 132;
Habsburg/Lopato 1994, cat. 78, p. 230 (ill.)

Exhibitions: Munich 1986–87; Lugano 1987, cat. 41, p. 64 (ill.);
Paris 1987, cat. 41, p. 60 (ill.); St. Petersburg/Paris/London 1993–94

The Forbes Magazine Collection, New York

— 252 —

OWL IN CAGE
Gold, agate, silver gilt, diamonds, pearls
H: 4⅛ inches
Marks: Fabergé, initials of workmaster Mikhail Perkhin, assay mark
of St. Petersburg 1896–1908

Housed in a silver gilt cage, the agate owl is perched
above a dish filled with tiny pearl "seeds."

Provenance: A La Vieille Russie, New York

Bibliography: Solodkoff 1984, p. 166 (ill.)

Exhibitions: ALVR 1983, cat. 426, p. 117, ill. p. 29; Lugano 1987,
cat. 59, p. 73 (ill.); Paris 1987, cat. 59, p. 69 (ill.)

The Forbes Magazine Collection, New York

— 253 —

AUTOMATED RHINOCEROS
Silver, gold
L: 2⅞ inches

This rhinoceros is comparable to one given to Queen Alexandra of England in 1909 for her sixty-fifth birthday by the lord chamberlain, Lord Howe (private collection, New York). A third automated rhinoceros, with a sapphire horn, was sold at Christie's, New York, on October 22, 1984, lot 676, and is now in a private collection in New Orleans.

Provenance: A La Vieille Russie, New York

Bibliography: Solodkoff 1984, pp. 24, 166, ill. pp. 4, 18, 166; Habsburg 1987, cat. 383, p. 209 (ill.)

Exhibitions: ALVR 1983, cat. 454, pp. 123–24, ill. p. 123; Munich 1986–87; Lugano 1987, cat. 56, p. 71 (ill.); Paris 1987, cat. 56, p. 67 (ill.)

The Forbes Magazine Collection, New York

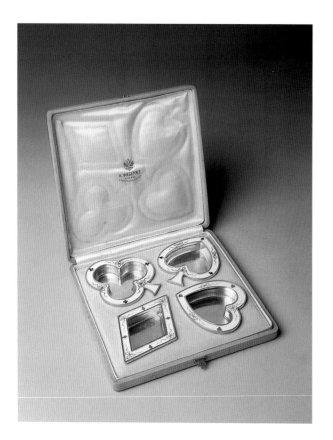

— 254 —

CARD-SUIT ASHTRAYS
Silver gilt, gold, enamel
H: (diamond) 3⅝ inches; (spade) 3¼ inches; (heart) 2¾ inches; (club) 3¼ inches
Marks: Imperial Warrant, initials KF, assay mark of Moscow 1896–1908, inv. no. 26535
Original fitted case with K Fabergé, Imperial Warrant, Moscow, St. Petersburg, Odessa

The four silver-lined ashtrays for bridge or other card games are cast as a diamond, heart, club, and spade. The decorative tied ribbons and the relevant suit are painted in either blue or red on the flat rim of each ashtray.

Provenance: Mrs. Hugh J. Chisholm Jr.; A La Vieille Russie, New York

Bibliography: Waterfield/Forbes 1978, p. 102, ill. p. 103; Solodkoff 1984, p. 179 (ill.); Kelly 1985, p. 18, ill. p. 19

Exhibitions: San Francisco 1964, cat. 161, p. 62

The Forbes Magazine Collection, New York

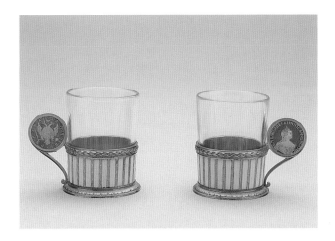

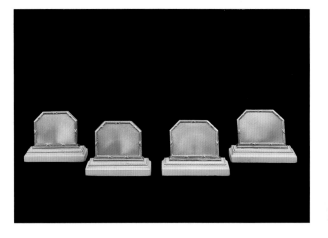

— 255 —

VODKA *CHARKI*

Gold, enamel, glass, rubles

H: 1¾ inches

Marks: Fabergé, initials of workmaster Mikhail Perkhin, assay mark
of St. Petersburg before 1896

The six *charki* (cups) in the set are in the form of miniature tea glasses.

Provenance: H. Harris; Mrs. Michael Pugh; Miss Woollcombe-Boyce

Bibliography: Bainbridge 1949, ill. 88; Bainbridge 1966, ill. 87;
Solodkoff 1984, p. 179 (ill.); Kelly 1985, p. 18, ill. p. 19

Exhibitions: Wartski 1953, cat. 249, p. 22; ALVR 1983, cat. 299, p. 94,
ill. p. 95; Lugano 1987, cat. 10, p. 46 (ill.); Paris 1987, cat. 10, p. 42 (ill.)

The Forbes Magazine Collection, New York

— 256 —

FOUR MENU HOLDERS

Silver gilt, enamel, holly

L: 2⅜ inches

Marks: K Fabergé, double-headed eagle, initials of workmaster
Anders Nevalainen, assay mark of St. Petersburg 1896–1908,
assay master A. Richter, 91, inv. no. 14435

Provenance: Countess Torby, née Countess Merenberg, wife of
Grand Duke Mikhail Mikhailovich; Mrs. R. L. Cameron;
Christie's, London, March 18, 1975, lot 161; Wartski, London

Bibliography: Waterfield/Forbes 1978, p. 102, ill. p. 103; Solodkoff 1984,
p. 180 (ill.); Kelly 1985, p. 16, ill. p. 17

Exhibitions: Forbes 1987–94

The Forbes Magazine Collection, New York

— 257 —

MARIA PAVLOVNA MIRROR
Silver, silver gilt, enamel, diamonds, mirror glass, wood
H: 8⅞ inches
Marks: Fabergé, initials of workmaster Victor Aarne, assay mark
of St. Petersburg 1896–1908

The monogram is that of Grand Duchess Maria Pavlovna (1854–1920), princess of Mecklenburg, who married Grand Duke Vladimir Aleksandrovich, brother of Alexander III, in 1874.

Provenance: Grand Duchess Maria Pavlovna; Sotheby's, London,
April 7, 1977, lot 49; Wartski, London

Bibliography: Solodkoff 1984, p. 171 (ill.); Kelly 1985, p. 16, ill. pp. 12, 16

Exhibitions: Forbes 1987–94

The Forbes Magazine Collection, New York

— 258 —

EGG BONBONNIÈRE
Gold, silver gilt, enamel, diamonds, rubies
H: 1⅞ inches
Marks: Initials of workmaster Henrik Wigström, assay mark of
St. Petersburg 1896–1908, assay master Iakov Liapunov

The bonbonnière originally would have been used to
hold small candies or pills.

Provenance: L. Desoutter, London; Mrs. L. Turnbull, England;
Christie's, London, December 8, 1965, lot 7

Bibliography: Waterfield/Forbes 1978, p. 36 (ill.); Forbes 1980, p. 18,
ill. p. 19; Solodkoff 1984, p. 186 (ill.); Kelly 1985, p. 16 (ill.)

Exhibitions: ALVR 1983, cat. 549, p. 140, ill. p. 139; Lugano 1987,
cat. 122, p. 118 (ill.); Paris 1987, cat. 122, p. 114 (ill.)

The Forbes Magazine Collection, New York

— 259 —

AESTHETIC-MOVEMENT CIGARETTE CASE
Gold, enamel, diamonds, sapphire
L: 3½ inches
Marks: Imperial Warrant, assay mark of Moscow before 1896,
inv. no. 11366

The enameled gold cigarette case is decorated with polychrome disks that have rose-cut diamond centers on a
white opalescent *guilloché* enamel ground. The design
was inspired by the aesthetic movement, an assimilation
of Japanese taste into the Arts and Crafts movement.

Provenance: Christie's, Geneva, November 17, 1983, lot 380

Bibliography: Solodkoff 1984, p. 174 (ill.); Kelly 1985, p. 16, ill. p. 17;
Habsburg 1987, cat. 469, p. 238 (ill.)

Exhibitions: Munich 1986–87; Lugano 1987, cat. 99, p. 97 (ill.);
Paris 1987, cat. 99, p. 93 (ill.)

The Forbes Magazine Collection, New York

— 260 —

STYLE-MODERNE CLOCK

Gold, enamel, silver, seed pearls

H: 5 inches

Marks: Fabergé, initials of workmaster Henrik Wigström, assay mark
of St. Petersburg 1896–1908; plaque inscribed "Murochka/on her
birthday/18 May 1907/Mirra"

The pink enamel dial of this clock in the modern style
has black Arabic numerals and gold hands and is cir-
cled by seed pearls. The face is set in a blue enamel circle, en-
closed by a white enamel crescent, and applied with a
gold plaque. The clock has a silver easel strut.

Provenance: Christie's, New York, March 14, 1984, lot 449

Bibliography: Solodkoff 1984, p. 178 (ill.)

Exhibitions: Lugano 1987, cat. 28, p. 55 (ill.);
Paris 1987, cat. 28, p. 51 (ill.)

The Forbes Magazine Collection, New York

— 261 —

POLAR STAR CLOCK

Gold, enamel, nephrite, silver, diamonds

H: 5¼ inches

Marks: Fabergé, initials of workmaster Mikhail Perkhin, assay mark of
St. Petersburg before 1896, inv. no. 546591

This star-shaped clock, its face surrounded by an enameled life ring, is thought to have been made for the imperial yacht *Polar Star.*

Provenance: Wartski, London; Dr. and Mrs. Leonard Slotover;
Christie's, Geneva, November 19, 1974, lot 278; Sotheby Parke Bernet,
New York, December 14–15, 1983, lot 512

Bibliography: Snowman 1962, pl. X; Habsburg/Solodkoff 1979, p. 77,
pl. 88; Solodkoff 1984, p. 177 (ill.); Kelly 1985, p. 23, ill. pp. 12, 23;
Solodkoff 1986, ill. p. 31; Habsburg 1987, cat. 510, p. 253 (ill.);
Hill 1989, p. 176, pl. 162

Exhibitions: Munich 1986–87; Lugano 1987, cat. 25, p. 53 (ill.);
Paris 1987, cat. 25, p. 49 (ill.)

The Forbes Magazine Collection, New York

— 262 —

PAIR OF TOILET BOTTLES
Glass, gold, enamel, amethysts, diamonds
H: 5⅛ inches (each)
Marks: Initials KF, assay mark of Moscow 1896–1908

An almost identical pair of toilet bottles with colored enamel stoppers is in the collection of Princess Margaret of England (see Snowman 1979, p. 28).

Provenance: Christie's, Geneva, November 30, 1982, lot 292

Bibliography: Solodkoff 1984, p. 178 (ill.); Kelly 1985, p. 16, ill. pp. 12, 17; Forbes 1986, ill. pp. 52–53; Hill 1989, p. 292, pl. 259

The Forbes Magazine Collection, New York

— 263 —

ROCAILLE OPERA GLASSES
Gold, enamel, diamonds, glass
L: 4¼ inches
Marks: Fabergé, initials of workmaster Mikhail Perkhin, assay master Iakov Liapunov, inv. no. 3945

These Louis XV–style opera glasses are enameled translucent pink and decorated with rococo motifs.

Provenance: Jan Skala, New York

Bibliography: Waterfield/Forbes 1978, p. 77 (ill.); Solodkoff 1984, pp. 30, 168 (ill.); Forbes 1986, p. 52 (ill.); Habsburg 1987, cat. 506, p. 251, ill. p. 252

Exhibitions: Munich 1986–87; Lugano 1987, cat. 69, p. 80 (ill.); Paris 1987, cat. 69, p. 76 (ill.)

The Forbes Magazine Collection, New York

— 264 —

IMPERIAL PRESENTATION CIGARETTE CASE
Gold, enamel, diamonds, paste brilliants
L: 3¾ inches
Marks: Fabergé, initials of workmaster August Holmström,
assay mark of St. Petersburg before 1896, inv. no. 1159;
interior inscribed "Ludwig Castenskiold"

Provenance: Presented by Czar Nicholas II to Ludwig Castenskiold,
equerry of the czar's grandfather, King Christian IX of Denmark;
Christie's, Geneva, November 30, 1982, lot 253

Bibliography: Solodkoff 1984, pp. 25, 174, ill. pp. 27, 174;
Kelly 1985, p. 16, ill. pp. 12, 17; Habsburg 1987, cat. 462, p. 237,
ill. p. 236; Habsburg/Lopato 1994, cat. 144, p. 279 (ill.)

Exhibitions: Munich 1986–87; Lugano 1987, cat. 98, p. 96 (ill.);
Paris 1987, cat. 98, p. 92 (ill.); St. Petersburg/Paris/London 1993–94

The Forbes Magazine Collection, New York

— 265 —

AMATORY FRAME
Gold, enamel, ivory
H: 4⅛ inches
Marks: Fabergé, initials of workmaster Mikhail Perkhin, assay mark
of St. Petersburg before 1896, inv. no. 45487

The frame contains a photograph of Czarina Maria Feodorovna and her sister, Queen Alexandra of England.

Provenance: Sotheby's Belgravia, London, November 6, 1975, lot 68
(with original photograph); A La Vieille Russie, New York

Bibliography: Waterfield/Forbes 1978, pp. 67, 143 (ill.);
Solodkoff 1984, p. 171 (ill.); Forbes 1986, ill. p. 52;
Habsburg 1987, cat. 495, p. 247, ill. p. 246

Exhibitions: Munich 1986–87

The Forbes Magazine Collection, New York

— 266 —

IMPERIAL PRESENTATION FRAME
Gold, rock crystal, enamel, diamonds, silver gilt, wood
H: 14⅝ inches
Marks: Fabergé, initials of workmaster Mikhail Perkhin, assay mark
of St. Petersburg 1896–1908, assay master Iakov Liapunov

The rock crystal panels of this frame are etched with lau-
rels and decorated with imperial crowns, Czarina Maria
Feodorovna's cipher, the imperial eagle, and musical and
amatory trophies. The strut is wrought in the form of an
M, the czarina's monogram, and is decorated with an
imperial crown. Presented by Czar Alexander III to his
wife, the frame contains a period print of a photograph
of their son, Nicholas II, wearing the Life Guard Hussars
uniform.

Provenance: Presented by Czar Alexander III to his wife,
Czarina Maria Feodorovna; Maurice Sandoz, Switzerland;
A La Vieille Russie, New York

Bibliography: Waterfield/Forbes 1978, p. 60 (ill.);
Solodkoff 1984, p. 170 (ill.)

Exhibitions: ALVR 1961, cat. 184, p. 62; ALVR 1968, cat. 322,
p. 122, ill. p. 123; V&A 1977, cat. L3, p. 71

The Forbes Magazine Collection, New York

267

268   269

271

270   272

273   275

274

276   279

277   278

280   281

282

— 267 —

MOSS AGATE EGG
Enamel, gold, diamonds
H: ¾ inch
Marks: Initials of workmaster Henrik Wigström, assay mark
of St. Petersburg 1896–1908

The egg is decorated to imitate moss agate in salmon
pink enamel over wintery brown foliage and surrounded
by a band of rose-cut diamonds.

Provenance: The Princess Royal (Victoria, daughter of Edward VII
and great-niece of Czarina Maria Feodorovna); Christie's, London,
June 28, 1966, lot 37; I. Freeman & Son, London and New York

Bibliography: Waterfield/Forbes 1978, no. 38, p. 38, ill. p. 39;
Forbes 1980, p. 32, ill. pp. 33, 41; Solodkoff 1984, p. 183 (ill.);
Hill 1989, p. 6, ill. on endpapers

The Forbes Magazine Collection, New York

— 268 —

UNION JACK EGG
Enamel, gold
H: ⁹⁄₁₆ inch
Marks: Initials of workmaster Gustav Lundell

The gold egg is enameled with the Union Jack on a white
ground. Like their larger counterparts, these egg charms
would have been exchanged on Easter with the greeting
"Christ is risen."

Provenance: Lansdell K. Christie, Long Island

Bibliography: Waterfield/Forbes 1978, cat. 18, p. 37 (ill.);
Forbes 1980, p. 44, ill. pp. 41, 45, back cover; Solodkoff 1984,
p. 181 (ill.); Hill 1989, p. 6, ill. endpapers

Exhibitions: Corcoran 1961, cat. 77, p. 50;
MMA 1962–65, L62.8.72 a–m

The Forbes Magazine Collection, New York

— 269 —

RED CROSS EGG
Enamel, gold
H: ½ inch
Marks: Initials A*H(?)

Czarina Alexandra Feodorovna and her daughters
worked for the Red Cross during World War I. The imperial family spent a large portion of its personal fortune
to support the Red Cross and other war efforts. An almost identical miniature egg was owned by Lansdell K.
Christie and is also in the Forbes Magazine collection
(see Solodkoff 1984, ill. p. 181).

Provenance: A La Vieille Russie, New York

Bibliography: Waterfield/Forbes 1978, no. 31, p. 38 (ill.);
Solodkoff 1984, p. 181 (ill.)

The Estate of Mrs. Roberta Forbes

— 270 —

ROMANOV BANNER EGG
Enamel, gold
H: ⁹⁄₁₆ inch
Marks: Initials of workmaster Fedor Afanassiev

The gold egg is enameled on one side with the Romanov
eagle on a yellow ground, and on the other with blue,
white, and red stripes. This egg was probably made to
commemorate the Russo-French alliance.

Provenance: Lansdell K. Christie, Long Island

Bibliography: Waterfield/Forbes 1978, cat. 16, p. 37 (ill.);
Forbes 1980, p. 48, ill. pp. 41, 49; Solodkoff 1984, p. 181 (ill.);
Hill 1989, p. 6, ill. on endpapers

Exhibitions: Corcoran 1961, cat. 77, p. 50;
MMA 1962–65, L.62.8.72 a–m

The Forbes Magazine Collection, New York

— 271 —

HELMET EGG
Purpurine, enamel, gold, silver
H: 1 inch

The egg was most likely made for the officers of the czarina's Guard Lancers, whose helmet caps the egg. The regiment was stationed in St. Petersburg.

Provenance: Lansdell K. Christie, Long Island

Bibliography: McNab Dennis 1965, p. 242 (ill.); Waterfield/Forbes 1978, cat. 21, p. 37 (ill.); Forbes 1980, p. 44, ill. p. 45, back cover; Solodkoff 1984, p. 180 (ill.); Hill 1989, p. 6, ill. on endpapers

Exhibitions: Corcoran 1961, cat. 77, p. 50; MMA 1962–65, L.62.8.72 a–m

The Forbes Magazine Collection, New York

— 273 —

TRELLISWORK FRAME EGG
Platinum, gold, diamonds, sapphires
H: ¾ inch
Marks: Initials of workmaster Alfred Thielemann

Provenance: A La Vieille Russie, New York

Bibliography: Solodkoff 1984, p. 183 (ill.)

The Forbes Magazine Collection, New York

— 275 —

MUSHROOM BASKET EGG
Gold, enamel
H: ¾ inch
Marks: Initials KF

Provenance: Christie's, Geneva, November 15, 1978, lot 411; A La Vieille Russie, New York

Bibliography: Habsburg/Solodkoff 1979, pl. 124; Solodkoff 1984, p. 182 (ill.); Solodkoff 1988, ill. p. 57; Hill 1989, p. 62, pl. 63

Exhibitions: Lugano 1987, cat. 133, p. 121, ill. p. 120; Paris 1987, cat. 133, p. 117, ill. p. 116

The Forbes Magazine Collection, New York

— 272 —

DUCAL CORONET EGG
Enamel, gold, diamonds
H: ⁹⁄₁₆ inch
Marks: Initials of workmaster Mikhail Perkhin, assay mark of St. Petersburg 1896–1908

Provenance: A La Vieille Russie, New York

Bibliography: Waterfield/Forbes 1978, cat. 36, p. 38, ill. p. 39; Solodkoff 1984, p. 183 (ill.)

The Forbes Magazine Collection, New York

— 274 —

CHICK EGG
Gold, enamel
H: ¾ inch
Marks: Initials KF

The gold egg is decorated with a chicken emerging from an egg on blue ground.

Bibliography: Waterfield/Forbes 1978, p. 39 (ill.); Forbes 1980, pp. 40, 48, ill. pp. 41, 49; Solodkoff 1984, p. 182 (ill.); Solodkoff 1988, ill. p. 57; Hill 1989, p. 62, pl. 62

Exhibitions: ALVR 1983, cat. 506, p. 138, ill. p. 137; Lugano 1987, cat. 134, p. 121, ill. p. 120; Paris 1987, cat. 134, pp. 116, 117

The Forbes Magazine Collection, New York

— 276 —

KINGFISHER EGG
Jasper, gold, diamonds
H: ¾ inch

Provenance: Christie's, Geneva, November 17, 1983, lot 335

Bibliography: Solodkoff 1984, p. 182 (ill.); Solodkoff 1988, pp. 58, 77, ill. p. 57

Exhibitions: Lugano 1987, cat. 132, p. 121, ill. p. 120; Paris 1987, cat. 132, p. 117, ill. p. 116

The Forbes Magazine Collection, New York

— 277 —
EGG IN LOUIS XVI STYLE
Gold, enamel
H: 9/16 inch
Marks: Initials of Alfred Thielemann(?), assay mark
of St. Petersburg 1896–1908

Bibliography: Waterfield/Forbes 1978, cat. 40, p. 39 (ill.);
Forbes 1980, ill. p. 45, back cover; Solodkoff 1984, p. 183 (ill.);
Hill 1989, p. 6, ill. on endpapers

The Forbes Magazine Collection, New York

— 278 —
IMPERIAL NAVY EGG
Gold, enamel
H: 9/16 inch

The gold-mounted red *guilloché* enamel miniature Easter
egg is painted with the flag of the imperial Russian navy.

Provenance: Grand Duke Aleksei Aleksandrovich, grand admiral
of the imperial Russian navy
Bibliography: Solodkoff 1984, p. 181 (ill.)

The Forbes Magazine Collection, New York

— 279 —
CHICK IN EGG-SHAPED PERCH
Amethystine quartz, gold, diamonds
H: ¾ inch
Marks: Initials of workmaster Fedor Afanassiev

Provenance: Christie's, Geneva, November 11, 1975, lot 183;
A La Vieille Russie, New York
Bibliography: Waterfield/Forbes 1978, p. 39 (ill.); Forbes 1980,
p. 46, ill. p. 47; Solodkoff 1984, p. 182 (ill.)

The Forbes Magazine Collection, New York

— 280 —
FISH EGG
Gold, rubies, pearl
H: ¾ inch
Marks: Initials KF

Provenance: Christie's, Geneva, November 11, 1975, lot 179;
A La Vieille Russie, New York
Bibliography: Waterfield/Forbes 1978, no. 46, p. 39 (ill.); Forbes 1980,
p. 44, ill. p. 45; Solodkoff 1984, p. 182 (ill.); Solodkoff 1988, ill. p. 57
Exhibitions: Lugano 1987, cat. 131, p. 121, ill. p. 120;
Paris 1987, cat. 131, p. 117, ill. 116

The Forbes Magazine Collection, New York

— 281 —
ANCHORS EGG
Enamel, gold
H: 9/16 inch
Marks: Initials of workmaster Erik Kollin

The gold egg is enameled blue and chased with a pair of
anchors.

Provenance: Lansdell K. Christie, Long Island
Bibliography: Waterfield/Forbes 1978, cat. 19, p. 37 (ill.); Forbes 1980,
ill. pp. 41, 45, back cover; Solodkoff 1984, p. 181 (ill.);
Hill 1989, p. 6, ill. on endpapers
Exhibitions: Corcoran 1961, cat. 77, p. 50;
MMA 1962–65, L.62.8.72 a–m

The Forbes Magazine Collection, New York

— 282 —
EASTER BUNNY EGG
Gold, aventurine quartz
H: ⅞ inch
Marks: Initials of workmaster August Holmström

Provenance: Christie's, Geneva, November 17, 1983, lot 331
Bibliography: Solodkoff 1984, p. 182 (ill.); Solodkoff 1988, ill. p. 57
Exhibitions: Lugano 1987, cat. 130, p. 121, ill. p. 120;
Paris 1987, cat. 130, p. 117, ill. p. 116

The Forbes Magazine Collection, New York

— 283 —

IMPERIAL RENAISSANCE EASTER EGG
Gold, agate, enamel, diamonds, rubies
L: 5¼ inches
Marks: Fabergé, initials of workmaster Mikhail Perkhin, assay mark
of St. Petersburg before 1896; dated 1894

This casket in the Renaissance style is the last of the eggs
made for Czar Alexander III, who died less than eight
months after its presentation. It is modeled after an
eighteenth-century casket by Le Roy, now in the Green
Vaults, Dresden (see Habsburg 1987, cat. 661). The
whereabouts and nature of the egg's surprise are unknown.

Provenance: Presented by Czar Alexander III to his wife, Czarina Maria
Feodorovna, Easter 1894; Armand Hammer, 1930; Mr. and Mrs. Henry
Talbot de Vere Clifton, England; Mr. and Mrs. Jack Linsky, New York;
A La Vieille Russie, New York

Bibliography: Bainbridge 1949, ill. 63; Snowman 1953, p. 78, ills. 291,
292; Snowman 1962, pp. 44, 84, pl. LXXII; Bainbridge 1966, ill. 64;
Waterfield/Forbes 1978, pp. 10, 13, 20, 22, 112, 130, 132–33, 135, 139,
ill. pp. 21, 116, dust jacket; Forbes 1979, p. 1236, pl. XV; Habsburg/
Solodkoff 1979, pp. 107, 117, 157, ills. 11, 137; Snowman 1979, p. 94 (ill.);
Forbes 1980, pp. 5, 7, 30, 61, ill. p. 31; Solodkoff 1984, pp. 12, 61, 107,
ill. pp. 68, 186; Kelly 1985, p. 14; Habsburg 1987, cat. 538, pp. 94–95,
102, 272, ill. p. 272; Solodkoff 1988, pp. 14, 31, 41, ill. p. 14

Exhibitions: Hammer 1939 (ill.); ALVR 1949, cat. 123, p. 14; Hammer
1951, cat. 156, p. 26, ill. p. 23; ALVR 1961, cat. 293, pp. 16, 92, ill. p. 90;
San Francisco 1964, cat. 148, pp. 38, 60, ill. pp. 39, 60; V&A 1977,
cat. L15, pp. 74–75, ill. p. 81; ALVR 1983, cat. 555, pp. 11, 16, 22, 144,
ill. p. 17; Munich 1986–87; Lugano 1987, cat. 117, pp. 16, 108–9,
ill. pp. 108–9; Paris 1987, cat. 117, pp. 12, 104–5 (ill.); San Diego/
Moscow 1989–90, cat. 4, pp. 13, 22, 40, 41, 89, 96 (ill.)

The Forbes Magazine Collection, New York
(not lent to New York)

— 284 —

IMPERIAL LILIES OF THE VALLEY EASTER EGG
Gold, enamel, diamonds, rubies, pearls, rock crystal
H: 7⅞ inches
Marks: Initials of workmaster Mikhail Perkhin, assay mark of
St. Petersburg before 1896; miniatures dated 1898

The surprise of the art nouveau–style Lilies of the Valley
egg is a trio of miniature portraits by Johannes Zehngraf
of Czar Nicholas II and his two eldest daughters, Grand
Duchesses Olga and Tatiana, which rise out of the egg
when a pearl "button" is turned. The date is engraved on
the reverse of the miniatures. The egg was discussed by
the jury of the 1900 Paris Exposition Universelle and is
visible in a photograph of the 1902 St. Petersburg exhibition held at the von Dervise House.

Provenance: Presented by Czar Nicholas II to his wife,
Czarina Alexandra Feodorovna, Easter 1898; purchased by
Emanuel Snowman for Wartski, London, ca. 1927

Bibliography: Bainbridge 1949, ills. 53, 54; Snowman 1953, p. 83,
pl. XXV; Snowman 1962, p. 88, pl. LXXIV; Bainbridge 1966, p. viii,
pls. 52, 56; Waterfield/Forbes 1978, p. 129, ill. p. 118; Forbes 1979,
pp. 1237–38, ill. p. 1237, pl. XVI; Habsburg/Solodkoff 1979, p. 157,
pl. 15; Snowman 1979, pp. 98, 140, ill. p. 98; Forbes 1980, pp. 5, 54, 63,
ill. pp. 55, title page, unnumbered page; Solodkoff 1984, pp. 13, 17,
64, 109, 126, 159, 187, ill. pp. 76, 127, 187; Kelly 1985, p. 14, ill. p. 25;
Forbes 1986, ill. p. 52; Habsburg 1987, pp. 94–95, 97; Solodkoff 1988,
pp. 31, 34, 42, ill. p. 32; Hill 1989, pp. 14, 58, pl. 35; Habsburg/
Lopato 1994, cat. 23, p. 187, ill. pp. 82, 187

Exhibitions: 1900 Paris Exposition Universelle; St. Petersburg 1902;
London 1935, cat. 585, p. 111; Wartski 1949, cat. 8, pp. 3, 10, frontispiece;
Wartski 1953, cat. 285, pp. 4, 24–25; V&A 1977, cat. O2, pp. 93, 132,
ill. p. 101; ALVR 1983, cat. 556, pp. 18, 144, ill. p. 143; San Diego/
Moscow 1989–90, cat. 8, pp. 17, 21, 48, 86, 99, 116, ill. pp. 24, 27, 48, 99;
St. Petersburg/Paris/London 1993–94

The Forbes Magazine Collection, New York
(lent to New York only)

— 285 —

IMPERIAL CORONATION EASTER EGG
Egg: Gold, enamel, diamonds, velvet
Coach: Gold, platinum, enamel, diamonds, rubies, rock crystal
L: (shell) 5 inches; (coach) 3 ¹¹⁄₁₆ inches
Marks: Initials of workmaster Mikhail Perkhin, assay mark of
St. Petersburg 1896–1908; "Wigström" scratched on interior of shell

The egg opens to reveal a removable miniature replica by George Stein of the coach used for the czarina's entry into Moscow in 1896. The color scheme of the egg is an allusion to the gold ermine trimmed robes worn by the imperial couple. A tiny egg, pavé-set with brilliants, once hung inside the coach. Beneath a portrait diamond set at the top of the egg, the monogram of Czarina Alexandra Feodorovna is emblazoned in rose-cut diamonds and rubies. The date 1897 appears beneath a smaller portrait diamond at the bottom of the egg. The egg is visible in a 1902 photograph showing items from the imperial collection at the von Dervise House, St. Petersburg.

Provenance: Presented by Czar Nicholas II to his wife, Czarina Alexandra Feodorovna, Easter 1897; purchased by Emanuel Snowman for Wartski, London, 1927

Bibliography: Bainbridge 1949, pp. 74, 76, pl. 58; Snowman 1953, pp. 48, 52, 81–82, pl. XXIV, dust jacket; Snowman 1962, pp. 52, 56, 86–87, pl. LXXIII, dust jacket (1974 ed.); Bainbridge 1966, pp. viii, 73, 75,

pl. 89, dust jacket; Waterfield/Forbes 1978, pp. 52, 129, ill. p. 118; Forbes 1979, pp. 1237–38, ill. 1237, pl. XVI; Habsburg/Solodkoff 1979, pp. 105, 107, 158, pls. 37, 126; Snowman 1979, p. 97 (ill.); Forbes 1980, pp. 5, 14, 62, ill. p. 15, unnumbered page; Solodkoff 1984, pp. 13, 17, 64, 65, 109, 126, 156, ill. pp. 9, 74, 186; Kelly 1985, p. 14, ill. pp. 14–15; Forbes 1986, ill. pp. 52–53; Habsburg 1987, cat. 539, pp. 12, 40, 94–95, 97–98, 272, 274, ill. p. 273; Solodkoff 1988, pp. 27–28, 34, 38, 43, 104, 119, ill. p. 35, dust jacket; Hill 1989, pp. 14, 57, pls. 31–32; Habsburg/Lopato 1994, cat. 110, p. 256, ill. p. 257

Exhibitions: 1900 Paris Exposition Universelle; St. Petersburg 1902; London 1935, cat. 586, p. 111; Wartski 1949, cat. 6, pp. 3, 10, ill. p. 31; Wartski 1953, cat. 286, p. 25; V&A 1977, cat. O1, pp. 12, 93, ill. p. 101; Munich 1986–87; Lugano 1987, cat. 119, pp. 11, 13, 113, ill. pp. 112–13; Paris 1987, cat. 119, pp. 6, 8, 109, ill. pp. 108–9; San Diego/Moscow 1989–90, cat. 7, pp. 14, 21, 46, 86, 98, ill. pp. 10, 46–47, 98; St. Petersburg/Paris/London 1993–94

The Forbes Magazine Collection, New York

— 286 —

IMPERIAL ORANGE TREE EASTER EGG
Gold, enamel, nephrite, diamonds, citrines, amethysts,
rubies, pearls, agate, feathers
H: 11¾ inches (open)
Marks: Fabergé; dated 1911

This object was inspired by French eighteenth-century
musical orange trees. The surprise concealed within the
orange tree is a mechanical bird, which emerges singing
when the correct orange is turned.

Provenance: Presented by Czar Nicholas II to his mother,
Dowager Empress Maria Feodorovna, Easter 1911; Wartski, London;
A. G. Hughes, England; Arthur E. Bradshaw; W. Magalow;
Maurice Sandoz, Switzerland; A La Vieille Russie, New York;
Mildred Kaplan, New York

Bibliography: Snowman 1953, pp. 96–97, ills. 334–35; Snowman 1962,
p. 102, pl. LXXVIII, ill. 363; Waterfield/Forbes 1978, pp. 8, 11, 13, 130,
132–33, 138, ill. pp. 26–28, 125, 138, dust jacket; Forbes 1979, pp. 1238,
1240, pl. XIX; Habsburg/Solodkoff 1979, pp. 107, 117, 131, 139, 157,
ills. 28, 139; Snowman 1979, p. 113, ill. p. 112; Forbes 1980, pp. 5, 22, 67,
ill. p. 23; Solodkoff 1984, pp. 12, 48, 65, 69, 126, ill. pp. 97, 187;
Kelly 1985, p. 14, ill. pp. 20–21; Forbes 1986, p. 86;
Solodkoff 1988, pp. 28, 42, ill. p. 28

Exhibitions: London 1935, cat. 582, p. 110; ALVR 1961, cat. 294, pp. 16,
92, ill. p. 93; ALVR 1968, cat. 369, p. 132, ill. p. 133; V&A 1977, cat. L4,
pp. 71–72, ill. p. 81; ALVR 1983, cat. 561, pp. 16, 22, 148, ill. p. 149;
Munich 1986–87, pp. 95, 97, 104, ill. p. 96; Lugano 1987, cat. 121, pp. 11,
16, 177, ill. pp. 116–17, cover; Paris 1987, cat. 121, pp. 12, 113,
ill. pp. 112–13; San Diego/Moscow 1989–90, cat. 20,
pp. 17, 22, ill. pp. 18, 72, 73, 109

The Forbes Magazine Collection, New York

— 287 —

PEDESTAL CLOCK
Nephrite, silver gilt
H: 6⅞ inches

An abbreviated inscription on the back plate (Ned-[elnyi]zav[od]) indicates that the clock can be wound to run for a week. An almost identical clock is in the collection of Baron Thyssen-Bornemisza (see Habsburg 1987, cat. 241, p. 170).

Provenance: A La Vieille Russie, New York

Bibliography: Solodkoff 1984, p. 177, ill. pp. 6, 177

The Forbes Magazine Collection, New York

— 288 —

WAR PRESENTATION BEAKER
Nephrite, silver
H: 3⅞ inches
Marks: Initials of workmaster Henrik Wigström,
assay mark of St. Petersburg 1896–1908; inscribed
"WAR/1914–1915/K FABERGÉ"

The medallions of this presentation beaker are embossed with the imperial eagle.

Provenance: Wartski, London

Bibliography: Solodkoff 1984, p. 173, ill. pp. 6, 173;
Habsburg/Lopato 1994, cat. 126, p. 269 (ill.)

Exhibitions: St. Petersburg/Paris/London 1993–94

The Forbes Magazine Collection, New York

— 289 —

CARD HOLDER
Nephrite, gold
L: 3 inches
Marks: Fabergé, initials of workmaster Mikhail Perkhin, assay mark
of St. Petersburg 1896–1908

The nephrite card holder is mounted in red and green
gold and stands on four bun feet.

Provenance: A La Vieille Russie, New York

Bibliography: Solodkoff 1984, p. 176, ill. pp. 6, 176

The Forbes Magazine Collection, New York

— 290 —

PEN TRAY
Bowenite, gold, enamel
H: 6½ inches
Marks: Fabergé, initials of workmaster Mikhail Perkhin, assay mark
of St. Petersburg before 1896, inv. no. 56200

Provenance: A La Vieille Russie, New York

Bibliography: Waterfield/Forbes 1978, p. 86, ill. p. 87;
Solodkoff 1984, p. 176 (ill.)

The Forbes Magazine Collection, New York

— 291 —

IMPERIAL PRESENTATION WRITING PORTFOLIO
Silver gilt, diamonds, leather, watered silk
H: 12½ inches
Marks: Fabergé, initials of workmaster Mikhail Perkhin, assay mark
of St. Petersburg before 1896

Provenance: Presented by representatives of the city of St. Petersburg to
Czar Nicholas II and Czarina Alexandra Feodorovna on June 22, 1896,
on the occasion of their entry into St. Petersburg during the coronation
festivities; Christie's, Geneva, May 1, 1974, lot 177

Bibliography: Koronatsionnyi sbornik 1899, vol. I, p. 394 (ill.);
Albert 1979, p. 11, ill. pp. 8, 10, cover; Waterfield/Forbes 1978, pp. 84,
132, 135, ill. p. 83; Solodkoff 1984, p. 172, ill. pp. 6, 172; Forbes 1986,
ill. p. 57; Hill 1989, p. 294, pl. 275; Habsburg/Lopato 1994,
cat. 109, p. 255 (ill.)

Exhibitions: St. Petersburg/Paris/London 1993–94

The Forbes Magazine Collection, New York

— 292 —

PERPETUAL CALENDAR
Nephrite, moonstones, silver gilt, gold, linen
H: 5¾ inches
Marks: Fabergé, initials of workmaster Mikhail Perkhin,
assay mark of St. Petersburg before 1896

The rectangular nephrite panel is set with four moonstones at the corners and three moonstones on the knobs
on either side which turn the dates for the calendar.

Provenance: Bentley & Co., London

Bibliography: Waterfield/Forbes 1978, p. 88 (ill.); Solodkoff 1984,
p. 175, ill. pp. 6, 175; Forbes 1986, ill. p. 57

The Forbes Magazine Collection, New York

— 293 —

CIRCULAR ASHTRAY
Bowenite, gold, rubies
Diam: 3½ inches
Marks: Initials of workmaster Mikhail Perkhin, assay mark of
St. Petersburg 1896–1908, assay master Iakov Liapunov, inv. no. 6133

Provenance: Countess Zouboff; Christie's, Geneva, May 1, 1974, lot 211;
A La Vieille Russie, New York

Bibliography: Waterfield/Forbes 1978, cat. 129, p. 100 (ill.);
Albert 1979, ill. p. 8, cover; Solodkoff 1984, p. 178, ill. pp. 6, 178;
Forbes 1986, ill. p. 56

The Forbes Magazine Collection, New York

— 294 —

IMPERIAL CYLINDER VASE
Nephrite, gold, rubies, diamonds
H: 4⅝ inches
Marks: Initials of workmaster Mikhail Perkhin, assay mark of
St. Petersburg 1896–1908, assay master Iakov Liapunov

Provenance: A La Vieille Russie, New York

Bibliography: Albert 1979, p. 11, ill. pp. 8, 10, cover;
Waterfield/Forbes 1978, cat. 125, p. 98 (ill.);
Solodkoff 1984, p. 179, ill. pp. 6, 179

The Forbes Magazine Collection, New York

— 295 —

PINK AGATE ASHTRAY
Agate, gold, enamel
Diam: 2¾ inches
Marks: Initials of workmaster Henrik Wigström, assay mark of
St. Petersburg 1896–1908, inv. no. 12311

The circular pink agate dish with a gold rim is enameled
in green with laurel and engraved with ribbon ties.

Provenance: Wartski, London

Bibliography: Waterfield/Forbes 1978, cat. 130, p. 100 (ill.);
Solodkoff 1984, p. 178, ill. pp. 6, 178

The Forbes Magazine Collection, New York

— 296 —
ROUND BELL PUSH
Bowenite, gold, enamel, diamonds, pearls, moonstone
H: 2¼ inches
Marks: Fabergé, initials of workmaster Mikhail Perkhin,
assay mark of St. Petersburg 1896–1908

Provenance: Juvel og Kunst, Copenhagen

Bibliography: Albert 1979, p. 8, ill. pp. 8, 10, cover;
Waterfield/Forbes 1978, cat. 104, p. 86 (ill.);
Solodkoff 1984, p. 178, ill. pp. 6, 178

The Forbes Magazine Collection, New York

— 297 —
OVAL BELL PUSH
Bowenite, gold, enamel, diamonds, garnet
H: 2¾ inches

Another unmarked bell push in white onyx is in the royal
collection at Sandringham, England, reproduced in
Snowman 1962, ill. 193.

Provenance: Sotheby's, London, November 9, 1964, lot 13;
Wartski, London

Bibliography: Albert 1979, p. 8, ill. pp. 8, 10, cover;
Waterfield/Forbes 1978, cat. 105, p. 86 (ill.);
Solodkoff 1984, p. 178, ill. pp. 6, 178

The Forbes Magazine Collection, New York

Fabergé Collectors Today

The author's twenty years as a Fabergé auctioneer and the results of recent sales demonstrate that there is a never-ending demand for the art of the Russian master. Collectors have become very discerning, warned off by the numerous forgeries that plague the market. Some specialize and collect, for instance, only cloisonné enamels or cigarette cases.

Among the current American collectors of note is John Traina, consultant in a variety of international businesses, world traveler, and author. Within a span of twenty years, Traina has amassed a unique collection of five hundred Russian works of art, including three hundred cigarette cases by Fabergé (see cat. nos. 18, 354–75, 377–83).

Joan Rivers, television personality and Broadway actress, is also a passionate Fabergé collector. Among her acquisitions, made primarily from Wartski, London, are a number of hardstone objects, various enamels, and a selection of jewelry (cat. nos. 339–50).

While Armand Hammer's pioneering marketing of Fabergé through department stores was eminently suc-cessful in its day, a sale of Fabergé objects fifty years later through Neiman Marcus in Dallas floundered. In the store's 1985 Christmas catalogue, four Fabergé items, priced from $9,500 for a gold-mounted topaz desk seal to $200,000 for a reversible oval box with articulated figures from Tchaikovsky's opera *The Queen of Spades*, reportedly went unsold. But America's love affair with Fabergé has endured well-nigh one hundred years and is here to stay.

Just how far Fabergé's art is diffused throughout America, sometimes unrecognized, is illustrated by the following incident. While examining objects for an auction house in 1991, the author was shown an exquisite, jeweled miniature Easter egg by the Russian master clearly worth more than $5,000. Asked for its provenance, the owner, a young lady in her twenties, said: "I picked it up for a dime in a garage sale in D.C." Her girlfriend had acquired its mate for the same amount. Today America is a country where imperial Fabergé Easter eggs are purchased for millions of dollars, while many of the jeweler's objects might still lie hidden, waiting to be rediscovered.

Catalogue

Fabergé Collectors Today

— 298 —

STURGEON-SHAPED BOWL
Silver
L: 23¾ inches
Marks: Imperial Warrant, assay mark of Moscow 1896,
assay master LO, inv. no. 6549

The sturgeon, ferocious in appearance, is naturalistically
formed and chased.

Bibliography: Habsburg/Lopato 1994, cat. 209

Exhibitions: St. Petersburg/Paris/London 1993–94

Gerald M. de Sylvar

— 299 —

IMPERIAL GRIFFIN CLOCK
Silver, bowenite
H: 10¼ inches
Marks: Imperial Warrant, initials of workmaster Julius Rappoport,
assay mark of St. Petersburg 1896–1908, inv. no. 60377,
French import marks

The rampant griffin of chased silver faces left, holding a
raised sword in its right paw and a clock, in lieu of a
shield, in its left paw. The oval bowenite base stands on
four stud feet. A presentation plaque is inscribed, "Offert

par S. M. Nicolas II. Prix du Tzar. Compiègne 1904. Cle-
ville." The clock is presumably a prize awarded by the
czar for an annual horse race run at Compiègne, France.
A number of such griffins, the emblem of the Romanov
family, are known to exist. Some were made to mark the
tercentenary in 1913. For other examples, see ALVR 1983,
cat. 108, p. 57; Habsburg/Lopato 1994, cat. 71.

William Dean Rasco

— 300 —

TEA AND COFFEE SET
Silver
H: (coffeepot) 5½ inches
Marks: Imperial Warrant, assay mark of Moscow before 1890
Original fitted case stamped with Imperial Warrant,
St. Petersburg, Moscow

Andre Ruzhnikov, Palo Alto, California

— 301 —

ROCOCO-STYLE TEA AND COFFEE SET
Silver
H: (coffeepot) 9⅜ inches
Marks: Imperial Warrant, assay mark of Moscow 1896–1908,
inv. no. 7751

Bibliography: Hill 1989, p. 225, pl. 215

Andre Ruzhnikov, Palo Alto, California

— 302 —

IMPERIAL PRESENTATION TROPHY
Silver
H: 13½ inches
Marks: Imperial Warrant, assay mark of Moscow 1908–17;
inscribed "First prize from her majesty"

Andre Ruzhnikov, Palo Alto, California

— 303 —

IMPERIAL PRESENTATION TROPHY
Silver
H: 16 inches
Marks: Imperial Warrant, assay mark of Moscow 1908–17

Andre Ruzhnikov, Palo Alto, California

— 304 —

IMPERIAL PRESENTATION JEWELRY BOX
Silver
W: 12½ inches
Marks: Imperial Warrant, assay mark of Moscow 1908–17

Provenance: Presented by Czar Nicholas II to the German chancellor
Theobald von Bethman-Hollweg (1856–1921) during his visit to
St. Petersburg in 1913

Bibliography: Winterfeld-Menkin 1942, p. 159

Andre Ruzhnikov, Palo Alto, California

— 305 —
CIGARETTE CASE IN NEO-RUSSIAN STYLE
Silver gilt, enamel
L: 3¼ inches
Marks: Imperial Warrant, assay mark of Moscow 1908–17

Andre Ruzhnikov, Palo Alto, California

— 306 —
CIGARETTE CASE IN NEO-RUSSIAN STYLE
Silver gilt, enamel
L: 3¼ inches
Marks: Imperial Warrant, assay mark of Moscow 1908–17

Andre Ruzhnikov, Palo Alto, California

— 307 —
CIGARETTE CASE IN NEO-RUSSIAN STYLE
Silver gilt, enamel
L: 4¼ inches
Marks: Imperial Warrant, overstruck initials of Fedor Rückert,
assay mark of Moscow 1908–17

Andre Ruzhnikov, Palo Alto, California

— 308 —

PENDANT WATCH IN LOUIS XVI STYLE
Gold, chalcedony, diamonds
L: 2¾ inches
Marks: Initials of workmaster Albert Holmström
Original fitted case stamped with Imperial Warrant, St. Petersburg,
Moscow, London; marked "Moser & Cie, no. 15151"

Andre Ruzhnikov, Palo Alto, California

— 309 —

CIRCULAR BONBONNIÈRE IN LOUIS XVI STYLE
Gold, enamel
Diam: 1¾ inches
Marks: Fabergé in English, London import marks, initials of
workmaster Henrik Wigström, assay mark of St. Petersburg
1896–1908, 72, inv. no. 24207

Andre Ruzhnikov, Palo Alto, California

— 310 —

SQUARE BELL PUSH
Silver gilt, enamel, moonstone
W: 2⅜ inches
Marks: Fabergé, initials of workmaster Henrik Wigström, assay mark
of St. Petersburg 1908–17, inv. no. 331133

Andre Ruzhnikov, Palo Alto, California

— 311 —

ENAMELED FRAME
Silver, enamel, pearls, ivory
H: 3¼ inches
Marks: Fabergé, initials of workmaster Mikhail Perkhin, assay mark
of St. Petersburg 1896–1908

For a Fabergé frame with a full-length miniature by
Vasilii Zuiev of the same lady, Mrs. Leo Neuscheller, née
Lucy Gilse van der Pals, see Habsburg/Solodkoff 1979,
p. 128, ill. 148.

Andre Ruzhnikov, Palo Alto, California

— 312 —

ENAMELED VANITY CASE
Silver gilt, gold, enamel, diamonds
L: 4 inches
Marks: Fabergé, initials of workmaster August Hollming,
assay mark of St. Petersburg 1896–1908, inv. no. 14882

Andre Ruzhnikov, Palo Alto, California

— 313 —
CIRCULAR DESK CLOCK
Silver gilt, gold, enamel, pearls, ivory
H: 4¼ inches
Marks: Fabergé, initials of workmaster Mikhail Perkhin, assay mark
of St. Petersburg 1896–1908

Andre Ruzhnikov, Palo Alto, California

— 314 —
SQUARE DESK CLOCK
Silver gilt, gold, enamel, ivory
H: 4 inches
Marks: Fabergé, initials of workmaster Mikhail Perkhin, assay mark
of St. Petersburg 1896–1908, inv. no. 45797

Andre Ruzhnikov, Palo Alto, California

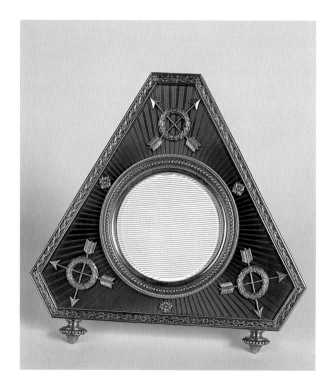

→ 315 ←

TRIANGULAR FRAME
Silver gilt, enamel, bone
H: 5¼ inches
Marks: Imperial Warrant, assay mark of Moscow
before 1896, inv. no. 4341
Original fitted case stamped with Imperial Warrant,
St. Petersburg, Moscow

Laurel wreaths and crossed arrows are applied to the red
guilloché enamel frame with cut corners.

Bibliography: Solodkoff 1988, p. 20

Louise and David Braver

→ 316 ←

JEWELED NEPHRITE FRAME
Nephrite, gold, enamel, rubies
H: 3⁵⁄₁₆ inches
Marks: initials of workmaster Henrik Wigström, assay mark
of St. Petersburg before 1896

A favorite Fabergé invention combines nephrite frames
with varicolored gold swags suspended from cabochon
rubies.

Louise and David Braver

— 317 —

SEMICIRCULAR LACQUER FRAME
Silver gilt, lacquer
H: 3⅜ inches

The frame contains an original photograph of Czarina
Alexandra Feodorovna.

Louise and David Braver

— 318 —

RECTANGULAR PALISANDER FRAME
Palisander, silver gilt, enamel
H: 7⅞ inches
Marks: Fabergé, initials of workmaster Anders Nevalainen, assay mark
of St. Petersburg 1896–1908

Louise and David Braver

— 319 —

SATINWOOD FRAME
Satinwood, silver gilt
H: 13½ inches
Marks: Fabergé, initials of workmaster Hjalmar Armfelt

The crowns of Russia and Spain decorate the frame,
which contains a photograph of Grand Duke Boris Vladimirovich and King Alfonso XIII of Spain, who wears
the uniform of a general of the Russian Lancers Regiment.

Provenance: Christie's, Geneva, April 27, 1977, lot 439;
Alan Hartman, New York

Louise and David Braver

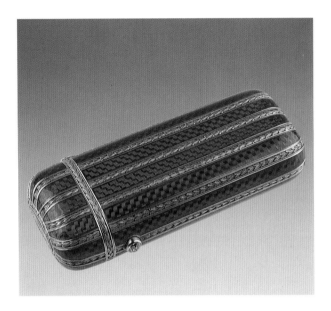

→ 320 ←

TUBULAR CIGAR CASE
Gold, enamel, diamond
L: 4⅛ inches
Marks: Fabergé, initials of workmaster Mikhail Perkhin, assay mark
of St. Petersburg before 1896, 72

The hinged oval case is decorated with alternating bands of red *guilloché* enamel and chased gold laurel leaves. The top and base are both adorned with a gold rosette. The push piece is a circular-cut diamond.

Private Collection

→ 321 ←

CIRCULAR CLOCK
Silver gilt, enamel, seed pearls, ivory
H: 4½ inches
Marks: Fabergé, initials of workmaster Mikhail Perkhin, assay mark
of St. Petersburg before 1896

The clock is decorated with a dark blue crescent moon on a white *guilloché* enamel ground. The eccentric white enamel dial has Arabic numerals and a seed pearl border. This clock is a variant of one in the Forbes Magazine collection by workmaster Henrik Wigström (cat. no. 260).

Provenance: Christie's, Geneva, May 11, 1982, lot 261

Private Collection

— 322 —

CIRCULAR ENAMELED BONBONNIÈRE
Gold, enamel
Diam: 2 3/16 inches
Marks: Fabergé, initials of workmaster Mikhail Perkhin, assay mark
of St. Petersburg 1896–1908

The warm orange enamel of the bonbonnière is painted
with dendritic motifs over a *guilloché* pattern of concentric circles and pellets. The *sablé* gold border is decorated
with green enamel leaves edged with white enamel pellets. For boxes of similar design, see cat. no. 205 and
Habsburg 1987, cat. 471.

Provenance: Wartski, London, 1946; Habsburg, Feldman,
Geneva, November 16, 1988, lot 80

Private Collection

— 323 —

TERRESTRIAL GLOBE
Silver gilt, gold, rock crystal
H: 4¾ inches
Marks: Initials of workmaster Erik Kollin, assay mark of
St. Petersburg before 1896, 84, inv. no. 43684

The silver gilt base with paw feet and flower swags is in
the mannerist style. The rock crystal globe is suspended
within a red gold graded stand. Frosted areas indicate the
continents. This object is virtually identical to a globe in
the collection of Queen Elizabeth II (Queen's Gallery
1995, p. 76).

Private Collection

— 324 —

ENAMELED GOLD FRAME
Gold, enamel, ivory
H: 2¾ inches
Marks: Fabergé, initials of workmaster Mikhail Perkhin, assay mark
of St. Petersburg before 1896

The shaped rectangular frame is of two-color gold and
blue *guilloché* enamel. Applied laurel leaf swags are suspended from a tied ribbon.

Private Collection

— 325 —

ROCK CRYSTAL HAND SEAL
Rock crystal, gold, enamel, seed pearls, chalcedony
H: 2½ inches
Marks: Initials of workmaster Henrik Wigström

The cylindrical handle rests on a flared pink *guilloché*
enamel base with two bands of seed pearls. The chalcedony seal face is engraved with the crowned cipher of
Grand Duke Konstantin Konstantinovich.

Provenance: Grand Duke Konstantin Konstantinovich;
Sir Charles Clore, London, Christie's, Geneva,
November 13, 1985, lot 62

Private Collection

— 326 —

CANE HANDLE
Gold, enamel, diamonds
H: 1⅜ inches
Marks: Initials of workmaster Mikhail Perkhin

The salmon pink *guilloché* enamel panels are painted with
trelliswork in sepia *camaïeu*. The borders are of rose-cut
diamonds and green enamel leaves; a single diamond is
in the center of each panel.

Private Collection

— 327 —

BLOODSTONE HAND SEAL
Gold, enamel, bloodstone, chalcedony
H: 3⁵⁄₁₆ inches
Marks: Fabergé, initials of workmaster Henrik Wigström

The seal has a pear-shaped bloodstone handle, a pink
guilloché enamel stand with palm-leaf and bright-cut
borders, and a chalcedony matrix.

Exhibitions: Helsinki 1980, cat. E15

Private Collection

— 328 —

STAMP BOX
Silver, enamel
L: 3½ inches
Marks: Imperial Warrant, assay mark of Moscow 1896–1908,
inv. no. 19873

The *guilloché* enamel panels are decorated with a central rosette and paterae. The stamp box has three slanted compartments.

Private Collection

— 329 —

PEAR-SHAPED GUM POT
Silver, gold, enamel, moonstone
H: 2 inches
Marks: Initials of workmaster Henrik Wigström, assay mark of St. Petersburg 1896–1908, assay master A. Richter, inv. no. 12602

Waved *guilloché* enamel decorates the body. The gadrooned gold cover has a cabochon moonstone finial.

Private Collection

— 330 —

MATCH HOLDER AND ASHTRAY
Silver, gold, enamel, nephrite, diamonds
H: 3 1/16 inches
Marks: Fabergé, initials of workmaster Victor Aarne, assay mark
of St. Petersburg 1896–1908
Original fitted case stamped with Imperial Warrant,
St. Petersburg, Moscow, Odessa

The half-moon-shaped ashtray is of nephrite. The match
holder is adorned with waved *guilloché* enamel panels.
One side has the monogram ZW set in diamonds.

Provenance: Lady Zia Wernher, Luton Hoo, England

Private Collection

— 331 —

RECTANGULAR GOLD FRAME
Gold, silver gilt, enamel, ivory
H: 4 1/4 inches
Marks: Fabergé, initials of workmaster Victor Aarne, assay mark
of St. Petersburg 1896–1908, inv. no. 2520

The frame has an oval aperture in a lozenge-shaped panel
of sunburst *guilloché* opalescent white enamel. The outer
panel is of waved lilac *guilloché* enamel, and the corners
are embellished with laurel wreaths.

Private Collection

— 332 —

LAPEL WATCH
Gold, enamel, diamonds
H: 2⅛ inches
Marks: Initials of workmaster August Holmström(?)

The opaque white enamel dial has blue Arabic numerals
and blue steel *flèche* hands. The opalescent pink *guilloché*
enamel case is ball shaped, and the bar brooch is *navette*
shaped. The chain is set with rose-cut diamonds. A drawing of the watch from the Holmström workshop, dating
from after 1908, is in one of two volumes with Wartski,
London (illustrated in Snowman 1993, p. 79). The wind-
ing mechanism of this watch model was invented by Paul
Ditisheim of La Chaux-de-Fonds, Switzerland, in 1896.

Provenance: A La Vieille Russie, New York

Bibliography: Snowman 1993, p. 79

Exhibitions: ALVR 1983, cat. 358

Private Collection

— 333 —

CLOCK-FRAME
Silver gilt, gold, enamel, wood, ivory(?)
H: 8½ inches
Marks: Fabergé, initials of workmaster Mikhail Perkhin, assay mark
of St. Petersburg 1896–1908

The panel is of opalescent pink moiré *guilloché* enamel.
The dial has a reed-and-tie border and is decorated with
gold ribbons and fruit swags. A miniature of a castle is
above the dial. The frame is further ornamented with a
gold and silver gilt quiver, laurel swags, ribbons, and
drapery.

Private Collection

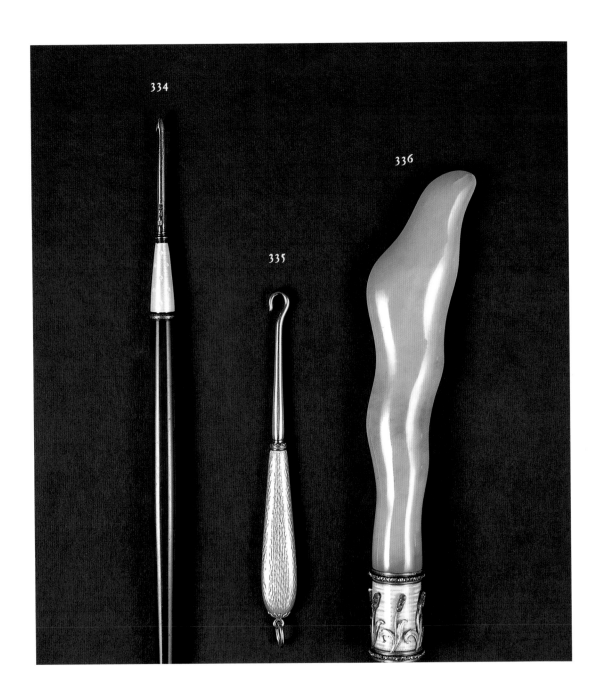

— 334 —

CROCHET HOOK
Gold, enamel, nephrite
L: 8¾ inches
Marks: Initials of workmaster Henrik Wigström

The nephrite handle of the gold hook has an opalescent white enamel band over a striped and dotted *guilloché* pattern and a palmetto border.

Provenance: Sir Charles Clore, London, Christie's, Geneva, November 13, 1985, lot 40

Private Collection

— 335 —

BUTTON HOOK
Gold, enamel
L: 4⅜ inches
Marks: Fabergé, initials of workmaster Henrik Wigström

The yellow gold hook has a pale blue *guilloché* enamel handle with a chased green gold palmetto band.

Provenance: Sir Charles Clore, London, Christie's, Geneva, November 13, 1984, lot 24

Private Collection

— 336 —

PARASOL HANDLE
Bowenite, gold, enamel, rubies
L: 6⅛ inches
Marks: Initials of workmaster Mikhail Perkhin, assay mark of St. Petersburg before 1896, inv. no. 57707

The handle is carved in the shape of a bean pod. Gold and ruby bullrushes are applied on the pale yellow *guilloché* enamel ground of the sleeve.

Private Collection

— 337 —

COLUMN FRAME
Nephrite, gold, enamel, diamonds
H: 3⅝ inches
Marks: Fabergé, initials of workmaster Victor Aarne, inv. no. 5158

The cylindrical nephrite column stands on three bun feet and is decorated with flower swags and draperies suspended from diamonds. The oval red *guilloché* enamel frame with rose-cut diamond border is flanked by palm sprays and surmounted by tied ribbons. For a frame of very similar shape from the Hillwood Museum, also by Aarne, see cat. 168.

Private Collection

— 338 —

NEPHRITE CIGARETTE CASE
Nephrite, gold, diamonds, rubies, sapphire
L: 3⅜ inches
Marks: Fabergé, initials of workmaster Mikhail Perkhin, assay mark of
St. Petersburg 1896–1908, inv. no. 4174

The nephrite case is adorned on one side with two floral
motifs set with a pear-shaped ruby and sapphire. The rim
of one side is set with alternating diamonds and rubies.

Private Collection

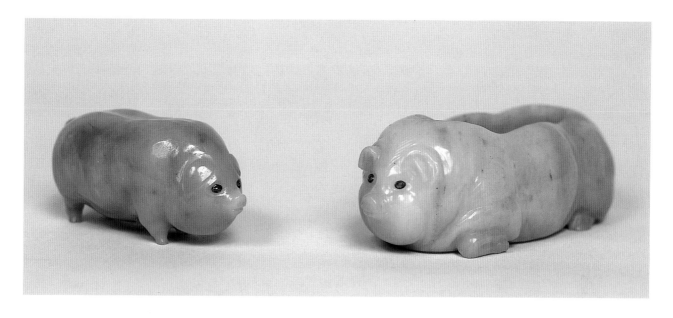

— 339 —
STANDING PIG
Aventurine quartz, rubies, gold
L: 2¾ inches

The standing figure of a rotund pig, like the next object, is carved from pink hardstone and has gold-mounted cabochon ruby eyes.

Provenance: Prince Andrei Romanov

Joan and Melissa Rivers (lent to New York and San Francisco only)

— 340 —
RECLINING PIG
Aventurine quartz, rubies, gold
L: 4¼ inches

Joan and Melissa Rivers (lent to New York and San Francisco only)

— 341 —
CYLINDRICAL BOX
Nephrite, gold, diamonds, sapphire
Diam: 1½ inches
Marks: Engraved Fabergé, inv. no. 21346

The cylindrical hardstone box has fleur-de-lys-shaped hinges. The clasp is set with rose-cut diamonds and a cabochon sapphire.

Joan and Melissa Rivers (lent to New York and
San Francisco only)

— 342 —
TRAPEZOIDAL BOX
Nephrite, gold, diamonds, rubies
L: 2½ inches
Marks: Engraved Fabergé

The hinges and clasp of this irregular-shaped box are in the form of diamond- and ruby-set C scrolls.

Joan and Melissa Rivers (lent to New York and
San Francisco only)

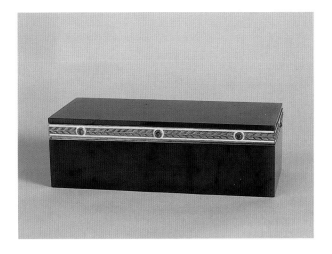

— 343 —

HOUSE-SHAPED BOX
Nephrite, gold, enamel, diamonds, rubies
L: 1⅞ inches
Marks: Fabergé, initials of workmaster Mikhail Perkhin, assay mark
of St. Petersburg before 1896

The hinged box has fleur-de-lys-shaped hinges and a
clasp set with diamonds and cabochon rubies. The rim of
the cover is set with rose-cut diamonds and trimmed with
a red and white enamel band.

Joan and Melissa Rivers (lent to New York and
San Francisco only)

— 344 —

OBLONG BOX
Nephrite, gold, enamel, rubies
L: 3¹⁵⁄₁₆ inches
Marks: Fabergé, initials of workmaster Henrik Wigström

The rim of the hinged box is decorated with a band of
chased-gold laurel leaves within opaque white enamel
borders, set with five cabochon rubies.

Joan and Melissa Rivers (lent to New York and
San Francisco only)

— 345 —

OWL-HEAD VODKA CUP
Agate, diamonds, gold, enamel
Diam: 1½ inches

Of reddish brown agate, the cup is carved as the head of
an owl with eyes of rose-cut diamonds in gold mounts.
The gold rim is trimmed with a green and white enamel
entrelac border.

Provenance: Grand Duchess Elizaveta Feodorovna, wife of
Grand Duke Sergei Aleksandrovich; Richard Stern, Geneva

Joan and Melissa Rivers (lent to New York and
San Francisco only)

— 346 —

BOX IN LOUIS XV STYLE
Nephrite, gold, enamel
Diam: 2½ inches
Marks: Fabergé, initials of workmasters Mikhail Perkhin and
Henrik Wigström, assay mark of St. Petersburg 1896–1908

The yellow gold cover of the circular nephrite box is
chased with an eagle (Zeus) and Cupid on a cloud, against
a pink *guilloché* enamel ground. The borders are chased
with bullrushes and scrolls.

Joan and Melissa Rivers (lent to New York and
San Francisco only)

— 347 —
DIAMOND PIN
Diamonds, gold
L: 1¼ inches
Marks: Initials of workmaster August Holmström, assay mark of
St. Petersburg before 1896

The central brilliant-cut black diamond, within a rose-
cut diamond border, is flanked by two pear-shaped diamonds in a yellow, white, and red gold mount.

Joan and Melissa Rivers (lent to New York only)

— 348 —
STAR SAPPHIRE BROOCH
Star sapphire, diamonds, platinum, gold
H: 1¼ inches
Marks: Illegible

The oval central stone within a border of diamonds is
surmounted by a ribbon knot set with diamonds. The
mount is platinum and yellow gold.

Provenance: Grand Duchess Vladimir

Joan and Melissa Rivers (lent to New York only)

— 349 —
AQUAMARINE BROOCH
Aquamarine, diamonds, platinum, gold
L: 1¼ inches
Marks: Initials of workmaster August Holmström

The central stone is surrounded by diamond-set openwork flowers within a border of diamonds. The mount is
platinum and yellow gold.

Joan and Melissa Rivers (lent to New York only)

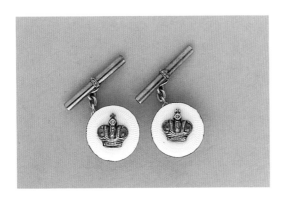

— 350 —

LADY'S ENAMELED CIGARETTE CASE
Gold, enamel, diamonds
L: 3⅜ inches
Marks: Fabergé, initials of workmaster Henrik Wigström,
assay mark of St. Petersburg 1908–17, 72

The rectangular central oval medallion has the monogram MR set with diamonds, within a diamond border. The case is further decorated with panels of white enamel stripes, an outer border of foliage and berries set with diamonds, and a medallion with a trophy of love.

Joan and Melissa Rivers (lent to New York and
San Francisco only)

— 351 —

IMPERIAL PRESENTATION CUFF LINKS WITH RUBIES
Gold, enamel, rubies, diamonds
Diam: ½ inch
Marks: Initials of workmaster August Hollming, assay mark
of St. Petersburg 1896–1908
Original fitted case with gilt imperial eagle

Provenance: Presented by Czar Nicholas II to the duke of
Saxe-Coburg-Gotha; Christie's, Geneva, May 12, 1980, lot 210

The Estate of James A. Williams

— 352 —

IMPERIAL PRESENTATION CUFF LINKS
Gold, enamel, diamonds
Diam: ½ inch
Marks: Initials of workmaster Alfred Thielemann
Original fitted case with gilt imperial eagle

Provenance: Christie's, Geneva, May 11, 1982, lot 312

The Estate of James A. Williams

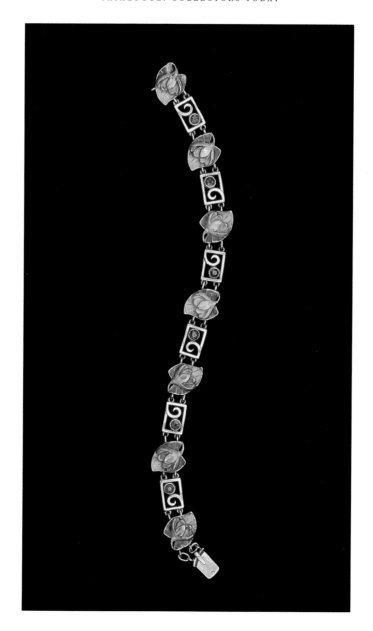

— 353 —

ART NOUVEAU BRACELET
Gold, enamel, sapphires
L: 7 inches
Marks: Initials KF, assay mark of Moscow 1896–1908,
assay master Ivan Lebedkin

The bracelet is formed of six water-lily motifs in cloisonné enamel, alternating with links of gold scrolls and
sapphires.

Private Collection

— 354 —

PALISANDER CIGARETTE CASE
Palisander, gold, sapphire
L: 3¹⁵⁄₁₆ inches
Marks: Fabergé, initials of workmaster Mikhail Perkhin,
assay mark of St. Petersburg before 1896, inv. no. 1289

This wooden cigarette case is of a simple but elegant
design.

Provenance: A La Vieille Russie, New York

John Traina

— 355 —

IMPERIAL PRESENTATION CIGARETTE CASE
Lacquer, gold
L: 4 inches
Marks: Fabergé, initials of workmaster Mikhail Perkhin, assay mark
of St. Petersburg before 1896

The Russian double-headed eagle on the cover of this
case indicates an imperial presentation.

John Traina

— 356 —

REEDED SILVER CIGARETTE CASE

Silver, sapphire

L: 3¾ inches

Marks: Imperial Warrant, assay mark of Moscow 1908–17

Original fitted case stamped with Imperial Warrant,

St. Petersburg, Moscow, Odessa

Provenance: Ermitage Ltd., London

John Traina

— 357 —

SILVER GILT CIGARETTE CASE

Silver gilt, enamel, gold, diamonds

L: 4½ inches

Marks: Fabergé, initials of workmaster Henrik Wigström,

assay mark of St. Petersburg 1908–17, inv. no. 22440;

interior inscribed "From Olaf 1912"

The case of moiré *guilloché* enamel has a diamond-set
thumb piece.

Provenance: Possibly Prince Alexander of Denmark
(later King Olaf V of Norway); Ermitage Ltd., London

John Traina

— 358 —

AUTOMOBILE CLUB CIGARETTE CASE
Silver
L: 3⅝ inches
Marks: Imperial Warrant, assay mark of Moscow 1908–17; inscribed
"Yeletz to Lipetzk, Yussa, driver P. A. Vedernikov, 1911"

The case is chased and engraved with the emblem of the
Moscow Automobile Club.

Provenance: Andre Ruzhnikov, Palo Alto, California

John Traina

— 359 —

CIGARETTE CASE IN NEO-RUSSIAN STYLE
Silver, rubies, sapphires
L: 4 inches
Marks: Imperial Warrant, assay mark of Moscow 1896–1908,
inv. no. 21133

The case is decorated with the chased head of a boyar
and a maritime motif. It is set with rose-cut rubies and
sapphires and has a cabochon sapphire push piece.

Provenance: Andre Ruzhnikov, Palo Alto, California

John Traina

— 360 —

SILVER PRESENTATION CIGARETTE CASE
Silver, diamonds, rubies
L: 3⅜ inches
Marks: Fabergé, initials of workmaster August Hollming,
assay mark of St. Petersburg 1908–17

Applied on one side are the entwined crowned initial K
and an anchor, either for Grand Duke Kirill Vladimirovich (1876–1938), captain in the Russian imperial navy
and commander of the cruiser *Oleg*, or for Grand Duke
Konstantin Konstantinovich (1858–1918), chief of the
Equipage of the navy.

Provenance: Andre Ruzhnikov, Palo Alto, California

John Traina

— 361 —

GOLD PRESENTATION CIGARETTE CASE
Gold, diamonds, enamel
L: 3 ¹⁵⁄₁₆ inches
Marks: Fabergé, initials of workmaster August Hollming, assay mark of
St. Petersburg 1896–1908, inv. no. 7443

The burnished exterior of this case is decorated on one
side with a red *guilloché* enamel disk containing a yellow
gold crowned cipher of Grand Duke Aleksei Aleksandrovich, son of Czar Alexander II, and admiral general
and supreme chief of the Russian imperial fleet.

Provenance: Grand Duke Aleksei Aleksandrovich;
Christie's, Geneva, November 11, 1990, lot 393

John Traina

— 362 —

IMPERIAL PRESENTATION CIGARETTE CASE
Gold, diamonds, enamel
L: 3⅝ inches
Marks: Fabergé, initials of workmaster Victor Aarne, assay mark of
St. Petersburg before 1896; interior inscribed in English "Presented to
Lieut. J. C. Harrison Scott Grey by H.M. the Emperor of Russia on the
occasion of his commanding the escort to His Majesty, Ballater
to Balmoral Sept. 22, Balmoral to Ballater Oct. 3, 1896"

The case was presented to the British escort officer on
the occasion of the visit of Czar Nicholas II, Czarina
Alexandra Feodorovna, and their first child, Olga, to
Queen Victoria in Balmoral in 1896 (for a photograph of
the visit, see Habsburg 1987, p. 20).

Provenance: Andre Ruzhnikov, Palo Alto, California

John Traina

— 363 —

ENGINE-TURNED ENAMELED CIGARETTE CASE
Gold, enamel, diamonds
L: 3⅝ inches
Marks: Fabergé, initials of workmaster Henrik Wigström, assay mark
of St. Petersburg 1908–17; interior inscribed "Merci February 18, 1942"

The case is decorated with white enamel stripes and blue
enamel Greek-key-pattern borders. The thumb piece is
set with diamonds.

Provenance: Given by Barbara Hutton to Cary Grant; Sotheby's,
Beverly Hills, California, November 17, 1987

John Traina

— 364 —

TWO-COLOR GOLD CIGARETTE CASE
Gold, enamel, diamonds
L: 3¼ inches
Marks: Imperial Warrant, assay mark of Moscow before 1896

The purple case is embellished with two-color gold
swags entwined with opaque white enamel zigzags. The
push piece is set with a rose-cut diamond.

Provenance: Gary Hansen, St. Louis, 1988

Exhibitions: ALVR 1983, cat. 195

John Traina

— 365 —

LADY'S GOLD CIGARETTE CASE
Gold, diamonds
L: 3 inches
Marks: Initials of workmaster Mikhail Perkhin, assay mark of
St. Petersburg before 1896; interior inscribed "Je voudrais être
une cigarette pour habiter un instant vos lèvres et puis m'éteindre"
(I would like to be a cigarette, to live for an instant on your lips,
and then go out).

The oblong reeded case has a diamond-set push piece.

Provenance: Ermitage Ltd., London

John Traina

— 366 —

CIGARETTE BOX IN LOUIS XVI STYLE
Gold
L: 4¼ inches
Marks: Fabergé, initials of workmaster Henrik Wigström, assay mark
of St. Petersburg before 1896, inv. no. 17765

The piece is in the manner of a Louis XVI snuffbox, with
an engine-turned pattern of waves and pellets and a
chased border of husks.

John Traina

— 367 —

ENGINE-TURNED GOLD CIGARETTE CASE
Gold, diamonds
L: 3⅝ inches
Marks: Fabergé, initials of workmaster Henrik Wigström, assay mark
of St. Petersburg 1908–17

Alternating panels of reeded red gold and engine-turned
green gold are separated by opaque white enamel bands.
Blue enamel stripes are on the top and sides; the thumb
piece is diamond set.

Provenance: Andre Ruzhnikov, Palo Alto, California

John Traina

— 368 —

RENAISSANCE-STYLE CIGARETTE CASE
Gold, sapphire
L: 3½ inches
Marks: Imperial Warrant, initials of workmaster Oskar Pihl,
assay mark of Moscow before 1896, inv. no. 4803

The case is chased with yellow gold scrolling foliage and
mythical birds on a pink *sablé* gold ground.

Provenance: Ermitage Ltd., London

John Traina

— 369 —

ENGINE-TURNED PRESENTATION CIGARETTE CASE
Gold, diamonds
L: 3⁵⁄₁₆ inches
Marks: Fabergé, initials of workmaster Henrik Wigström,
assay mark of St. Petersburg 1896–1908

The name Elizaveta and the dates 1886 and 1904 are set
in diamonds on one side.

Provenance: Said to have been presented by Elizaveta Feodorovna
(Elisabeth, princess of Hessen-Darmstadt), wife of Grand Duke Sergei
Aleksandrovich and sister of Czarina Alexandra Feodorovna, to her
husband, uncle of Czar Nicholas II; A La Vieille Russie, New York

John Traina

— 370 —

NEPHRITE CIGARETTE CASE
Nephrite, gold, emerald
L: 3¾ inches
Marks: Initials KF, assay mark of Moscow before 1896

The carved nephrite box with rounded sides is decorated with green gold laurel swags and red gold ribbons. It has an emerald push piece.

Provenance: Sotheby Parke Bernet, New York, June 12, 1986, lot 290

John Traina

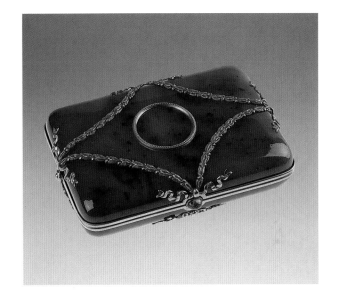

— 371 —

NEPHRITE PRESENTATION CIGARETTE CASE
Nephrite, gold, enamel
L: 3⅜ inches
Marks: Fabergé, initials of workmaster Henrik Wigström, assay mark of St. Petersburg 1896–1908; reverse inscribed XXV

The nephrite case has a central roundel with the monogram MP under an imperial crown on a pink enamel ground.

Provenance: Habsburg, Feldman, New York, April 21, 1991, cat. 21

John Traina

— 372 —

ROCOCO-STYLE CIGARETTE CASE
Silver gilt, enamel, gold, diamonds
L: 3¾ inches
Marks: Initials of workmaster Mikhail Perkhin, assay mark
of St. Petersburg before 1896

The blue moiré *guilloché* enameled case is applied with
rococo scrolls inset with rose-cut diamonds.

John Traina

— 373 —

IMPERIAL PRESENTATION CIGARETTE CASE
Silver gilt, enamel, diamonds
L: 3⅞ inches
Marks: Initials of workmaster August Hollming, assay mark
of St. Petersburg 1896–1908
Original fitted case stamped with Imperial Warrant,
St. Petersburg, Moscow

The eccentric *guilloché* sunburst centers on a chased gold
imperial eagle and rose-cut diamond. The push piece is
set with faceted diamonds.

Provenance: Presented by the Imperial Cabinet on behalf of Czar
Nicholas II to Eduard Vella in May 1902, for services rendered
at the Russian consulate in Malta; Christie's, Geneva,
November 17, 1993, lot 310

John Traina

— 374 —

ENAMELED GOLD CIGARETTE CASE
Gold, enamel, diamonds
L: 3½ inches
Marks: Fabergé, initials of workmaster Mikhail Perkhin, assay mark
of St. Petersburg 1896–1908

The case is of pink enamel over a *guilloché* enamel ground
of reeds and pellets. On one side is a princely crown. The
lip has a diamond border, and the push piece is diamond-
set.

John Traina

— 375 —

ENAMELED SILVER CIGARETTE CASE
Silver, enamel, gold, diamonds
L: 3¾ inches
Marks: Fabergé, initials of workmaster Henrik Wigström, assay mark
of St. Petersburg 1896–1908

The crowned monogram FS is applied on one side of this
green enameled case.

Provenance: Prince Juan Fulco di Savoia, Spanish ambassador to
Russia, 1887–91; Christie's, New York, April 16, 1985, lot 227

John Traina

— 376 —

SILVER GILT VANITY CASE
Silver gilt, enamel, sapphires, ivory, glass
L: 3½ inches
Marks: Fabergé, initials of workmaster August Hollming,
assay mark of St. Petersburg before 1896, inv. no. 16256;
interior engraved "S. Sch."

Of brilliant emerald green enamel, the vanity case has
three compartments, containing an ivory tablet, a mirror,
and a pencil. The four thumb pieces are set with cabochon sapphires. The interior is decorated with a princely
crown.

Provenance: Panzer Collection; Christie's, New York,
October 1993, lot 153

John Traina

— 377 —

TUBULAR GOLD CIGARETTE CASE
Gold, enamel, diamonds
L: 3 7⁄16
Marks: Fabergé, initials of workmaster August Hollming, assay mark
of St. Petersburg 1896–1908

The mauve enamel case is set with rose-cut diamonds on
the thumb piece.

Exhibitions: ALVR 1983, cat. 189, ill. p. 73

John Traina

— 378 —

TUBULAR SILVER GILT CIGARETTE CASE
Silver gilt, enamel, diamonds
L: 3¾ inches
Marks: Fabergé, initials of workmaster Henrik Wigström, assay mark
of St. Petersburg 1908–17, London import marks

The red enameled case opens at the sides to reveal a
striker plate and a match compartment.

Provenance: Andre Ruzhnikov, Palo Alto, California

John Traina

— 379 —

IMPERIAL PRESENTATION CIGARETTE CASE
Silver gilt, enamel, ruby, emerald, sapphire, diamonds
L: 3⅝ inches
Marks: Fabergé, initials of workmaster August Hollming,
assay mark of St. Petersburg 1908–17

The case is of steel gray enamel over a *guilloché* sunburst.
One side is decorated with a Monomakh crown set with
a ruby, a sapphire, and rose-cut diamonds. (The original
Monomakh crown was used at the coronation of the first
Romanov czar.) The push piece is set with a diamond.

John Traina

— 380 —

IMPERIAL PRESENTATION CIGARETTE CASE
Silver gilt, enamel, diamonds, ruby, sapphire
L: 3¾ inches
Marks: Fabergé, initials of workmaster August Hollming,
assay mark of St. Petersburg 1908–17
Original fitted case

Provenance: Christie's, New York, June 3, 1986, lot 372

John Traina

— 381 —

IMPERIAL PRESENTATION CIGARETTE CASE
Gold, enamel, diamonds
L: 3¾ inches
Marks: Fabergé, initials of workmaster A. Holmström,
assay mark of St. Petersburg 1896–1908, inv. no. 1158
Original fitted case with gilt imperial eagle

The decoration is strawberry red enamel over a *guilloché*
sunburst centering on a diamond-set imperial crown.

Provenance: Presented by Czar Nicholas II to Pavel Kaczkovsky,
a high-ranking civil servant at the court, on the eve of the coronation,
May 25, 1896; Sotheby's, Geneva, May 19, 1994, lot 251

John Traina

— 382 —

IMPERIAL PRESENTATION CIGARETTE CASE
Silver gilt, enamel, diamonds
L: 3½ inches
Marks: Fabergé, initials of workmaster August Hollming,
assay mark of St. Petersburg 1908–17
Original fitted case with gilt imperial eagle

The case of royal blue enamel over a *guilloché* sunburst is
decorated on one side with a central diamond-set imperial eagle. It has a diamond-set push piece.

Provenance: Presented by Czar Nicholas II to the chief police inspector
Henrik Madsen in Copenhagen; Christie's, Geneva,
November 17, 1983, lot 381

John Traina

— 383 —

IMPERIAL PRESENTATION CIGARETTE CASE
Silver gilt, enamel, seed pearls, gold
L: 4 inches
Marks: Initials of workmaster Henrik Wigström, assay mark of
St. Petersburg 1896–1908; interior inscribed "Nicky Alix 15.VI.1907"

This oval case is enameled in emerald green over a moiré
guilloché pattern. It has a chased two-color gold palmetto border. The rim is set with a row of seed pearls.

Provenance: Presented by Czar Nicholas II and Czarina Alexandra
Feodorovna to a member of the Swedish royal family;
Ermitage Ltd., London

John Traina

— 384 —

CIRCULAR TRAY
Nephrite, gold, enamel, diamonds
W: 10¾ (at handles)
Marks: Fabergé, initials of workmaster Mikhail Perkhin,
assay mark of St. Petersburg before 1896

Nephrite trays from Fabergé's workshop exist in two shapes: circular and rectangular with rounded short sides. All of them are by Mikhail Perkhin, and with one exception, they are all in the rococo style. The largest extant nephrite tray is the circular example in the Forbes Magazine collection (cat. no. 250), presented at the coronation of Nicholas II by the dignitaries of St. Petersburg. Another example, similar to the present one but larger, was in a private collection in England (Habsburg/Lopato 1994, cat. 169).

John Traina

— 385 —

NOTE BLOCK AND PENCIL
Silver, bowenite, pencil
H: 5⅞ inches
Marks: Fabergé, initials of workmaster Julius Rappoport,
assay mark of St. Petersburg 1896–1908

The silver cover has a bowenite plaque decorated with
rococo openwork scrolls and rocaille.

Provenance: Gift of John Traina

Fine Arts Museums of San Francisco, 1991.42a–b

Appendix I

"Fauxbergé"

Over the last sixty years in the United States and Russia, the forging of Fabergé objects has become a well-developed industry of frightening proportions.[1] Tens of thousands of imitation pieces have been fashioned and sold, mostly to gullible collectors. Some fakes have found their way into reputable museums.

It appears that the earliest forged Fabergé in the United States can be traced to Armand Hammer. According to his brother Victor, Armand worked hand in hand with Anastas Mikoyan, Stalin's trade commissar, organizing sales of genuine Russian treasure on behalf of the Bolsheviks throughout the 1930s. From Mikoyan Armand received "Fabergé" hallmarking tools: "Side by side with the Soviet-owned Fabergé we sold our own perfectly hallmarked Fabergé pieces and kicked back commissions on both to Mikoyan. In 1938 we had a very big Fabergé sale and sold so many real pieces and so many counterfeits we grossed millions."[2] The proof of Hammer's activities is to be found in several major American museums and private collections, where many flowers sold by him are but poor Art Deco–style imitations (see p. 338).

In the late 1960s "Fauxbergé" from Soviet Russia permeated the Western market. African and Middle Eastern diplomats returned from Russia with their diplomatic bags full of genuine late-nineteenth- and early-twentieth-century Russian cloisonné enamels, most bearing forged Fabergé hallmarks, alongside hardstone figures copied from well-known Fabergé models. Some auction houses apparently were led astray by a number of clever animal sculptures, which were reputed to be the work of a first-class Russian craftsman.[3]

A collection of more than one hundred pieces of Fauxbergé left Russia in the late 1970s in the suitcases of a Russian émigré. For a time domiciled in Bel Air, California, the collection was promoted as the "World's Finest and Largest Private Collection of Art Masterpieces by Carl Fabergé" and changed hands at least once in the United States. It was last offered for sale to this author in Geneva by an unsuspecting Armand Hammer in 1987.

As recently as 1994 the New Brunswick Museum, St. John, Canada, was obliged to recatalogue and downgrade more than one hundred "Fabergé" objects received as a gift in the 1980s. Courageously, as an example, the museum put its Fauxbergé and genuine objects on view, side by side, thus offering the public a first and most welcome opportunity to compare forged and authentic items.[4] The works at the museum originated primarily from Russian workshops situated in Brooklyn, New York. These fakes, dubbed by this author as the work of the "Brooklyn Forger," are often touted by self-styled Russian emigrants with thick accents, who travel with suitcases full of such objects, which they offer as "imperial." One Texan collector is known to be the proud owner of 165 such works, all crafted by the Brooklyn Forger's workshop.

When viewed individually, present-day forgeries are capable of leading the unsuspecting buyer astray. Shown en masse, they display an instantly recognizable style. Many have shapes that are non-Russian and/or postdate

World War I. Although most Fabergé objects are one of a kind, forgers often produce easily detectable copies of existing, well-documented originals. Fabergé selected from a palette of 145 enamel hues, but forgers restrict themselves primarily to scarlet and sometimes pale blue, green, mauve, or white. While only a small number of genuine Fabergé pieces were made for the use of the imperial family, many forgeries are adorned with imperial ciphers, double-headed eagles, or crowns.

A closer look at hallmarks frequently gives the careless forger away. Many a modern counterfeit has been hallmarked with incompatible punches. For instance, a number of fakes bear the initials of workmaster Mikhail Perkhin, who is known to have died in 1903, or of Victor Aarne, who left St. Petersburg for Finland in 1904, combined with assay marks corresponding to the years 1908 through 1917. Other pieces have received marks that are contrary to their very nature. Thus modern Moscow-style cloisonné enamel objects often carry initials of St. Petersburg craftsmen who specialized exclusively in *guilloché* enamels. Whereas some forgers have produced faithful replicas of Russian hallmarks, others have carelessly given only approximate renditions of the originals.

More subjective perhaps, because less scientific, are determinations of authenticity based on quality. If some forgeries are blatantly obvious and poor caricatures of Fabergé's art, others are more daring and sophisticated. Yet the juxtaposition of even an ambitious forgery with any original shows, especially under magnification, that they are worlds apart. No forger has been able to attain the glossy perfection of the enameled surfaces for which Fabergé was so justly celebrated. Recent products are pockmarked and uneven, with enamels often overflowing the bordering channels.

Fabergé's complicated varicolored gold swags, in which the virtuosity of the chaser is best exemplified, are rarely attempted by forgers. In Fabergé's workshops even simple laurel or palmetto borders, when mechanically produced, were carefully hand finished; the forger's attempts are invariably left grainy. Small details that give away the emulator also include carelessly drilled hardstone surfaces, with chipped orifices; poorly finished, badly cut screws and nuts; and uneven, sloppy mounts for seed pearls or semiprecious stones. In Fabergé's time even the simplest objects took many days to produce, with many hours spent polishing the finished object. Today the time, or the money, is rarely spent on such painstaking work.

One exception to this rule was the celebrated case of the Nicholas II Equestrian egg, traditionally held to have been a present from Czarina Alexandra Feodorovna to Nicholas on the occasion of the Romanov tercentenary in 1913. This jeweled and enameled Easter egg, reproduced in several early monographs and certified as genuine by more than one expert, was acquired by Iranian collector Iskander Aryeh in Geneva in 1976 for 550,000 Swiss francs. By 1985, when Aryeh decided to sell the egg, newly published archival sources excluded the alleged imperial provenance. Aryeh sued the auction house, and rumor put the out-of-court settlement at $5 million.

The following pages contain thirty-one items lent by the New Brunswick Museum, St. John, Canada, from their study collection. The collection includes many forgeries acquired in good faith by a Canadian collector and given to the museum between 1986 and 1990. A final object has been lent by the Brooklyn Museum, New York. All thirty-two objects bear spurious hallmarks.

The intention of this appendix of forged Fabergé objects is to make the future collector fully aware of the many pitfalls that await him or her. Chances are that unless they are offered by a reputable dealer or auction house, Fabergé items available on the American market today are forgeries.

— Géza von Habsburg

NOTES

1. For the most recent discussion of Fauxbergé, see Géza von Habsburg, "Fauxbergé," *Art & Auction* 16, no. 7 (February 1994), pp. 76–79.

2. Carl Blumay with Henry Edwards, *The Dark Side of Power: The Real Armand Hammer* (New York: Simon and Schuster, 1992), p. 106.

3. Yuri Brokhin, *Hustling on Gorki Street: Sex and Crime in Russia Today* (New York: Dial Press, 1975), pp. 162–85.

4. For a discussion of the New Brunswick Museum forgeries, see Géza von Habsburg, in Solodkoff 1995, pp. 42ff.

386. PERFUME BOTTLE
Silver gilt, gold, enamel, diamond; h. 2⅝ inches

The forger used the shape of a Fabergé brush pot for a perfume bottle.

New Brunswick Museum, St. John, Canada, 986.9.408

387. INKWELL
Silver gilt, enamel, gold, diamonds; h. 2⅝ inches

The forger "married" a bell push and a brush pot, adding superfluous embellishments.

New Brunswick Museum, St. John, Canada, 986.14.8

388. BRUSH POT
Silver gilt, enamel, gold, sapphire; h. 2 inches

This well-imitated Fabergé object is given away by its fake hallmarks.

New Brunswick Museum, St. John, Canada, 986.9.432

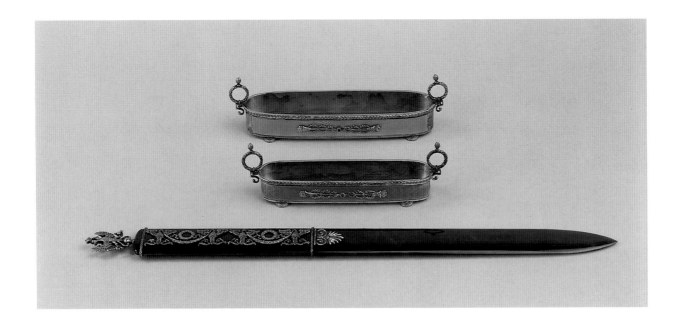

389. OVAL PEN TRAY
Silver gilt, enamel, rubies; l. 7 inches

The pen tray is an unrecorded shape in Fabergé's oeuvre.

New Brunswick Museum, St. John, Canada, 986.9.428

390. OVAL PEN TRAY
Silver gilt, enamel, rubies; l. 6⅛ inches

See the object above.

New Brunswick Museum, St. John, Canada, 986.9.429

391. LETTER OPENER
Nephrite, silver gilt; l. 15⅜ inches

This is one of hundreds of such poor "imperial" objects.

New Brunswick Museum, St. John, Canada, 990.44.18

392. CYLINDRICAL BRUSH POT
Silver gilt, gold, enamel, sapphire, diamonds; h. 2⅞ inches

This tapering, cylindrical form is an unrecorded shape for a brush pot in Russia.

New Brunswick Museum, St. John, Canada, 990.44.11

393. CYLINDRICAL BOX
Silver gilt, gold, enamel, diamonds; h. 1½ inches

This box is an overembellished, non-Russian shape.

New Brunswick Museum, St. John, Canada, 990.44.17

394. PERFUME BOTTLE
Silver gilt, enamel, sapphire, rubies; h. 2⁷⁄₁₆ inches

Plain burnished mounts, instead of chased leaf borders, give away this otherwise well-executed forgery.

New Brunswick Museum, St. John, Canada, 986.9.434

395. CYLINDRICAL BOX
Silver gilt, gold, enamel, diamonds, rubies; h. 1¹⁵⁄₁₆ inches

The box is another "imperialized," overembellished, and non-Russian object.

New Brunswick Museum, St. John, Canada, 990.44.8

396. CYLINDRICAL BRUSH POT
Silver gilt, enamel, diamonds; h. 2⅞ inches

This shape did not exist in Fabergé's oeuvre.

New Brunswick Museum, St. John, Canada, 990.44.10

397. TWO-HANDLED CUP
Nephrite, silver gilt, gold, enamel, diamonds, rubies; h. 3⅝ inches

This successfully imitated object is betrayed by its hall-marks.

New Brunswick Museum, St. John, Canada, 990.44.16

398. NEPHRITE VASE
Nephrite, silver gilt, rubies; h. 5⅞ inches

The "imperial" portraits and the bad quality of the neph-rite and gold chasing are characteristics of this workshop.

New Brunswick Museum, St. John, Canada, 990.44.15

399. RECTANGULAR CIGARETTE CASE
Nephrite, silver gilt, gold, enamel; h. 3⅜ inches

This piece is a free imitation of a cigarette case in the Traina collection (see cat. no. 371).

New Brunswick Museum, St. John, Canada, 989.182.13

400. OVAL SNUFFBOX
Nephrite, silver gilt, gold, enamel, diamonds; l. 2⅞ inches

The spurious marks suggest an "imperial" provenance for this poor-quality box.

New Brunswick Museum, St. John, Canada, 989.182.14

401. OVAL NEPHRITE BOX
Nephrite, enamel, gold, rubies, diamonds; l. 2⅝ inches

This is an "imperial" box of very poor quality.

New Brunswick Museum, St. John, Canada, 986.14.30

402. TERCENTENARY BOX
Silver gilt, enamel, diamonds; w. 4 3/16 inches

The box is a very poor rendering of an object made to commemorate three hundred years of Romanov rule.

New Brunswick Museum, St. John, Canada, 990.44.7

403. SQUARE BOX
Silver gilt, gold, enamel, diamonds; w. 3 3/16 inches

This box is an obvious, slightly enlarged copy of an imperial presentation snuffbox in the Victoria and Albert Museum, London (see Habsburg/Lopato 1994, cat. 107).

New Brunswick Museum, St. John, Canada, 990.44.6

404. CIRCULAR BOX
Silver gilt, gold, enamel, rubies, diamonds; diam. 3 1/4 inches

The box is a very poor quality forgery with an "imperial" eagle.

New Brunswick Museum, St. John, Canada, 986.9.430

405. CIRCULAR BONBONNIÈRE
Silver gilt, enamel, diamonds; diam. 1 15/16 inches

This bonbonnière is another case of a wrong type of object for an "imperial" presentation.

New Brunswick Museum, St. John, Canada, 986.9.431

406. CIGARETTE CASE
Silver gilt, enamel, rubies, diamond; l. 4 1/16 inches

The cigarette case is another "imperialized" item.

New Brunswick Museum, St. John, Canada, 986.9.409

407. RECTANGULAR CIGARETTE BOX
Silver gilt, enamel, diamonds; l. 3 7/8 inches

Plain rims (instead of elaborately chased), an odd *guilloché* pattern in the medallion, and nineteenth-century-style griffins help identify this object as a forgery.

New Brunswick Museum, St. John, Canada, 986.9.410

409

408

410

411

408. CIRCULAR FRAME

Silver gilt, gold, enamel, diamonds, glass, bone; diam. 4 inches

The forgers freely adapted a Fabergé design for a clock (see cat. no. 321) and made it into a frame.

New Brunswick Museum, St. John, Canada, 986.14.11

409. FRAME

Silver gilt, enamel, bone; h. 4¼ inches

The frame is another "imperialized" item of exceedingly poor quality.

New Brunswick Museum, St. John, Canada, 986.14.9

410. TRAPEZOIDAL FRAME

Silver gilt, enamel, diamonds, glass, bone; h: 4⅜ inches

The frame's atypical shape and very poor engine turning help classify this object as a fake.

New Brunswick Museum, St. John, Canada, 989.182.19

411. OVAL FRAME

Silver gilt, enamel, glass, bone, rubies; h. 4¼ inches

An "imperial" jeweled crown and an apparently French eighteenth-century miniature do not render this object genuine.

New Brunswick Museum, St. John, Canada, 986.14.9

412. CIRCULAR BOX

Silver gilt, gold, enamel, diamonds; diam. 1⅝ inches

This and the three other boxes shown here that are done in the forger's preferred red enamel are ridiculous, "imperialized" fakes.

New Brunswick Museum, St. John, Canada, 989.182.15

413. CIRCULAR BOX

Silver gilt, gold, enamel, diamonds; diam. 2⁷⁄₁₆ inches

This overembellished, "imperialized" box is otherwise quite a successful forgery.

New Brunswick Museum, St. John, Canada, 986.14.6

414. OVAL BOX

Silver gilt, gold, enamel, diamonds; l. 1⁹⁄₁₆ inches

New Brunswick Museum, St. John, Canada, 989.182.17

415. RECTANGULAR BOX

Silver gilt, gold, enamel, diamonds; l. 1⅜ inches

New Brunswick Museum, St. John, Canada, 989.182.18

416. OBLONG BOX

Silver gilt, gold, enamel, diamonds; l. 1⁹⁄₁₆ inches

New Brunswick Museum, St. John, Canada, 989.182.16

417. WILD STRAWBERRY PLANT

Chalcedony, jasper(?), gold, nephrite, onyx, glass; h. 5 inches

The plant has white chalcedony blossoms with yellow stone centers and berries in red jasper(?). Gold stalks bear nephrite leaves. The plant stands in a striated white onyx pot, which contains simulated earth in the form of colored glass shards. The piece bears spurious marks of Fabergé and the initials of workmaster Henrik Wigström.

This is a good example of the dozens of forged flowers sold chiefly in the 1940s (some by Armand Hammer) that are included in several major American institutions and private collections.

The Brooklyn Museum, New York, bequest of
Helen B. Sanders, 78.129.16

Appendix II

Acquisitions by Americans at Fabergé's London Shop, 1907–1917

Our knowledge of Fabergé's London clients is based chiefly on two sales ledgers that survive from his London shop. (For a discussion of the London ledgers, see Géza von Habsburg, in Habsburg/Lopato 1994, pp. 124–31.) They cover the period from October 6, 1907, until January 9, 1917, and the sale of almost ten thousand objects, jewels, and items of gold and silver. The lists indicate every sale effected by the London branch, the date of acquisition, name of buyer, and a short description of the object, along with its stock number, sales price in pounds sterling, and cost price in rubles. The names of Fabergé's European celebrity customers, including virtually all the kings and queens of Europe, are contained together with numerous representatives from the *Almanach de Gotha* (the *Who's Who* of European royalty and nobility) as well as both the old and new moneyed class.

Although much attention has been paid previously to European royalty and celebrity customers of Fabergé in London, this appendix lists for the first time a selection of the numerous American customers who between 1907 and 1917 acquired Fabergé objects, some in large quantities, others with more restraint. Many of these objects were bought to be presented as gifts locally and might have ended in the hands of non-American recipients. Others doubtless crossed the ocean on board some private yacht or luxury steamer. This appendix lists more than 450 purchases made by sixty-eight customers who are certainly, or most probably, American. One hopes this list will help to identify some of the described objects that are still in the United States.

Since many buyers were entered in the original ledgers only by surname, this appendix includes just those names that are particular to America, or instances where an American origin is indicated. Thus many possible American buyers might have been eliminated inadvertently. In some cases a choice had to be made between two or more possible buyers. In other cases the salesman committed mistakes in spelling a name or in the transcription of initials, thus making errors in identification possible. In each case the likeliest candidate has been selected. The *New York Social Register* (1908–19) has been extensively consulted, as have the obituary columns of the *New York Times*. A selected list of other references consulted follows the appendix.

Italic names are listed as in the ledgers; the years of purchase are indicated after the names. This list is alphabetized by head of household or most prominent family member, with family members grouped below. The value of the U.S. dollar barely fluctuated between 1907 and 1917: £1 was the equivalent of $4.87.

The following abbreviations appear in the ledger: bl = blue; bonbon = bonbonnière; brills = brilliants; cab = cabochon; cal = calendar; chrys = chrysoprase; cig, cigtte = cigarette; compt = compartment; d, dk = dark; diads = diamonds; en, enal, enl = enamel(ed); eng = engraved; gld = gold; lt = light; m = mecca; medln = medallion; mts = mounts; nepp, neph = nephrite; opl = opalescent; opq = opaque; ornt = ornament; pendt = pendant; plt, plat = platinum; prls = pearls; rasp = raspberry; roses = rose-cut diamonds; sapp(s) = sapphire(s); sil, silr = silver; sq = square; stl = steel; tort = tortoiseshell; umb = umbrella; wh, wht = white.

A

Mrs. J. J. Astor, 1909, 1911, 1913, 1914, 1916

Ava Lowle Willing (1869–1958) of Philadelphia married John Jacob Astor IV (1864–1912) in 1891. She was active in New York and London society and entertained Edward VII and members of British nobility in her country house and in Mayfair. In 1910 she divorced Astor, who two years later died in the sinking of the Titanic. In 1919 she married Lord Ribblesdale (d. 1925). The mother of William Vincent Astor (1891–1959) and Ava Alice Astor (1902–56), she was noted for her beauty and ability as a sportswoman.

Cig. Case. Dk. blue Enl. on silver garlds & roses, no. 16834, £17/10

Cig. case, raspberry enl. gold mounts, 1 rose, no. 18918, £25/15

Cig. case, oval, blue opal. enamel, ornts, no. 18044, £21/15

Reenamelling own green en: Cig. case, no. RO239, (nett) £7

Repairing & reenamelling own green Cigtte. case, no. RO342, (nett) £9

Pencil, steel grey enl., no. 22320, £3/10

Do, blue enamel, no. 22591, £3/10

Cig. case, long, oval, steel grey enal. gold mts. roses, no. 22843, £23

Cigtte. case, gold, sap. cab., no. 24476, (nett) £55

Capt. J. J. Astor, 1916

John Jacob Astor V, Baron Astor of Hever (1886–1971), was born in New York. He was the son of First Viscount William Waldorf Astor (1848–1919) and Mary Dahlgren Paul of Philadelphia (1853–94) and the younger brother of Waldorf Astor.

The Astors established residence in England in 1890. He is listed in the ledger as living at St. James Square, London, in 1916, the year of his marriage to Lady Violet Mary Elliot Mercer Nairne, daughter of the earl of Minto and widow of a fellow officer, Major Lord Charles Mercer Nairne. Astor was brought up as an Englishman and with his brother attended Eton and Oxford. He was wounded in World War I. Chairman of the London Times for many years, he also served as a member of Parliament.

Brooch, pink opal / enamel and roses, no. 79845, £15/10

Hairpins (2) blond tort- / shell, brills & roses in plat, no. 97571, £175

Elephant, lapis lazuli, no. 24612, £12/10

Mrs. J. J. Astor, 1916

The wife of John Jacob Astor V is listed as Mrs. J. J. Astor and also as Lady Violet Astor.

Papercutter, nephrite, no. 22932, £8/15

Waldorf Astor, 1908, 1909

Second Viscount Waldorf Astor (1879–1952) was the eldest son of First Viscount William Waldorf Astor (1848–1919) and his Philadelphia-born wife Mary Dahlgren Paul (1853–94). Astor was born in New York, but by 1890 his family had settled in England. In 1906 he married Nancy Langhorne Shaw, an American divorcée. The couple entertained Edward VII and his mistress, Mrs. Keppel, at Clivenden in Buckinghamshire, the country estate given to them by his father. From 1910 to 1918 Astor was member of Parliament for Plymouth, and on the death of his father he became a peer. In the 1930s Clivenden was the gathering place of the pacifist and pro-Hitler "Clivenden Set."

Egg. Owl. Grey Chalcedony Gold Legs Garnet Eyes, no. 81098, £4/15

Ditto, ditto, White Chalcedony, ditto, ditto, no. 81097, £4/15

Ditto, Lt. Blue Enl., £13

Ditto

Ditto

Ditto, white, ditto

Ditto

Ditto

Ditto, Pink, ditto

Ditto, Salmon, ditto

Ditto, Lt. Green, ditto

Ditto, Nephrite Small, £10

1 Link, neph. 1 Brill, roses (added to own 3/4 pair Links), £5

Crochet hook, amaranth lt. blue enamel, 1 sapp. fancy, no. 18037, £4/5

Cig. case, lt. blue en: wht. leather, no. S9523, £10

Umb. top, pink enl. gold mount, no. 18752, (sold) £5/5

Mrs. W. Astor, 1911, 1914

Nancy Witcher Langhorne (1879–1964) of Virginia married Robert Gould Shaw in 1897. She divorced Shaw in 1903 and moved to England. In 1906 she married Waldorf Astor, heir to the $110 million Astor fortune. John Singer Sargent's 1907 portrait of her is well known, as are the images of her sister Irene, the model for the Gibson Girl. Known for her energy and sharp tongue, Lady Astor had an international reputation as a hostess and as the first woman to serve in the House of Commons (1920–45), where she championed the rights of women and children.

Reenamelling, own Mouthpiece, inv. no. RO243, £5/8

B

Jules S. Bache, 1910

Jules S. Bache (1861–1944) was born in New York to Semon Bache and Elizabeth von Praag of Nürnberg, Germany. He entered the banking house of Leopold Cahn & Co. in 1880 and became its head in 1892. The bank, which had branches in London and Mexico City, was renamed J. S. Bache & Co. He married Florence Rosalee Scheftel in 1892. The Bache collection of old masters was given to the Metropolitan Museum of Art, New York, in 1940.

Cig. case, oval, white opl. enal. gold mts. roses, no. 19659, £23/5

Miss Barnes, 1908

Mildred Barnes Bliss (ca. 1880–1969), born in New York City, was the daughter of Demas Barnes (d. 1888) and his second wife, Anna Dorinda Blaksley, who subsequently married William H. Bliss. Educated in Paris, Mildred married her stepfather's son, the diplomat Robert Woods Bliss (see *R. Woods Bliss*) in 1908. She probably made her Fabergé purchases in spring 1908, when she returned from abroad. In a 1914 settlement she received over $4 million of the family fortune, made from her father's patent medicine. Bliss was a noted horticulturist, collector, patron of the arts, and generous philanthropist.

Paperknife, grey birds eye oxyde ribbed silver caps, no. S17325, £2

Gordon Bennett, 1911

James Gordon Bennett Jr. (1841–1918), was the son of the New York publisher James Gordon Bennett and Henrietta Agnes Crean from Ireland. Brought up in Europe, he entered the U.S. navy in 1861. After the Civil War he managed his father's newspaper, the *New York Herald*. In 1867 he founded the *Evening Telegram* and in 1887 established the Paris edition of the *New York Herald*. He maintained three homes, in France and in America, including a villa in Newport, Rhode Island, and spent much time on his yacht, *Lysistrata*. He was involved in both the world of sports and European society. In 1914, in Paris, he married the former Maud Potter of Philadelphia, widow of Baron George de Reuter. Among his known peculiarities was his love of owls. His only purchase from Fabergé was the owl listed below.

Owl, grey jadeite, gold feet, 2 brilliants, no. 20992, nett £65

R. Woods Bliss, 1912, 1913

Robert Woods Bliss (1875–1962), the son of William H. Bliss, was born in St. Louis. A career diplomat, he was secretary to the embassy in St. Petersburg in 1904, aide at the embassy in Paris in 1905–6 (both posts under Ambassador R. S. McCormick), and secretary to the American legation in Brussels in 1908, the year he married Mildred Barnes. Later postings included The Hague, Stockholm, and Buenos Aires. The Blisses collected Byzantine and pre-Columbian art of the Americas. Their historic Washington, D.C., home, Dumbarton Oaks, was given to Harvard University in 1940.

Buttons (3), 1 moonstn. gold, n.n., £10

Mrs. Woods Bliss, 1913, 1914

See *Miss Barnes*.

Links, moonstones & gold, n.n., £15

New gold & green en. leaves to own model "daffodil" & new gold rim in base, RO414, (nett) £4 (Paris)

Miss Bliss, 1908

Jade, (chinese) cabochon, n.n., £65

Cigtte. holder case, lilac enal. gold mts 72°, no. 22494, £8

Menthol-case blue grey mauve enamel., no. 17890, £5/5

Thermometer case, red enl., no. 17889, £11

Miss Brice, 1907

Miss Brice was possibly Helen Olivia Brice (d. 1950), the daughter of Senator Calvin Stewart Brice (1845–98) and Katherine

Olivia Meily. Her father, a railroad lawyer and entrepreneur, was elected senator from Ohio in 1890 and upon retirement moved to New York. She is listed in the *New York Social Register* of 1908 as residing at 693 Fifth Avenue with other members of the family. She died unmarried at her home at 960 Fifth Avenue.

> Cig. Case for lady. Gold fluted, 1 Sapph., no. 15393, £19/5

Mrs. Walter Burns, 1907, 1908, 1911

Mary Lyman Morgan (1844–1919), the sister of J. Pierpont Morgan Sr. (1837–1913), in 1867, in London, married Walter Hayes Burns (d. 1897) of New York. After the death of her husband she helped to receive and entertain Morgan's guests in London. On March 7, 1908, Queen Alexandra, her daughter Victoria, the Princess Royal, and her sister Dowager Empress Maria Feodorovna were received by Morgan and Mrs. Burns at Prince's Gate. She had a son, Walter, and a daughter, Mary, later Viscountess Harcourt.

> Tiepin - Mecca - Roses, no. 82809, £6/15
>
> Buckle, round, dark blue enl. centre. green & wht. opq. en., border green gold ornts., no. 17793, £11/15
>
> Umb. Top, blue en: 1 sapp, no. 17393, £5/5
>
> Umb. top, wht. opl. enl. 1/2 prls. mirror, puff etc., no. 15236, (nett) £10

C

Mrs. G. Cornwals West, 1911

Mrs. George Cornwallis West, née Jennie Jerome (1854–1921), better known as Lady Randolph Churchill, was the Brooklyn-born second daughter of Leonard Jerome (1817–91) and Clarissa Hall (1825–95). Her father, the financial speculator known as the "king of Wall Street" and "father of the American turf," organized the grand ball in honor of the Prince of Wales's visit to the United States in 1860. In 1874 she married Lord Randolph Henry Spencer Churchill (d. 1895), second son of the seventh duke of Marlborough. Her first-born son was Sir Winston Churchill (1874–1965). After the death of her husband, she married George Cornwallis West in 1900. They were divorced in 1914. She then reverted to her title, Lady Spencer Churchill, which she retained after her 1918 marriage to Montagu Porch. Many important men were enamored of her, including Edward VII.

> Pencil, white opl. en., no. 13981, £4/5

C. T. Crocker, 1911

"Colonel" Charles Tempelton Crocker (1884–1948) was the son of Charles Frederick Crocker of San Francisco and Jennie Easton. He was the grandson of Charles Crocker, one of the "Big Four" who built the Central Pacific Railroad. Crocker was known as a yachtsman, explorer, author, composer, and patron of the arts. In 1911 he married Hélène Irwin, and the couple are thought to have voraciously collected artworks during their two-year honeymoon in Europe. Part of the "ultra-fashionable" class of San Francisco, they took first place as hosts to nobility. Between 1912 and 1917 the Crockers built Uplands, a $1.6 million, thirty-nine room mansion at Rancho Las Pulgas, California, designed by Willis Polk in the neo-Renaissance style. The Crockers were divorced in 1925.

> Cig. case, oval, gold 56° white opq. en: inlaid 2 calcedonies, roses, no. 20805, £175
>
> Cig. case, oval, white opal. en. gold mts etc., no. 21518, £23/10

Mrs. C. T. Crocker, 1913

> Cig. case, red & green gold guilloche; white opq. enl., no. 22979, £65/10

Miss Crocker, 1908

> Cig. case, Dk. enl. gold stripe. Moonstone, no. 15685, £32
>
> Matchbox, Lilac enl. rose, no. 9002, £8/5
>
> Cig. case Steel bl. enl. moonstone, no. 16091, £14/10

Lady Bache Cunard, Mrs. E. Cunard, 1907, 1908, 1910, 1916

Maud Burke (d. 1948) was born in San Francisco. In 1895 she married the grandson of the founder of the Cunard steamship line, Sir Bache Cunard (1851–1925), a prominent member of the English hunting and polo set. Lady Cunard called herself Emerald, mingled with royalty, and as a popular hostess noted for her wit and exuberance participated in London's literary and artistic scene. She was a close friend of George Moore and the conductor Sir Thomas Beecham.

> Cig. Case oval. white opaq. en. Roses, no. 15577, £23/5
>
> Calendar. Pink En. & Garland, no. 12622, £20/10
>
> Owl. Nat Agate & gold Perch gold & white onyx, no. 13922, £16/5
>
> Frame. Onyx 1/2 Pearls Arrows & Garlands, no. 12950, £12/15
>
> Returned: Umb. Top, plain pink Enl. & Gold / Purchased by Lord Elphinstone 17 July 07, no. 13554, (amount allowed) £4/15

Returned: Pencil. Plain Green Enl / Purchased by W. Callendar 17 July 07, no. 13243, (amount allowed) £2/14

Stud Pearl Lt. Blue Enamel, no. 82439, £6/9

Cig. case, white opal / enl. bent, gold mts. roses, no. 19814, (nett) £20

Powderpuff case, pink en, no. 23436, £20

Bonbon, white opl. enal. etc., no. 23782, £20

Return: Powderpuff case, egg, pink en, no. 23436, £20

Returned: Bonbon, white opl. enal, etc., no. 23782, £20 (acquired December 12th by Mrs. Leeds, for £30)

D

Florence Davis. See *Marchioness of Dufferin (& Ava)*.

Mrs. J. W. Dixon, 1912

Mrs. J. W. Dixon was possibly Charlotte Hopkins (d. 1957), the wife of Joseph W. Dixon, chairman of the executive committee of the American Securities Corporation and national vice president and director of the American Voluntary Services in New York.

Cigtte. case, grey enal., no. 22461, £21

Stamp box, ditto, no. 22462, £9/19

W. Earl Dodge, 1911

William Earl Dodge IV (d. 1924) was the son of William Earl Dodge III (1858–86) and Emeline Harriman (d. 1938). Dodge, who married Jessie Sloan, was a scion of the Phelps-Dodge family of New York, whose worldwide metal and copper mining interests created vast fortunes. His grandfather William E. Dodge Jr. (1832–1903) was one of the founders of the American Museum of Natural History and the Metropolitan Museum of Art.

Cig. case, pink opq, en: matt, 2 white opl. enl. rims, gold, roses, etc., no. 13540, (nett) £35

Anthony Drexel, 1909, 1911, 1912, 1913, 1914

Colonel Anthony Joseph Drexel Jr. (1864–1934) was the son of Anthony Joseph Drexel (1826–93) and Ellen Rozet (1832–91) of Philadelphia, and grandson of Francis Martin Drexel (1782–1863), the Austrian-born portrait painter and banker who founded the firm of Drexel & Company. In 1886 he married Margarita Armstrong, who divorced him in 1917. Much of his time was spent abroad, and he was well acquainted with both

King Edward VII and Kaiser Wilhelm II. Princess Daisy of Pless in her diary records a visit to St. Petersburg in 1901 while traveling on Drexel's steam yacht *Margaretta*, named for his daughter. He also owned the yachts *Sayonara* and *Aloma*.

Cig. case, dk. blue enamel place for matches, roses, gold mounts, no. 18000, £29/5

Umb. Top, nephrite, pink enamel, roses, no. 13605, £29

Umb. handle, nephrite frog, white opl. en. roses, no. 19083, £30

Pendant, neph: diads, no. 90844, £35

Pendt, neph. br. roses, no. 90842, £30/10

Chain, long, platinum, no. II 7405, £9/10

Cig. case, blue enal., no. 21988, £21

Ditto, nephrite, roses, no. 21998, £50

Cig. case, silver, 1 sapp., no. 20606, £11

Clock, neph: white opl. enl., no. 21910, £55

Bonbon, chinese jade &., no. 22770, £32

Pendant, amethyst drop, roses & plat. chain, no. 97817, £20

Umb. top, pink enamel, no. 23287, £11

Lipsalve tube, lt. mauve en:, no. 22937, £8/10

Clock, neph. white enl. on gold, gilt silver mts, no. 24240, £35

Pencil, cutter, blue enl., no. 19108, £5/5

Mrs. Anthony Drexel, 1907, 1909, 1910, 1911, 1913

Margarita Armstrong (1869–1948) of Philadelphia married Anthony Joseph Drexel Jr. in 1886. For many years they resided in London, where they were popular in court circles. The Drexels had four children. Their daughter Margaretta married Viscount Maidstone in 1910 and became Countess of Winchelsea and Nottingham. After her divorce from Drexel, Margarita married Lieutenant Colonel Brinsley Fitzgerald of the British Army.

Tie pin, 1 Mecca + Roses, no. 81770, £3/15

Own Umbrella top repaired, no. RO131, £15

Cig. case, square, gold, fluted and roses, no. 19502, £30

Matchbox, red gold 56°, green 72°, 1 sap. cab., no. 16597, £11/15

Matchbox, gold, 1 sapp:, no. 14203, £8/15

A. J. Drexel Esq. Jr., 1912, 1914

Anthony Drexel (1887–1946), the son of Anthony Joseph Drexel Jr. and Margarita Armstrong (and also referred to as Jr.), was born in Philadelphia and educated in England. In 1910 he married Marjorie Gwynne Gould (d. 1955), daughter of George Jay Gould and granddaughter of the financier Jay Gould. Her father spent $200,000 on her coming-out party in

1909. The Drexels had homes in Philadelphia and abroad. A partner in the brokerage firm of Ligget & Drexel, Anthony Drexel had a seat on the New York Stock Exchange until 1918. He was the owner of the 238-ton steel yacht *Queen of Scots*.

> Cigtte. Holder, light blue opal enamel & amber, no. 15807, £3/10
> Matchbox, mauve enl., no. 22711, £7

Marchioness of Dufferin (& Ava), 1909, 1916

Florence Davis (1867–1918) was the daughter of John H. Davis, a New York banker, and Theresa Sievwright, residing at Washington Square. In 1893 she married the second marquis of Dufferin and Ava, Terence Temple-Blackwood (b. 1866), the ambassador to Russia, Turkey, Italy, and France. They resided at Cadogan Square, London, in 1910. The marchioness was prominent among American society in London.

> Elephant, rock crystal, no. 15296, £11/15
> Returns: Cig. holder, amber and green enamel, no. 15808, £3
> Return: Bonbon, jade, diads. rubies, no. 22583, £20

Miss Dupont, 1908

Miss Dupont was probably Amy du Pont (1880–1962) of Wilmington, Delaware. She was the daughter of Eugene and Amelia du Pont and a great-granddaughter of Eleuthère Irénée du Pont (1771–1834), founder of the E. I. du Pont de Nemours chemical business. A noted equestrian and horse breeder, Amy du Pont was a sponsor of the national horse show in New York. One of the wealthiest women of her era, she was a generous philanthropist and patron of the arts.

> Egg, plain blue enl., £13
> Pencil, lt. blue enl.: gold, no. 15212, £4/15
> Egg, mauve enl. plain, n.n., £13
> Returned: Pencil, blue enl. & gold, no. 17375, £4/15
> Egg, plain blue enl., £13
> Pencil, lt. blue enl., no. 15212, £4/15
> Egg, mauve enl. plain. £5/8

F

Mr. Philip Foster, 1909

A Mr. Philip Lawrence Foster of West 44th Street, New York, is listed in the *New York Social Register* as being abroad in 1908.

> Cig. case, amaranth, gold catch & tinder, no. 17790, £3/10

G

Chas. T. Garland, 1914

Charles Tuller Garland (d. 1921), the son of James A. Garland and Anna Louise Tuller of New York, married Margaret Williams (d. 1918). He resided in 1908 at Moreton Morell, Warwickshire, England. A millionaire, sportsman, and racehorse owner, Garland became a British citizen in 1914, the year of his Fabergé acquisition.

> Brooch, lapis lazuli, roses, no. 90271, £11

Mr. John Work Garrett, 1910

John Work Garrett (1872–1942), the son of T. Harrison Garrett (1848–88) and grandson of Baltimore & Ohio Railroad president John Work Garrett (1820–84), was born into a wealthy Baltimore banking family but preferred a diplomatic career. He was an avid coin collector and an ardent bibliophile. In 1908 he married Alice Warder (d. 1952) of Washington, D.C. Garrett was appointed first secretary to the American embassy in Rome, where in 1910 he made the Fabergé purchases recorded in the London ledgers under "Rome Trip." (At that time the exchange rate was $1 to 5.2 lire.) Twenty years later he returned to Rome as ambassador. The Garretts' Baltimore home, Evergreen House, was left to Johns Hopkins University with its art collection and rare book library.

> Pig, white onyx, no. 13752, Lire 295
> Bell Push, fish, nephrite 2 meccas and roses, no. 15658, Lire 1,235
> Bonbonniere, white opl. enl. on gold, rims in white opq. enl. and 1/2 pearls, 5 mossagates and roses, no. 18725, Lire 2,275
> Order: Necessaire, mauve enl. engrd. white opq. en: rims roses in catch, no. 20132, £40

Mrs. Ogden Goelet, 1907, 1912

Mary R. Wilson (1855–1929) was the daughter of Southerners Richard T. Wilson and Melissa Clementine. In 1878 she married Ogden Goelet (d. 1897), a scion of the old New York multimillionaire real estate family. Her sister Grace Wilson became Mrs. Cornelius Vanderbilt III (see below). Another sister, Belle, married Sir Michael Herbert, a British ambassador to the United States. Mary was the mother of Robert Goelet and of Mary, called May, duchess of Roxburghe (see below), who paid for her acquisitions at Fabergé. The Goelets, who entertained lavishly in London and Newport, Rhode Island, and aboard their yacht, included among their distinguished guests Edward, Prince of Wales, and Grand Duke Boris Vladimirovich of Russia. Mrs. Goelet once paid Yvette Guilbert £600 to break a contract in Paris and come sing for Edward VII in Cannes.

> Bracelet chain Plat + Red Gold, no. 4739, £20/10, paid for on May 2nd by the Duchess of Roxburghe
>
> Pencil Pink Enamel, no. 14807, £14/15
>
> Match Box. Blue En. 1 Rose, no. 14419, £8/5
>
> Ditto Pink En. ditto, no. 14399, £8/5 (paid May 7th 08 by Duchess of Roxburgh)
>
> Cig. case, grey agate & mts. sq. cut rubies & roses, no. 22219, £60
>
> Cig. case, var. gold, fluted, no. 21968, £60

Mrs. Robert Goelet, 1908, 1910, 1911

Harriet Louise Warren (d. 1912) in 1879 married Robert Goelet III (1841–99), brother of Ogden Goelet. She lived on Fifth Avenue and traveled extensively on board her yacht *Nahma*, on which she entertained Kaiser Wilhelm II and King Edward VII. She was the mother of Beatrice (d. 1902), immortalized by John Singer Sargent in his canvas *Child with a Parrot*. At the time of her Fabergé purchases, the two main branches of the Goelet family together held one of the largest real estate fortunes in the world.

> Pencil. Red Enamel, no. 14866, £4/15
>
> Ditto small, no. 11449, £3/5
>
> Ditto Blue Opal. En. + Gold Orns., no. 13314, £4
>
> Cigtte. case, d. mauve, enl. gold rims, 1 sap., no. 15157, £21
>
> Matchbox, nephrite, no. 18056, £13/10
>
> Bracelet, chain, red and green gold, no. II 8355, £7/10
>
> Cig. case, lt. blue en. engd. gold stripes & gold mts. moonstone, no. 20021, £23/10
>
> Matchbox, pink siberian orletz, gold mts, no. 19706, £11
>
> Matchbox, lt. blue enl. stripes, no. 20842, £10
>
> Cig. case, black, green opq. & wht. opq. enal. in stripes, gold, 1 ruby, no. 20924, £34/10
>
> Matchbox, ditto, 20925, £13/13

G. Gould Esq., 1912, 1914

G. Gould was possibly Gerald Blenkiron Gould (1890–1953) of Detroit, married to Leah Curtiss of Tarrytown, New York. He was associated with the Fuel Engineering Company in 1911 and was a member of American societies of mining, metallurgical, and mechanical engineers.

> Pendant, orletz, diads., no. 93218, (nett) £58
>
> Pendant, platm. emerld. "scarab," 1 brill, roses, etc., no. 97577, £36

Mrs. Gerald Gould, 1913

> Egg, orletz, on gold chain, n.n., £1/6/6

R. S. Grant Esq., N.Y., 1909

R. S. Grant was possibly R. Suydam Grant (d. 1912), a stockbroker residing at Gramercy Park, New York. His niece, Adela Beach Grant, was the wife of the seventh earl of Essex. In 1915 she inherited $591,000 from his estate according to the earl's *New York Times* obituary.

> Hat Pin, white opl. enl., no. 85413, £5/15

Mrs. Robert Grant, 1910

Mrs. Robert Grant was possibly Priscilla Stackpole of Boston, who had just married her childhood friend Robert Grant, the son of the Boston lawyer and author of the same name and Amy Galt Grant. Beginning in 1910 the couple resided in England for eighteen years while Robert Grant was a partner in, and the American representative for, the firm of Higginson & Company, the independent English branch of Boston's Lee, Higginson Company.

> Cig. case, place for matches, white opl. enamel, gold rim and roses, no. 20156, £21/10
>
> 2 Studs, 2 cab. sapps. roses (1 part set of three), no. 79508, (nett) £9/10

H

The Princess Hatzfeldt, 1907, 1908, 1910, 1911, 1912, 1913, 1916

Clara Prentice (1862–1928) of Sacramento, California, was adopted by her aunt, the first wife of railroad tycoon Collis P. Huntington (1820–1900). In 1889 she married Prince Francis von Hatzfeldt-Wildenburg, an impecunious nobleman given to extravagance and gambling. Having inherited a fortune of $6 million, she assumed a prominent position in English society. The princess, without her husband, was often invited for dinner with Edward VII.

> Lipsalve Tube (small), Fluted Gold, 1 sapphire, no. 15815, £2
>
> Cig. Case. Ashroot. Gold Mts. Roses, no. 15251, £7/15
>
> Ditto Birch of Karelia. Gold Clasp. Tinder, no. 15181, £12/15
>
> Cig. case Neph. gold mountings Ruby, no. 16124, £40/15
>
> Cig. case Wh. opal. enl. 1 sapp. cab., no. 17194, £20
>
> Cig. case, tchinar, 1 sapp., no. 16939, £4/15
>
> Ditto red enl. 1 sapp., no. 17291, £15/5

Ditto mauve enl. roses, no. 17268, £29/5

Ditto gold, fluted, var. sap., no. 12010, £41/15

Ditto gold, sapphire, no. 13336, £28/10

Pocketbook, white leather, gold ornamts., no. 16193, £8/15

Ditto yellow, ditto, no. 16195, £8/15

Ditto red, ditto, no. 19194, £8/15

Papercutter, mahogany, lt. green & wht. opl. enl. gold. 1 M'stone, no. 15671, £7/15

Papercutter, wht. birds eye red enamel, gold rim, no. S.17194, £4/15

Papercutter, silver lizard on white birds eye wood, no. S.16505, £3

Papercutter, pear tree, white opl. enl. gold mount, no. 17988, £4/10

Pencil, wht. opl. en: gold garlds., no. 17538, £6/10

Ditto lt. blue, ditto, no. 17542, £6

Clock, dark blue enamel, no. 17275, £25/10

Match Box, round, flat, mauve enl. & 1 sapp., no. 17092, £7/15

Cig. case, long, red & green fluted, 1 sapphire cab. no. 19110, £40

Cig. case, gold 56, polished, ribbed, roses, no. 18110, £30

Box, nephrite, rims gold, white opaque en: 1 ruby and roses, no. 18587, £46/15

Clock, small raspberry enamel, white opaque enl. rims, gold mounts, no. 19297, £31

Cig. case, square, bent green & red gold, roses, no. 19503, £38/10

Paperknife, thin neph. white opal. enl. roses, no. 17588, £31

Calendar Frame, in nephrite, green gold, no. 18041, £23/5

Calendar Frame, in nutwood, pink enamel silver gilt mountings, no. 18381, £14

Smelling Salts Bottle, glass, light blue enamel and gold rims, no. 19141, £10

Visiting card case, in green leather, white enamel & ornaments, no. 18105, £8/5

Cig. case, square, bent, red gold ribbed, roses, no. 19504, £38

Papercutter, amaranth, lt. green enl. engd. gold ornt., no. 19599, £10

Badmington, ye. brown leather, gold ornts., roses, no. 17119, £8/5

Cal. Frame, grey bird's eye, lt. red en: gilt silver mts., no. S18383, £14

Cal. Frame, raspberry enal. silver gilt rims, no. 18500, £8/5

Cal. Frame, dk. blue enl. silver gilt rims & mounts, no. S.17320, £1410

Cal. Frame, small, lt. blue enl. gilt silver mts., no. S.18387, £8/15

Cal. Frame, small pink enamel, silver gilt rims, no. S.18388, £8/15

Cal. Frame, peartree, lt. green en. silver gilt rims, no. S.18382, £14

Cal. Frame, amaranth, wht. opl. en: silver gilt mts. no. S.18384, £14

Bonbon, gold 72°, 1 mossagate, dk. green enal. roses & rubies, no. 10845, £53

Clock, small, pink & white enl. stripes 1/2 pearls, gold rims etc., no. 19857, £41

"Oroto" Fountain pen, violet enl. gold mts., no. 19756, £8/15

Pencil, & paperknife, lilac enal. gold mts., no. 20507, £5/5

Seal, nephrite, gold, no. 14132, £19/5

Ashtray, neph. gold red enal. & roses, no. 21479, £23

Box, nepp: gold, rubs. no. 21457, £40

Cal. Frame, pink en:, no. 20868, £13/10

Bell-push, silr. "bear," no. S20068, £8/10

Mirror, wht. bird's eye, no. S20217, £8/2

Paperknife, neph. red gld., no. 8988, £12

Ditto, neph: gold, no. 16549, £15

Cigtte. case, gold 72° & roses, no. 21942, £47

Returned: Cig. case, gold, 72° & roses, no. 21942, £47

Ashtray, nephrite, etc., no. 22765, £30

Returned: Ashtray, orletz & gold, no. 22767, £30

Noteblock, cherry tree root, pink enamel, silver gilt mts., no. S.22402, £15/15

Paperweight, snail, silver on nephrite slab, no. S.15253, £14

Arthur Platt Howard, 1908

Arthur Platt Howard who was married to Annie M. Legg, resided abroad in 1908.

Cig. case, eng. under mauve enl. garlands & roses, no. 16838, £20/5

Brloque Basket. roses with gold, no. 83328, £5/5

Bracelet Gold chain. Pearls, no. 82654, £10/10

Egg Pendt. mecca. roses. red enl., no. 80472, £7/15

Links Green enl., no. II 3181, £3/5

[All above items returned.]

Mrs. Hughes, 1908, 1910, 1911, 1912

Mrs. Hughes was possibly Mrs. John M. Hughes (Cornelia Hilton), who resided at Harrow Weald Park, England, as of 1901.

Egg, blue & Wh opaq Enl. no. II 4963, £1/5

Ditto, Lilac Enl., n.n., 13/-

Egg, silver lt green & mauve e., o.d., £1/8

Egg, sil. mat, white opq. enl., o.d., £1/8

Egg, white opl. white & grey opq. en: & gold, o.d., £1/10

Egg, green, lt. blue & lt. green & white opq. enal., o.d., £1/4

Egg, blue enamel, o.d., 13/-

Egg, red & white enal., d.n., £1/9

Egg, dk. blue enal., d.n., 13/-

Egg, brown enal, d.n., 13/-

Miss Hutton, 1909

Miss Hutton was possibly a daughter of Gaun M. Hutton (1848–1916), resident of Baltimore and Newport, Rhode Island. He was a former American vice consul in Russia who married Celeste Marguerite Winans, a Baltimore cousin of Walter Winans (see *W. Winans*).

Lipsalve tube, blue opal. enamel & rose, no. 12609, £6/15

Mrs. Hazen Hyde, 1913

Marthe Leishman (d. 1944) was the daughter of John G. Leishman (d. 1924), an American ambassador to Switzerland, Turkey, and Germany, and Julia Crawford Leishman. In 1904 she married Count Louis de Goutant-Biron (d. 1907). In 1913, in Paris, she became the first wife of James Hazen Hyde (1876–1959), who was the son of Henry Baldwin Hyde, the founder of the Equitable Life Assurance Society. Their one child was named for his grandfather. They were divorced in 1918. A longtime resident of New York, Marthe Hyde died at her home on Park Avenue.

Lipsalve tube, pink enl, no. 21770, £9

Frame, grey birds eye wood, polished sil rim, no. S.20260, £7/10

J

Mrs. Jay, 1907, 1908, 1909, 1910

Mrs. Jay was probably Lucie Oelrichs Jay (1854–1931), the daughter of Henry Oelrichs, a New York shipping magnate. In 1878 she married Colonel William Jay (1841–1915), a Civil War veteran, lawyer, gentleman farmer, and founder of the New York Coaching Club. The family often traveled to London, where they had many friends in the Edwardian social set, including the duchess of Marlborough (Consuelo Vanderbilt).

Cig. case, green en. + garnet, no. 14039, £11/15

3 Buttons, wht. opl. enl. & gold border. own 3 lapis stones, no. RO95, £6/5

1 Ring, gold, setting own stones: 1 emerald 13 brills, no. RO100, £4/10

22 Pearls (9 cts.), £39

3 Buttons, 3 meccas, green en:, no. 87729, £10

Ring, platinum, own brills and cut rubies, no. RO133, £10/10

Repairing own 3 buttons (gratis)

Making one nephrite part with gold leaves and rose to own Links, RO162

Links, nephrite, repaird. new gold rims added, no. RO184

Lady Johnstone, 1908, 1909, 1912

Antoinette Eno Pinchot, the daughter of James Wallace Pinchot and Mary Jane Eno of New York, married Sir Alan Johnstone (1859–1932), a diplomat, in 1893. He was the British minister to Copenhagen from 1905 to 1910 and until 1917 represented Britain at The Hague, where he and his wife were particularly popular. Lady Johnstone was the sister of Gifford Pinchot, the governor of Pennsylvania, and of Amos Richards Eno Pinchot (see *Mrs. A. Pinchot*).

Links, 4 meccas & roses in half plat (to match RO90), no. 86150, £27/10

Own brooch, 1 mecca and roses, 1 rose added. brooch cleaned, no. RO90, £2/6

Nephrite part added to own red en: portion of Umbrella Handle, no. RO126, £8

Match box, nephrite, red enamel & roses, no. 14244, £17/10

Cig. case, nephrite, white enamel, rubies, ornaments, no. 17072, £37

Box, 1 nephrite; mts. ornts. in gold 72° & roses, no. 21515, nett £85

K

Mrs. H. M. Kelly, 1914, 1915

Helen M. Kelly (1884–1952) was the former wife of Frank Jay Gould (divorced), of Ralph Thomas (deceased), and of Prince Vlora of Albania (divorced).

Necklace, 30 cut sapps (lt. blue) & roses in sil-plat, no. 97511; Pendant, 2 cut sapps. (lt. blue) 3 brills & roses, no. 97512, (sold together) £375

Earrings, 2 brills & brills, no. 90020, £725

Returned: Pendant necklace, cut sapps, diamonds, roses, no. 97511, £300

L

Madam W. B. Leeds, 1913, 1914, 1915, 1916

Nancy Mary (May) Stewart (1873–1923) was the daughter of W. E. Stewart. Her first husband was George Worthington, and her second was William Bateman Leeds (1861–1908), the "tin-plate king," who bought the Vanderbilt mansion Rough Point in Newport, Rhode Island. Celebrated for her extravagance, she used to return to the United States after each visit to Europe laden with trunks full of expensive Parisian dresses. As a widow she resided at Grosvenor Square in London and entertained royally. Her social sponsor was Lady Paget (see *Lady Arthur Paget*). She made an $80,000 contribution to the great Shakespeare ball, at which Prince Felix Yusupov, Anthony Drexel (see above), and Lady Paget took part, and at which Mrs. Leeds danced as Cleopatra in a costume sewn with rubies, emeralds, and diamonds. Her portrait was painted by Giovanni Boldini. She lost a much publicized lawsuit with U.S. Customs concerning a pearl necklace acquired in Paris, which she declared at $220,000, but which had cost her $340,000. She tried to import the necklace as "loose stones" at 10 percent duty to avoid the 60 percent duty due. In 1920 she married Prince Christopher of Greece (1888–1940). Leeds was one of the Fabergé's most important clients in London, having acquired sixty-five pieces, chiefly between 1915 and 1916. Her son William B. Leeds Jr., in 1921 married Princess Xenia of Russia, daughter of Grand Duke Georgi Aleksandrovich.

Matchbox, silver, 1 sap, no. S.S 21818, £8/10

Cigtte. case, oval, gold 72°, white opq. inlaid enamel 2 white calcedonies on pink foil, roses in plat., no. 22498, £220

Returns: Cig. case, quartz, diads. in plt., no. 23488; ditto, dark blue enal., no. 20706 (together), £80/10

Cannes: New half to own pink orletz Cigtte. case, etc., no. RO393, (nett) £14

Frame, lt. mauve enal., no. 97193, £27

Clock, lapis lazuli in two parts, nephrite wreath with chrysoliths & roses set in platinum; gold mts., no. 24697, £50

Ashtray, nephrite, rim in white opq. & black enl; 14 cut rubies; gold mts., no. 21334, £25

Kovsh, nephrite, gold ornts., no. 23328, £80

Box, red enal. gold mts., no. 20379, £50

Clock, neph. gold ornts. no. 22241, £75

Clock, pourpourine, etc., no. 25007, £50

Clock, yellow & mauve enl., no. 9420, £45

Clock, pink orletz, enl. gold &, no. 24293, £40

Papercutter, neph. mauve & white opq. & gold mt. etc., no. 22661, £30

Frame, red enal. gilt silver ornts. no. S.21162, £29

Scent bottle, glass, blue & white opl. enal. top. Wedgwood medln., no. 24425, £24

Brooch, aqua. brills & roses, no. 94843, £200

Cig. case, lapislaz. brills, platm., no. 23977, £120

Matchbox, ditto, no. 23978, £60

Cigtte. case, gold, white opal enal & green enamel &, no. 22645, £90

Cigtte. case, oval, gold & red enl. 2 mossagates, diamonds &, no. 15881, £65

Bonbon, neph. gold mt. enal. painted view Stratford Church, no. 17257, £65

Bonbon, white opal. enl. Wedgwd., no. 23782, £30

Papercutter, nephrite, gold & white opq. enal. 1 ruby, no. 24105, £28

Papercutter, neph. white opl. enal. gold rims 1 cut ruby & roses, no. 22208, £26

Papercutter, Chinese jade, gold mts. white opq. & steel blue enal. & roses in plattm., no. 24661, £30

Papercutter, nephrite, 1 mecca, no. 24419, £35

Bulldog, obsidian, collar in gold & white opq. enamel, no. 23475, £68

Cigtte. case, dark blue opal. enal. on gold 72°, amber holder, match compartmt., no. 20751, £75

Cigtte. case, gold 72°, blue opq. enamel inlaid, match compt. diads in platm. catch, no. 24948, £160

Mistletoe Sprig, nephrite stem & leaves matt rock crystal berries, lapis laz. pot, no. 23370, £45

Clock, mauve enal. 1/2 pearls, no. 20795, £30

Clock, blue enal. sil-gilt mts., no. 24446, £22

Ashtray, jadeite, gold rim lilac & white opq. enamel, no. 22896, £19

Seal, nephrite, roses, 4 sapps., no. 22691, £20

Bonbon, neph. gold mts. roses, no. 22583, £28

Clock, lt. green & yellow painted enal. 1/2 pearls &, no. 23119, £85

Cigtte. case, red gold & plat., no. 24403, £3

Match Box, ditto, no. 24404, £35

Necessaire, pink enal. gold etc., no. 23900, £78

Inkstand, nephrite & gold, no. 16501, £83

Box, pink orletz, gold & enal, no. 23134, £75

Boston Terrier, orletz &, no. 24044, £65

Sweet pea, orletz, onyx, jade &, no. 23431, £60

Jessamine, onyx, jade, gold &, no. 23922, £60

Cigtte. case, jade diads. in plat, no. 20965, £60

Clock, white opq. enl. & gold, no. 25744, £60

Bonbon, gold, engd. enl. & gold, no. 24207, £45

Cigtte. case, rock crystal etc., no. 22602, £40

Ashtray, pink orletz & gold, no. 23700, £28

Bonbon, silver, black enal. etc., no. 23508, £26

Elephant, grey calcedony, no. 19021, £20

Scent flacon, glass, grey enl., no. 24662, £15

Salts Flacon, glass, blue enl., no. 24424, £11

Salts Flacon, glass, pink enl., no. 25836, £12

Bonbonniere, lapislaz. diads etc., no. 25006, £75

Links, engd. amethysts & roses, no. 97393, £40

Narcissus, jade, gold, enal etc. no. 13029, £40

Cigtte. Ashtray, brown orletz 2 jade Elephants, no. 17768, £80

Links, white opq. enl. gold stripes, 4 brills, sq. cut sapps., no. 93131, £28

Pencil, white opq. bombe enl., no. 23750, £11

Elephant, grey jasper, no. 24606, £20

Elephant, nephrite, no. 24608, £20

Elephant, pink orletz, no. 24610, £12/10

Return: Pencil, white opq. enamel, no. 23750, £11

Mrs. John Leslie, 1910

Leonie Blanche Jerome (1859–1943) was the youngest daughter of Leonard Jerome (1817–91) and Clarissa Hall (1825–95) and sister of Lady Randolph Churchill (Jennie Jerome, see *Mrs. G. Cornwals West*). She married Lieutenant John Leslie of the British grenadier guards. The Leslies were listed at London addresses in 1908 and 1917.

Hatpin, pink enal. gold ornts. steel pin, no. II 7634, £2/2

Hatpin, d. blue, ditto, no. II 7635, £2/2

Cig. case, oval, grey enl. gold mts. roses, no. 2075, £23/10

Pencil, steel grey en:, no. 20618, £4/5

Returns: Cig. case, oval, pink opl. enamel, roses, no. 19399, £28/10

Cal Frame, small, lt. blue, enl. sil. mts., no. S18387, £6

M

Duchess of Manchester, 1907, 1908, 1909, 1910

Helena A. Zimmerman was the daughter of Eugene Zimmerman (1845–1914), railroad mogul of Cincinnati, Ohio. In 1900 she married William Angus Drogo Montagu, ninth duke of Manchester.

Fan Pink en. + gold ornaments, no. 14479, £32

Returned: Match Stand, Stone & Silver Gilt, no. S14374, £5

Baby Lion, no. 16855, £32/5

Bear, grey obsidian, no. 18696, £29/5

Elk, gold horns, no. 14314, £17/10

Mrs. Bradley Martin, 1907, 1911

Cornelia Sherman (d. 1920) was the daughter of Isaac Sherman, of Buffalo, whose fortune was made in lumber and barrel staves. She married Bradley Martin of New York (1841–1913).

The Martins became part of the "ultra-fashionable" class in New York. In 1897 they gave a notorious masquerade ball at the Waldorf Astoria, at which Cornelia wore a stomacher that had belonged to Queen Marie Antoinette (see fig. 11, p. 32). The ball, which cost over $350,000, and the publicity surrounding it raised their real estate taxes so high that they took up permanent residence in Britain. They rented the Seafield Estate Balmacaan in Scotland, where they entertained up to seventy guests at a time during the shooting season. Their daughter, Cornelia, married the earl of Craven in 1893, thus assuring them of a social position in London.

Magnifying Glasses. Jadeite Red En. Glass, Gold & Roses, no. 1295, £17/10

Lorgnon. Lt Blue wh opl. En. Roses, no. M3393, £40/15

Pocket Mirror. Pink wh. opaq En. Gold Garlands, no. 15529, £17/10

Heron. Calcedony. Gold Legs, no. 15396, £23/5

Motor Pin. Pink En. 1 Brill. Roses, no. 81760, £20/10

Ditto Lt Blue wh opaq. En. 1 Ruby Roses, no. 82660, £17/10

Tie Pin. 1 Mecca. Red Enamel, no. 82593, £3/10

Ditto. 1 Ditto Wh. opaq. En. & Green En., no. 83293, £4/15

Ditto. 1 Ditto Wh. opaq. En. & Gold, no. 83290, £4/15

Ditto. 1 Ditto Wh. opaq. En. & Gold, no. 83291, £4/15

Cig. Case. Wh. opal. En. 1 Sapphire, no. 15163, £14/10

Ash Tray. Pink Orletz. Wh. opq. + Green Enamel, no. 15872, £3/10

Lorgnon. Tortoiseshell Gold & Roses, no. 9764, £27/5

Lorgnette. Pink + Green En. & Roses, no. 12906, £17/10

Gum Bottle. Lt. Blue En. 1 M. Stone, no. 15018, £7/15

Links. White Opal. En. & Roses, no. 82845, £19/5

Pendant. 1 Mecca [illegible]. Wh. Opaq. En., no. 82548, £10/10

Umbrella Top Wh. Opal Lt. Blue Opaq. En. 1 Roses, no. 14910, £11/15

Cig. Holder Amber Green En., no. 15808, £3/10

Pencil, steel blue enal., no. 22352, (nett) £5/5

Returned in exchange: Pencil, stl. blue enamel, no. 22663, £4/15

Bradley Martin Esq.

Fan Pink en. & gold ornaments, no. 14479, £32

H. F. McCormick, 1913

Harold Fowler McCormick (1872–1941) of Chicago was the son of Cyrus Hall McCormick (1809–84), who invented the reaping machine that revolutionized farming. In 1895 he married Edith Rockefeller (d. 1935; see fig. 6, p. 29), daughter of

John D. Rockefeller; they were divorced in 1921. In 1922 McCormick married Ganna Walska, who acquired the Duchess of Marlborough Easter egg (cat. no. 8) in Paris in 1926.

Seal, owl, white onx, no. 23266, £18

Scentbottle, blue enal, no. 22499, £16

Vinaigrette, white opl. en:, no. 22679, £11

Stampbox, blue & yellow enamel stripes etc., no. 21765, £11

Miss Meade, 1907, 1908, 1909

Miss Meade was a shopping companion of Walter Winans (see *W. Winans*).

Locket, pink enamel, no. 81283, £174

Necessaire, Pink enamel + 5 Roses, no. 14748, £44/15

Brooch 1 Chrys. brills (small very fine & expensive) & roses, no. 84863, £81/10

1 pr. Earrings 2 Chrys 2 brills simple gold hooks, no. 84864, £7

Repairing her Collier, lapis lazuli, Moonstones, Turq. & Malachites

Egg Pendant Mecca roses 1 Brill (wreath), no. 81006, £8/15

Ditto, no. 81005, £8/15

Long Chain, gold, 16 matrix Turq. natural blue, no. 84879, £43/10

Long Platinum Chain, no. II 5899, £7/15

1 Sapphire, blue, cut, no. S29/32, £516

Mrs. Moore, 1914

Ada Waterman Small (ca. 1859–1955) was married to William H. Moore (1848–1923) in 1879. In a long, spectacular career in corporate organization, he amassed millions, which enabled his wife to travel, collect, and endow. Her bequests included $500,000 and a collection of Chinese art to Yale University and works of art valued at $92,000 to the Metropolitan Museum of Art. She made her Fabergé purchases in Cannes, at an exchange rate of $1 to 5.19 French francs.

Watch-chain, gold & platm., no. II 10993, 125 Francs, £5

Watch, gents, gold 18ct, blue enamel circle, n.n., 510 Francs, £20/8

Cigarette case, mauve, enal. leather sheath, no. 12859, 256 Francs, £10/5

J. J. Morgan, 1908

John Junius Morgan (d. 1942) was the son of Reverend John B. Morgan and Juliet Pierpont Morgan (b. 1847), and the nephew of the financier J. Pierpont Morgan (1837–1913). He lived in Paris with his father in 1908, the year he made his Fabergé purchases.

Pencil Lt. green enl. roses, no. 14804, £7

Brooch Lt. blue en: roses, garlds., no. 82783, £10

Mrs. C. A. Munn, 1912, 1914

Mary Astor Paul (1889–1950) was the daughter of James William Paul Jr. (1851–1908) and Frances Drexel (1852–92), and the granddaughter of financier Anthony Joseph Drexel Sr. (1826–93), all of Philadelphia. Her expensive 1906 debut, the "butterfly ball," was remembered as a disastrous affair. In 1909 she married Charles Alexander Munn of Radnor, Pennsylvania. They were divorced in 1930. In 1934 she married Jacques Allez. A resident of France from 1922 until her death, she was awarded the American Medal of Freedom and the French Legion of Honor for her work with the French Resistance during World War II. Her daughter-in-law, Dorothy Munn, daughter of Alma Spreckels of San Francisco, in 1969 donated to the California Palace of the Legion of Honor a silver group by Fabergé (cat. no. 39).

Cig. case, red gold, no. 22888, (nett), £40

Cig. case, oval, white opl. en, no. 23248, £21

Ditto, long, yellow, enl, no. 23901, £25

P

Lady Arthur Paget, 1907, 1908, 1909, 1910, 1911, 1912, 1913, 1914, 1915, 1916

Mary Fiske Stevens (b. 1853), known as Minnie, was the daughter of Paran Stevens (d. 1872), a wealthy Boston hotelier, and his second wife, Harriet Reed (d. 1895). The family moved to New York in the 1860s. Edward, Prince of Wales, who stayed at the Stevenses' Fifth Avenue hotel on his visit to America, entertained Minnie and her mother at Sandringham and Marlborough House when they took up residence in England after her father's death. In 1878 she married Arthur Henry Paget of the Scots guards, who was later knighted. The Prince of Wales was godfather to one of their three sons. As Lady Paget, Minnie was very much at the center of Edwardian and Anglo-American society. Fabergé's first patron in London, she arranged an exhibition of his wares at a bazaar held at Albert Hall June 21–23, 1904, in aid of the Royal Victoria Hospital for Children. Queen Alexandra attended the bazaar and purchased a jade scent bottle and an enamel and diamond cigarette holder at Lady Paget's stall of Fabergé objects. In 1910 the Pagets resided at Belgrave Square in London.

Cig. Case. Ebony + Roses, no. 15626, £4/5

Frame. Brown Orletz. Gold. + Pearls, no. 13868, £3/5

Crochet Hook, wht. birds' eye, mauve & wht. opal. enl. green gold ornt. 1 M'stone, no. 17686, £4/25

Bonbonniere, red opl. enamel on gold 72° rims in white opq. and green enamel & chased gold, no. 16716, £74

Returned: Notebook; pink and lt. green enl. roses, gold ornt., no. 13000, £23/8

Cigtte. case, oval, dk blue enal. gold, roses, no. 20706, £23/10

Cig. case, lt. blue enl. rims white opq. enl: 2 mossagates, 1 mecca & gold mts., no. 19930, £42/15

Frame, nephrite & engd. mauve enamel, no. 16420, £46/15

Cig. case, grey agate, gold mts, 4 cut emer. 7 cut rubies & 2 brills in platinum, no. 21684, £58

Ashtray, 1 sib. orletz pR wht. opq., en: roses, no. 19868, (nett) £20

Returned: Mirror, pear blue en: no. S20216, £13/10; Cal. Frame, pink en:, no. 20868, £20

Cig. case, orletz & diads., no. 21711, £68

Matchbox, dk. blue enl., no. 22835, £17

Cig. case, silver, 1 sap., £11/15

Cig. holder case, stl. blue enal. amber holder, no. 21866, £22/10

Cig. holder case, blue en:, no. 22490, £8

Pencil, stl. blue enal, no. 22344, (nett) £5

Returned: Frame, wht. maple, silver, no. S.21310, £5

Cig. case, quartz, two parts, 1 sap. cab. & roses in platm., no. 23488, £75

Cig. holder Case, blue en:, no. 21866, £22/10

Cig Case, neph, rubies, roses, no. 21453, £54

Cig. case, green opl. enal on gold, 2 cameos, roses, &, no. 23080, £85

Jade Walking-stick handle made to own mount & the latter restored, etc., no. RO393, nett £2

Returned: Umb. top (with powderpuff case), pink opl. enamel, no. 23287, £8

Cigtte. case, oval, lt. blue opaque enal. & roses, no. 24176, £21

Chimpanzee, petrified wood, no. 24223, £55

Cigtte. case, gold. black, green & red inlaid enals. roses &, no. 24600, £195

Box, porpourine, red & green gold rim, roses &, no. 24687, £130

Box, pink Siberian orletz, gold mts. green & white enal, no. 21807, £35

Kitten, yellow quartz, etc., no. 22993, £25

Horn Owl, petrified wood, yellow sapps in eyes &, no. 23583, £65

Match Stand, silver ape, red opal. enamel, no. S15245, £11

Menu Stands (2), rasp. enal., no. 21958, £25

Mrs. A. Pinchot, 1912, 1913

Gertrude Minturn, of New York, was the daughter of Robert Bowne Minturn and a Miss Shaw. In 1900 she married Amos Richards Eno Pinchot (1873–1944), a grandson of a captain in Napoleon's army. He was a well-known political activist and a founder of the Progressive party. His sister was Antoinette Eno Pinchot (see *Lady Johnstone*). The couple had two children and lived on Park Avenue. In 1919 they were divorced.

Links, lt. grey en. diads, no. 96123(?), £36

Pencil, red, black & green e., no. 23747, £13

Princess E. de Polignac, 1912

Winarette Eugenie Singer (1865–1943) was born in Yonkers, New York. She was the daughter of Isaac Merritt Singer (1811–75), the sewing machine manufacturer, and his second wife, Isabelle Boyer Summerville. Brought up in England and France, "Winnie" was a musically gifted patroness of young composers and writers. A marriage to Prince Louis de Scey Montbeliard was annulled. In 1893 she married fifty-nine-year-old Prince Edmond de Polignac (d. 1901), who shared her interests in modern music, art, and literature. Their salon was frequented by composers Gabriel Fauré and Claude Debussy and the young writer Marcel Proust.

Cig. case, wht. opl. enl. roses "Doge's Cap" with crown in rubies and gold, no. RO85, £23/15

Clara Prentice. See *The Princess Hatzfeld*.

R

Mrs. Whitelaw Reid, 1907, 1908

Elizabeth Mills (1858–1931) was the only daughter of Darius Ogden Mills (1825–1910) and sister of Ogden Mills. She and her brother inherited equal shares of the $50 million fortune their father left. After her marriage in 1881 to the newspaper publisher and diplomat Whitelaw Reid (1837–1912), she became a well-known hostess in London's Edwardian society and New York's political and publishing circles. She was an active philanthropist and distinguished humanitarian and served as chairperson of the American Red Cross in Britain during World War I. Her husband was special ambassador at the coronation of King Edward VII in 1902 and ambassador to the Court of St. James, 1905–12. The couple entertained at Dorchester House on an unprecedented scale.

Umbrella Top, Mauve En. 1 Chrysolite, 1/2 pearls, no. 15502, £9/10

Buckle, gold. wht. opaq. enl., no. 16785, £10/10

Pencil, green enamel, no. 17373, £4/15

Ditto mech. mauve enl. red gold point, no. 17429, £5/15

Miss Rider (USA), 1914, 1915

Egg-breloque, jadeite, 3 brills in silver-pltn., no. 98323, £2/15

Mrs. Rider

Cross, matt gold, no. II 7690, £2/10

Duchess of Roxburghe, 1907, 1908, 1910

Mary (May) Wilson Goelet (1879–1937) was the daughter of Ogden Goelet (see *Mrs. Ogden Goelet*). May had been a brides-maid at the marriage of Consuelo Vanderbilt to the duke of Marlborough in 1895, and in 1903 she married Henry John Innes-Ker, eighth duke of Roxburghe (1876–1932), in the same Fifth Avenue church. She became one of the leading hostesses of London and a friend of King Edward VII and Queen Alexandra, and of King George V and Queen Mary. Her only child, Alastair Robert Innes-Ker, the marquess of Beaumont, was born in 1913.

Match Box Turq. En. 1 Rose, no. 14496, £7/15

Ditto, white en., no. 12644, £7/10

Cig. case oval, lt. green enl. re-enameled & 1 gild rim added, no. RO76, £1/2

Match Box, lilac en: 1 sapp., no. 17419, £8

Cig. case, fluted silver 91°, 1 sapphire, no. S14452, £7/15

Links, lt Green enamel, no. 85417, £4

Cig. case, flat, blue opal enamel (like no. 17282), no. 1792, £11/15

Cig. case, square, red gold ribbed, roses in catch, no. 19508, £32/15

Powder Puff, flat, gold, wht. opq. en: & gold rims, no. 19368, £32/15

Matchbox, raspberry enl. wht. opq. en. rims, gold Mounts & ring, 1 rose, no. 19666, £8/15

Cig. case, lt. blue enamel gold stripes, 1 Moonstone, no. 19498, £23/5

Cig. case, flat, place for matches, lt. blue en: roses, no. 19245, £19/10

Frame, mauve enal., no. 16369, £13/10

Cig. case, flat, mauve enal. roses, place for matches, no. 19246, £19/10

Cig. case, peartree wood, gold & roses, no. 14003, £8/15

Cigtte. box, grey bird's eye wood, gold ornts., no. 20396, £10

Box, pink orletz, mts. & rims in gold, green, white opal and white opq. enl., no. 20848, £35/5

Cig. case, green, black & white opq. enl. 1 ruby, no. 19764, £35

Matchbox, ditto, no. 19765, £14/10

Barette, white opal. enl. & lt. blue en: 1/2 pearls, no. 90058, £4/10

S

Winarette Eugenie Singer. See *Princess E. de Polignac.*

Count Louis Szechenyi, 1907, 1908

Count Louis Szechenyi (d. 1938) in 1908 married Gladys, daughter of Cornelius Vanderbilt II (1843–99) and Alice Claypoole Gwynne.

Cig. Case. Green En Roses. Two calcedonies in pink mouth piece 2 quills, monogram A.W.A., no. RO61, (nett) £110

Button. Neph. + Brills added to 3/4 Pair Links, no. RTO50, £2/15

Alterations to chains (gratis) 1 Button neph. & 1 brill added to 3/4 pair Links & 1 stud, £2/15

T

Mrs. Payne Thompson, 1911

Edith Blight (d. 1941) in 1897 married at Newport, Rhode Island, Virginia-born sportsman William Payne Thompson (1872–1922). They lived at Longfields in Westbury, Long Island, and were abroad in 1912. Edith was an artist who painted under her maiden name. She later lived in England.

Pencil, grey en: gold, no. 20034, £3/10

Ditto, dk. pink. ditto, no. 20036, £3/10

Edward Tuck Esq. (Monte Carlo), 1914

Edward Tuck (1842–1938) was a banker and philanthropist. He was born in Exeter, New Hampshire, the son of Congressman Amos Tuck. In 1872, in Paris, he married Julia Stell (d. 1929) of Baltimore. They settled permanently in Paris in 1890. His gifts to France included an art collection valued at $5 million, hospitals, schools, and parks. Edward and Julia Tuck were showered with high honors and special awards by the French government. Tuck established the business school at Dartmouth College, New Hampshire, that bears his father's name. He died in Monte Carlo. At the time that Tuck made his Fabergé purchases in Monte Carlo, the U.S. dollar was worth 5.19 French francs.

Bracelet, silver, 2 cut Saphs., no. 96862, 520 Francs

Bellpush, rock crystal Elephant on jadeite pedestal, no. 23976, 1,625 Francs

Brooch, rasp. enl. brills, etc., no. 93458, 600 Francs

Brooch, 2 pink meccas & diads. no. 93804, 820 Francs

Brooch, pink orletz, 1 brill, roses, no. 93809, 385 Francs

Brooch, pink mossagate 4 cut sapphires & roses, etc., no. 97430, 895 Francs

Buttons (3), moonstones, gold, no. 96897, 250 Francs

Chain, long, red & green gold, no. II 10835, 420 Francs

Earrings, 2 moonstones & diads, no. 95879, 880 Francs

Model of lapwing, agate, no. 15397, 520 Francs

Papercutter, neph. pink en:, no. 20204, 527 Francs

Pendant, blue mecca, brills & roses, plat chain, no. 94894, 794 Francs

Pendant, brills & roses, 1 mec, no. 95568, 780 Francs

Pendant, rock crystal "icicle," brills & roses in plat., no. 96718, 1,760 Francs

Seal, agate owl, neph, gold, no. 21357, 985 Francs

Seal, owl, white quartz, etc., no. 14113, 530 Francs

V

Mrs. Cornelius Vanderbilt, 1909, 1913

Grace Wilson (1870–1953) was born in New York of Southern parents. In 1896 she married Cornelius Vanderbilt III (1873–1942), against the wishes of his parents, Cornelius Vanderbilt II (1843–99) and Alice Claypoole Gwynne. Grace became a famous hostess in New York and Newport, Rhode Island, and was said to have entertained more members of European royal houses than any other woman in the United States. Her nephew was R. Thornton Wilson (see cat. no. 44). One sister, Mary, married Ogden Goelet (see *Mrs. Ogden Goelet*), another, Belle, married Sir Michael Herbert, brother of the earl of Pembroke. Grace Vanderbilt's niece, Mary, married the duke of Roxburghe (see *Duchess of Roxburghe*). The Vanderbilts resided at Beaulieu, their Fifth Avenue mansion, kept a home in Newport, and traveled on their yacht, *North Star*.

Crochet Hook, white wood / red & white enamel 1 rose, no. 18036, £4/5

Crochet Hook, satinwood / blue & wht. en. green gold, 1 rose, no. 18038, £4/15

Egg, pink enamel, roses, no. 80680, £8

Ditto, mecca, green & wht. en. roses, no. 80682, £8

Cig. case, white birds eye / gold catch, 1 sapp. tinder, no. 15536, £4/5

Sleevelinks, double white / opal enal. sq. cut sapphires, no. 95459, £19/10

Mrs. W. K. Vanderbilt, 1909

Virginia Graham Fair (d. 1935) was born in San Francisco, the daughter of millionaire James Graham Fair (1831–94), one of the original discoverers of the Comstock Lode. "Birdie" married William K. Vanderbilt II (1878–1944) in New York in 1899. His sister Consuelo had married the duke of Marlborough in 1895. The Vanderbilts separated in 1909 and were divorced in 1927. A noted hostess, Virginia Vanderbilt maintained a Gothic-style residence on Fifth Avenue and owned an important racing stable.

"Uncle Sam" white onyx hat / shirt & trousers, obsidian / coat, orletz face, grey & red / enamel waistcoat, gold / watchchain & buttons, no. 17714, £60 nett

Polar Bear, white onyx, no. 18324, £26/10

B. van Voorhis, 1907, 1909, 1910

Bartow W. van Voorhis lived at the Union Club, New York, in 1908. In the years of Voorhis's purchases at Fabergé, a Mrs. Bartow W. Voorhis is listed care of the Rothschilds, Paris.

Small Cup. Old Russian. Misc. Sapphs., no. 14177, £4/15

Bonbonniere, dark blue enl:, no. 17942, £8/15

Hatpin, violet enl. ball gold ornts. gilt steel pin, no. II 7631, £2/2

Hatpin, raspberry, ditto, no. II 7632, £2/2

Hatpin, mauve enaml 1 mecca, steel gilt pin, no. 88374, £2/5

Bonbonniere, green opal. enamel, & rose, no. 9747, £8/15

Smelling Salts bottle, glass, grey enal. white opaq. enl. rims, gold mounts, 1 chrysoprase, no. 19805, £11/15

Tray, jadeite, blue & wh. e., no. 22156, (nett) £18

W

Mrs. Jn. Ward, 1908, 1916

Jean Templeton Reid (1884–1962) was the only daughter of Whitelaw Reid (1837–1912), editor of the *New York Tribune* and ambassador to the Court of St. James, 1905–12, and Elizabeth Mills Reid (see *Mrs. Whitelaw Reid*). In 1908, in a London wedding attended by royalty, she married John Hubert Ward (d. 1938), the second son of the earl of Dudley, equerry in ordinary to Edward VII and later equerry to Queen Alexandra. He was knighted in 1917.

Cig. Holder, amber & red en:, no. 16960, £6/10

Flower, Vase, Violets, no. 11510, £32

Cig. case, oval, wht. op. enl. on silver, 2 calcedonies on pink folium, roses, no. 17014, £49/10

Pencil, brown enal. roses, no. 19670, £4/15

W. Winans, 1907, 1908, 1909

Walter Winans (1852–1920) was born and educated in St. Petersburg. He was the son of the American William Louis Winans, one of the founders of the Moscow–St. Petersburg Railroad. Winans was an author, sportsman, sculptor, horse exhibitor, and world champion rifleman. He apparently visited the United States once, in 1910, for the national horse show in New York. He married a Miss Belcher of Hove, England. His shopping companion at Fabergé was a Miss Meade (see above). Winans resided at Surrendam Park, Kent, from 1907 to 1910.

Cig: case. var: gold. 1 sapph., no. 10161, £58

Pendant. Brills, 1 Emerald cab. + Roses, no. 78240, £267

Note Book. White Leather. Gold rims, Lt. Green + Pink. En. pencil in gold + Mecca, no. 15882, £20/10

Long Chain. Pink En. + Pearls, no. 77070, £65

Ditto White Opal. + Pink En. Both Gold with Slide, no. 82646, £26/5

Binocle (Opera Glass) Pink painted Enamel, wh opaq rims gold mtgs, no. 16589, £49/5

Clasp Roses, Garnets. opaq. Enl. Roses, no. 11689, £75/10

Hat Pin Chrysophrase Snake in Roses. 1 Ruby, no. 83597, £40/15

Menthol Holder to hang white opaq Enl. 2 Meccas, no. 16037, £14/10

Bracelet—twisted Gold 94°, no. II 1173, £21

Ditto Gold 94°, 2 sapp, no. 79791, £43/10

Small Platinum Chain, n.n., £2/15

Egg—Mauve Opaq. Enl. Roses, no. 82326, £15/15

Ditto Roses "pave.", no. 78268, £22/15

Locket & Chain Turq. bl opal enl. brills & roses with plat. & brill chain, no. 81252, £215

Safety Pin 1 chrys 1 rose gold, no. 81750, £4/15

Cross, gold, no. 44854, £6/10

Bracelet solid gold 94° 2 snakes, no. II 5824, £28

Comb. big. Tortoise Shell Lt. Green enl. roses, no. 81532, £79/10

Comb. big Tort. Shell Blue opaq. enl. roses, no. 81530, £37/15

Hat. Pin. Green Chryso. Roses, no. 82165, £40/10

Pair of Combs. Tort. brills, no. 82015, £171

Barette. Lt. bl. opal enl. 1 mecca, roses, no. 84874, £23/5

Earrings 2 Emeralds (cab) 8 brills, no. 77822, £232

Fan of Ostrich Feathers. Pink Enl. edges of wht. opq. enl. roses handle of mountain (rock) crystal and mirror, no. 17348, £90

Hat Pin, 1 mecca, gold, roses, no. 79364, £52

Powder Puff Box, pink opal. enl. gold chain, swivel puff, mirror, no. 17500, £26/5

Menthol Holder, silver, engd. mauve enl. chain, garlds. roses and 1 mecca, no. 16677, £9/15

Kovsh, filigre enamel with Siberian Stones, no. 18357S, (nett) £12/10

Mrs. Stuart Wortley, 1909

Virginia Schley was the daughter of Admiral Winfield Scott Schley of the U.S. navy (1839–1909) and Ann Rebecca Franklin. In 1891 Miss Schley married Ralph Granville Montagu-Stuart-Wortley (d. 1927).

Own Bracelet repaired, 1 own rose reset. 2 added, no. RO138, £2/5

Z

Helena A. Zimmerman. See *Duchess of Manchester.*

REFERENCES

Amory, Cleveland. *Who Killed Society?* New York: Harper & Bros., 1960.

Batterbury, Michael. *On the Town in New York from 1776 to the Present.* New York: Scribner, 1973.

Bierne, Francis F. *The Amiable Baltimoreans.* New York: E. P. Dutton, 1951.

Birmingham, Stephen. *California Rich.* New York: Simon and Schuster, 1980.

————. *Our Crowd: The Great Jewish Families of New York.* New York: Harper & Row, 1967.

Blatzell, E. Digby. *Philadelphia Gentlemen: The Making of a National Upper Class.* Philadelphia: University of Pennsylvania Press, 1979.

Cannadine, David. *The Decline and Fall of the British Aristocracy.* New Haven, Conn.: Yale University Press, 1990.

Decies, Elizabeth Wharton Beresford. *"King Lehr" and the Gilded Age.* Philadelphia: J. P. Lippincott, 1935.

Dictionary of American Biography. 17 vols. and 8 suppls. New York: Scribner's, 1927–74.

Dictionary of National Biography. 22 vols. and 11 suppls. London and New York: Oxford University Press, 1885–1993.

Erenberg, Lewis A. *Steppin' Out 1890–1930: New York Night Life and the Transformation of American Culture*. Westport, Conn.: Greenwood Press, 1981.

Ervin, Robert, ed. *Baltimore 1729–1929: Two Hundredth Anniversary*. Baltimore, 1929.

Fielding, Daphne. *Those Remarkable Cunards, Emerald and Nancy*. New York: Atheneum, 1968.

Golby, Gerard. *Dupont Dynasty*. Secaucus, N.J.: Lyle Stuart, 1984.

Hibbert, Christopher. *The Royal Victorians: Edward VII, His Family and Friends*. Philadelphia: J. P. Lippincott, 1976.

Hoyt, Edwin P. *The Vanderbilts and Their Fortunes*. Garden City, N.Y.: Doubleday, 1962.

Nichols, Charles Wilbur de Lyon. *The 469 Ultra-Fashionables: A Social Guide Book and Register to Date*. New York: Broadway Publishing Co., 1912.

Satterlee, Herbert Livingston. *J. Pierpont Morgan: An Intimate Portrait*. New York: Macmillan, 1939.

Sinclair, Andrew. *Corsair: The Life of J. Pierpont Morgan*. Boston: Little Brown, 1981.

Sinclair, David. *Dynasty: The Astors and Their Times*. New York: Beaufort Books, 1984.

Vanderbilt, Arthur, II. *Fortune's Children: The Fall of the House of Vanderbilt*. New York: William Morrow, 1989.

Waldrop, Frank C. *McCormick of Chicago: An Unconventional Portrait of a Controversial Figure*. Engelwood Cliffs, N.J.: Prentice Hall, 1966.

Who's Who. London: Adam and Charles Black; New York: Macmillan, 1911.

Who Was Who in America: 1897–1942. Vol. 1. Chicago: A. N. Marquis, Co., Inc., 1942.

Bibliography

BOOKS AND ARTICLES

Albert 1979
Albert, S. J. "The Fantastic Forbes Fabergé Collection." *American Collector* 10, no. 1 (January 1979), pp. 8–11.

Art News 1936
"From the Hermitage: The Work of Fabergé." *Art News* 35, no. 6 (November 7, 1936), p. 16.

Bainbridge 1934
Bainbridge, Henry C. "Russian Imperial Gifts: The Work of Carl Fabergé." *Connoisseur*, May/June 1934, pp. 299–348.

Bainbridge 1935
Bainbridge, Henry C. "The Workmasters of Fabergé." *Connoisseur*, August 1935, pp. 88ff.

Bainbridge 1939
Bainbridge, Henry C. "Russian Imperial Easter Gifts: The Work of Carl Fabergé." *Connoisseur* 93, no. 393 (May 1934), pp. 299–306.

Bainbridge 1949
Bainbridge, Henry C. *Peter Carl Fabergé: Goldsmith and Jeweller to the Russian Imperial Court*. New York and London: B. T. Batsford, 1949.

Bainbridge 1966
Bainbridge, Henry C. *Peter Carl Fabergé: Goldsmith and Jeweller to the Russian Imperial Court*. Rev. ed. London: Spring Books, 1966.

Balsan 1952
Balsan, Consuelo Vanderbilt. *The Glitter and the Gold*. New York: Harper, 1952; London: William Heinemann, 1953.

Booth 1990
Booth, John. *The Art of Fabergé*. Secaucus, N.J.: Bloomsbury, 1990.

Comstock 1936
Comstock, Helen. "Imperial Easter Egg by Fabergé, 1903." *Connoisseur* 98, no. 423 (November 1936), p. 284.

Cooper 1963
Cooper, Douglas, ed. *Great Private Collections*. New York: Macmillan, 1963.

Curry 1995
Curry, David Park. *Fabergé*. Richmond: Virginia Museum of Fine Arts, 1995.

Demerest 1983
Demerest, Michael. "The Affable Elegance of Fabergé." *Time*, May 2, 1983.

D'Otrange 1953
D'Otrange, M. L. "New York Auction Report." *Connoisseur* 131, no. 531 (June 1953), pp. 139–40.

Fagaly 1972
Fagaly, William A. *Treasures by Peter Carl Fabergé and Other Master Jewelers: The Matilda Geddings Gray Foundation Collection*. New Orleans: The Matilda Geddings Gray Foundation, 1972.

Forbes 1979
Forbes, Christopher. "Fabergé Imperial Easter Eggs in American Collections." *Antiques* 115, no. 6 (June 1979), pp. 1228–42.

Forbes 1980
Forbes, Christopher. *Fabergé Eggs: Imperial Russian Fantasies*. New York: Abrams, 1980.

Forbes 1986
Forbes, Christopher. "Imperial Treasures." *Art and Antiques*, April 1986, pp. 52–57, 86.

Garvey 1945
Garvey, Marian. "Clocks by a Russian Jeweler." *The Complete Collector* 5, no. 7 (May 1945), pp. 2–4.

Gems and Minerals 1961
"Fabulous Jewels by Fabergé." *Gems and Minerals* (March 1961), pp. 16–18.

Habsburg 1986
Habsburg, Géza von. *Fabergé: Hofjuwelier der Zaren*. Munich: Hirmer Verlag, 1986.

Habsburg 1987
Habsburg, Géza von. *Fabergé: Jeweler of the Czars*. Geneva: Habsburg, Feldman, 1987; New York: Vendome Press, 1988.

Habsburg 1994
Habsburg, Géza von. *First Impressions: Carl Fabergé*. New York: Abrams, 1994.

Habsburg/Lopato 1994
Habsburg, Géza von, and Marina Lopato. *Fabergé: Imperial Jeweler*. New York: Abrams, 1994.

Habsburg/Solodkoff 1979
Habsburg, Géza von, and Alexander von Solodkoff. *Fabergé: Court Jeweler to the Tsars*. New York: Rizzoli, 1979.

Hammer 1932
Hammer, Armand. *The Quest of the Romanoff Treasure*. New York: William Farquhar Payson, 1932.

Hawley 1967
Hawley, Henry. *Fabergé and His Contemporaries: The India Early Minshall Collection of the Cleveland Museum of Art*. Cleveland: Cleveland Museum of Art, 1967.

Haydon 1967
Haydon, Harold. *Great Art Treasures in America's Smaller Museums*. New York: G. P. Putnam's Sons, 1967.

Hill 1989
Hill, Gerard, ed. *Fabergé and the Russian Master Goldsmiths*. New York: Hugh Lauter Levin Associates, 1989; distributed by Macmillan.

Keefe 1993
Keefe, John W. *Masterpieces of Fabergé: The Matilda Geddings Gray Foundation Collection*. New Orleans: New Orleans Museum of Art, 1993.

Kelly 1985
Kelly, Margaret. *Highlights from the Forbes Magazine Galleries*. New York: Forbes, Inc., Publishers, 1985.

Koronatsionnyi sbornik 1899
Koronatsionnyi sbornik (Coronation Collection). St. Petersburg: Ministerstvo Impeatorskogo dvora, 1899.

Lesley 1976
Lesley, Parker. *Fabergé: A Catalog of the Lillian Thomas Pratt Collection of Russian Imperial Jewels*. Richmond: Virginia Museum of Fine Arts, 1976.

Lopato 1984
Lopato, Marina. "New Light on Fabergé." *Apollo*, n.s., 119, no. 263, pp. 43–49.

Lopato 1991
Lopato, Marina. "Fabergé Eggs. Re-dating from New Evidence." *Apollo*, n.s., 133, no. 348 (February 1991), pp. 91–94.

McCanless 1994
McCanless, Christel Ludewig. *Fabergé and His Works: An Annotated Bibliography of the First Century of His Art*. Metuchen, N.J., and London: Scarecrow Press, 1994.

McNab Dennis 1965
McNab Dennis, J. "Fabergé's Objects of Fantasy." *Metropolitan Museum of Art Bulletin*, n.s., 23 (March 1965), pp. 229ff.

New York Sun 1936
"Royal Red Cross Treasure." *New York Sun*, October 31, 1936.

Pfeffer 1990
Pfeffer, Susanna. *Fabergé Eggs: Masterpieces from Czarist Russia*. New York: Hugh Lauter Levin Associates, 1990; distributed by Macmillan.

Ross 1952
Ross, Marvin C. *Peter Carl Fabergé: Illustrated with Objects from the Walters Art Gallery*. Baltimore, Md.: Walters Art Gallery, 1952.

Ross 1965
Ross, Marvin C. *The Art of Peter Karl Fabergé and His Contemporaries: Russian Imperial Portraits and Mementoes. The Collections of Marjorie Merriweather Post*. Norman: University of Oklahoma Press, 1965.

Snowman 1952
Snowman, A. Kenneth. *The Art of Carl Fabergé*. Boston: Boston Book and Art Shop, 1952.

Snowman 1953
Snowman, A. Kenneth. *The Art of Carl Fabergé*. London: Faber and Faber, 1953.

Snowman 1962
Snowman, A. Kenneth. *The Art of Carl Fabergé*. Rev. ed. London: Faber and Faber, 1962.

Snowman 1966
Snowman, A. Kenneth. *Eighteenth-Century Gold Boxes of Europe*. London: Faber and Faber, 1966.

Snowman 1979
Snowman, A. Kenneth. *Carl Fabergé, Goldsmith to the Imperial Court of Russia*. London: Debrett; New York: Viking, 1979.

Snowman 1993
Snowman, A. Kenneth. *Fabergé: Lost and Found, The Recently Discovered Jewelry Designs from the St. Petersburg Archives*. New York: Abrams, 1993.

Solodkoff 1984
Solodkoff, Alexander von, ed. *Masterpieces from the House of Fabergé*. New York: Abrams, 1984.

Solodkoff 1986
Solodkoff, Alexander von. *Fabergé Clocks*. London: Ermitage, 1986.

Solodkoff 1988
Solodkoff, Alexander von. *Fabergé*. London: Pyramid, 1988.

Solodkoff 1995
Solodkoff, Alexander von. *Fabergé: Juwelier des Zarenhofes*. Heidelberg: Brans, 1995.

Stolitsa y Usadba 1916
Stolitsa y Usadba (Town and Country, Petrograd), April 1, 1916.

Swezey 1980
Swezey, Marilyn Pfeifer. "In Celebration of a Bicentennial: Fabergé's Imperial Easter Egg of 1903." *Arts in Virginia* 20, no. 3 (Spring 1980), pp. 22–31.

Taylor 1983
Taylor, Katrina V. H. *Fabergé at Hillwood*. Washington, D.C.: Hillwood Museum, 1983.

Waterfield 1973
Waterfield, Hermione. *Fabergé from the Forbes Magazine Collection*. New York: Charles Scribner's Sons, 1973.

Waterfield/Forbes 1978
Waterfield, Hermione, and Christopher Forbes. *C. Fabergé: Imperial Easter Eggs and Other Fantasies*. New York: Charles Scribner's Sons, 1978.

Williams 1980
Williams, Robert C. *Russian Art and American Money*. Cambridge: Harvard University Press, 1980.

Winterfeld-Menkin 1942
Winterfeld-Menkin, Joachim von. *Jahreszeiten des Lebens*. Berlin, 1942.

EXHIBITIONS

ALVR 1949
Peter Carl Fabergé: An Exhibition of His Works, A La Vieille Russie, New York, 1949.

ALVR 1961
The Art of Peter Carl Fabergé, A La Vieille Russie, New York, 1961.

ALVR 1968
The Art of the Goldsmith and Jeweler, A La Vieille Russie, New York, 1968.

ALVR 1983
Fabergé: A Loan Exhibition, A La Vieille Russie, New York, 1983.

Cooper Union 1954
Enamel, New York, Cooper Union for Art and Decoration, 1954.

Corcoran 1961
Easter Eggs and Other Precious Objects by Carl Fabergé. Washington, D.C.: Corcoran Gallery of Art, 1961.

Florida 1995
Five Centuries of Russian Art, St. Petersburg, Florida, Museum of Fine Art, 1995.

Forbes 1987–94
Fabergé Silver from the Forbes Magazine Collection, Forbes Magazine Collection, New York, 1987–94.

Hammer 1937
Fabergé: His Works, Hammer Galleries, New York, 1937.

Hammer 1939
Presentation of Imperial Russian Gifts by Carl Fabergé, Hammer Galleries, New York, 1939.

Hammer 1943
500 Years of Russian Art, Hammer Galleries, New York, 1943.

Hammer 1951
A Loan Exhibition of the Art of Peter Carl Fabergé, Hammer Galleries, New York, 1951.

Hammer 1952
Hammer Galleries, New York, 1952.

Helsinki 1980
Carl Fabergé and His Contemporaries, Helsinki, Museum of Arts and Crafts, 1980.

Houston 1994
The World of Fabergé: Russian Gems and Jewels, Houston Museum of Natural Science, 1994.

London 1935
Exhibition of Russian Art, Belgrave Square, London, 1935.

Lord and Taylor 1933
The Hammer Collection of Russian Imperial Art Treasures from the Winter Palace, Lord and Taylor, New York, 1933.

Lugano 1987
Fabergé Fantasies: The Forbes Magazine Collection, Villa Favorita, Lugano-Castagnola, Switzerland, 1987.

MMA 1962–65
Metropolitan Museum of Art, New York, 1962–65.

Munich 1986–87
Fabergé: Hofjuwelier der Zaren, Kunsthalle der Hypokulturstiftung, Munich, 1986–87.

NCMA 1979
Treasures from the Virginia Museum Collection Featuring the Fabergé Collection, North Carolina Museum of Art, Raleigh, 1979.

New Orleans 1971
Fabergé: The Matilda Geddings Gray Foundation Collection, New Orleans Museum of Art, 1971.

Paris 1987
Fabergé Orfevre à la Cour des Tsars: The Forbes Magazine Collection, Musée Jacqemart-André, Paris, 1987.

PFAC 1981
Russian and Imperial Art, Peninsula Fine Arts Center, Newport News, Virginia, 1981.

Queen's Gallery 1995
Fabergé, Queen's Gallery, Buckingham Palace, London, 1995.

SAM 1984
Arts of Imperial Russia, Seattle Art Museum, 1984.

San Diego/Moscow 1989–90
Fabergé: The Imperial Eggs, San Diego Museum of Art; Armory Museum, State Museums of the Moscow Kremlin, 1989–90.

San Francisco 1964
Fabergé: Goldsmith to the Russian Imperial Court, M. H. de Young Memorial Museum, San Francisco, 1964.

St. Petersburg 1902
Von Dervise House, St. Petersburg, 1902.

St. Petersburg/Paris/London 1993–94
Fabergé, Imperial Jeweller, State Hermitage Museum, St. Petersburg; Musée des Arts Décoratifs, Paris; Victoria and Albert Museum, London, 1993–94.

V&A 1977
Fabergé, 1846–1920, Victoria and Albert Museum, London, 1977.

WAG 1959
Walters Art Gallery, Baltimore, 1959.

WAG 1982
Walters Art Gallery, Baltimore, 1982.

WAG 1984
Walters Art Gallery, Baltimore, 1984.

WAG 1995
Walters Art Gallery, Baltimore, 1995.

Wartski 1949
A Loan Exhibition of the Works of Carl Fabergé, Wartski, London, 1949.

Wartski 1953
Carl Fabergé: Wartski Coronation Exhibition, London, 1953.

Zurich 1989
Carl Fabergé: Kostbarkeiten Russischer Goldschmiede der Jahrhundertwende, Museum Bellerive, Zurich, 1989.

Index